Reality Television and Class

Edited by Helen Wood and Beverley Skeggs

A BFI book published by Palgrave Macmillan

First published in 2011 by
PALGRAVE MACMILLAN

on behalf of the

BRITISH FILM INSTITUTE
21 Stephen Street, London W1T 1LN
www.bfi.org.uk

There's more to discover about film and television through the BFI. Our world-renowned
archive, cinemas, festivals, films, publications and learning resources are here to inspire you.

Palgrave Macmillan in the UK is an imprint of Macmillan Publishers Limited, registered in
England, company number 785998, of Houndmills, Basingstoke, Hampshire RG21 6XS.
Palgrave Macmillan in the US is a division of St Martin's Press LLC, 175 Fifth Avenue, New
York, NY 10010. Palgrave Macmillan is the global academic imprint of the above companies
and has companies and representatives throughout the world. Palgrave® and Macmillan®
are registered trademarks in the United States, the United Kingdom, Europe and other
countries.

Cover design: keenan
Text design: couch
Images from *Győzike*, © RTL Klub; *Cathy Come Home*, © BBC; *Underage and Pregnant*, © BBC

Set by Cambrian Typesetters, Camberley, Surrey
Printed in China

This book is printed on paper suitable for recycling and made from fully managed and
sustained forest sources. Logging, pulping and manufacturing processes are expected to
conform to the environmental regulations of the country of origin.

British Library Cataloguing-in-Publication Data
A catalogue record for this book is available from the British Library
A catalog record for this book is available from the Library of Congress
10 9 8 7 6 5 4 3 2 1
20 19 18 17 16 15 14 13 12 11

ISBN 978–1–84457–397–4 (pb)
ISBN 978–1–84457–398–1 (hb)

Contents

Acknowledgments

We would like to thank Joanne Whitehouse-Hart for all her fabulous help with preparing the manuscript and Luna Glucksberg for her help with the book's preparation. We would also like to thank the authors for their diligence, patience and for managing our requests as editors. The final delivery of this book has come about alongside other arrivals for a number of the contributors – so welcome Jakey, Lina, Liina and Max. Thank you authors for your hard work during these new challenges. Thanks to Rebecca Barden at the BFI for originally recognising that reality television *is* about class.

Helen would like to thank colleagues at De Montfort University for their ongoing support, in particular Stuart Hanson, Simon Mills, Stuart Price, Diane Taylor and Andrew Tolson. Thanks to Rachel Moseley and Helen Wheatley for their genuine comradeship and for putting up with my work on this book as we start a new venture. Thank you to Albert and Pauline Wood, as always. Thanks to 'tough guy' Phil for making me see sense and for calming me down, and thanks to Max for being absolutely brilliant and not too clingy. Bev would like to thank colleagues at Goldsmiths University, Ken and Doreen Skeggs, and the gorgeous Jeremy. Helen would like to thank Bev for making her say more and Bev would like to thank Helen for making her say less!

Notes on Contributors

Mark Andrejevic is a Research Fellow at the Centre for Critical and Cultural Studies, University of Queensland. He is the author of *Reality TV: The Work of Being Watched* (Rowman and Littlefield, 2004) and *iSpy: Surveillance and Power in the Interactive Era* (University Press of Kansas, 2007) as well as numerous journal articles and chapters on surveillance, popular culture and interactive media.

Anita Biressi is Reader in Media Cultures at Roehampton University, London. Her research interests include discourses of crime and criminality and law and order in the media, media ethics, popular journalism and tabloid culture, media spectacle, reality programming, documentary and factual film and television. Anita is currently undertaking further research in the areas of class politics and reality television; media spectacle and documentary film. Her new book (with Heather Nunn), *Class in Contemporary British Culture*, is forthcoming from Palgrave Macmillan.

Lisa Blackman is a Reader in Media and Communications at Goldsmiths, University of London. She works at the intersection of body-studies and cultural theory and is particularly interested in subjectivity, affect, the body and embodiment. She has published three books in this area: *Hearing Voices: Embodiment and Experience* (Free Association Books, 2001), *Mass Hysteria: Critical Psychology and Media Studies* (with Valerie Walkerdine, Palgrave, 2001) and *The Body: The Key Concepts* (Berg, 2008). Her fourth book, *Immaterial Bodies: Affect, Embodiment and Mediation*, is forthcoming (Sage, 2012). She is also the editor of the journal *Body & Society* (Sage) and a co-editor of the journal *Subjectivity* (Palgrave).

Nick Couldry is Professor of Media at Goldsmiths University of London. He is a participant in the Goldsmiths Leverhulme Media Research Centre and the author or editor of seven books including *The Place of Media Power: Pilgrims and Witnesses of the Media Age* (Routledge, 2000), *Inside Culture* (Sage, 2000), *Media Rituals: A Critical Approach* (Routledge, 2003), *Contesting Media Power: Alternative Media in a Networked World* (Rowman and Littlefield, 2003, co-edited with James Curran) and most recently *Media Consumption and Public Engagement: Beyond the Presumption of Attention* (Palgrave Macmillan, 2007).

Karmen Erjavec is an Associate Professor at the Faculty of Social Sciences, University of Ljubljana, Slovenia, where she teaches Mass Communication, Media and Minorities and Media Education. Her main research interests include critical discourse analysis, media and minorities/nationalism/ racism, and media education.

Laura Grindstaff is Associate Professor of Sociology and the Director of the Consortium for Women and Research at UC Davis. Her teaching and research focus on popular culture, cultural studies, feminist theory and ethnographic methods. She is the author of *The Money Shot: Trash, Class, and the Making of TV Talk Shows* (University of Chicago Press, 2002), as well as various essays on reality media and other key sites in American popular culture. She is currently completing a book on cheerleading with her co-author Emily West.

Anikó Imre is Associate Professor of Critical Studies in the University of Southern California's School of Cinematic Arts, Los Angeles. Her work revolves around film and new media theory, global television, national and transnational media, post-coloniality, global consumption and mobility, studies of identity and play, media education, and European media. She is the author of *Identity Games: Globalization and the Transformation of Media Cultures in the New Europe* (MIT Press, 2009), editor of *East European Cinemas* (Routledge, 2005) and *The Blackwell Companion to East European Cinema*, and co-editor of *Transnational Feminism in Film and Media* (Palgrave, 2007) and *Popular Television in Eastern and Southern Europe* (Routledge, 2011).

Tania Lewis is a Senior Research Fellow in Sociology at La Trobe University, Victoria, Australia. She is the author of *Smart Living: Lifestyle Media and Popular Expertise* (Peter Lang, 2008), editor of *TV Transformations: Revealing the Makeover Show* (Routledge, 2009) and co-editor (with Emily Potter) of *Ethical Consumption: A Critical Introduction* (Routledge, 2010). Her current research is on sustainable lifestyles, green citizenship and ethical consumption. She is also a chief investigator on a four-year (2010–13) comparative study of lifestyle-advice television in Asia funded by the Australian Research Council.

Vicki Mayer is Associate Professor of Communication at Tulane University, New Orleans. Her work on media producers and production cultures has appeared in many journal articles, and in the following books: *Below the Line: Producers and Production Studies in the New Television Economy* (Duke, 2011), *Production Studies: Cultural Studies of Media Industries* (Routledge, 2010) and *Producing Dreams, Consuming Youth: Mexican Americans and Mass Media* (Rutgers, 2003).

Heather Nunn is Professor of Culture and Politics and Director of the Centre for Research in Film and Audiovisual Cultures at Roehampton University, London. Research interests include reality television and factual programming, political representation and the media, cultural politics, gender, feminism and the media, national identity, formations of class and nation, images of childhood. Her new book (with Anita Biressi), *Class in Contemporary British Culture*, is forthcoming from Palgrave Macmillan.

Gareth Palmer is Professor of Media in the School of Media, Music and Performance at the University of Salford, Greater Manchester. He has worked on the subject of reality television since the 1990s. He published *Discipline and Liberty* with Manchester University Press in 2003. More recently, his work has focused on lifestyle television. In 2008, he published a collection of papers entitled *Exposing Lifestyle Television* for Ashgate. Palmer continues to undertake practical work – most recently a large-scale production with the people of Salford entitled 'New Mornings, Old Streets' funded by the Learning Revolution Transformation Fund.

Beverley Skeggs is Professor of Sociology at Goldsmiths, University of London. She held the Kerstin Hesselgren Professorship in Gender Studies at Stockholm University in 2007. She has worked in the areas of women's studies and cultural studies as well as sociology. Her books include: *Issues in Sociology: The Media* (with J. Mundy, 1992), *Feminist Cultural Theory: Production and Process* (1995), *Formations of Class and Gender: Becoming Respectable* (1997), *Class, Self, Culture* (2004); *Sexuality and the Politics of Violence* (co-authored with Les Moran, 2004) and *Feminism after Bourdieu* (co-edited with Lisa Adkins, 2004).

Lisa Taylor is Principal Lecturer in Media and Cultural Studies at Leeds Metropolitan University. She is co-author (with Andrew Willis) of *Media Studies: Texts, Institutions and Audiences* (Blackwell, 1999) and has published on film and media theory. More recently, her publications have been concerned with issues of class, taste and lifestyle television. Her book *A Taste for Gardening: Classed and Gendered Practices* was published by Ashgate in 2008.

Andrew Tolson is Professor of Media at De Montfort University, Leicester. His main research interest is in the analysis of broadcast talk (speech communication on TV and radio), with a particular interest in news and political communication, and celebrity interviews, talk shows and reality TV. His most recent book is *Media Talk: Spoken Discourse on TV and Radio* (Edinburgh University Press, 2006).

Annabel Tremlett is a Senior Lecturer at the University of Portsmouth, Hampshire. Her research interests include looking at the way minority groups are represented in European contexts, both in public discourses and local practices. She is an ethnographer with particular experience of working with Roma minorities in Hungary, including over six years of in-depth experience in community projects and fifteen months of ethnographic fieldwork. She has published in a variety of journals and books on representations of Roma minorities in the media, popular culture, academia, the European Union, and also on a local 'ordinary' level.

Imogen Tyler is a Senior Lecturer in Sociology at Lancaster University, Lancashire. Her work focuses on social identities, mediation and inequalities. This chapter emerged out of a Leverhulme-funded research project, 'Revolting Subjects: Marginalisation and Resistance', and a monograph, *Revolting Subjects* (Zed Books), is forthcoming. Other recent publications include: 'Naked Protest: The Maternal Politics of Citizenship and Revolt', *Citizenship Studies* (forthcoming), 17(2); 'Pregnant Beauty: Maternal

Femininities under Neoliberalism', in *New Femininities: Postfeminism, Neoliberalism and Identity* (with B. Bennett, 2011); 'Celebrity Chav: Fame, Femininity and Social Class', *European Journal of Cultural Studies* (2010), 13(3); and 'Designed to Fail: A Biopolitics of British Citizenship', *Citizenship Studies* (2010), 14(1).

Zala Volčič works in the Centre for Critical and Cultural Studies at the University of Queensland. In addition to work on her current manuscript, which deals with the role of the media in the construction of national identities in the Balkans, other projects include writings on media commercialisation, public television, social movements and media education. She has written extensively on the role of the media in the Balkans.

Valerie Walkerdine is Distinguished Research Professor in the School of Social Sciences, Cardiff University. She has worked on issues of class, gender and media and popular culture for a number of years. Her books on these topics include the following: *Democracy in the Kitchen: Regulating Mothers and Socialising Daughters* (Virago, 1989); *Schoolgirl Fictions* (Verso, 1991); *Daddy's Girl: Young Girls and Popular Culture* (London/Cambridge, MA: Macmillan/Harvard University Press, 1997); *Growing up Girl: Psychosocial Explorations of Gender and Class* (London/New York: Palgrave/NYU Press, 2002) and *Children, Gender, Video Games: Towards a Relational Approach to Multi-Media* (London: Palgrave, 2007).

Brenda R. Weber is Associate Professor of Gender Studies at the University of Indiana, Illinois. She has published widely on gender, media and representation. Her latest book, *Makeover TV: Selfhood, Citizenship and Celebrity* (2009), is published by Duke University Press.

Helen Wood is Reader in Media and Communication at De Montfort University, Leicester. She is author of *Talking with Television* (University of Illinois Press, 2009), co-editor of the *CCCS Working Papers in Cultural Studies* (Routledge, 2007) and the book *Reacting to Reality Television* (with Beverley Skeggs) is forthcoming from Routledge. She has published widely on popular television, audiences and methodology in journals such as *Media, Culture and Society, Cinema Journal* and the *European Journal of Cultural Studies*.

1/Beverley Skeggs and Helen Wood

Introduction: Real Class

'Is it really about class?'

This was the question often asked when we presented our research at various seminars and conferences throughout the duration of our reality television project, 'Making Class and Self through Televised Ethical Scenarios'.[1] The project, rather unusually since David Morley's (1980) audience research on *The Nationwide Audience*, foregrounds issues of class in both textual and audience analyses. The fields of media studies and sociology have sometimes been rather reticent to acknowledge that *all* representations are at some level always about class. Television in particular, with its stories of everyday lives and 'ordinary people', represents the structure of social relationships, from the most intimate to the most global, which are *always* in one way or another *about* class.

Journalists have not been so hesitant. They have regularly and repeatedly pointed to the class dimensions at work in reality television, referring to them as classed pantomimes and morality plays. In the US, James Wolcott laments that 'Reality TV wages class warfare and promotes proletarian exploitation' (*Vanity Fair*, December 2009), while in the UK, Decca Aitkenhead reports:

> No one knew that reality television could turn a person's world upside down; reinvent a gobby young *Big Brother* girl from Bermondsey as a millionaire princess, or turn a council estate *Wife Swap* mum into a national hate figure. Nor did anyone realise that the class system would devour the genre, letting all our old prejudices run riot in the new cultural shorthand for vulgarity and exhibitionism. (*Guardian*, 15 June 2009)

While class may have, until recently, been 'uncool' in public debate and in the academy, reality television has made it spectacularly visible across our screens. Let us start with some obvious observations. First, there are many popular critical commentaries in which reality television as 'trash' inscribes a set of assumptions about participants and viewers based upon hierarchies of culture, taste and person-value. Second, the idea that reality television represents a crisis in civic public culture is largely framed around its inversion of public and private spheres in which matters of the everyday and the 'ordinary' are made centre stage. The term 'ordinary' is one of the many euphemisms used to stand in for 'working class', because in many different nations it is no longer fashionable to speak about class identifications (Bromley 2000; Savage 2003; Sayer 2005). Locating the drama at the site of the 'ordinary' also suggests a greater purchase on the 'authentic' – a route informed by social-realist critique in documentary and film – which is often problematically associated with race and class formations (Gilroy 1990; Biressi and Nunn 2005). Third, in terms of the participants *on* reality television programmes, there is an over-representation of the working class, precisely because of their cultural and economic situation. Mimi White (2006), for instance, commenting on the American programme *Cheaters* (2000–), notes how the $500 payment skews the class profile decisively, so much so that there is clearly a level of class exploitation at work. This is a point that is often obscured by the apparent democratising potential of reality television as access is opened out to members of the public. Fourth, the supposed access to a 'better life' and even to celebrity through reality television reinvents the myths of social mobility that abound in neo-liberal political culture. As chapters of this book address, the contours of celebrity themselves evoke a language of class antagonism around taste distinctions and judgments of talent which often result in the emergence of working-class celebrities as hate figures. It is ironic that lifestyle and reality television espouse mobility and choice at precisely the same time as the gap between rich and poor widens and social mobility rates remain stagnant, or even point downwards in the UK and the US (Brunsdon 2003; Andrejevic 2004).

Finally, many programmes specifically promote and develop formats of class antagonism (*Wife Swap*, *Holiday Showdown*, *The Simple Life*). Some develop the Pygmalion story where the working class are exposed as inadequate and in need of training in middle- or upper-class etiquette standards (*Ladette to Lady*, *My Fair Lady*) or even in commodity culture (*From Asbo Teen to Beauty Queen*), or must prove their worth in terms of deserving financial aid or benefit (*Secret Millionaire*, *How the Other Half Live*, *Benefit Busters*). Others pit working class against aristocratic culture (*What the Butler Saw*), or set the aspirational against the abject working class (*Wife Swap*); some identify deficient working-class practices and bodies (*Supernanny*, *What Not to Wear*, *You Are What You Eat*, *Honey We're Killing the Kids*) or revel in apparently pathological abjectness (*Ibiza Uncovered*, *Jersey Shore*, *Geordie Shore*). While extensive research has already pointed out that many lifestyle programmes promote and establish middle-class standards as normative and universal (Biressi and Nunn 2008; Lewis 2008; Palmer 2004; Ringrose and Walkerdine 2008; Taylor 2005; McRobbie 2004).

For these reasons, we think it is important to discuss television's intervention in class formations, particularly at a time when political rhetoric is diverting the blame for structural inequality onto per-sonal, individualised failure (Skeggs 2004a). And this is the main problem. How do we explain this awkward tension between what is obvious to many newspaper commentators and critics and the sensitivities around a bold discussion of class that exist elsewehere? bell hooks argues:

> Nowadays it is fashionable to talk about race or gender; the uncool subject is class. It's the subject that makes us all tense, nervous, uncertain about where we stand. In less than twenty years our nation has become a place where the truly rich rule. At one time wealth afforded prestige and power, but the wealthy alone did not determine our nation's values. While greed has always been a part of American capitalism, it is only recently that it has set the standard for how we live and interact in everyday life. (hooks 2000: vii)

A huge amount of rhetorical effort has gone into denying the existence of class, which makes sense as the privileged and those who represent them protect their interests. So in the UK, we have witnessed the denial of 'class' and 'society' by Conservative Prime Minister Margaret Thatcher and the denial of the 'social' by Conservative Prime Minister John Major. New Labour has claimed that 'the class war is over', with Prime Minister Tony Blair and his deputy stating, 'we're all middle class now' (curiously, while Deputy John Prescott was simultaneously being laughed at for his lack of language skills). Both UK governments (not that there was much difference between them – Margaret Thatcher claims her 'greatest achievement' was New Labour) over a period of thirty years have put a great deal of effort into delegitimating and reducing the power of trade unions. While in the US, the power of the state, expressed through McCarthyism, meant that to speak class was to be in serious danger of appearing anti-American (Weir 2007), an issue that reared its ugly head in the recent attack on Frances Fox Piven by the *Fox TV* news host, Glenn Beck (see Harris 2011).

When we have talked about reality television outside of the UK, we have sometimes met the response that class is a peculiarly British preoccupation, both on the shows and for British academics. But as Alessandra Stanley, writing in *The New York Times* about humiliation on US reality shows, suggests, 'the novelty lies in heightening the clash between the upper middle class and blue-collar America, a leitmotif of previous reality shows that has now become prominent' (23 April 2003). It is clear that some of the preoccupations on British reality television, with settings such as finishing schools and manor houses, hark back to a particular national formation (although *What the Butler Saw* aired on US PBS in 2003 as *The Manor House* with fairly good ratings).

Part of the impetus for this book comes from the recognition that class relationships have very different national inflections and we have included contributions from post-socialist Europe, Australia, as well as the US and UK. The main differences, which various chapters will go on to flesh out, lie in the history of the vernacular expression of class rather than in its theoretical explanation. In the UK/European traditions, class relations are usually spoken through antagonism, with a longer historical tradition of the celebration of working-class culture evident in the UK (Vicinus 1974; Vincent 1981). In the US, incorporation rather than antagonism structures the vernacular, which is founded in the myths of the American Dream where everyone who works is coded as middle class. This is complicated further by the categorisation of working-class black Americans as 'poor' and antagonism displaced onto struggles for civil rights, which also explains the need to racialise those outside the structures of work as 'white trash' (Wray and Newitz 1997). In Eastern Europe, socialism and ideals of the collective worker as inscribed by the state are being shed in the move to market economies. Such rapid transformation means that any mention of class is seen as retrograde, working against the progress of the nation (see Volčič in this volume). Interestingly, Australia has inherited some of the UK vernacular traditions where the history of British transportation haunts the class relations of the present. Discourses of Australia have historically been founded upon myths of egalitarianism that have been filtered through narratives of the rural 'man of the bush' (Western 1991). However, no matter how much effort goes into denial through political rhetoric, popular culture repeatedly returns like the repressed to the issue of class and has become one of the major conceits (or structuring absences) of reality television. As formats travel across national boundaries, we see a bizarre mix of antagonism and incorporation, exclusion and abjection, but nearly always with the reification of individual volition as the solution to all problems.

Perhaps reality television's amplification of class can exist precisely *because* of the dominant rhetoric that class is less significant than it once was. The ever-mutating genre exists alongside political rhetoric and the claims of academic theory that in late-capitalist consumer-driven societies, class as a category is irrelevant or in decline: Ulrich Beck and Elisabeth Beck-Gernsheim (2002), for instance, describe class as a 'zombie category', a haunting but irrelevant nuisance that gets in the way of understanding individualisation. Dominant shifts in social theory around individualisation, which have sometimes been applied to explain the rise of ordinary people on television, suggest the decline of class as a salient category. These propositions are underpinned by the notion that because class formations have been altered by the decline in manufacturing industry and the rise of the service sector, the articulation of a class consciousness has disappeared with the decline in power of the unions, leaving us all able to refashion our 'mobile selves' in relation to a more flexible job market. We have been at pains to point out that such theories contribute to a new *ideology* of class, which occludes the causes of class (Skeggs 2004a; Wood and Skeggs 2008; Skeggs and Wood 2009).

If class *consciousness* is not what it once was, class *inequality* is certainly increasing. (As we write in 2011 from the British context, the UK coalition government's campaign to reduce the national debt involves a series of harsh cuts in public funding which will be felt most by the poorest of society. Unemployment is at 7.9 per cent and one in five young people between sixteen and twenty-five are now unemployed.[2] In the USA, the unemployment figure rose from 5 to 9 per cent between 2008 and 2010.[3]) New capitalist modes of production only reorganise those that cannot mobilise themselves around the shifting job market, leaving many – the so-called underclass 'chavs' in the UK, or the 'white trash' and racialised 'poor' of the US – related to the mode of production by their very alienation from it, discarded (literally and metaphorically) as the 'waste' of the 'system'.

Another explanation for the hesitancy around class is that media and cultural studies have responded to post-structuralist critiques of 'reductionism' and 'essentialism' (Morley 2009). Analyses of media and class were stymied by criticism of an overly reductive application of Marx's version of ideology which relied on the base/superstructure model (Murdock 1997). Assuming the base as the economic force which underpins and therefore determines the superstructure (the ideas of a society) is to oversimplify the tensions and complex relationships between the economy of culture and the cultural economy in social relations of production. Morley (2009) argues that Marxist analyses often read texts as simple 'reflections' of the ideas of the ruling classes, offering crude assumptions about the successful imposition of dominant ideologies, largely through a reading of Althusser's (1971) model of interpellation. Given this kind of determinism overburdened by explicating ideology, there was a retreat from the practice of making critical judgments about cultural products, as cultural studies in particular pursued the ordinary and the vernacular with zeal (Murdock 1997).

One answer has been to argue for the renewed relevance of political economy, and reality television has been evaluated in terms of its congruence with the capitalist economy of television production: cheap programming which is easily formatted and exported (Raphael 2004). This cues us into the fact that media are both mode of production *and* cultural narrative. Moreover, technological advances and developments in the industry have meant that these two elements have become even more intricately entwined as production is more and more part of the text, and audiences become more and more involved in production. Nowhere is this more visible than in reality television's ongoing integration into other media platforms. As Mike Wayne (2003: 143) argues about the *Big Brother* phenomenon, '"text" is really too narrow a word', since it is 'haunted by the unequal exchanges of value, power and ethics which are indispensable to capitalism'.

What Is Reality Television?

Debates about what exactly constitutes reality television are extensive within television production, journalism, marketing discourse and academic analyses. Su Holmes and Deborah Jermyn (2004) detail how reality television is far too diverse to be contained within a specific genre, drawing on techniques from light entertainment, lifestyle, daytime TV, talk shows, documentary and melodrama, in which key skills in television production shift from direction to casting and editing. It is precisely its hybridity and the speed with which it replicates itself that makes it difficult to define and pin down (Holmes 2008). However, Nick Couldry argues for maintaining the term 'reality television' because of its suggestiveness about the myth of the mediated centre: 'presenting itself as the privileged "frame" through which we access the reality that *matters to us as social beings*' (Couldry 2003: 58; our emphasis). We would further argue for keeping the term for what it indexes about the appearance of the material world in texts – for its contribution to the spectacularisation of class relations.

Reality television has often been cited as having antecedents in social-realist observational documentary in the UK (for a good account, see Biressi and Nunn 2005 or Bruzzi 2006), and in the social experimental tradition of liberal education in the US (see McCarthy 2004). Early examples include observational documentaries such as Paul Watson's *The Family* (1974) and in the US *An American Family* (1972). Later developments, potentially fuelled by the economic pressures on the television industry (Raphael 2004), saw observational cop shows like *America's Most Wanted* (1988) in the US and *Police, Camera, Action* (1994) in the UK. A new era of 'formatted documentary' (Hill 2007) was quick to develop, while exportable shows like *Big Brother* (2000), *Survivor* (2000) and *Idol* (2001) created lucrative franchises that were sometimes termed 'event' programming. At the same time, the mainstreaming of what were once daytime concerns into primetime television saw the feminisation of the schedule and the rise of lifestyle and makeover television (Moseley 2000). At the end of the 1990s and into the 2000s, shows like *Changing Rooms* (1997), *What Not to Wear* (2002), *Extreme Makeover* (2002) and *Extreme Makeover: Home Edition* (2003) offered transformative solutions to tired bodies, homes and gardens. These shows have begun to evolve into programmes with an even more strident moral/pedagogic agenda like *Supernanny* (2004), *You Are What You Eat* (2004), *The Biggest Loser* (2004) and *Honey We're Killing the Kids* (2006), largely promoted by Channel 4 and BBC 3 in the UK, and by The Learning Channel in the USA. For a more detailed discussion of the gender and classed elements of the pedagogic agenda in the numerous versions of makeover television, see Weber (2009). The reality landscape now looks incredibly diverse, with pedagogic shows surviving among game and dating permutations such as *The Bachelor* (2002), shows which urge the reform of loutish men (*Tool Academy*, 2009), to those about relations with pets (*It's Me or the Dog!*, 2005), along with shows about heroic (working-class) masculinity (*Deadliest Catch*, 2005) and numerous challenges for celebrities (*I'm a Celebrity, Get Me Out of Here!*, 2002, and *Dancing with the Stars*, 2004).

Faced with such a range of programmes, defining the rise of the genre has proved difficult. For a time, the term 'docusoap' was used as a catch-all phrase (Bruzzi 2006; Dovey 2000; Kilborn 2003), but the event-focused lack of narrative structure and short timescale of many programmes called into question the soap element, while the formatted, melodramatic generation of conflict challenged the documentary elements. John Corner (2002) proposes that reality television is best viewed as part of television's 'post-documentary context', a contradictory cultural environment where viewers, participants and producers are less invested in absolute truth and representational ethics, and more interested in the space that exists between reality and fiction, in which new levels of representational play and reflexivity are visualised.

The establishment of lifestyle programming and its insistence on the exploration of the personal and intimate has given momentum to changes in documentary formats. One of the prevailing techniques from the makeover show is the camera's primary interest in the *reaction* to the situation, rather than the action – what Charlotte Brunsdon (2003: 10) calls 'the changed grammar of the close-up', where television evokes rather than represents. Rachel Moseley describes how:

> Make-over shows ask the audience to draw on a repertoire of personal skills, our ability to search faces and discern reaction (facilitated by the close-up) from the smallest details – the twitch of a muscle, an expression in the eye – a competence suggested by Tania Modleski as key to the pleasure of soap opera's melodramatic form. These programmes showcase the threatening excessiveness of the ordinary ... These are precisely instances of powerful spectacular uber-ordinariness. (Moseley 2000: 314)

The regularity and importance of the close-up across all reality programmes, coupled with ironic music and juxtapositional editing, register the close proximity reality programming has to melodrama and its manipulation of affect. Private lives are transformed into public spectacle through an emphasis upon drama and performance over information. Helen Piper (2004) usefully offers us the phrase 'improvised drama' to describe how the banal observations of a series like *Wife Swap* (2003–9) are turned into moments of dramatic intensity.

The melodramatic tension of much reality television suggests more potential in the form beyond initial disappointment with a lack of documentary point of view. Holmes and Jermyn's (2007) analysis of the ambiguities present in *Wife Swap* suggest that the focus on the struggles of the individual and their everyday labours reveals the very constructedness of 'typical' gender identities. While John Corner (2006: 73) suggests that it 'exposes some of the rhythms, tensions, and contradictions of everyday living and indeed the structures of wealth, class and culture in ways not open to more conventional [documentary] treatments'. Participants and viewers are at least opening themselves up to the possibility of re-imagining the routine and the everyday as they wrestle with aspects of discontent.

What is therefore interesting is *how* reality television forces class back onto the agenda. Whereas people 'in' the media were out of reach and belonged to a set of privileged elites, now the reliance on so-called 'ordinary' people as participants in all manner of games, trials and transformations, who allow their own behaviours and practices to be observed and recorded for entertainment, shifts the terms of debate. Holmes and Jermyn (2004) note that the one consistent feature of reality television is how the issues of cultural value continually plague the discussion, which is partly to do with this emphasis on what Francis Bonner (2003) calls 'ordinary everydayness'.

Some suggest that the use of 'ordinary' people is democratising, others that it is exploitative. The use of the term 'ordinary' should immediately alert us to the political archaeology latent in the word: as mentioned above, Roger Bromley (2000) proposes that 'ordinary' is one of the many euphemisms to emerge after thirty years of political rhetoric and academic theory claiming the demise of class, as a substitute for the term 'working class'. The class profile of those appearing on reality television is skewed towards the working class, which also reflects more widespread trends in participatory media which have altered the class and gendered dynamics across media more generally (see Griffen-Foley 2004).

Whereas previous analyses of social-realist documentary and drama could comfortably draw out the dominant position in the text, when media had a more obvious relationship with the state, or with other modes of capitalism, in reality television we are faced with questions of *self* representation, as well as representation. Increased access to the media has not necessarily produced access to full participation in democracy, or even more control over the semiotic forms of power, which calls for a re-evaluation of recognition politics (see also Fraser 1999; McNay 2008). This is an era, Graeme Turner (2010) argues, where the media has become so powerful that it operates in its own interest and where participation in media entertainment is a very different process to 'participatory democracy'. Now media do not just work to 'represent' cultural identities, rather they have the power to create them, as we see in the various permutations and values attached to forms of celebrity. Wood (2009) has argued elsewhere that television has interactive ways of establishing meaning with viewers which extend beyond models of representation. We must therefore look for other ways, *as well as* through representation, in which social inequalities are embedded into mediated processes (Wood 2010).

If the media occupies a mythical 'centre', as proposed by Nick Couldry (2003), we need to reassess how it functions. For Jack Bratich (2007), reality television is not just about the *representation* of society and culture, but a more ingrained *intervention* into those fields. Unpaid participation in media has collapsed the distance from which we might once have seen it as an ideological force operating from 'out there'. One response to the failings of ideology to fully explain ambiguities in media texts in the 1990s was to deploy postmodern critiques which talked about irony and playfulness. While reality television certainly plugs into that trajectory, the further collapse of modernist boundaries of production and consumption, and of text and audience, ironically put class, and more problematically ideology, back in the spotlight. Class inequality has offered up a convenient short cut to narrative oppositions in the absence of traditional scripting. Now that reality television inscribes 'performing oneself' as labour, what kinds of alienation might we be experiencing? To tell dramas through 'real' people marks the editing and (sometimes) scripting of people as processes which attach value to certain modes of performance and behaviour over others. This is why so many out-dated forms of class antagonism, like the use of finishing-school teachers to control recalcitrant pupils (as in *Ladette to Lady*, 2005–), can be resurrected without much curiosity. What modes of antago-nism are at work when people perform themselves? Do we see new mediated forms of struggle where self-performance is the new 'spirit' which fuels profit accumulation? 'Real life' is broken down and commodified into forms of spectacle, encoding certain ways of seeing ourselves and seeing others which is constitutive (not just representative) of social hierarchies and distinctions. In the inter-ests of lucrative entertainment, class is back, presented in new (mediated) ways.

Given that class has for some years now been marginal to the analyses of media texts, we think it useful first to offer a summary of class theories. We hope this will help to guide the reader through the rest of the book. We then explain some of the extant work on class and reality television and offer a route through the structure and chapters of the book.

What Is Class?

The term 'class' is one of the most spoken, denied, euphemised and confusing terms bandied about in public culture and remains integral to the vernacular, from popular culture to government rheto-ric and academic writing. In a UK MORI (1995) poll, over 50 per cent of the population specified that they 'felt' working class, but had huge problems defining what this meant. In a UK MORI (1997) poll for the TV programme *World in Action*, of those surveyed, 75 per cent of people said they were conscious of living in a society divided by class. And in 2002 in a UK MORI poll, 66 per cent of people surveyed claimed to feel 'working class and proud of it'. Nearly 50 per cent believed that Britain was more divided by class today than it was in 1979, and 70 per cent said they believed 'the class system is harmful to us and those around us'. More bizarrely, the 2002 poll also found that 55 per cent of those who would be categorised as middle class by occupation claimed to have 'working-class feelings'.

Sociologists Payne and Grew (2005) suggest that these uncertainties around 'knowing' and 'feel-ing' whether one is of a certain class, or whether one experiences society as classed, persist because class is incredibly hard to define and has come to stand in for so many things. Since the Ancient Greeks, the term 'class' has operated to include and exclude, to mark through classification and ma-terialise inequalities, in an effort to organise and constitute understandings of value. The term is also used as a way of explaining *all* social organisation and is intimately tied to other complex under-standings of nation, sexuality, race and gender. Payne and Grew maintain that in order to answer 'what is class?' would require a complex sociology essay, which explains why lay people have so much difficulty pinning down the definition. Below is our attempt to summarise the main arguments.

Class-ifications are never neutral terms, but emerge as the result of particular power interests that then get consolidated into abstract explanations. While they are shaped by interest groups in the social and material conditions of their emergence, they are also reinforced by their citation, their performative function and the struggles for legitimation that take place across different sites of institutionalisation such as welfare, law, education and the media. Therefore, there are always struggles over the definitions of class-ifications and the power relations which instate and reinforce inequality. Social and media theorists are part of this legitimation/institutionalisation process and the current state of debates about class in social and cultural theory demonstrates the range of interests and perspectives at stake between those who want to use and organise around the category for purposes of social justice, and those who want to deny the existence of class to hide and legitimate their own privilege (see Savage 2003 and Skeggs 2004a for a development of these debates).

Put most simply, the term class explains distributive inequality through economic differentiation. For industrialised societies, class has been formed around the basis of capitalism, distinguishing between those who do, and those who do not, have access to the means of production. Yet even this is not straightforward, as key forms of economic organisation such as imperialism and colonialism, which established our current global economy, were indivisible from their moral legitimation – 'the civilising mission'. For Max Weber ([1904] 1930), the project of capitalism was inseparable from its 'spirit' – that of Christianity – which was central to organising the labouring body and soul. The labouring body has been entwined with ideas about gender and sexuality. Capitalism shapes the divisions of labour – as raced, gendered and classed – not through the direct imposition of a model of perfect profit accumulation, but in negotiation with other histories of structured power such as patriarchy.

In this summary of the historical legacies that inform the use of the concept of class, we examine what is at stake in these particular definitions. Hopefully, this will enable the reader to identify why class is a still a significant analytical lens for media analysis. It also draws attention to how ideas were transported into different spaces, via Marx and later Weber, in the making of national cultures, such as the Puritanism of the US, the communism of Eastern Europe and the 'have a go' denial of class in Australia, as demonstrated by the chapters in this book.

Marx and Weber

There are two major theoretical/political trajectories in the development of class as a concept. These are abstractions about how class works – its causes and its manifestations – rather than understandings of empirical experience. The first, Marxist, approach prioritises the role of exploitation and struggle in the making of classes and social relations more generally. The second focuses on class hierarchies and status without reference to struggle and exploitation (see Cannadine 1998). For Marxists, class has a number of distinctive features: class is a *relationship* – i.e. it is always relative to other groups – and the relationship is *antagonistic* because it is always based on exploitation and control. Therefore, class is always about the struggle between groups over control, in which the exploiters and exploited fight it out. The antagonism is always formed in the process of *production*, and class is an *objective* relationship. For Marx, the ideas of society are always the ideas of the ruling class who have the means to put them into effect (access to the symbolic). It does not matter how people think about their subjective location (identity); rather, the location of people is entirely determined according to economic relationships of exploitation (Callinicos and Harman 1987).

The emphasis on antagonism means that, for Marx, class relations are *the* dynamic of history. This is epitomised by the struggle between those trying to extract (surplus) value from workers' labour power and the attempt by workers to restrict this extraction and wrestle back control over their time and energy. The form of this relationship of exploitation may change over time. For example, the development of the service economy and mutations into financialisation are not based on a direct labour relationship (e.g. sub-prime mortgages – see the brilliant analysis by Gary Dymski 2009), but ultimately, the relationship is always based on a struggle over the extraction and protection of value from bodies.

In Weber's ([1904] 1930) development of Marx, he shows how Calvinism's incitement to continual toil in order to generate one's place in heaven produced great dividends for capital. This analysis involved not just the imposition of the 'ideas of the ruling class' as Marx proposed, but a 'spirit' diffused through all our social relationships, including what we think of as our soul or subjectivity. In the US, we can see how the 'American Dream' operates as a 'spirit of capitalism', a pseudo-religious incitement deployed to similar effect to make im/possible future success the means for enduring harsh labour conditions in the present and as a way of closing down alternative legitimate ways of being.

For Marx and Engels, it is the bourgeoisie that calls into existence the modern working class – the proletarians – 'who live only so long as they find work and who find work only so long as their labour increases capital' (Marx and Engels [1848] 1968: 51). In their analysis, class is a description of the conditions of existence of labour under capitalism. Class consciousness is not about identifying with a category but of recognising the exploitative conditions of one's existence. Weber ([1904] 1930) diluted the emphasis on exploitation and talked instead of 'life chances' and access to 'resources', and therefore many theorists have used Weber to develop ideas of status. The 'economic class' versus 'social status' dialectic has shaped two further directions: the insistence on politics and culture as major influences over class formation (Gramsci 1971; Williams 1961) and the insistence on the importance of consumption, rather than production (Veblen [1899] 2008), to the conditions of existence. Studies which focus on consumption often draw upon Weberian status hierarchies, where class becomes a marker of difference rather than a sign of exploitation.

While both Marx and Weber point to inequalities, Marx is more concerned with the practices through which those with resources reproduce their advantage. For Marx, one person's advantage is another's disadvantage: the capitalist exists to exploit the labourer; the material welfare of one group causally depends on the material deprivations of the other (see Wright 1997). For Marx, these advantages are institutionalised in law (property relations) and enforced (if challenged) through violence (the police/army) and by ideological state apparatuses, of which the media are but one.

Measuring and Class-ifying

Marx's perspective is radically different to the other major etymology of the concept of class. This perspective sees no need for a revolution, but concerns itself with the precise nature of classification, employment 'aggregates', status and how to best conceptualise occupational groups in a hierarchical order. It began in 1665 with William Petty, who set out to calculate the value of the 'people' of England for taxation purposes, and was carried over to the US for administrative purposes.

Petty is attributed with devising what is now known as the 'political arithmetic' tradition of class analysis in order to enumerate what was otherwise unmeasurable (Poovey 1995). A person was conceptualised as a quantifiable, knowable, hence *governable object* tightly linked to national formations. James Thompson (1996: 26) documents how, throughout the eighteenth century, there was a 'drive toward an abstract and consistent and therefore predictable representation of exchange, that is, toward (new) scientific, quantitative, and mathematical modelling'. This tradition led to the British Government's Registrar General's five categories of social class based on the collation of occupational groups from professional/managerial to unskilled, which has recently expanded to include seven new categorisations, to take into account economic changes, such as the decline of the manufacturing industry and the rise of the service industry.

Emphasis on measurement and calculation deflects attention away from the reasons for inequality and into a methodological debate about how best to measure, as if divisions were the result of mathematical formulae. The significant difference between the two main perspectives is cause and effect: one tries to explain why classes come into effect, while the other measures the end product of historical social relations. Central to both is paid work: labour as a force which shapes all relations, and work organised into occupations for measurement. Feminist critiques point out that exploitation through paid labour is only one way in which capitalism operates, highlighting the significance of domestic labour for social reproduction which sustains exploitation by providing and servicing the workforce (Hartmann and Sargent 1981). Feminists have also critiqued the political arithmetic tradition arguing that measuring women's social class by the husband's and father's occupation is inadequate (see Crompton 1993; Stanworth 1984). There is some agreement, however, over the notion that even if children are not immediately born into work categories, they are born into classed routes, through access and exclusion. Most theorists of class agree that inheritance of social position at birth is the key to future trajectory.

These epistemological etymologies of the concept of class are premised on both understanding 'objective' social relationships (economic possibilities, means of production, divisions of labour, measurement of status differences) and, in some cases, attempting to understand how class consciousness comes into being (for Marx) and how the soul is generated from the spirit of capitalism (for Weber). The abstraction from the objective into the subjective (economic position will lead to a certain consciousness/soul) gives rise to huge theoretical complications and confusions when we try to understand class as a lived experience. Epistemological abstractions do not fit the ontological experiences, or even the mediation of lived experiences. The difficulty is exacerbated when we try to weave a third key thread into understandings of class: morality. And morality leads us into very different vernacular traditions in national expressions of class.

Morality and Culture

Definitions of class often entwine ideas of a person's moral as well as economic value (Skeggs 1997, 2004a; Sayer 2005). As pointed to earlier, classifications have long fluctuated between moral and economic criteria. At certain periods in history, class was definable primarily by economic, monetary and market value; at others, it was defined in relation to moral behaviour. During the 1850s and 1860s, for instance, there was less talk of working class and middle class, and more focus on the deserving and undeserving poor, of 'respectable artisans and gentlemen as emphasis was placed on moral rather than economic criteria' (Crossick 1991: 61). In the play for power and legitimation by the newly emergent middle class, morality became more central to defining class. Adam Smith (1757) the proponent of political economy, for instance, advanced the concept of economic self-interest as a moral (religious) imperative, one that now exerts its presence as a 'truth'.

It is not until the early nineteenth century that the term class regularly appears in discourse and is consolidated in descriptions of society. Some theorists argue that the term emerged to coincide with the rise of the 'middle sort' (Williams 1988). Dror Wahrman (1995) maintains that the crucial moment for fixing the idea of the middle class in Britain occurred around the time of the 1832 *Reform Act*, where the need for political representation allowed the middle class to be consolidated as a group. One of the central issues concerns the question of who had access to the symbolic means to legitimate themselves. Significantly, for this book, Terry Eagleton (1989: 22) notes how in order to legitimate their own claims for power, the middle class used the expression of 'taste' and the generation of distinctive cultures: 'the ultimate binding force of the bourgeois social order [were] habits, pieties, sentiments and affections' to which *they* attributed higher moral value. Displays of culture and morality were the means by which the middle class became recognisable, and claims to high culture and taste continue to be mechanisms for promoting distinction and exclusion (see Bourdieu [1979] 1986). We will explore Bourdieu's proto-Weberian analysis in more detail below, as it under-pins the analysis of many of our authors.

The emergence of the term working class is subject to a similarly contested debate. Lynette Finch documents how in Australia, class emerged from the middle-class colonial welfare administrators as a category to define the urban poor. Carrying with them British definitions, they developed their own interpretations and categorisations that were particularly gendered and conceived through the interpretation of the behaviour of women from the urban slums:

> The range of chosen concerns through which middle-class observers made sense of the observed, included references to: living room conditions … drinking behaviour … language (including both the type of things which were spoken about, and the manner in which they were referred to – literally the types of words used); and children's behaviour. (Finch 1993: 10)

As she notes, these were *moral*, gendered references where political arithmetic and morality combine through methods of observation. In an equally detailed historical analysis of British imperial discourse, Ann McClintock suggests that the concept of class has a historical link to more generalisable 'Others', who were known through the concept of degeneracy, a term applied as much to classifying racial 'types' as to the urban poor:

> The degenerate classes, defined as departures from the normal human type, were as necessary to the self-definition of the middle class as the idea of degeneration was to the idea of progress, for the distance along

the path of progress travelled by some portions of humanity could be measured only by the distance
others lagged behind. (McClintock 1995: 46)

Domestic servants, for instance, were often depicted by the racialised imagery of degradation – of
contagion, promiscuity and savagery. As Friedrich Engels ([1844] 1958: 33) notes of the working class,
it is 'a physically degenerate race, robbed of all humanity, degraded, reduced morally and intellectually to bestiality'. Engels' description, used in his case to advocate for social justice, is delimited by the
prevailing gendered and raced discourses of his time which semiotically attach degeneracy to the
working classes. In the bourgeois claim for moral legitimacy, domestic servants, in particular, became
the projected object and location for dirt (see also Walkerdine in this volume). They were explicitly
associated with the care of back passages, and the generalised poor came to be represented as
excrement. Osbourne's pamphlet on 'Excremental Sewage' in 1852 represents the working class as
a problem for civilisation, as sewerage that contaminates and drains the nation (Yeo 1993).
Moreover, Nancy Armstrong (1987) notes how fears of women's bodies as carriers of degeneracy
and contagion as the constitutive limit to proper personhood held particular significance for the
Puritans in the establishment of America.

Gender, race and sexuality amalgamate in all class definitions. As McClintock puts it, 'the invention of racial fetishism became central to the regime of sexual fetishism which became central to the
policing of the "dangerous classes"' (McClintock 1995: 182). This was all premised on protecting and
drawing boundaries around economic interests through moral and cultural visibilities. Foucault, for
instance, notes how the middle class, struggling to find the means to define themselves, used reference to commodification to regulate sexuality as a means of social identification:

The middle class thus defined itself as different from the aristocracy and the working classes who spent,
sexually and economically, without moderation … It differed by virtue of its sexual restraint, its monogamy
and its economic restraint or thrift. (Foucault 1979: 100)

Economic metaphors abound, enabling us to see how the discourses of the economy infuse discourses of class, race, gender and sexuality, often by integrating moral categories of value such as
aspiration and degeneracy.

However, value can only be realised though its use and exchange. For instance, through property and social contracts we see bodily value distributed and traded. The marriage contract legally
institutionalises heterosexuality as the legitimate structure for the organisation of both gender and
sexuality (and many would argue class relations through the consolidation of property relationships),
which instead of operating through an antagonistic structuring dynamic relationship (like class)
reveals an agreement drawn up at an intimate level that secures unequal power relationships
(Pateman 1988). The heterosexual contract reveals that class, race, gender and sexuality do not work
as equivalent and compatible categories. While it could be argued (as many feminists have) that men
exploit (but are dependent upon) women through their domestic labour, we also know that many
women voluntarily contract into that exploitation. This exploitation is different to the employment

contract, since it is enabled through ideas about romance and love, although, as Kipnis (1993) and Evans (2003) have documented, these contracts are always entwined with economic and cultural exchange relationships. Bourdieu (1977) maintains that the marriage contract is a key site for the misrecognition of power, a mystificatory device that makes intimacy appear as if it exists in a different space to capital exchange. And it is to Bourdieu that we now turn.

Bourdieu

Drawing on Weber's modifications of Marx, Pierre Bourdieu (1985, 1987) takes up the legacy of life chances, status and (market) exchange by using metaphors of capital – economic, social, symbolic and cultural – as they accrue over time and space in different composition and volume, to describe how the middle classes reproduce their interests. His is a theory of social reproduction: the transmission of power and advantage that operates through processes of capital accrual and misrecognition of power. It is not a theory of direct exploitation but of legitimation, showing how one class gains advantage through institutionalised processes of exclusion (such as education and taste) and, by doing so, enact a form of symbolic violence. In the process, the excluded are also symbolically misrecognised as responsible for their own exclusion. He enables us to see how the middle classes amass resources while continually excluding others by installing boundaries around their advantage. These distinctions exclude and extend beyond the law, seeping into all social relationships.

Bourdieu's theories provide exceptional explanatory power (empirically and theoretically) for understanding how middle-class privilege remains unchallenged. As we have shown elsewhere, his ideas are particularly valuable for understanding formations of power and legitimation, but are much less useful for understanding the power-less (Skeggs 2004b). For instance, working-class culture is rendered valueless because it can rarely be capitalised upon in the fields of exchange (Boyne 2002). Likewise, gender has less value by default, as the fields of exchange are premised on masculine structural power (Bourdieu 1977). Skeggs (2011) has proposed elsewhere a development of Bourdieu's model into an understanding of 'person-value' in order to see how those who are not born into the middle class generate alternate value-chains in different spaces of exchange. Bourdieu has also been accused of reinforcing the very categories that he set out to unearth (Cook 2003), for just as he describes the taste culture of the middle classes, he also legitimises that culture *as* middle class (Rancière 1983).

Bourdieu offers us a useful frame to understand middle-class power and *legitimation*. Mike Savage (2003) and Marilyn Strathern (1992) take this analysis further, demonstrating how values and cultural practices traditionally associated with the middle class and reliant on access to forms of cultural capital, such as educational leisure activities, eating and speaking, are not only convertible into value but are also increasingly becoming *the* normative, generating what Savage identifies as the new 'particular-universal'. He proposes that this echoes the larger social shift that occurred in the late twentieth century due to changing formations of deindustrialisation in the West. Strathern also demonstrates, through a study of English kinship, how normative value is given to specific middle-class practices. These practices, she argues, have come to increasingly define the Western social itself, marking out the proper against which the constitutive limit is established.

We can see this manifested, in particular, through what we call the 'normative performative', the iteration of the norm through bodily practices which enact the proper as if normal and habitual. When Judith Butler (1990) suggests that discursive performa*tives* and embodied performa*nces* are both modes of citationality, she opens up the 'demand to perform'. Later in this introduction, we will explore how this relates to reality television and new visual imperatives to perform the norm. We might see this performance demand as just the latest form in a long line of historical techniques used to make the working class publicly 'appear' and be made accountable through specific ways of telling and doing. For instance, Carolyn Steedman (2000) details how the working class had to learn to historically tell themselves in front of law, generating legally fashioned classed subjectivity in order to receive poor relief. Telling was structured through moral redemptive narratives (influenced by Christianity), which enabled the working class to show that they were redeemable and hence 'deserving'. This leads Steedman to argue that ideas of self for the working class were shaped by legal interlocution and state welfare. Stanley Aronowitz (2004) also argues that power not only includes the ability to exclude, but also the ability to set the terms of the social through the telling of the past, present and future.

How do we trace these elements of social relations based on inequality, premised on forms of judgment, value and exchange, and which inscribe modes of performance through the contours of the shifting landscape of reality television?

Theorising Class and Reality Television

The majority of recent work on reality television draws upon a Foucauldian frame using Nikolas Rose (1989) to chart the imperatives to self-governance as part of a broader neo-liberal political agenda which accompanies the repeal of state support (e.g. Ouellette 2004; Ouellette and Hay 2008; Palmer 2003). Particularly apparent in lifestyle and makeover television, middle-class tastes and values are normalised (Palmer 2004; Taylor 2005; Karl 2007; Karl and Doyle 2008) and offered as pedagogic guidance to those who are deemed to be failing in the skills of self-work and self-development that are necessary in the precarious 'new economy' (McRobbie 2004). In this vein, Samantha Lyle (2008) argues that a programme like *Wife Swap* assumes a 'middle-class gaze' as viewers are encouraged to judge normative behaviour. We have contributed to that debate by arguing that the lack of historical context given to the participants' situations in reality television texts means that the consequences of social and material forces are played out through the immediacy of the genre. Participants' failures, and sometimes their successes, are coded as psychological traits at the level of individual responsibility. While class inequality as an *explanation* is occluded from the text, it is a different step to suggest that this is evidence that class is now a zombie category that has been *replaced* by life narratives. Rather, we point out that imperatives to selfhood and responsibilisation are themselves an ideology, visible in other sites such as law and education, where the blame for inequality is shifted onto those at a disadvantage (Wood and Skeggs 2008).

Explanations which utilise the governmentality thesis of Rose (1989) have been criticised for adopting a functionalist explanation of the media, assuming that the pedagogic mode of governance is easily passed on to audiences (Morley 2009), and drawing attention away from television's role in new forms of capital exploitation. As one of the most effective global industries for generating new sources of revenue, television has been highly adept at finding new markets: enabling new forms of exploitation through opening out the previously 'private' forms of intimate life (the rise and rise of the reality television format); challenging traditionally protected labour markets (flexible contracts for those working in the industry, and the blurring of the boundaries between employees and participants – see Jost 2011); and establishing new terms of market exchange with audiences (pay-per-view, for instance). Attention on governance can deflect attention away from the reason *for* governance, which is to lubricate the operations of capital.

We need to take into account the mutability of capital and class relations as we think about reality television. One further development of Bourdieu has taken an interesting direction by extending the Marxist idea of value-extraction. These theorists circumnavigate the determinism of Marx by showing how as capital finds new routes, 'lines of flight', and new forms of exploitation, we must recalibrate our understandings of exploitation. Laura Grindstaff (2002) and Eva Illouz (2003, 2007), for instance, note how new fields of value production have emerged through talk-show television. Grindstaff's research shows how the production process is geared towards 'the money shot' – the heightened dramatic moment when guests lose control. She argues that while this gives media 'access' to those once excluded, it only allows working-class participants to speak and 'rant' in certain ways under particular conditions, reproducing class difference in the process. Similarly for Illouz, shows like *Oprah* (1986–2011) exploit a 'culture of pain and misery'. 'Ordinary' peoples' performances of emotion generate audience viewing figures, producing not just symbolic violence (through humiliation and shaming) but also straightforward exploitation and the extraction of economic value. Oprah Winfrey has amassed a huge fortune by positing herself as the ultimate commodity in self-management through a whole media empire (Illouz 2003).

More recently, Hollows and Jones (2010) note the rise and marketability of 'the moral entrepreneur' as a new category of media celebrity. In a discussion of the British TV chef Jamie Oliver, who is responsible for reality programmes like *Jamie's School Dinners* (2005), they argue that Oliver produces value through promoting a mixture of morality and commodity, offering the solution to social problems through the market. Like Oprah, Oliver (and his sponsor Sainsbury's supermarket) has accumulated huge profits through identifying those in need of moral reform: symbolic denigration and exploitation that converts into economic capital. Likewise, Mark Andrejevic (2004) documents the value and exploitation involved in new forms of surveillance where reality television can be posed as 'the work of being watched'. He points to the double value that can be extracted from programmes – in the exchange itself for television's profit, and in the information that participants give up about themselves which is useful to the broader market, a process which further acculturates us into accepting systems of surveillance.

These new forms of exploitation and their mediation lead us into debates about the significance of affect to the forms of labour that make such exploitation more intense, subtle and directed to and from women, and from which it is less easy to be alienated as it operates in the field of intimate relationships (Skeggs 2010). Illouz (2007) maintains that economic relationships have become deeply emotional, while close intimate relationships have become increasingly defined by economic models of bargaining, exchange and equity – or what she calls 'emotional capitalism' and 'cold intimacy'. However, it could be argued that sentiment in other forms, especially romantic novels and their development into women's magazines, have always offered a space of value production (see Thompson 1996; Berlant 2008). We argue that it is the use of unpaid 'ordinary people' marshalled from audiences into production regimes that intensifies the possibilities for exploitation.

Reality television therefore extracts value in different ways from the performances of the unpaid participants. This is not so far removed from the 'enforced narratives' of working-class telling that Carolyn Steedman describes above, which have now been extended by reality television into full-blown 'enforced performances'. The telling is now accompanied by detailed doing, where numerous acts of behaviour are put on display as reality participants publicly perform (for entertainment value, not legal interlocutors) the performance demands of the programme.

As we referred to earlier, pace Butler, performatives are unconscious repeated gendered and classed enactments, while performances are full-blown conscious actions. What we often see on reality television is the performative made explicit. That which is meant to be normative, a citational form of social reproduction, becomes writ large as its component parts are revealed through ungovernable bodies and embodied excessive performances that cannot be controlled by the demands that have called them into effect. Participants are called on by producers to 'be themselves', 'only more so', in what Kitzman calls 'an economy of recognition' (cited in Grindstaff 2011). So when wives are swapped in Wife Swap, or participants are holed up together in the Big Brother house, or forced to undertake group tasks to get a job on The Apprentice (2005–), we see taken-for-granted unconscious performatives made into conscious deliberations and acts, as they are called into a public televised performance. Participants often fail to explain their behaviour when they are suddenly called to account for themselves to camera for conditions that are beyond their control in the 'happenstance' of reality programming (Wood and Skeggs 2008). Editing and ironic voiceover often focus in on the symbols of failure in what we have previously termed 'the judgment shot' (Skeggs, Thumim and Wood 2008, and see Tyler in this volume).

If class is performative in the same way as gender and heterosexuality, then it is routinely performed through the bodily hexis or habitus. As Bourdieu (1986) argues, repeated bodily movements and habits reveal class position, such as the bent body of the farm labourer. Bodily dispositions that appear as natural, normal and habituated are exposed through performance demands. Class inequalities in access to resources are revealed by the TV producers' demand for people in need of transformation: the abject are expected to perform their abjection and the excessive are asked to perform their excess in order to display their need for transformation and education in the normative. Reality television through full-blown performance demands reveals classed and gendered bodies in the making and unmaking (see also Holmes and Jermyn 2008). Here, in the focus on the 'immediacy' of reality television, and in the tension over what will happen next, participants can surprise us as 'affect seeps beyond containment', which all of course enhances the entertainment value. It is precisely this revealing and opening out of the normative performative that we also found in our audience research. We found that viewers did not always take up the middle-class gaze or even the pedagogic incentive to self-govern, but would make assessments of value based on their own experiences, resources and capitals. The affective immediacy of the text often brought about surprising connections that reached beyond the symbolic violence of the programmes. All of which makes us challenge the functionalist approach to reality television which assumes that governance works (Skeggs, Wood and Thumim 2008; Wood, Skeggs and Thumim 2008; Skeggs and Wood 2008; Wood and Skeggs 2011; Skeggs and Wood forthcoming).

Real Class in This Volume

When *we* refer to class, we deploy these legacies to speak about class relations as:

- exploitation, where one group's advantage is another's loss
- generated through different forms of exchange, where the moral and the economic work through each other to produce new forms of value
- part of the changing moral 'spirit' of capitalism, where the 'self-investment' ethic shapes the neo-liberal capitalist dream
- the struggle over the establishment of middle-class values as normative and universal, which are made explicit through marking the constitutive limit
- a process of inscription written on bodies, which may appear as individualised and psychological failure but is in fact bodily habitus, produced as a direct result of social positioning.

We have therefore used these explanations to shape our collection, and the chapters which follow offer the reader a route through various positions on reality television's relationship to class. We have organised the volume into three subsections: Mediated Exchange and Judgment; Normalisation, Aspiration and Its Limits; Performing and Feeling Class.

Part One: Mediated Exchange and Judgment

This section opens the book by setting out some of the frames and terms of exchange. Who is positioned as having value? How are we invited to make judgments of value? And how do these judgments play out through their mediation? The chapters note how social problems are rerouted through the reality formats, which entice particular performances. Identifying 'the threat to the nation' becomes a powerful device which enables attention to be diverted away from issues of class, while still performed through its idioms. In situations of rapid social transformation, the 'proper subject' is fought over in heightened moral debates about reality television. The chapters on post-socialist reformation show how the terms of exchange are not euphemised but made explicit by the evocation of dangerous pasts. They reveal a precarious situation in which talking about class remains difficult while traditional cultural arbiters of taste attempt to hold on to the power to frame moral value. This situation is fully resolved in post-colonial Australia, where it is the performance of labour that is evaluated as the sign of the good national subject. In many of the papers, labour is seen as a personal disposition rather than a structuring division upon which the distribution of capital is based. The chapters set out how class formations on reality television work as structuring absences that are 'systematically displaced' onto other relationships (see Grindstaff in this volume).

By revisiting his arguments about the myth of the mediated centre in relation to Sennett and Cobb's (1977) work on the hidden injuries of class, Nick Couldry in Chapter Two shows how new class processes on reality television embed forms of moral judgment as a normalised set of relationships. Drawing on Max Weber's ideas of transparency, he maintains that people cannot see the connection between their class position and its causes because of the de-symbolisation of working-class culture which enables the legitimation of middle-class standards (Parkin 1972). The 'hidden hand' of the market system enables reality television to make real social problems nothing more than part of the game or the format (see Biressi in this volume on programmes which intervene in unemployment, and Tyler in this volume for those which deal with teenage pregnancy). This goes some way to explaining the curious way in which class is both visible and invisible, present and yet denied across reality television, to which many of our authors allude.

In Chapter Three, Andrew Tolson, draws on a high-profile UK instance when a normalised set of classed judgments were meted out against Jade Goody (white working-class participant and at some time both a national love and hate figure) in the infamous bullying of Shilpa Shetty (middle-class Asian participant) debacle on UK *Big Brother*. As he explains, Jade represents the 'threat' of demotic celebrity, a working-class woman who used the media system to considerable material advantage. Her outburst towards Shilpa was publicly registered as a threat to national propriety, not class antagonism (which echoes the chapters by Andrejevic, Imre and Tremlett, and Weber in this volume), and was punished accordingly. By conducting a close reading of the transcript of the argument, Tolson reveals how it erupted through the moves made on both sides, and demonstrates clearly how language works as resource where cultural capitals are exchanged. Here, reality television offers a platform for 'unruly civility' which evokes class pathologisation to the advantage of 'good' television.

In Chapter Four, Mark Andrejevic reminds us of the different national frames that manifest around class on reality television as he compares the US and Australian versions of *Border Security*. He details the paradoxes at the heart of making spectacular that which is an unequally distributed resource – mobility. The programmes foreground the radical differences in mobility for different classed and raced groups. The 'border anxiety' expressed by the programme, which profiles airline passengers, enables viewers to recognise the differences between good and bad travellers. Bad (illegal) mobility enables class differences to be seen as a national threat, and viewers are educated to spot the differences by inhabiting the position of security guard. Elsewhere, Andrejevic (2004) has noted the significance of surveillance in the control of risk, and here he demonstrates how surveillance works to exclude people from sources of value. Class politics are transferred onto the threat to the nation represented by the 'outsider' through neo-liberal populism. What is interesting is that those *with* mobility capital – 'business class' travellers – are curiously invisible. Potentially, *invisibility* in media terms is now the more powerful resource, while the visible 'demotic celebrity' (Jade) is duly punished, and following Couldry, hiding power is the name of the game.

Zala Volčič and Karmen Erjavec in Chapter Five discuss the Slovene celebrity reality show *The Farm*, where the communal work space of the rural idyllic farm provides the backdrop to a recognisable reality competition involving various tasks. Here, the old 'spirit' of socialist collective work is marked in sharp contrast to the new forms of neo-liberal self-work espoused by the celebrity participants. The show seems to offer an insight into the rapid transformation and uneven development in Slovenia towards a more neo-liberal state. Myths of social mobility focused on the individual abound in the text and are celebrated by the young audiences of the show. This occurs while the reality of deepening class inequality is denied in public and academic discourse as out of step with the progress of the nation. In post-socialist Slovenia, class cannot be spoken, as it represents the old tradition from which the modern individual must perform their distance.

In Chapter Six, Aniko Imre and Annabel Tremlett discuss the Roma celebrity Győzike, a pop star who has consolidated his fame and fortune through reality television. The authors point out the difficulty in transferring some of the American and Anglocentric models which have thus far been used to explain reality television to the Hungarian context. While the star represents the kind of demotic celebrity discussed by Turner (2010), he is also representative of the Roma underclass which has been savaged by the rise of capitalism in Eastern Europe, demonstrating how discourses of class are also entwined with discourses of race. The rapid rise of commercial television in Hungary is accompanied by the rhetoric of the anxious intellectual elite who, in their play to hold onto power in times of change, are embroiled in a problematic moral dialectic of value. Again, this reality television programme comes to represent some of the difficult negotiations around class, race and national identity in a period of uncertain social transition.

Tania Lewis in Chapter Seven shows how in *MasterChef Australia* (2009–) media economic logics are not just about representation at the level of the symbolic (Turner 2010), but about how performances of value are made through labour and ethnicity. Labour stands in as a personal disposition rather than as a form of exploitation central to the formation of class relations. By promoting ethnicity as part of the romantic ethic of work (aspirational ethnicity as the new spirit of capitalism), in which subjects are ordinary, amenable and willing, working becomes the sign of the good national subject rather than a class relation. This operates against the background of precarious job markets where *MasterChef Australia* foregrounds ethnic 'cosmopolitanism' to 'pave over class differences'.

Part Two: Normalisation, Aspiration and Its Limits

This section shows how the 'normative performative' is key to the making of class relations. New 'aspirational' reality television encapsulates the normative performative at its most alluring as a new wave of reality television, particularly from the US, foregrounds wealth and privilege. In this way, we see how aspiration is commodified and is firmly embedded as a branding process in which bodies are supposed to erase the signs of their labour. But there are tensions in trying to evade the realities of labour, as becomes clear when reality programmes enter into realms such as the labour market, and the myth of transformation available to all is exposed. There are limits to the normalisation process, and in deficit crisis times in Western economies some programmes are struggling to rebrand their pitch. In property programmes, the performance of greed (making more capital through capital) has to be rerouted not just in case it looks morally suspect, but also because property is less likely to realise a return in the present climate. Turning the home into a place of sanctuary instead of profit capitalises on new shifts to affect in class formations of the performative normative.

Lisa Taylor opens this section in Chapter Eight with an analysis of the aspirational lifestyle reality show *The Hills* (2006–) which offers a very different and glamorous aesthetic compared to many other reality shows. She points to the visual allure of the show in which gender shapes dramatic life dilemmas and material wealth is the unacknowledged backdrop to success. No questions are asked about how these young women can afford and access such luxuries, as the historical context of privilege is denied and the dilemmas of the heterosexual contract distract attention. The stars are successful in their ability to self-promote while denying the resources that allow them to do so, which Taylor argues, *pace* bell hooks cited earlier, indexes the inevitability of wealth and privilege at the centre of national value.

Gareth Palmer picks up this thread of self-promotion as an extension of capital's 'line of flight' in Chapter Nine, which draws out the similarities between lifestyle shows like *10 Years Younger* (2003) and *What Not to Wear* and advertising styles. He proposes that the call to aspiration and transformation is straightforwardly promoted through the use of tried and tested advertising techniques which equate selling products with selling selves. He describes how TV stations have to maintain their brand by promoting the experience of pedagogical empowerment, 'watch this and learn how to transform yourself into something good'. Yet he also points to how the body reveals the limits to this incitement to labour as type, amount and possibilities for investment expose the gendered and classed dynamics of the self-branding imperative.

Anita Biressi in Chapter Ten analyses the paradoxes produced by the programme *Benefit Busters* (2009) which follows the extension of reality television into promoting social enterprise initiatives which aim to help people find employment. Such programmes reiterate historical notions of the 'deserving' and 'undeserving' poor through the discourse of social entrepreneurialism in which the modern individual must continually 'enterprise up' their capital to develop future potential. But economic reality spoils the makeover narrative of transformation as high unemployment and unwilling employers mean that the programme struggles to contain the 'truth' within the format. Biressi shows that some things exceed the model of transformation, and that while the show makes an effort to deny class, it is structural inequality after all which breaks open and reveals the conceit of the narrative frame.

In Chapter Eleven, Brenda R. Weber highlights how gender and class produce an explosive mix in the mythical narrative of the American Dream. In a number of chapters in this book, the blogosphere emerges as a site where vitriolic hate directed towards reality participants is poured out at the same time that viewer ratings rise. Indeed, affects of hate are lucrative. Weber looks at this phenomenon in the context of 'octo-mum' Kate Gosselin, who exposes the limits to the American Dream which promotes success as open to all. Using her motherhood as a route to celebrity and material wealth invites an outpouring of moral invective. By promoting the private life of her eight children, Gosselin flouts the game's gendered rules of propriety. While celebrity might be more available, this does not mean that it offers access to symbolic power, since it is clear throughout the book that celebrity operates through a series of class oppositions that delimit taste and value. Gosselin is the constitutive limit to good motherhood. As in the case of Jade and Győzike, the affective reactions of the public are only harnessed further by the media machine to its own advantage as they drive up the media hype.

In Chapter Twelve, the final chapter in this section, Heather Nunn writes of a shift on British television from property to retreat television. Struggling to contain the trope of property investment as a means for profit in the face of the sub-prime scandal and the global downturn, UK programming has come to reflect a shift in investments in the home for the middle classes. Nunn examines the emergent role of the home as a positive investment in 'hope'. Reality television has repackaged its property programmes so that they offer affective security rather than financial insecurity – promoting a synaesthetic sanctuary in an insecure world. Divorcing the home from property and finance, Nunn argues, offers an intervention in a larger political re-imagining of sites of enrichment rather than sites of loss. We see reality television again emerging as part of a much larger attempt at national political reformation by which we are incited to assuage the disappointments of capital. Choice and investment are mobilised here as comfort rather than aspiration.

Part Three: Performing and Feeling Class

This section of the book extends our analysis by examining reality television as a node in sociality, part of the social lives that we live, connecting us as bodies through the various forms of exchange and value-codings that make up class. A television production is one moment in this process. It feeds into and from the interconnected social relations in which we are located, to ourselves and to others, through affect, knowledge and bodily dispositions, but also through our feelings and experience of class over time and social space. The performances interrogated in this part of the book vary, from students attempting to become either performers or participants, to the enforced performances required by radically different US reality television programmes, to reality television participants' 'talking back' to their own performances through social networking sites, and to reality television's mobilisation of shame and pride as both historical and social.

Vicki Mayer in Chapter Thirteen draws on her research into the labour of the casters (the people who scout, select and promote participants) for reality television programmes and the labour of her students who attempt to work and perform in the reality television industry. Mayer was perfectly placed to discuss her students' (and her own) experiences and ambivalent feelings about reality television 'work' as they try and negotiate 'contradictory class locations' as both exploited and exploiter (Wright 1997) in radically different spaces of exchange. All the students had a clear knowledge of class and taste distinctions as they assessed which shows had value. They aimed for programmes that would enhance their already accumulated capitals and worked hard to perform their fit with the programmes' requirements and the casters' capitals. The interrogative nature of casting – asking questions about sex and sexuality, traumas, psyches and embarrassment – can be seen to be working at the minutiae of the episteme of class.

Exploring the 'performance logic' of reality programming in the US, Laura Grindstaff in Chapter Fourteen shows how the new televised environment capitalises on performances of class. Like Mayer, Grindstaff also investigated workers and participants on reality programmes. She discusses *Jersey Shore* (2009, a docusoap made for MTV about Italian Americans in New Jersey), where participants are expected to perform their class and ethnicity through excessive behaviour, leading her to propose that these cartoon-like behaviours are the equivalent of modern-day minstrelsy as they perform a 'trash face'. This face involves excessive expressiveness and is accompanied by a 'trash body' of which fat is the visible sign, pointing to the failure to achieve normative respectable restraint. Grindstaff argues that this is politics at the level of caricature, not surprising in a neo-liberal economy in which as economic inequalities become more stark, cultural caricatures offer a method for encapsulating distinctions. Both Mayer and Grindstaff note the simultaneous denial of the existence of class through the American Dream while programmes are highly structured through class relationships.

Imogen Tyler also exposes the caricatured nature of British reality television through an analysis of 'Chav Mum' TV in Chapter Fifteen. This is not a traditional analysis of cheap television that amplifies stereotypes because it cannot come up with anything more challenging. Rather, it explores the whole social ensnaring process by which TV producers trap young mothers into performing a 'class act' with promises that are never met. Drawing on interviews with the mothers themselves, Tyler shows how they become aware of the negative loading of the filming and the editing process. They then transcode and reanimate their own images through the networking sites that led to the misrecognition of their value in the first place. This is a class value battle fought through the same circuits by which they were ensnared.

Also pointing to locations in time, space and circuits of value, in Chapter Sixteen Valerie Walkerdine analyses how affect is mobilised through class relationships on reality television. Walkerdine demonstrates how the shame and humiliation imposed upon television participants (to reveal their need for transformation) does not just work at the level of the ideological/discursive/representational. It also works through an affective register as shame is carried across history by transgenerational transmission from mother to daughter. By referencing the representation of working-class women historically as the source of dirt and disorder, she suggests that shame has already been embodied by working-class television participants and viewers through maternal transmission before they come into contact with the television. Women are predisposed to feel the shame of their historical value-positioning. This chapter directs us to the continued significance of historical materialism to ideas about which bodies count and how affects are carried through to the present. Walkerdine maintains that anxiety in the present is likely to be a result of positional insecurity in the past, where the gendered body is the transmissional link for classed experience.

Lisa Blackman pushes the deployment of affect in another direction in Chapter Seventeen by detailing how a British reality television programme called *The Choir* (2009) attempted to get people from a working-class area to work together to compete in a choir-singing contest. She analyses how singing together produced a form of collective sociality which transformed (historically produced) shame into pride, an act, she argues, that moves us from a singular individual understanding of television as a form of governance to something much more social and expansive. Like Walkerdine,

Blackman notes the significance of intergenerational transmission of class relations. But she gives us hope that it is not only the negative affects of shame, humiliation and anxiety that are historically transmitted. Through what she describes as 'performative routedness', ideas of revalued community can be regenerated and retained against the backdrop of incessant incitements to aspiration and individuality in a climate of increasing inequality and decreasing job opportunities.

Class is no longer the 'hidden injury' in exactly the same way that Sennett and Cobb proposed in 1977 and we hope this book fuels a more sustained analysis of the ways in which class formations are increasingly mediated.

Notes

1. Funded by the ESRC. Our findings are accessible at: <http://www.esrc.ac.uk/my-esrc/grants/RES-148-25-0040/read>.
2. See <http://www.bbc.co.uk/news/business-12477563> accessed 17 February 2011.
3. See <http://www.tradingeconomics.com/Economics/Unemployment-Rate.aspx?Symbol=USD> accessed 17 February 2011.

Bibliography

Althusser, L. (1971) *Lenin and Philosophy and Other Essays* (London: New Left Books).

Andrejevic, M. (2004) *Reality TV: The Work of Being Watched* (Oxford: Rowman and Littlefield).

Armstrong, N. (1987) 'The Rise of the Domestic Woman', in N. Armstrong and L. Tennenhouse (eds), *The Ideology of Conduct: Essays on Literature and the History of Sexuality* (London: Methuen), pp. 96–141.

Aronowitz, S. (2004) *How Class Works: Power and Social Movement* (New Haven, CT: Yale University Press).

Beck, U. and E. Beck-Gernsheim (2002) *Individualisation: Institutionalised Individualism and Its Social and Political Consequences* (London: Sage).

Berlant, L. (2008) *The Female Complaint: The Unfinished Business of Sentimentality in American Culture* (London/Durham, NC: Duke University Press).

Biressi, A. and H. Nunn (2005) *Reality TV: Realism and Revelation* (London: Wallflower Press).

——— (2008) 'Bad Citizens: The Class Politics of Lifestyle Television', in G. Palmer (ed.), *Exposing Lifestyle Television* (Aldershot, Hants.: Ashgate), pp. 15–24.

Bonner, F. (2003) *Ordinary Television* (London: Sage).

Bourdieu, P. (1977) *Outline of a Theory of Practice* (Cambridge: Cambridge University Press).

——— (1985) 'The Social Space and the Genesis of Groups', *Theory and Society*, 14(6): 723–44.

——— ([1979] 1986) *Distinction: A Social Critique of the Judgement of Taste* (London: Routledge).

——— (1987) 'What Makes a Social Class? On the Theoretical and Practical Existence of Groups', *Berkeley Journal of Sociology*, 32: 1–18.

Boyne, R. (2002) 'Bourdieu: From Class to Culture', *Theory, Culture and Society*, 19(3): 117–28.

Bratich, J. (2007) 'Programming Reality: Control Societies, New Subjects and the Powers of Transformation', in D. Heller (ed.), *Makeover Television: Realities Remodelled* (London: I.B. Taurus), pp. 6–22.

Bromley, R. (2000) 'The Theme That Dare Not Speak Its Name: Class and Recent British Film', in S. Munt (ed.), *Cultural Studies and the Working Class: Subject to Change* (London: Cassell), pp. 51–69.

Brunsdon, C. (2003) 'Lifestyling Britain: The 8–9 Slot on British Television', *International Journal of Cultural Studies*, 6(1): 5–23.

Bruzzi, S. (2006) *New Documentary*, 2nd edn. (London/New York: Routledge).

Butler, J. (1990) *Gender Trouble: Feminism and the Subversion of Identity* (London: Routledge).

Callinicos, A. and C. Harman (1987) *The Changing Working-Class: Essays on Class Structure Today* (London: Bookmarks).

Cannadine, D. (1998) *Class in Britain* (New Haven, CT/London: Yale University Press).

Cook, J. (2003) 'Culture, Class and Taste', in S. Munt (ed.), *Cultural Studies and the Working Class: Subject to Change* (London: Cassell), pp. 97–113.

Corner, J. (2002) 'Performing the Real', *Television and New Media*, 3(3): 255–70.

——— (2006) 'Analysing Factual TV: How to Study Television Documentary', in G. Creeber (ed.), *Tele-visions: An Introduction to the Study of Television* (London: BFI), pp. 60–73.

Couldry, N. (2003) *Media Rituals: A Critical Approach* (London: Routledge).

Crompton, R. (1993) *Class and Stratification: An Introduction to Current Debates* (Cambridge: Polity).

Crossick, G. (1991) 'From Gentlemen to the Residuum: Languages of Social Description in Victorian Britain', in P. J. Corfield (ed.), *Language, History and Class* (Oxford: Blackwell), pp. 150–78.

Dovey, J. (2000) *Freakshow: First Person Media and Factual Television* (London: Pluto Press).

Dymski, G. A. (2009) 'Racial Exclusion and the Political Economy of the Subprime Crisis', *Historical Materialism*, 17: 149–79.

Eagleton, T. (1989) 'The Ideology of the Aesthetic', in P. Hernadi (ed.), *The Rhetoric of Interpretation and the Interpretation of Rhetoric* (Durham, NC/London: Duke University Press), pp. 75–86.

Engels, F. ([1844] 1958) *The Condition of the Working-Class in England* (St Albans, Herts.: Panther).

Evans, M. (2003) *Love: An Unromantic Discussion* (Cambridge: Polity).

Finch, L. (1993) *The Classing Gaze: Sexuality, Class and Surveillance* (New South Wales, Australia: Allen and Unwin).

Foucault, M. (1979) *The History of Sexuality: Volume One, an Introduction* (London: Penguin).

Fraser, M. (1999) 'Classing Queer: Politics in Competition', *Theory, Culture and Society*, 16(2): 107–31.

Gilroy, P. (1990) 'One Nation under a Groove: The Cultural Politics of "Race" and Racism in Britain', in D. T. Goldberg (ed.), *Anatomy of Racism* (Minneapolis: University of Minnesota Press), pp. 263–83.

Gramsci, A. (1971) *Selections from the Prison Notebooks of Antonio Gramsci* (London: Lawrence and Wishart).

Griffen-Foley, B. (2004) 'From *Tit-Bits* to *Big Brother*: A Century of Audience Participation in the Media', *Media Culture and Society*, 26(4): 533–48.

Grindstaff, L. (2002) *The Money Shot: Trash, Class and the Making of TV Talk Shows* (Chicago: University of Chicago Press).

——— (2011) 'Just Be Yourself – Only More So: Ordinary Celebrity in the Era of Self-Service Television', in M. K. Kraidy and K. Sender (eds), *The Politics of Reality Television: Global Perspectives* (Abingdon, Oxon.: Routledge), pp. 44–59.

Harris, P. (2011) 'Frances Fox Piven defies death threats after taunts by anchorman Glenn Beck'. Available at: <http://www.guardian.co.uk/media/2011/jan/30/frances-fox-piven-glenn-beck> accessed 10 February 2011.

Hartmann, H. and L. Sargent (1981) *The Unhappy Marriage of Marxism and Feminism* (London: Pluto).

Hill, A. (2007) *Restyling Factual TV* (London: Routledge).

Hollows, J. and S. Jones (2010) '"At least he's doing something": Moral Entrepreneurship and Individual Responsibility in *Jamie's Ministry of Food*', *European Journal of Cultural Studies*, 13(3): 307–22.

Holmes, S. (2008) '"A term rather too general to be helpful": Struggling with Genre in Reality TV', in L. Geraghty and M. Jancovich (eds), *The Shifting Definitions of Genre* (Jefferson, NC/London: McFarland), pp. 21–39.

Holmes, S. and D. Jermyn (2004) 'Introduction', in S. Holmes and D. Jermyn (eds), *Understanding Reality Television* (London/New York: Routledge), pp. 1–32.

———— (2007) '"Ask the fastidious woman from Surbiton to hand-wash the underpants of aging Oldham skinhead …": Why Not *Wife Swap*?', in Thomas Austin and Wilma de Jong (eds), *Rethinking Documentary: A Documentary Reader* (Maidenhead, Berks.: Open University Press), pp. 59–74.

hooks, b. (2000) *Where We Stand: Class Matters* (New York/London: Routledge).

Illouz, E. (2003) *Oprah Winfrey and the Glamour of Misery* (New York: Columbia University Press).

———— (2007) *Cold Intimacies: The Making of Emotional Capitalism* (Cambridge: Polity).

Jost, F. (2011) 'When Reality TV Is a Job', in M. Kraidy and K. Sender (eds), *The Politics of Reality Television: Global Perspectives* (London/New York: Routledge), pp. 31–43.

Karl, I. (2007) 'Class Observations: "Intimate" Technologies and the Poetics of Reality TV', *Fast Capitalism*, 2(2). Available at: <http://www.uta.edu/huma/agger/fastcapitalism/2_2/karl.html> accessed 26 July 2011.

Karl, I. and J. Doyle (2008) 'Shame on You: Cosmetic Surgery and Class Transformation in *10 Years Younger*', in G. Palmer (ed.), *Exposing Lifestyle Television* (Aldershot, Hants.: Ashgate), pp. 83–99.

Kilborn, R. (2003) *Staging the Real: Factual TV Programming in the Age of Big Brother* (Manchester: Manchester University Press).

Kipnis, L. (1993) *Ecstasy Unlimited: On Sex, Capital, Gender and Aesthetics* (Minneapolis: University of Minnesota Press).

Lewis, T. (2008) *Smart Living: Lifestyle Media and Popular Expertise* (New York: Peter Lang).

Lyle, S. (2008) '(Mis)recognition and the Middle Class/Bourgeois Gaze: A Case Study of *Wife Swap*', *Critical Discourse Studies*, 5(4): 319–30.

McCarthy, A. (2004). '"Stanley Milgram, Allen Funt and me": Postwar Social Science and the "First Wave" of Reality TV', in S. Murray and L. Ouellette (eds), *Reality TV: Remaking Television Culture* (New York: NYU Press), pp. 19–39.

McClintock, A. (1995) *Imperial Leather: Race, Gender and Sexuality in the Colonial Context* (London: Routledge).

McRobbie, A. (2004). 'Notes on "What Not to Wear" and Post-Feminist Symbolic Violence', *Sociological Review*, Special Issue on Feminism after Bourdieu, 52(2): 97–109.

Marx, K. and F. Engels ([1848] 1968) *Manifesto of the Communist Party* (London: Lawrence and Wishart).

Morley, D. (1980) *The Nationwide Audience: Structure and Decoding* (London: BFI).

———— (2009) 'Mediated-Classifications: Representations of Class and Culture in Contemporary British Television', *European Journal of Cultural Studies*, 12(4): 487–508.

Moseley, R. (2000) 'Makeover Takeover on British Television', *Screen*, 41(3): 299–314.

Murdock, G. (1997) 'Base Notes: The Conditions of Cultural Practice', in M. Ferguson and P. Golding (eds),
    Cultural Studies in Question (London: Sage), pp. 86–101.

Ouellette, L. (2004) ' "Take responsibility for yourself": *Judge Judy* and the Neo-Liberal Citizen', in S. Murray
    and L. Ouellette (eds), *Reality TV: Remaking Television Culture* (New York: NYU Press), pp. 231–50.

Ouellette, L. and J. Hay (2008) *Better Living through Television* (Oxford: Blackwell).

Palmer, G. (2003) *Discipline and Liberty: Television and Governance* (Manchester: Manchester University Press).

———— (2004) ' "The New You": Class and Transformation in Lifestyle Television', in S. Holmes and D. Jermyn
    (eds), *Understanding Reality Television* (London: Routledge), pp. 173–90.

Parkin, F. (1972) *Class Inequality and Political Order* (St Albans, Herts.: Granada Publishing).

Pateman, C. (1988) *The Sexual Contract* (Cambridge: Polity).

Payne, G. and C. Grew (2005) 'Unpacking "Class Ambivalence": Some Conceptual and Methodological Issues
    in Accessing Class Cultures', *Sociology*, 39(5): 893–910.

Piper, H. (2004) 'Reality TV, *Wife Swap* and the Drama of Banality', *Screen*, 45(4): 273–86.

Poovey, M. (1995) *Making a Social Body: British Cultural Formation 1830–1864* (Chicago: Chicago University
    Press).

Rancière, J. (1983) *The Philosopher and His Poor* (Durham, NC/London: Duke University Press).

Raphael, C. (2004) 'The Political Economic Origins of Reali-TV', in S. Murray and L. Ouellette (eds), *Reality TV:
    Remaking Television Culture* (New York: NYU Press), pp. 123–40.

Ringrose, J. and V. Walkerdine (2008) 'Regulating the Abject: The TV Make-over as a Site of Neo-Liberal
    Reinvention towards Bourgeois Femininity', *Feminist Media Studies*, 8(3): 227–46.

Rose, N. (1989) *Governing the Soul: The Shaping of the Private Self* (London: Routledge).

Savage, M. (2003) 'A New Class Paradigm? Review Article', *British Journal of Sociology of Education*, 24(4): 535–41.

Sayer, A. (2005) *The Moral Significance of Class* (Cambridge: Cambridge University Press).

Sennett, R. and J. Cobb (1977) *The Hidden Injuries of Class* (Cambridge: Cambridge University Press).

Skeggs, B. (1997) *Formations of Class and Gender: Becoming Respectable* (London: Sage).

———— (2004a) *Class, Self, Culture* (London: Routledge).

———— (2004b) 'Introducing Pierre Bourdieu's Analysis of Class, Gender and Sexuality', in L. Adkins and
    B. Skeggs (eds), *Feminism after Bourdieu* (Oxford: Blackwell), pp. 19–33.

———— (2010) 'The Value of Relationships: Affective Scenes and Emotional Performances', *Feminist Legal
    Studies*, 18(1): 29–51.

———— (2011) 'Imagining Personhood Differently: Person Value and Autonomist Working-Class Value
    Practices', *Sociological Review*, 59(3): 579–94.

Skeggs, B. and H. Wood (2008) 'The Labour of Transformation and Circuits of Value "around" reality TV',
    Continuum: Journal of Media and Cultural Studies 22(4): 559–72.

———— (2009) 'The Moral Economy of Person Production: The Class Relations of Self-Performance on Reality
    Television', *Sociological Review*, 57(4): 626–44.

———— (forthcoming) *Reacting to Reality Television: Performance, Audience and Value* (London/New York:
    Routledge).

Skeggs, B., H. Wood and N. Thumim (2008) ' "Oh goodness, I am watching reality TV": How Methodology
    Makes Class in Multi-Method Audience Research', *European Journal of Cultural Studies*, 11(1): 5–24.

Smith, A. (1757) *Theory of the Moral Sentiments* (London: Liberty Press).

Stanworth, M. (1984) 'Women and Class Analysis: A Reply to Goldthorpe', *Sociology*, 18(2): 153–71.

Steedman, C. (2000) 'Enforced Narratives: Stories of Another Self', in T. Cosslett, C. Lury and P. Summerfield (eds), *Feminism and Autobiography: Texts, Theories, Methods* (London: Routledge), pp. 5–40.

Strathern, M. (1992) *After Nature: English Kinship in the Late Twentieth Century* (Cambridge: Cambridge University Press).

Taylor, L. (2005) ' "It was beautiful before you changed it all": Class, Taste and the Transformative Aesthetics of the Garden Lifestyle Media', in D. Bell and J. Hollows (eds), *Ordinary Lifestyles: Popular Media, Consumption and Taste* (Maidenhead, Berks.: Open University Press), pp. 113–27.

Thompson, J. (1996) *Models of Value: Eighteenth Century Political Economy and the Novel* (Durham, NC: Duke University Press).

Turner, G. (2010) *Ordinary People and the Media: The Demotic Turn* (London: Sage).

Veblen, T. B. ([1899] 2008) *The Theory of the Leisure Class*, e-book. Available at: <www.forgottenbooks.org>.

Vicinus, M. (1974) *The Industrial Muse: A Study of Nineteenth Century British Working Class Literature* (London: Croom Helm).

Vincent, D. (1981) *Bread, Knowledge and Freedom: A Study of Working-Class Nineteenth Century Autobiography* (London: Europa Publications).

Wahrman, D. (1995) *Imagining the Middle-Class: The Political Representation of Class in Britain, c. 1780–1840* (Cambridge: Cambridge University Press).

Wayne, M. (2003) *Marxism and Media Studies: Key Concepts and Contemporary Trends* (London: Pluto Press).

Weber, B. (2009) *Makeover TV: Selfhood, Citizenship and Celebrity* (Durham, NC: Duke University Press).

Weber, M. ([1904] 1930) *The Protestant Ethic and the Spirit of Capitalism* (London: George Allen and Unwin).

Weir, R. (2007) *Class in America* (Westport, CT: Greenwood Press).

Western, J. (1991) 'Class in Australia: The Historical Context', in J. Baxter, M. Emmison and J. Western (eds), *Class Analysis in Contemporary Australia* (Melbourne, Australia: Macmillan), pp. 14–22.

White, M. (2006) 'Investigating *Cheaters*', *The Communication Review*, 9: 221–40.

Williams, R. (1961) *Culture and Society 1780–1950* (Harmondsworth: Penguin).

———— (1988) *Keywords: A Vocabulary of Culture and Society* (London: Fontana).

Wood, H. (2009) *Talking with Television: Women, Talk Shows and Modern Self-Reflexivity* (Urbana: University of Illinois Press).

———— (2010) 'From Media and Identity to Mediated Identity', in M. Wetherell and C. Mohanty (eds), *The Identities Handbook* (London: Sage), pp. 258–76.

Wood, H. and B. Skeggs (2008) 'Spectacular Morality: Reality Television and the Re-Making of the Working Class', in D. Hesmondhalgh and J. Toynbee (eds), *Media and Social Theory* (London: Routledge), pp. 177–93.

———— (2011) 'Reacting to Reality TV: The Affective Economy of an "Extended Social/Public Realm"', in M. K. Kraidy and K. Sender (eds), *The Politics of Reality Television: Global Perspectives* (Abingdon, Oxon.: Routledge), pp. 93–107.

Wood, H., B. Skeggs and N. Thumim (2008) ' "It's just sad": Affect, Judgement and Emotional Labour in Reality Television Viewing', in S. Gillis and J. Hollows (eds), *Feminism, Domesticity and Popular Culture* (London/New York: Routledge), pp. 135–50.

Wray, M. and A. Newitz (1997) *White Trash: Race and Class in America* (New York: Routledge).

Wright, E. O. (1997) *Class Counts: Comparative Studies in Class Analysis* (Cambridge: Cambridge University Press).

Yeo, E. (1993) *The Contest for Social Science in Britain: Relations and Representations of Gender and Class* (London: River Oram Press).

PART ONE

Mediated Exchange and Judgment

2/Nick Couldry

Class and Contemporary Forms of 'Reality' Production or, Hidden Injuries of Class 2

The opacity of how power operates in society is hardly a new problem. In modern societies, where resources are allocated largely by the 'hidden hand' of a market system, this opacity is intensified, making the regular inequalities that result from that allocation difficult to perceive as such (Parkin 1972: 161). According to Max Weber, common class interests (based on shared positions in that allocation) are grasped only if there is a 'transparency of the connections' between the causes and the consequences of the 'class situation' (Gerth and Mills 1991; quoted in Parkin 1972: 162). The growing scalar complexity of economic and labour relations, combined with the decline of institutions for organising labour (trade unions) and of a whole family of narratives for making sense of social action in terms of class (socialism), has made it still more difficult to produce effective narratives of class in late modernity.[1] This is a general, and not a specifically national, problem; obviously, it is not something for which direct responsibility can be laid at media's door.

If there is a *specific* problem in the relations between contemporary media institutions and class, then the problem must lie elsewhere: not in media's failure to sustain an account of class based in inequalities of resource distribution, but in the *specific ways* in which that story fails to be told. Contemporary forms of 'reality' production (reality TV) require attention because, at least in the UK, they embed new mechanisms for publicly reproducing class difference in an increasingly unequal society. Media are also built on their own distinctive form of inequality (privileged access to the means of representing reality: Carey 1989; Couldry 2000). In reality TV, the broader 'hidden injuries' of media power (Couldry 2001a) cross with the distinctive hidden injuries of class, first diagnosed famously by Richard Sennett (Sennett and Cobb 1972): hence, my subtitle, 'Hidden Injuries of Class 2'.

The surface features of this process have already been carefully analysed by media scholars.[2] The faultline of class has been traced from TV shows that 'make over' anything from homes to dress sense (Palmer 2004; Philips 2005), to generalised reality games such as *Big Brother* (Holmes 2004; Biressi and Nunn 2005: 149–52), to the most obviously classed subgenre of media pedagogy, the cookery programme (Palmer 2005: 178; Strange 1998). Two important background factors have been widely recognised, the first more than the second: first, the basis of 'reality TV' formats everywhere in the economic benefits, in increasingly competitive national and global TV markets, of their low costs, high audience interactivity and easily transposable formats (Kilborn 1994; Magder 2004);

and second, in the UK and USA at least, the societal background of increasing inequality,[3] decreasing *upward* social mobility[4] and (in terms of general features of popular culture) increasing cultural *de-differentiation*. The last factor deserves immediate comment. In a cultural context where it is both notable and strategically important for a member of the Royal Family (Prince William) to wear jeans and trainers, the symbols of 'ordinary' fashion, it is perhaps not surprising to see the same royal, six years later, hailed as 'King of the Chavs', when he attended an army training party in mock-working-class ('chav') clothing:[5] 'difference' needs in the end to be marked. The only odd thing is that this event was reported in a newspaper whose readership is principally working class.

In what follows, I endorse the argument that reality TV reinforces, rather than challenges, class differentiation in Britain: helping to 'mould and to legitimate our class membership' (Palmer 2004: 189), enforcing a model of 'judgement and classification' (Biressi and Nunn 2005: 151), and providing a new 'stage for the dramatizing of contemporary class relations' (Wood and Skeggs 2008: 181). The notable expansion of opportunities for non-media professionals to appear in media formats in Britain (and many other countries) over the past fifteen years does not represent *in itself* a new form of politics,[6] let alone an actual reversal of class inequality: the question is always the terms on which such expanded access has been made available.

I hope to contribute to the debate by asking two additional questions. First, what is it about reality TV – understood not so much as a media text or format, but as a social process (something one set of social actors do to another) – that generates its contribution to the reproduction of *class in particular*? And, second, what is it about reality TV's insertion in a wider mechanism of representational authority (television, 'the media') that enables this work of reproducing, indeed renewing, class difference to occur without protest? For perhaps the most striking thing about the public debate in contemporary Britain on reality TV and class is an apparent tolerance for a marked increase in class abuse (directed 'downwards', not 'upwards'). The voice of the working-class subject is on this point mostly silent, at least in public discourse. We need to focus then not only on the reproduction of class, but on the *naturalisation* of this reproduction. I acknowledge that this gives less emphasis to the inevitably greater variety and complexity that emerges when we look at the detailed workings of a large range of reality TV texts, let alone at the reactions of individual and collective audiences. But this emphasis is, I believe, justified: we need to understand the machine of reality TV in all its symbolic force, before we turn to those subtleties. Inevitably, my argument is focused on the classed realities of a particular society, the UK, with some cross-references to the USA, but the mechanisms uncovered will also, I hope, be of potential relevance to some other societies.

Hidden Injuries of Class I

My argument starts out from Richard Sennett's analysis of the distinctive, hidden injuries with which class is associated. These hidden injuries are broader than inequalities of taste or 'cultural capital' (Bourdieu 1984),[7] although taste is one key means by which those injuries are reproduced.

There were at least three ways in which 1970s sociologists explained how, from the perspective of the working or dominated class, inequality is reinforced through culture, taking further the insight that perceptions of inequality are based on 'relative deprivation' – that is, lack relative to the perceived situation of relevant reference groups (Runciman 1972: Chapters 2 and 3). Paul Willis' ethnographic account emphasised, at least for working-class boys, how a positive culture of solidarity and resistance at school exactly *trained* those boys not to take jobs that would change their position in the work hierarchy (Willis 1978). Pierre Bourdieu took a different direction, using statistical data to track the patterning of taste across all class fractions in a system that *objectified* the unequal distribution of cultural capital and hid its basis in underlying economic and social inequality (Bourdieu 1984). Richard Sennett also started from inequalities in education, but traced their consequences into working-class US men's accounts *of themselves*.

Richard Sennett and Jonathan Cobb's 1972 book *The Hidden Injuries of Class* examined the damage that class inequality, embedded through the education system and division of labour, did to individual members of the American working class. They discuss a manual labourer 'Rissarro' who 'believes people of a higher class have a power to judge him because they seem internally more developed human beings … He feels compelled to justify his own position [in relation to them]' (Sennett and Cobb 1972: 25). While it is difficult to believe, nearly four decades since that fieldwork, that the point of comparison and difference would today be expressed in quite these terms ('formal education' versus 'manual labour'), Sennett's diagnosis of how objective inequalities come to make painful *subjective* sense is perhaps the most durable account of how class is culturally reproduced, as well as the most apposite for understanding class reproduction in reality TV.

Sennett bypasses two explanatory principles that have in the past four decades become difficult to sustain – the existence of hermetically sealed subcultures (Willis) and the existence of a clearly hierarchised field of cultural production and taste (Bourdieu) – and relies only on the subject's internalisation of others' capacity to *judge* him or her, and on that capacity's assumed basis in an achieved level of *personal development*. Sennett and Cobb insist that this vulnerability to judgment is not based in any positive respect for those imagined judges (Rissarro, they say, feels a revulsion towards 'educated people') (Sennett and Cobb 1972: 25) or in any negative self-devaluation (they point out that Rissarro believes in the dignity of his own manual labour). The problem lies, instead, in the internalisation of a model of self-development ('a higher form of self-control') (ibid.: 23), on terms which guarantee that the working-class man is always positioned as having a lack, and the middle-class man is always positioned as having the capacity to judge and fill that lack. Educators, educated and the whole school system become a machine of class reproduction, producing injuries that deepen and, by deepening, further naturalise class difference. The result is to disable a working-class voice that could translate its basic sense of self-respect into a public discourse of self-development to rival dominant understandings of the developed human being – an asymmetry of narrative resources that Axel Honneth later called 'de-symbolisation' (Honneth 1995: 213–17), although (to be clear) this de-symbolisation of the working class is not incompatible with the re-symbolisation of other classes.

I want to argue that in Britain, reality TV operates something like a system of de-symbolisation in this sense, even though it appears on one level to give voice to so-called 'ordinary people'. I will base my argument not on any specific judgments of class-related taste made in reality TV (there are plenty of those, but they are variable, and their object is not always the working class), but rather on the *mechanism of judgment* that reality TV comprises. The de-symbolisation of the working class through reality TV has brought with it a re-symbolisation of other class positions: for example, new pedagogical roles for middle-class and upper-middle-class performers such as Nigella Lawson and Davina McCall; however, I do not have space to pursue this here.

Before going further, it is important first to clarify what is, and what is not, distinctive about the hidden injuries of class. Other forms of inequality involve hidden injuries, whether based on race, gender, age or sexuality.[8] If anything, Fanon (1986) and Du Bois' ([1903] 1989) accounts of racism offer more vivid accounts of hidden injuries. And, since hidden injuries work in the territory of the self, they inevitably have some connection with the languages available for self-assessment: think of Du Bois' famous definition of 'double consciousness' as the 'sense of always looking at one's self through the eyes of others' (Du Bois 1989: 3), or Jean Améry's less well-known account of the 'total social determination' that derives from old people's submission to others' discourses about themselves (Améry 1994: 67). Nor is class uniquely characterised by an occlusion of authentic self through a system of self-transformation whose tools all lie in the hands of the dominant: at different periods of history, both gender and race have been managed through the 'mask' of education (Viswanathan 1990; Gilligan 1982). What distinguishes the hidden injuries of class is that class is tied to differences that are *not* 'automatically' marked on the body, differences that, to some degree, *must* be elicited *in the course* of the attempt at self-development. Just as a narrative of solidarity based on class is difficult to initiate (because there is nothing simple in common it can point to) (Parkin 1972: 161), so a narrative of individual self-transformation can be imposed from the outside rather easily (because there is no simple difference that it is seen to disrespect). In the 'violence' (Biressi and Nunn 2005: 151) committed in service of the hidden injuries of class, there is *always* an alibi.

Mechanisms of Judgment

Sennett and Cobb could not have anticipated that the *imagined* mechanisms of judgment on which the hidden injuries of class rely would become *objectified* in an entertainment format broadcast nationally with the full authority of major media institutions behind it. I shall come to the broader media setting in the next section. Let's focus first on what reality TV's format does to class's hidden injuries.

What reality TV does not do is expose those injuries and so potentially demystify class difference. Rather, as much commentary on reality TV has emphasised, this genre reinforces class-related differences, exposing working-class people to the judgment (often harsh, insulting, undermining) of those from different class-positions.[9] But that is only the beginning: for in the process of enabling and legitimating class-based judgment in an entertainment format, reality TV also brings into being a social mechanism – whose workings are on public view, with little, if any, apparent challenge – that *objectifies* the judgments that Sennett and Cobb's subjects had internalised in imaginary form. Whereas Rissarro 'believes people of a higher class have a power to judge him because they seem internally more developed human beings', reality TV confirms this as a fact. TV schedules provide endless models of how such judgments are made, and how people, including working-class participants, accept such judgments, and the 'expertise' that underlies them. Even if the injuries of class remain hidden, one mechanism for inflicting them is now out there, celebrated in public.

A complicating factor is that, in the social process of reality TV, the judging is not done only by the television experts, but by audiences who, as research has shown, take up the programmes' invitation to judge, albeit with some ambivalence (Hill 2007; Skeggs, Thumim and Wood, 2008). Potentially, there is a more democratic process at work here, but it would only work to challenge the hidden injuries of class if the mechanisms of judgment were themselves exposed to challenge. *Reality TV's mechanism of judgment is doubly mystified:* first, because it is embedded in a form of play whose rules, like the rules of any game, are not explicitly open to challenge while the game is being played;[10] second, because, through the rhetorical invitation of the reality TV text (its implied claim to access 'shared' reality), its judgments carry an assertion of universal relevance and authority – they are judgments about 'the way things are' for all of us. I will return to this deeper underpinning of reality TV's authority later, since it helps explain the format's success in making its strange mechanisms acceptable. Let's concentrate first on just how bizarre those workings are, as seen from a broader social perspective.

The judgment process that reality TV enacts is striking for four reasons. The first is that such judgments are accepted by the participants and by the audiences who watch their outcomes. Why should it be acceptable to see people confronted with humiliating comment and self-images? Let's acknowledge the sheer difficulty of 'ordinary' citizens challenging the media process,[11] but let's also assume that the genre of reality TV could not have expanded so rapidly unless there was a significant body of opinion who regarded its judgment mechanisms as somehow 'right', or at least as justified by a larger goal (that of transforming participants into something 'better'). If there are ethical issues raised by this process, they are seldom voiced. The resulting normalisation of personal judgment in public culture is significant: the intersection between changing norms of the neo-liberal workplace and this wider authorisation to judge the lives of others is also striking,[12] even if we must avoid a neat functionalist explanation of the coincidence. We now live in societies where, within the authorising frame of media institutions, people are allowed to harshly judge and embarrass others in public without the judged having the opportunity to respond, let alone question the basis of the judgment. To say 'it's only entertainment' is to miss the point: that this is an actual process which *serves as* 'only' entertainment, a process that under other conditions might be challenged.

The second strange aspect of reality TV's mechanisms of judgment is the authority on which it relies. At one end, there are the widely acknowledged experts who judge participants, and demonstrate what they need to do to be expert (for example, celebrity cooks judging cooking programmes): a master-class format, where wide agreement on the value of the knowledge to be imparted licenses a degree of tension and difficulty for the participants. Then there are 'experts' in domains where the value of expertise is at least open to question because there may be differing regimes of value at stake: for example, the so-called experts on programmes about property transformations and clothing makeovers, the psychologists on *Big Brother* (as if one could be 'expert' about anything so artificial!) and Sir Alan Sugar, the 'expert' host on the UK's *The Apprentice* (2005–). Finally, there are programmes which apply the expert-participants model to domains where arguably there is no expertise at all, or at least none that can be plausibly displayed under the conditions required by a short television programme: for example, programmes which, in individualised form, seek to address general social problems, such as unemployment (Channel 4's *Who Knows Best*, 2010, and BBC 1's *Famous, Rich and Jobless*, 2010). In this last type, the very *idea* that anyone could have the expertise and authority to judge or alter someone's capacity for employment is highly questionable. And yet this is what the entertainment format requires us to believe.

This leads us to the third strange thing characteristic of the authorised judgments of reality TV: that anything *like* a competitive entertainment format could be considered an adequate way to address the issues arising in the domains where reality TV's judgments are meted out. While it is unsurprising to see advice about hair, dress sense or body image being imparted through a narrative that focuses on the possibility of individual self-transformation (as Simmel was the first to note, fashion is a language for competitive self-differentiation), it is odd to see *general social problems* (family breakdown, unemployment, and the like) treated in a similarly individualised and game-based way (see Biressi in this volume). The situation was once different: a long tradition of realist documentary sought to present social issues in vivid but still general form (Biressi and Nunn 2005: Chapter 2). As Biressi and Nunn note, reality TV redefines what it is that television 'reveals': no longer the 'previously hidden condition of the working classes' but now *the individual*'s path to realising how, by applying an expert's existing knowledge, they can transform themselves along anticipated lines (ibid.: 36). Reality TV focuses on how to 'manage the self and one's immediate environment rather than the social', even though this individualised transformation is portrayed as plausible only by reference to assumed 'social, psychological, political and historical truths' (ibid.: 5) and on the basis of an assumed 'social' or collective authority that legitimates reality TV's games.

Fourth (and this is less strange than inherent to the televisual setting), television spectacle, by its usual emphasis on the display of emotion and emotional interaction, foregrounds the aspects of judgment which are, for quite different reasons, most wounding: not the process of reasoning that led up to the judgment, or its retrospective rationalisation, or the discussions of bystanders, but the emotion of the acts of judging and receiving judgment themselves. In other words, anger, contempt, dismissal on the one hand, and distress, humiliation and shame on the other. Reality TV, as part of the broader spectacularisation of everyday life (Wood and Skeggs 2008), effortlessly foregrounds the aspects of judgment which hurt most: the face-to-face exchange of emotions which register the moment of judging. As a result, reality TV does more than naturalise the judgments of class that, in another era, were 'hidden' and privately internalised: it naturalises the force and violent interchange of those judgments and installs them as a 'fact' of public life.

In these various ways, reality TV establishes an alternative model of social knowledge in ways particularly suited to reinforcing the hidden injuries of class: first, by *acting out* in public the judgment process whose injuries an earlier sociology had treated as hidden; and second, by *supplanting* general accounts of social, political and economic conditions (accounts that, because general and impersonal, might be questioned by anyone from whatever class position) and replacing them with a new mode of social 'knowledge' (speculative, but vouchsafed by the sequenced witnessing of the reality format). In the new mode, social knowledge is assumed to result when we see an individual submitting to various artificial transformation procedures in order to reach a pre-formatted result. Such *pre-formatting* of the social outlaws from the start any possibility of discovering life-conditions beyond the format. The institution of game-based judgment and evaluation as the privileged tool for social knowledge has a specific implication for the hidden injuries of class, for it silently reproduces, as 'nature' beyond investigation, many external factors that predispose some groups to be judged 'better' than others: for example, language skills, obesity, levels of education.[13] Meanwhile, the media institutions that once sought to visualise such factors as general problems for popular discussion now concentrate their efforts on selling programme formats that turn the consequences of such problems into reality games. The result is to install a form of cultural pedagogy (Giroux 2000) whose authority has rarely been accounted for, let alone justified.

The Ritual Setting

As I write, a respected social commentator (Alison Benjamin, editor of broadsheet newspaper the *Guardian*'s society pages) complains that recent reality TV formats dealing with unemployment and employability 'fail … to highlight the [new UK Coalition] government's flawed approach to tackling unemployment' (*Guardian*, 11 August 2010). If ever there was a social problem tied to the hidden injuries of class, it is unemployment, but the problem is that the reality TV formats Benjamin describes (including *Who Knows Best* and *Famous, Rich and Jobless*) cannot in principle deliver the types of policy reflection she quite rightly wants to see somewhere in the media. As reality games that focus on the fates and characters of individuals, they only masquerade as social knowledge, even though they are broadcast by major media institutions (BBC, Channel 4) within a public service remit. How can such a gulf between the apparent purpose of television formats (to capture 'reality') and their actual formats be sustained?

We need to turn here to the 'ritual' dimensions of reality TV, and indeed other types of media (Couldry 2003). There are three distinct levels on which reality TV works as a media format and which, taken together, help explain the otherwise implausible work that reality TV does to reinforce the hidden injuries of class.

First, reality TV in all its varieties is produced and consumed within a longer and much larger social construction that I have called 'the myth of the mediated centre' (Couldry 2003: Chapter 3; 2006a: Chapter 2). This is the social construction of centralised media ('the media' in common parlance) as our privileged access point to the 'central realities' of the social world, whatever they are. This 'myth' builds on an underlying myth that society has a 'centre'. Assuming that society operates on the basis of many overlapping concentrations of resources, 'the myth of the centre' is the idea that this organisational centre, which will always in practice be complex (that is, the site of multiple, competing forces: political, economic, social, cultural), is also a centre *of social values and coherence*. The myth of the centre (with all of its functionalist baggage) is inseparable from the myth of the *mediated* centre: the myth that media institutions are our privileged, or central, access point to the social 'centre'. The myth of the mediated centre is a pervasive feature of media discourse: media are consistently telling us that they speak 'for us', express 'our values'. This myth is now under considerable pressure from many directions: the proliferation of media interfaces, the declining economic viability of at least older models of media production (such as the newspaper), the growth of alternative social 'centres', such as social networking sites. But there are too many institutions with a lot at stake in the myth of the mediated centre for it simply to be abandoned (Couldry 2009); considerable efforts are likely to be made to sustain it, even if in new forms. Indeed, I would see reality TV as one important means of doing precisely that, reclaiming media's privileged access to some important shared 'reality' by incorporating performances from members of the audiences themselves. The circularity of this process does not matter, since, like any hermeneutic circle, it is based practically in a way of organising things *as if* its claims were true.

Second, the myth of the mediated centre is reproduced, not in the abstract but through certain key categories that have a general organising force.[14] One category in the media case is that of the 'media' person/thing/event which is treated as automatically of higher value than any person, thing or event not in the media: the specific distinction between 'media' and 'ordinary person' overlaps with the notion of celebrity.[15] This is important, since the 'ordinary person' is after all the defining origin and target of reality TV's narratives. I will come back to the 'ordinary person' in a moment. More important at a general level for stabilising the genre of reality TV is the category of 'reality' itself (Couldry 2003: Chapter 6). In itself, of course, it makes no sense to claim that the singular productions of a particular media institution based in a particular site with finite resources amount to 'reality', especially in today's environment where production is almost entirely outsourced to an unstable chain of suppliers. That the notion of 'reality TV' has been sustained in industry and general discourse for so long is evidence, I suggest, that the term is based on a category in Durkheim's sense, and marks the special connection that media presentations are assumed to have with an underlying shared reality in common. In previous work, I have tended to write at this point of media's assumed link to 'the social', but 'social' is exactly the term that is increasingly at issue in the diffused accounts of contemporary life that reality TV provides. I will return to this point at the end. The claim to 'reality', based as it is in an underlying category distinction between 'media' and 'non-media' or 'ordinary' worlds, is linked with an equally important claim associated with television since its early days: the claim of 'liveness'. Liveness is a term that does ideological work (Feuer 1983), claiming for TV – and increasingly the whole range of interconnected media linked through television – a special connection to a shared reality, enacting this in versions of reality TV with climactic competitions such as *Big Brother* (Couldry 2003: 106; Turner 2010: 13).

It is from these core categories that the basic discourse and rhetorical claims of reality TV are constructed. However, reality TV could not have been such a successful format unless it had worked these categories into a process with meaning in its own right, a transformation that stood in for something wider: in other words, a ritual. This is the third and crucial level on which the status of reality TV is sustained. In reality TV, two types of transformation are overlaid on each other: the basic transformation of the 'ordinary person' (not yet in the media) into a 'media person' by virtue of their appearance on the show; and second, the transformation of the ordinary person's inchoate existence into the underlying 'reality' that media claims to reveal in all its 'potential'. The transformations enacted through reality TV thus answer two types of constructed need: the collective need for access to a shared 'reality', and the individual need for access to media exposure. The latter addresses what elsewhere I have called the 'hidden injuries' of the media frame (Couldry 2001a): that is, the sense of symbolic exclusion that comes from living in societies dominated by the narrative outputs of media institutions that benefit from huge inequalities of *symbolic* (as well, of course, as economic) resources. The attractions of reality TV's call to participation in societies distinguished by such symbolic inequality, as well as other deep inequalities of recognition, must be taken very seriously.[16] They are further reinforced by the general culture of gossip and scandal that a spectacular process of judgment brings inevitably in its wake.

The linkage of *media's* 'hidden injuries' (as I call them) to class are not straightforward, since any of us who is not part of 'the media' is injured in this new sense. But in practice, there is a tighter, if still only partly understood, linkage to class, derived from the wider economic logic of mass-media production in the digital age. TV's increasing reliance on short-term employment contracts – or even in early career no contract or pay at all – and the general collapse of any career structure for all but the most successful entrenches persistent inequalities in the types of people who *can* participate in the media industries, except through the spectacle of reality TV. Unless you have considerable private resources, reality TV's judgment machine is effectively your only route to 'breaking into television', and, as we have seen, it comes at a high price.

Conclusion

Reality TV emerged as a form in global television through a range of disparate factors that are likely to underpin reality media's continued role across multiple platforms in the next decade. Elsewhere, I have called reality TV a 'figuration' in Norbert Elias' sense, to reflect the many cross-cutting interdependencies that underlie it: economic pressures, threats to broadcasters' institutional legitimacy, a deficit of social recognition, a growing crisis of governmental legitimacy (Couldry 2010, quoting Elias [1939] 1994).

As Graeme Turner (2010) has recently argued, the largest transformation in global media is the increased emphasis on selling *entertainment* as opposed to any more political strategy (binding together or educating the nation, sustaining public values). In this new environment, there is every reason to think that reality TV's cheap model of entertainment based on formatting games for individual's self-transformation will continue to be exported and renewed. If so, its pervasive re-narrativisation of the everyday world will be even more securely installed. As Turner points out for television in general, the outcome is ideological, 'like an ideological system but without an ideological project' (Turner 2010: 25), a machine that re-describes social processes in regular ways, yet is based in no intent to influence the social. That machine, as it operates in Britain, assigns roles of judge and judged broadly according to class, unequal roles that are taken on under the guise and alibi of social 'reality'.

The politics of reality TV are not then accidental. Indeed, we can go further. In countries dominated by neo-liberal discourse, reality TV's politics intersect with a neo-liberal view of the social domain as the site for the individual's competitive self-transformation[17] and, in Britain at least, with an actual social world characterised by less mutual support, more aggression and growing insecurity and inequality (see Couldry 2010). But crucially, those politics do not depend on any intent of class oppression. No intent is needed to maintain in place a public mechanism for objectifying the hidden injuries of class, once it has been installed; meanwhile, reality media's vestigial sense of the 'social' affords no space from where a broader critique of that mechanism could be mounted. It will require, therefore, more than a cultural politics to name and challenge reality TV's new hidden injuries for what they are.

Notes

1. And indeed many other forms of political narrative: see Bauman (2001:9).
2. For important analyses of class in reality TV, see Palmer (2005), Philips (2005), Biressi and Nunn (2005), Wood and Skeggs (2008), as well as the recent surveys by Morley (2009) and Turner (2010: Chapter 3).
3. Institute of Fiscal Studies figures, reported by Giles (2009); on the USA, see Greenhouse (2009).
4. Goldthorpe and Jackson (2007). As Morley (2009: 499) notes, British television's (including reality TV's) portrayal of what Marx would have called the 'lumpen proletariat' coincides with the more permanent marginalisation of large groups from the labour market in Britain since the 1980s.
5. Respectively, *The Sun*, 17 June 2000, discussed in Couldry (2001b: 225–6), and *The Sun*, 10 April 2006, discussed in Harris (2006).
6. Turner (2010: 2, 173) makes a similar broad point well.
7. On Bourdieu and reality TV, see Palmer (2004: 176–9) and McRobbie (2008).
8. Compare Couldry (2010: 117–24) for an overview of the literature.
9. See references in note 2 above.
10. Compare Couldry and Littler (2011) on *The Apprentice* (UK version).
11. Compare Couldry (2006a: 137–9).
12. Compare Couldry (2006b, 2008).
13. For valuable commentary outside reality TV on the continuing links between social and economic resources and poor language skills, obesity and low educational attainment, see Toynbee (2004a and b) and Webber and Butler (2007).
14. I am working here via an analogy with Durkheim's analysis of the social bases of religion (Durkheim [1915] 1995). For more detail, see Couldry (2000: 14–16; 2003: 6–9).
15. Compare Holmes (2004).
16. Compare Couldry (2010: 81–2).
17. See Palmer (2003), Couldry (2006b, 2008), McCarthy (2007) and Ouellette and Hay (2008).

Bibliography

Améry, J. (1994) *On Aging* (Indianapolis: Indiana University Press).

Bauman, Z. (2001) *The Individualized Society* (Cambridge: Polity).

Biressi, A. and H. Nunn (2005) *Reality Television: Realism and Revelation* (London: Wallflower Press).

Du Bois, W. E. B. ([1903] 1989) *The Souls of Black Folk* (New York: Bantam).

Bourdieu, P. (1984) *Distinction* (London: Routledge).

Carey, J. (1989) *Communication as Culture* (Boston: Unwin Hyman).

Couldry, N. (2000) *The Place of Media Power* (London: Routledge).

———— (2001a) 'The Hidden Injuries of Media Power', *Journal of Consumer Culture*, 1(2): 155–79.

———— (2001b) 'Everyday Royal Celebrity', in D. Morley and K. Robins (eds), *British Cultural Studies* (Oxford: Oxford University Press), pp. 221–34.

———— (2003) *Media Rituals: A Critical Approach* (London: Routledge).

———— (2006a) *Listening beyond the Echoes: Media, Ethics and Agency in an Uncertain World* (Boulder, CO: Paradigm Press).

———— (2006b) 'La Téléréalité ou le théâtre secret du néoliberalisme', *Hermes*, Special Issue on Economy and Communication, 44: 121–8.

———— (2008) 'Reality TV, or the Secret Theatre of Neoliberalism', *Review of Education, Pedagogy and Cultural Studies*, 30(1): 3–13.

———— (2009) 'Does "the Media" Have a Future?', *European Journal of Communication*, 24(4): 437–50.

———— (2010) *Why Voice Matters: Culture and Politics after Neo-Liberalism* (London: Sage).

Couldry, N. and J. Littler (2011) 'Work, Power and Performance: Analysing the "Reality" Game of *The Apprentice*', *Cultural Sociology*, 5(2): 263–79.

Durkheim, E. ([1915] 1995) *Elementary Forms of Religious Life* (Chicago: Chicago University Press).

Elias, N. ([1939] 1994) *The Civilising Process* (Malden, NH: Blackwell).

Fanon, F. (1986) *Black Skin, White Masks* (London: Pluto).

Feuer, J. (1983) 'The Concept of Live Television', in E. A. Kaplan (ed.), *Regarding Television* (Los Angeles: American Film Institute), pp. 12–22.

Gerth, H. and C. Wright Mills (1991) *From Max Weber* (London: Routledge).

Giles, C. (2009) 'Record level of inequality hits Labour's image', *Financial Times*, 8 May.

Gilligan, C. (1982) *In a Different Voice* (Cambridge, MA: Harvard University Press).

Giroux, H. (2000) *Stealing Innocence* (New York: St Martin's Press).

Goldthorpe, J. and M. Jackson (2007) 'Intergenerational Class Mobility in Contemporary Britain: Political Concerns and Empirical Findings', *British Journal of Sociology*, 58(4): 525–46.

Greenhouse, S. (2009) *The Big Squeeze*, 2nd edn. (New York: Anchor Books).

Harris, J. (2006) 'Bottom of the class', *Guardian*, G2 section, 11 April.

Hill, A. (2007) *Restyling Factual TV* (London: Routledge).

Holmes, S. (2004) '"All you've got to worry about is the task, having a cup of tea and doing a bit of sunbathing": Approaching Celebrity in *Big Brother*', in S. Holmes and D. Jermyn (eds), *Understanding Reality Television* (London: Routledge), pp. 111–35.

Honneth, A. (1995) *The Fragmented World of the Social* (Albany: SUNY Press).

Kilborn, R. (1994) '"How real can you get?" Recent Developments in "Reality" Television', *European Journal of Communication*, 9(4): 421–40.

McCarthy, A. (2007) 'Reality Television: A Neoliberal Theatre of Suffering', *Social Text*, 25: 93–110.

McRobbie, A. (2008) *The Aftermath of Feminism* (London: Sage).

Magder, T. (2004) 'The End of TV 101: Reality Programs, Formats and the New Business of Television', in S. Murray and L. Ouellette (eds), *Reality TV* (New York: NYU Press), pp. 137–56.

Morley, D. (2009) 'Mediated Class-ifications: Representations of Class and Culture in Contemporary British Television', *European Journal of Cultural Studies*, 12(4): 487–508.

Ouellette, L. and J. Hay (2008) *Better Living through Reality TV* (Malden, NH: Blackwell).

Palmer, G. (2003) *Discipline and Liberty: Television and Governance* (Manchester: Manchester University Press).

———— (2004) '"The New You": Class and Transformation in Lifestyle Television', in S. Holmes and D. Jermyn (eds), *Understanding Reality Television* (London: Routledge), pp. 173–90.

Parkin, F. (1972) *Class Inequality and Political Order* (St Albans, Herts.: Granada Publishing).

Philips, D. (2005) 'Transformation Scenes: The Television Series Makeover', *International Journal of Cultural Studies*, 8(2): 213–29.

Runciman, W. G. (1972) *Relative Deprivation and Social Justice* (Harmondsworth: Penguin).

Sennett, R. and J. Cobb (1972) *The Hidden Injuries of Class* (New York: Norton).

Skeggs, B., N. Thumim and H. Wood (2008) '"Oh goodness, I am watching reality TV": How Methods Make Class in Audience Research', *European Journal of Cultural Studies*, 11(1): 5–24.

Strange, N. (1998) 'Perform, Educate and Entertain: Ingredients of the Cookery Programme Genre', in C. Geraghty and D. Lusted (eds), *The Television Studies Book* (London: Arnold).

Toynbee, P. (2004a) 'We can break the vice of the great unmentionable', *Guardian*, 2 January.

———— (2004b) 'Inequality is fattening', *Guardian*, 28 May.

Turner, G. (2010) *Ordinary People and the Media* (London: Sage).

Viswanathan, G. (1990) *Masks of Conquest: Literary Study and British Rule in India* (London: Faber).

Webber, R. and T. Butler (2007) 'Classifying Pupils by Where They Live: How Well Does This Predict Variations in Their GCSE Results?', *Urban Studies*, 44(7): 1229–54.

Willis, P. (1978) *Learning to Labour* (Aldershot, Hants.: Gower).

Wood, H. and B. Skeggs (2008) 'Spectacular Morality: "Reality" Television, Individualization and the Remaking of the Working Class', in D. Hesmondhalgh and J. Toynbee (eds), *The Media and Social Theory* (London: Routledge), pp. 177–93.

3/Andrew Tolson

'I'm common and my talking is quite abrupt' (Jade Goody): Language and Class in *Celebrity Big Brother*

We demanded grittier, dirtier, more offensive television and nowhere better can this be seen than on *Big Brother* ... Jade Goody epitomised such a hunger. Not Jade herself, but what we wanted Jade to do for the audience ... The producers ... had picked up that the audience's appetite for uncomfortable, degrading material had grown and they weren't going to go against their audience ... (Anna Nolan 2010)

Demotic Celebrity and 'Unruly Incivility'

In a 'First Person' article published in the *Observer* (6 June 2010) to coincide with the start of the final season of *Big Brother* on Channel 4, UK, Anna Nolan (who came second in the first series in 1999) offers some retrospective thoughts on the significance of the show. She reminds her readers that there was a time when this form of reality TV was promoted as a type of social experiment, but even then the contestants knew they were performing. What subsequently became apparent to Anna and her fellow contestants was the way *Big Brother* constructed narrative scenarios to create 'personalities out of all of us ... The Z-list celebrity had been born'. Nolan then continues, in typical journalistic fashion, to draw parallels between this phenomenon and the zeitgeist of the decade. 'The noughties were years of affluence and greed' whose spirit of excessive indulgence found its way into the trajectory of the show. Driven by audience demand, the 'personalities' became more eccentric and their performances more shocking. As the above quotation confirms, it was Jade Goody, according to Nolan, more than any other contestant, who personified these developments.

Here I want to reassess some aspects of Jade Goody's celebrity persona, linking it not to the zeitgeist but rather to the social and cultural arguments that underpin this book.[1] In this context, Goody is selected here as a case study of certain discourses and strategies of representation that foreground questions of social class. In particular, I am connecting here with Beverley Skeggs' discussion of the 'monstrous' white working-class femininity, made visible in the phenomenon of the 'hen party' and constructed in the distinction between 'respectable' and 'abject' forms of working-class culture (Skeggs 2005). At the high point of her celebrity, before it was finally redeemed by her public-spirited but ultimately losing battle with cancer, Goody's persona was both defined by and revolved around these discourses of class. Initially regarded as an ignorant, vulgar object of ridicule (Rahman

2008), but nevertheless crucially as 'true to herself', Goody's subsequent celebrification was seen, at least in some quarters, as an exemplary aspirational narrative. She represented, in the UK, the triumph of 'demotic celebrity' (Turner 2004), which she appeared to achieve without compromising her original identity. To some sections of the reality TV audience, Goody's popularity was precisely based on her seeming indifference to middle-class norms of taste and cultured behaviour, as she continued, despite her material success, to demonstrate a 'ghetto rat' authenticity (Skeggs and Wood 2008).

In his latest discussion of 'ordinary people and the media', Turner (2010), building on Skeggs' arguments, suggests that some participants in reality television demonstrate a spirit of 'fighting back' or resistance to its dominant norms of 'compulsory individuality'. This involves rejecting middle-class judgments of 'good subjectivity' which many reality TV shows, through their transformational narratives, are designed to promote (Taylor 2002; Palmer 2004). Turner takes Ozzy Osbourne as his example of the 'unruly incivility of the demotic', but this is a phrase that might equally apply to Jade Goody. By exploiting this territory successfully to build a celebrity career, perhaps Goody had begun to believe her own publicity when, in 2007, she was invited to return to *Celebrity Big Brother*. Certainly, a 'monstrous' femininity was demonstrated there, conforming to most of Skeggs' characteristics of 'hen-party' culture: 'loud, white, excessive, vulgar, disgusting ...', and if this was a strategic demonstration of a particular version of working-class identity, it spectacularly backfired in the 'racist bullying' incidents that developed.

In this chapter, I shall take Goody's appearance in *Celebrity Big Brother* 2007 as an exemplary instance of the kind of behaviour Skeggs and Turner are discussing. There are two reasons for wishing to revisit this infamous moment in Jade Goody's celebrity career. The first is simply that this might be taken as the classic display of 'unruly incivility' on British TV. It seems to confirm a version of white working-class culture as 'racist ... and a blockage to global modernity' (Skeggs 2005), which is how the bullying of Shilpa Shetty was first interpreted and then morally condemned by the British national press. However, the second reason to look again at this incident is to foreground a particular academic interest. As an analyst of media discourse, I believe there are insights to be gained by examining such incidents in detail as instances of broadcast talk (Tolson 2006). From this perspective, participants can be seen to be engaged in a performance of talk which is 'doubly articulated' (Scannell 1991). That is to say, it is not only 'discourse-in-interaction' (Schegloff 1999) and thus amenable to Conversation Analysis (or CA), it is also on display in a public arena for consumption by an 'overhearing audience' (Heritage 1985). In this case, some sections of the overhearing audience were highly critical of the behaviour of Goody (and her associates), including her use of language in the context of her class background.

'Racist Bullying'

For those who might have missed it (and they will be few), the incidents that comprised this notorious media event can be briefly summarised. During the second week of the show, from Monday, 15 January 2007, there was growing public concern, expressed in complaints to the TV channel and its regulator Ofcom, about the treatment of the Bollywood actress Shilpa Shetty by two groups of housemates. The first group was Goody's family (mother and boyfriend), while the second included two other white female contestants, Danielle Lloyd (a model) and Jo Mears (pop singer). Jade Goody herself was leading protagonist in both these groups, and the accusation was that racist comments were being made about Shetty, initially as asides, but then increasingly to her face. On Wednesday, 17 January, the edited highlights featured an extended verbal confrontation between Goody and Shetty (with Lloyd and Mears also present) in what became known as the 'Oxo cubes' row. Ostensibly, this began as a complaint that Goody had used all the stock cubes, ordered by Shetty, in her cooking (such is the banality of life in the *Big Brother* household); however, it developed into a sustained personal attack on Shetty, largely instigated by Goody, which proved to be the defining moment of the programme and, for a time, Jade Goody's career.

Much of the ensuing furore was orchestrated, not surprisingly, by *The Sun* newspaper. 'Racist bullying' was the interpretation offered by *The Sun* in its front-page headlines on Wednesday, 17 January, before the Oxo cubes argument was transmitted. In the same edition, it was also reported that the MP Keith Vaz had tabled a motion in the House of Commons attacking racism on television, and that an unprecedented number of viewers were complaining to Ofcom and Channel 4. By 18 January, according to *The Sun*, the situation had escalated into a 'race war with India', as representatives of the Indian Government made formal complaints and street protests occurred in Indian cities. The former Chancellor Gordon Brown, on an official visit to India, was obliged to comment, as was Tony Blair at Prime Minster's Questions. Blair spoke about 'opposing racism in all its forms', though he conceded that he had not seen the show. That 'Shilpa's treatment is bullying' was taken as a given in *The Sun*'s editorial on 18 January, with 'millions of people here and in India think[ing] it is something more repugnant than that – racism'.

Ultimately, in its inimitable fashion, *The Sun*'s editorial of 19 January nailed its true colours to the mast. Its developing campaign to evict Jade Goody took on a nationalistic urgency:

> Let's root out Big Bruv bigot
> TONIGHT is a moment of truth for Britain
> Out of nowhere, a Channel 4 show watched by a few million has erupted from being a bit of a laugh to a defining moment in the way Britain is seen by the rest of the world.
>
> Make no mistake. Much more hangs on tonight's *Celebrity Big Brother* eviction vote than the issue of whether Jade Goody or Shilpa Shetty stays in the house. At stake is whether we are happy to be seen as a nation willing to tolerate vile bullying and foul-mouthed yobbishness. That is why *The Sun* urges every reader who loves Britain to pick up a phone and make sure the ghastly Jade Goody is kicked out tonight.

Sure enough, with its army of readers duly mobilised, Jade Goody was evicted on 19 January, by an 82 per cent majority. In its editorial on 20 January, *The Sun* proclaimed that this was 'the most important vote in Britain since the last General Election', the political significance of which politicians themselves seemed to recognise. On the opposite page, Gordon Brown, still in India, was said to endorse *The Sun*'s campaign, urging voters to demonstrate that 'Britain is a nation of tolerance and fairness'.

Clearly, there was a consensus here, not only that Jade's bullying of Shilpa was out of order, but more significantly that it was representative precisely of that kind of 'antisocial behaviour' that was the focus for public revulsion as well as much New Labour social policy.[2] Moreover, the 'authoritarian populism' of *The Sun*'s approach to these events seemed to be echoed in the knee-jerk reaction of some of the political comment: 'I think this is racism being presented as entertainment – I think it is disgusting' (Tessa Jowell). Apparently then, a national community was speaking with one voice against a perceptible threat to its identity.

Escalating Oppositional Argument

There were alternative views expressed by other commentators, particularly in the broadsheet press, to which we will return later. There was even, in the *Guardian* (17 January 2007), just one hint of dissent. Perhaps because of her jaundiced view of the programme as a whole (she walked out of a previous edition of *Celebrity Big Brother*), Germaine Greer's criticism extended to all the main protagonists, including Shilpa herself. Greer reminded her *Guardian* readers that 'Shilpa is a very good actress'. Passing critical comment on her manner and demeanour, Greer suggested that Shilpa was in control of her self-presentation, and moreover she knew how to exploit this in the 'disorienting' atmosphere of the show. 'Everyone hates her because she wants them to. She also knows that if she infuriates people enough, their innate racism will spew forth' (Greer 2007: 12).

That, of course, was pure journalistic speculation and possibly intentionally mischievous. Beyond what she could see on TV, Greer had no access to Shilpa's motives or understanding of the situation. Furthermore, that Shilpa herself might be implicated in these events does not excuse them, from a moral or political point of view. What it does begin to do, however, is open up the issue of 'racist bullying' to a more complex kind of analysis. We can start to explore this if we examine the incidents that occurred in the programme as instances of broadcast talk.

Before we look at some of the details of the transcript, it will be helpful to consider various general points about forms of argumentation. To begin with, if argument can be defined as a 'speech genre' (as distinct, for example, from joking or storytelling), then, as Schiffrin (1985) has pointed out, there are two broad subcategories, namely 'rhetorical' and 'oppositional' forms. Rhetorical arguments develop through a series of propositions designed to persuade; oppositional arguments are confrontational, designed to dispute a position held by another speaker. Clearly, in these terms, the argument between Jade and Shilpa is oppositional, but it is also a particular type of opposition. It is not, for instance, the type of 'sociable argument' also discussed by Schiffrin (1984) where participants are enjoying arguing as a way of bonding with each other. Nor, precisely, is this the sort of 'confrontation talk' analysed by Hutchby (1996) in his study of radio phone-ins. That type of argument focuses on the pursuit of controversy over a topic, whereas this kind of argument is *personal*.

Some additional considerations are usefully summarised by Hutchby (1996). Generally, as CA has shown, the 'preferred' (i.e. default) protocol for oppositional arguments in ordinary conversation is that they will involve mitigation, to indicate that 'aggravated' disagreements are 'dispreferred', and to attend to the 'face' of co-participants. In some forms of broadcast talk, unmitigated disagreements can develop, but only because participants can be secure in the knowledge that they are contained within a format (such as the 'panel interview') that will be managed by an independent third party, the panel interviewer or chair (Greatbatch 1992). Even in confrontational talk shows like *The Jerry Springer Show* (1991–), which possibly this incident most closely resembles, contestants engage in 'spectacular confrontation' (Hutchby 2006) on the basis that there are bouncers to protect them and that Springer himself is ultimately in control (Lunt and Stenner 2005). In *Celebrity Big Brother*, however, contestants are engaged in argument which is extremely 'aggravated' and without much in the way of mitigation, either at the level of ordinary conversation or provided by the format in which it occurs.[3]

Transcript

(Note that, for reasons of space and word length, some lines are omitted.[4])

Extract 1

```
    Jade:   Shilpa you didn't only order the Oxo cubes that's really
            stupid to say
    Shil:   'Scuse me?
    Jade:   You didn't really only order the Oxo cubes [...
5   Shil:                                      [I didn't say
            I owned them I just I didn't say I owned them [I only
            asked you if you'd used them
    Jade:                                         [Did you
            say (.) You did not say I only ordered Oxo cubes [did
10          you say that?
    Shil:                                    [Jade I
            don't want to fight. You want to get argumentative it's
            fun for you please go on be my guest [I don't want to do
            that it's not my style
15  Jade:                              [Did you say I only
            ordered Oxo cubes? Did you say I only ordered Oxo cubes?
    Shil:   My life doesn't run for this TV show maybe it runs for
            [you please be my guest
    Jade:   [Now you're contradicting yourself you're pathetic
20          you're pathetic you're pathetic you're absolutely
            pathetic [you're pathetic=
    Shil:           [You must be pathetic
    Jade:                         =my opinion of you is you're
            pathetic [and a fake that is my opinion of you you're
25          pathetic and a fake
```

Shil: [You know what is pathetic you actually blamed
                 all that chicken going to waste only because of me. What
                 about all the times that I have cooked?

Jade: Yeh and I've ate it I never said the <u>cur</u>ry went to waste
30   did I 'cos everyone ate it I'm saying that the chicken
          went to waste. You're saying [you only ordered Oxo cubes

Extract 2

60   Shil: Ah (.) you know what I don't need to dignify this stupid
                    stupid argument. It may be fun [for you Jade

          Jade: [caused by you caused by
                    you 'cos you said the only thing you ordered was Oxo
65   cubes [which is an out and out lie out and out lie

          Shil: [Oh please shut up (.) shut up

          Jade: No I won't shut up. You shut up

          Shil: Shut up

          Jade: You shut the fuck up. Who the fuck are you to tell me to
70   shut up? You [might be some princess in fucking
                    neverland=

          Shil: [Don't use don't' use that language with me
                    Jade

75   Jade: =but I don't give a shit. You're not a
                    fucking princess here. You're a normal housemate like
                    everybody else everybody else. And you need to come to
                    terms with that and don't lie. Don't lie about things.
                    Why come and say the only thing I ordered was Oxo cubes?
80   Why lie? Why lie? You had the shopping list stuck in
                    between your legs for the whole task Why lie? Do not
                    tell me to shut up. Shut yourself up (2.0) Or go and
                    fucking cry and put your glasses on, Go on go in the
                    diary room for another eight times GO ON (1.0) You're a
85   liar. You're a liar and you're a fake you're a liar
                    (3.0)

          Shil: I'm not even [going to say anything

          Jade: [You're not in neverland here you're not no
                    princess here you're normal [You are normal Shilpa=

90   Shil: [Who said I'm a princess

          Jade: =and
                    learn to live with it you are normal

	Shil:	[Jade I <u>am</u> normal
	Jade:	[Don't come to me tell me=
95	Jerm:	Just forget it, just forget it
	Jade:	=the only thing you ordered [to
		Jermaine] She had a go at me because I used me and
		Danielle used four Oxo cubes. This was the only thing I
		ordered off the shopping list. [THAT'S A LIE
100	Shil:	[I ordered the condiments.
		Oh please get some learn some manners. You know what?
	Jade:	Learn some manners learn some manners
	Shil:	[Yes (…)
	Jerm:	[Forget it forget it forget it forget it forget it forget it
105		forget it forget it forget it …
	Jade:	[(…) I DON'T WANT MANNERS TO YOU I DON'T WANT MANNERS
		TO YOU I DON'T WANT MANNERS TO YOU. You know what you
		need some real life in your life. That's what you need.
		You're just so stuck up your own arse you can't think of
110		anything else other than your own fucking life.
	Shil:	I'm stuck up?
	Jade:	Yeh you are. You're so far up your arse you can smell
		your own shit (.) You're fucking ridiculous (.) You're a
		liar and you're a fake (3.0)

Particularly on the part of Jade Goody, what we seem to have here is an aggravated, personal (and abusive) type of oppositional argument. To use lay terminology, at a certain point Jade seems to have 'lost it', she is 'off her head' with rage. From a discourse analytic point of view, to adopt a term first used in Greatbatch's account of the 'panel interview', but which can also be applied to debate programmes (Tolson 2006), I will define this as a type of argumentative *escalation*, with a characteristic structural form. It consists of two main sequences of talk, the boundary between these occurring on line 66. Up to that point, Jade is making an accusation about a specific incident and demanding a confession or an apology, which Shilpa duly delivers (omitted here). From line 66 onwards, however, the salience of that incident recedes, and Jade's discourse becomes a torrent of generalised personal abuse. She is shouting at the top of her voice, using increasingly obscene language and seems to be out of control in what one might term argumentative 'flooding out' (Goffman 1974).[5]

However, if we also consider this as a form of 'discourse-in-interaction', some further observations can be made. Clearly, Jade could be described as the chief protagonist, but as in any conversational interaction this is not all one-sided. Shilpa herself plays a significant role in both sequences, a role which is neither passive nor simply reactive. In the first sequence, Jade makes repeated accusations ('Did you say …') punctuated by escalating personal insults ('you're pathetic', 'fake', 'a liar').

She also uses devices such as the personal 'footing preface' ('I'm saying', 'I'm asking you') which rein-forces the personal nature of the confrontation.[6] At first, however, Shilpa refuses to respond directly to these accusations. Instead, she answers questions with questions, repeatedly produces meta-statements ('My life doesn't run for this TV show') and is not above trading some of the milder insults, though with a degree of mitigation ('You must be pathetic').

In the second sequence (i.e. after line 66), Jade becomes increasingly personal and abusive, employing contrastive characterisations ('You're not a princess, you're a housemate'), repeated rhetorical questions ('Why lie? Why lie?') and extended obscene metaphors. On one level, it is possible to interpret this as conventional *Big Brother* ideology: that in this context, all participants are equal and the way to get on is to 'be yourself' without pretence or pretension (Jones 2003). However, as the escalation develops, there are many instances of overlapping talk, and at the height of the 'flooding out' (lines 102–7), all participants are talking at once without reference to what the other, at that point, is saying. What is Shilpa's role in this escalation? In line 66, it is Shilpa who first abandons the interrogative for the imperative ('Shut up'). And there are some moments (marked by extended pauses in the transcript, for example at line 86) where Jade's 'flooding out' seems to exhaust itself, only for Shilpa to continue with metastatements which provoke Jade to further reaction.

So the fact that this discourse analysis shows that *both* participants (though perhaps not equally) are contributing to the escalating argument at the very least raises some questions about 'bullying' – if by that we mean the *unilateral* mistreatment of some human beings by others. I want to suggest, however, that there are two further critical points here, the first of which develops a theoretical implication of CA. If the argument between Jade and Shilpa is jointly produced, with each party play-ing a constitutive role, it is also evident, to adopt another CA term, that its sequences are 'locally occasioned' in so far as the strategies and responses of both participants are finely attuned to the evolving situation. The CA perspective sees this as a basic form of social order. As Schegloff argues, 'structures of sociality' obtain even where 'divergent interests, beliefs, commitments or projects among humans … [are] realized as conflict, disagreement, misunderstanding and the like' (Schegloff 1999: 427). Extended sequences of aggravated opposition would seem to constitute the extreme-case scenario for Schegloff's position, but even here, as this analysis shows, locally occasioned 'struc-tures of sociality' are in evidence.

But what sort of 'sociality' is being constructed? A second line of critical thinking is suggested by Ben Rampton's work on social class and verbal stylisation (Rampton 2003, 2006). There is of course a substantial tradition of sociolinguistic research on language and class (Morley 2009), but it is not necessary to claim that Goody and Shetty are operating with versions of 'restricted' and 'elaborated' codes (Bernstein 1971).[7] Rather, what they seem to be reproducing is the 'cultural semantic' which Rampton (following Cohen 1988) argues has been mapped onto class distinction in England since the eighteenth century, and which he observes in the verbal stylisations of 'posh' and 'cockney' used by modern London teenagers. Here the semantic dichotomies of high–low, mind–body and reason–emotion are mapped onto shifts of accent in everyday speech situations. Class is not directly referred to, or spoken explicitly, rather it is performed by switching between normal and 'posh' or 'cockney' voices. In such verbal stylisations, speakers demonstrate their reflexive awareness of and response to relations of power and subordination. On *Celebrity Big Brother*, it is Shilpa who speaks 'posh' and Jade who speaks 'cockney' but together they are enacting a cultural semantic legacy of class stratification deeply embedded in Western/industrialised societies.

Language and Class

But if the cultural distinction between 'posh' and 'cockney' can be used as a resource by Rampton's teenagers, it is also available as an ideological framework for interpreting events such as these. Following the Oxo cubes incident, the critical reaction to Jade's performance began to develop beyond the immediate accusation of racism. In editorials and special features, journalists offered their judgments and interpretations, and from the perspective of this chapter what is most interesting is that many of these focused on two factors which became connected. First, Goody was widely condemned for her excessive verbal behaviour (or 'foul-mouthed yobbishness' according to *The Sun*); and second, this was repeatedly related to her class origins.

Primarily, it was commentary in the conservative tabloids and mid-market papers that was most critical of Goody's use of language. Typical of these were two comments in the *Daily Mail* (19 January 2007) which ranged from a critical observation by columnist Sam Greenhill that 'she is not very intelligent and not very good with words', to forthright condemnation from the pundit Amanda Platell: 'She is a vicious guttersnipe, her mind and prejudices as filthy as her language.' Earlier, in the *Daily Star*, erstwhile TV presenter Vanessa Feltz contrasted Goody's unacceptable behaviour with Shetty's eloquence; and it is interesting that in both commentaries language use is seen not simply as an indicator of cultural difference or levels of education, but also as definitive of personality, or, perhaps more precisely, personal moral character:

> The fact that Shilpa is better educated, more successful, far more eloquent – even in her second language –
> and in every conceivable way a more accomplished, more compassionate human being than they will ever
> be is completely and utterly lost on them. (Vanessa Feltz, *Daily Star*, 18 January 2007)

From this point, it then became clear that an alternative line of interpretation to the 'racist bullying' scenario was developing. Particularly in the broadsheet press, some commentators argued that the housemates' behaviour towards Shetty was a product of ignorance and envy, rather than racism per se, and this was itself a reflection of differences of social class. In these arguments, moral condemnation was accompanied by reflections on forms of social behaviour where Goody and her accomplices were explicitly typecast. For middle-class commentators, Goody represented precisely the 'monstrous' white working-class femininity that Skeggs (2005) describes, in which vicious language (with a cockney accent) is just one audible feature of a generalised disgust:

> Most of the time I think the housemates open their mouths without thinking. They seem to be stupid
> rather than wilfully unpleasant. (Janet Street-Porter, *The Independent*, 18 January 2007)

> While the gobby Bermondsey girl had legions of fans, the Jade we've been watching on *Big Brother* is a different matter – a foul mouthed bully spewing vitriol at the Bollywood star Shilpa Shetty … this was probably much more of a class war than it was a race one. (Barbara Ellen, *Observer*, 21 January 2007)

> We wonder if there is any real evidence of racism here. Isn't it more about class, and the fact Miss Shetty's thick and foul-mouthed British housemates are jealous of her superior intelligence, grace and good manners? (*Daily Mail*, Comment, 18 January 2007)

> Jade's behaviour has been disgusting, but I feel sorry for her, if only because we have seen her reverting to type – precisely the kind of woman whom she has struggled to escape. (Kathryn Flett, *Observer*, 21 January 2007)

> Nastiness and ignorance is a way of life for girls like this … [they] are using Shilpa's race to abuse her, but their cruel bullying is actually about class. (David Seymour, *Daily Mail*, 18 January 2007)

> Does that make them racist? What they're doing is more about class than race. She's posh. They're lowlifes who don't want to eat 'foreign muck'. It's prejudiced but it's everyday stuff on the streets of London or Bradford. (Derek Laud, *The Sun*, 18 January 2007)

When she was taken to task, initially in the *Big Brother* Diary Room but also, following her eviction, in press interviews, Goody herself began to make the link between language use and class. The quotation that appears in the title of this chapter comes from a Diary Room scene on the day of the Oxo cubes incident, and here cross-cultural differences in ways of speaking are elided with the class identity Goody wants to project. At this early stage, it would seem that she is defending herself:

> She erm she said something along the lines of erm 'you should change your tone by the way you talk to me'. And I thought no. She went 'my tone is different to yours'. And I was like 'yeh your tone is different to me because you're Indian and you're quite soft within your speaking. I'm common and my talking is quite abrupt'. (Diary Room, 17 January 2007)

Later, however, as the case for her defence became increasingly shaky, Goody's self-reflections took on a more confessional character. Momin Rahman's critical analysis of 'Jade's Confession' argues that it operated as a strategy of rehabilitation for the fallen celebrity (and by extension for the show) by 'demonstrating the interiority of the star as one who is a victim' (Rahman 2008: 143). In Goody's case, she was able to claim to be a victim of her own ignorance, of her social background and of her own personality failings in the emotional intensity of the show. Rahman's key point is that the discourse of 'victimhood' displaces intentional racism, deflecting racist behaviour onto other causes with which the audience can empathise. That might be the case, but it is also interesting that Goody's self-presentation included learning lessons about ways to argue in which, again, forms of verbal behaviour are implicitly if ambivalently linked to social class:

I just thought when anyone has an argument they sounded like I did erm I now know that's not the case. (Diary Room, 20 January 2007)

I've never blamed my past for anything I've done but I don't know any other way. My only way to argue is to shout – to get louder and louder so I can't hear what they're saying. (*News of the World*, 21 January 2007)

In this way, then, a dominant discourse about language and class was reproduced both in the journalistic commentary and in Goody's confession. In this discourse, some uses of language are condemned as pathological. They are seen as manifestations of ignorance and inferior moral character. They are consistently and explicitly related to social class, if not the poverty of the 'abject' working class, then certainly the 'class envy' of the disadvantaged for their cultural superiors. According to this discourse, the right way to deal with these problems is to recognise their limitations on a personal level, and to accept that there are other more appropriate ways to speak and to argue. In this process, what Deborah Cameron (1995) identified as the ideology of 'verbal hygiene', the cultivation of normatively acceptable and appropriate communicative practices, has now become a feature of the self-transformation agenda of UK reality TV.

'Confrontainment' or 'Belligerent Broadcasting'

However, if this ideology displaces the charge of racism, it also sidesteps any more complex consideration of arguments of this kind. Let us try to develop this by making, initially, two simple empirical observations. The first is to repeat the point that if Shilpa Shetty displays 'educated eloquence', she is also significantly implicated in the development of the escalating argument with Jade Goody. She doesn't walk away, but defends herself by trading retorts and metastatements that only serve to enrage Jade further. The second observation is that escalating arguments of this kind are quite common on *Big Brother*. There have been occasions when housemates have been removed for their own safety, and in 2006 a celebrity contestant, Michael Barrymore, pursued precisely such an argument with fellow housemate, the model (younger, female) Jodie Marsh. On this occasion, however, he was not roundly vilified (though he was criticised by Germaine Greer, 2006, in the *Guardian*). Rather, Barrymore's outburst was seen as part of a process of working through his own personality 'issues', confronting his 'demons' etc., and he came second in the final vote.

In their research on the reality TV audience, Wood, Skeggs and Thumim (2009) present evidence which suggests that 'spectacular moments of emotional turmoil' might be a generic feature of many such programmes. One of their respondents (Ruby) makes precisely this point when discussing the reality TV show *Wife Swap* – and, indeed, she focuses on different ways of being argumentative. She suggests that intense emotional confrontation is understandable in some contexts:

… Cos I think sometimes you've got to go through all that anger and fighting and shouting and screaming at each other to, unfortunately you know you've got to go through it to find out the answer to solve the problem, it's part of the process. And yes we'd all love to be able to sit around a table and make notes and

say well I disagree with this … *but life ain't like that.* You do have to scream and shout sometimes to be
heard you know it's an invasion of your life, you know it's their home and someone's coming in you know
and saying right I'm going to change it. Well of course they scream and shout and there are tears and you
know swearing and … slamming doors … (Wood, Skeggs and Thumim 2009: 142–3)

No doubt there are differences between a stranger invading your domestic space and confrontations between housemates in *Big Brother*. Moreover, Ruby clearly recognises here that 'shouting and
screaming at each other' is not the preferred form that arguments should take. However, the broader
point is that there is now a genre of reality TV in which such confrontations are frequent and perhaps have a purpose. The staging of conflict is an essential part of the package.

Furthermore, because these situations are initially unscripted, and participants are performing
'being themselves', they are not contained as they might be in more conventional forms of drama.
Certainly, there is the opportunity to omit excessive and potentially offensive behaviour in subsequent editing, where the highlights narrative is created, but as Rahman (2008) (and other commentators at the time) have noted, Endemol/Channel 4 did not avail themselves of this opportunity,
rather they chose to exploit it. Rahman's explanation for this is not simply that editors were negli-
gent, but rather that they were and are committed to a 'dialectics' of celebrity where 'ridicule' is constantly available as a strategy of representation, which is the other side of the coin to 'respect'.
Part of the audience's fascination with celebrities is the ever-present possibility of their losing face.

So arguably, Jade and Shilpa were performing a generic narrative scenario in a format where
emotional conflicts of this sort are preferred. We can recall Anna Nolan's point about 'the audience's
appetite for uncomfortable, degrading material'. In her book on television discourse, Nuria Lorenzo-
Dus (2009) discusses 'the rise of spectacular incivility' or 'confrontainment' as a pervasive feature of
contemporary TV. In particular, she highlights the way that direct personal arguments with studio
audience participation, as featured in many talk shows, have found their way into the domain of news
and current affairs. However, personal confrontations, involving insults, obscenities, put-downs and
sundry 'face-threatening acts', are now widely seen in talent shows and lifestyle/makeover programming as well as talk shows and reality TV. For other commentators, this constitutes a general rise in
what has been termed 'belligerent broadcasting'.[8] This is programming that deliberately challenges
norms of civility and politeness, possibly in the pursuit of confrontainment, but more generally con-
firming a competitive, cut-throat and self-seeking neo-liberal individualism which Jade Goody, on one
level, represented.

In her commentary on the 'new incivility' in American public discourse, Robin Tolmach Lakoff
(2003) points out that this can be found well beyond the confines of broadcasting, in politics and in
everyday life. She speculates that this might reflect a break up of cultural consensus, which is neither
historically unprecedented nor one-dimensional in its effects. It may be the focus for conservative
cultural lament, a nostalgia for patrician middle-class cultural hegemony – but one consequence of
the social shift she describes is the entry of voices into the public sphere that previously would never
have been heard. If in some cases these voices seem coarse, vulgar or disruptive, this may be a consequence of their struggle for recognition. As with many such arguments, there may be an element

of sanguine liberalism here that ignores, for instance, the exploitation of these voices by forces (such as TV companies) outside their control. Also, as the treatment of Jade Goody (as opposed to Michael Barrymore) showed, it is necessary to recognise that such voices are evaluated differently according to perceptions of gender and class. This case study seems to confirm that there is a particular stigma attached to the 'incivility' of white, lower-working-class women. However, although it is not possible to sanction all that went on in *CBB* 2007, it is also tempting to conclude that the unified, even hysterical vilification of Jade Goody was indicative of the challenge to traditional norms of public discourse that some forms of reality TV make possible.

Notes

1. A preliminary version of this article was given as a paper at the Ross Priory Seminar on Broadcast Talk, University of Strathclyde, May 2007. I am grateful for the comments of co-participants.

2. Dealing with 'antisocial behaviour' was a key aspect of the New Labour Government's moral agenda for tackling 'social exclusion' in the late 1990s. For an incisive analysis of the rhetoric underpinning this policy, see Norman Fairclough's *New Labour, New Language?* (2000), Chapter 2. Fairclough argues that 'exclusion' displaces 'poverty' as the focus for New Labour's authoritarian approach to social welfare.

3. I think it is interesting, however, that as the argument reaches its most 'aggravated' level (from line 86) Jermaine Jackson tries to intervene. Unlike the bouncers on *The Jerry Springer Show*, it is not his job to do so, but there may be some circumstances, in confrontations such as these, where an altruistic third party is prompted to self-select.

4. The transcript presented here uses some of the conventions of CA notation for transcription – in particular, overlapping talk, pauses, 'latching' of utterances and LOUDER speech (cf. Hutchby and Wooffitt 1988). However, some parts of some sequences of overlapping talk are indistinguishable and thus impossible to transcribe. These are indicated by three dots enclosed by round brackets thus: (…).

5. 'Flooding out' is a term used by Goffman to refer to instances of emotional disturbance where a speaker loses self-control. Typical forms of flooding out include bursting into tears, or uncontrollable fits of laughter, though in *Frame Analysis* Goffman also refers to anger in this context (1974: 350ff.).

6. As distinct, for example, from the 'token argument preface' used in football phone-ins where arguments are framed as 'sociable' (Tolson 2006). One way of distinguishing between forms of oppositional argument might be to examine the prefaces through which speakers establish their argumentative footings.

7. There is not the space here to develop a critique of Bernstein. Suffice it to say that there is a basic conceptual difference between his structuralist theory of 'codes' and the more flexible and creative definition of 'stylisation' as used by Rampton and other contemporary sociolinguists.

8. 'Belligerent broadcasting' was the focus for the 2009 Ross Priory Seminar on Broadcast Talk, at the University of Strathclyde. Currently, members of that seminar are preparing papers on this topic for publication.

Bibliography

Bernstein, B. (1971) *Class, Codes and Control*, Vol. 1 (London: Paladin).
Cameron, D. (1995) *Verbal Hygiene* (London: Routledge).

Cohen, P. (1988) 'The Perversions of Inheritance: Studies in the Making of Multi-Racist Britain', in P. Cohen and
      H. Bains (eds), *Multi-Racist Britain* (Basingstoke, Hants.: Macmillan), pp. 9–120.

Fairclough, N. (2000) *New Labour, New Language?* (London: Routledge).

Goffman, E. (1974) *Frame Analysis: An Essay on the Organization of Experience* (New York: Harper & Row).

Greatbatch, D. (1992) 'The Management of Disagreement between News Interviewees', in P. Drew and
      J. Heritage (eds), *Talk at Work: Interaction in Institutional Settings* (Cambridge: Cambridge University Press),
      pp. 268–301.

Greer, G. (2006) 'Lay off poor Jodie, you big bullies', *Guardian* [online], 13 January. Available at:
      <www.guardian.co.uk/media/2006/jan/13/realitytv.bigbrother> accessed 13 January 2006.

——— (2007) 'Why does everyone hate me?', *Guardian* [online], *g2*, 17 January. Available at:
      <www.guardian.co.uk/culture/tvandradioblog/2007/jan/17> accessed 17 January 2007.

Heritage, J. (1985) 'Analyzing News Interviews: Aspects of the Production of Talk for Overhearing Audiences',
      in T. van Dijk (ed.), *Handbook of Discourse Analysis*, Vol. 3 (London: Academic Press), pp. 95–117.

Hutchby, I. (1996) *Confrontation Talk: Arguments, Asymmetries and Power on Talk Radio* (Mahwah, NJ: Lawrence
      Erlbaum Associates).

——— (2006) *Media Talk: Conversation Analysis and the Study of Broadcasting* (Maidenhead, Berks.: Open
      University Press).

Hutchby, I. and R. Wooffitt (1988) *Conversation Analysis* (Cambridge: Polity).

Jones, J. (2003) 'Show Your Real Face', *New Media & Society*, 5(3): 400–21.

Lakoff, R. T. (2003) 'The New Incivility: Threat or Promise?', in J. Aitchison and D. M. Lewis (eds), *New Media
      Language* (London: Routledge), pp. 36–44.

Lorenzo-Dus, N. (2009) *Television Discourse: Analysing Discourse in the Media* (Basingstoke, Hants.: Palgrave
      Macmillan).

Lunt, P. and P. Stenner (2005) '*The Jerry Springer Show* as an Emotional Public Sphere', *Media, Culture & Society*,
      27(1): 59–81.

Morley, D. (2009) 'Mediated Class-ifications: Representations of Class and Culture in Contemporary British
      Television', *European Journal of Cultural Studies*, 12(4): 487–508.

Nolan, A. (2010) '*Big Brother* changed my life, but the time is right for it to bow out', *Observer* [online],
      6 June 2010. Available at: <http://www.guardian.co.uk/tv-and-radio/2010/jun/06/big-brother-bows-out>
      accessed 31 January 2011.

Palmer, G. (2004) '"The New You": Class and Transformation in Lifestyle Television', in S. Holmes and D. Jermyn
      (eds), *Understanding Reality Television* (London: Routledge), pp. 173–90.

Rahman, M. (2008) 'Jade's Confession: Racism and the Dialectics of Celebrity', *Social Semiotics*, 18(2): 133–48.

Rampton, B. (2003) 'Hegemony, Social Class and Stylisation', *Pragmatics*, 13(1): 49–83.

——— (2006) *Language in Late Modernity: Interaction in an Urban School* (Cambridge: Cambridge University
      Press).

Scannell, P. (1991) 'Introduction: The Relevance of Talk', in P. Scannell (ed.), *Broadcast Talk* (London: Sage),
      pp. 1–13.

Schegloff, E. A. (1999) 'Discourse, Pragmatics, Conversation', *Discourse Studies*, 1(4): 405–35.

Schiffrin, D. (1984) 'Jewish Argument as Sociability', *Language in Society*, 13: 311–35.

——— (1985) 'Everyday Argument: The Organization of Diversity', in T. Van Dijk (ed.), *Handbook of Discourse Analysis*, Vol. 3 (London: Academic Press), pp. 35–46.

Skeggs, B. (2005) 'The Making of Class and Gender through Visualizing Moral Subject Formation', *Sociology*, 39(5): 965–82.

Skeggs, B. and H. Wood (2008) 'The Labour of Transformation and Circuits of Value "around" Reality TV', *Continuum: Journal of Media and Cultural Studies*, 22(4): 559–72.

Taylor, L. (2002) 'From Ways of Life to Lifestyle: The Ordinari-ization of British Gardening Lifestyle Television', *European Journal of Communication*, 17(4): 479–93.

Tolson, A. (2006) *Media Talk: Spoken Discourse on TV and Radio* (Edinburgh: Edinburgh University Press).

Turner, G. (2004) *Understanding Celebrity* (London: Sage).

——— (2010) *Ordinary People and the Media: The Demotic Turn* (London: Sage).

Wood, H., B. Skeggs and N. Thumim (2009) '"It's just sad": Affect, Judgement and Emotional Labour in "Reality" Television Viewing', in S. Gillis and J. Hollows (eds), *Feminism, Domesticity and Popular Culture* (London: Taylor and Francis), pp. 135–50.

4/Mark Andrejevic

Managing the Borders: Classed Mobility on Security-Themed Reality TV

One episode of the successful Australian reality show *Border Security: Australia's Front Line* provided viewers with a primer on profiling airline passengers who claim to be business travellers: do their passports provide evidence of frequent travel? Are they dressed like corporate executives in expensive business suits? Are they carrying BlackBerrys? Is their English fluent – or close to it? Unfortunately for the four Vietnamese citizens attempting to enter Australia on business visas, they failed on all counts. Thanks to actor Grant Bowler's voiceover, viewers learn that the four were targeted by officers in the customs zone because they did not look the part of business travellers. It turns out that the passengers were 'low-level employees' of the company they claimed to represent, using fraudulently obtained business visas to come to Australia to find work.[1] By the end of the episode, the show suggested that justice had been served and the nation protected from a potentially harmful incursion: the four travellers' visas were revoked and they were all returned to Vietnam on the next flight.

What was striking about this episode was not the detection and capture of Asian economic migrants – a recurring theme in the series – but the way in which it highlighted a persistent *absence* in the show's vignettes of visa violators: images of actual business travellers. There are recurring character-types on the Australian show, but business travellers do not feature prominently among them. For the most part, the show focuses on people seeking work without a visa, low-level drug smugglers who are down on their luck enough to risk their freedom and, in some cases, their bodies for a cash payoff; travellers with felony convictions trying to convince customs officials to let them into the country; Asian travellers with exotic foods hidden in their luggage; and American tourists smuggling snack food, as if unaware that Australia is riddled with 7-Elevens and McDonald's. The real corporate executives with the BlackBerrys and business suits, however, remain outside the reality TV frame, presumably moving frictionlessly across borders, failing to trigger the scrutiny of *Border Security* spotters or the TV cameras that capture their activities. In this regard, the class-based language so familiar to air travel takes on a more literal cast. Business class does not just refer to fully reclining chairs and chilled flatware, but also to a particular type of mobility in the era of globalisation.

In marking these distinctions between varying abilities to fulfil the economic and security criteria for border crossing, *Border Security* illustrates Doreen Massey's observation about the classed nature of mobility in an era of so-called space–time compression: 'different social groups and differ-ent individuals are placed in very distinct ways in relation to those flows and interconnections' (Massey 1993: 62). To speak of this distinction in terms of class is to point out the structured differ-ences in access to consumer goods (including leisure travel) and productive resources that distin-guish between business travellers, tourists and 'illegal' migrants. As David Morley has noted, in the era of globalisation, borders do not disappear or become irrelevant, but serve as a sorting mechanism for flows of information, goods and people, with differential permeability based on access to resources, 'financial or other' (Morley 2000: 197). Different levels of access reflect and reproduce power relations:

> Different social groups have distinct relationships to this anyway-differentiated mobility: some are more in
> charge of it than others; some initiate flows and movement, others don't; some are more on the receiving
> end of it than others; some are effectively imprisoned by it. (Massey 1993: 62)

And, I would add, even *literally* imprisoned as a result of it. Prison is part of the *Border Security* scenery: a typical episode signs off with a description of the prison sentences meted out to one or more of the felons caught up in the 'surveillant assemblage' (Haggerty and Ericson 2000: 605) at the border – an assemblage comprised of human spotters, sniffer dogs, video cameras, body searches, metal detectors, X-ray scanners and drug detection kits.

Much has been made in recent scholarly work on reality TV of its disciplinary function: the forms of self-governance, performance, self-training and responsibilisation it models and enacts (for example, Palmer in this volume and Palmer 2003; Ouellette 2004; Ouellette and Hay 2008). Furthermore, as Bev Skeggs and Helen Wood have compellingly demonstrated, the neo-liberal emphasis on techniques for self-management serves to background issues of class. They note that in the post-industrial era,

> Self-responsibility and self-management … become key features of the 'new' reflexive self. 'Reality' television
> which foregrounds the display of self-performance by 'ordinary' people doing 'ordinary everydayness' with
> new levels of televisual representational play offered us the perfect site for exploring self-making, self-
> legitimation and the supposed demise of class. (Skeggs and Wood 2009: 628)

Although the recent spate of border-themed reality shows in the UK (*Customs*, 2008–11), the US (*Homeland Security USA*, 2009), Australia (*Border Security: Australia's Front Line*, 2004–) and New Zealand (*Border Patrol*, 2002) complement disciplinary models of responsible citizenship with the intrusion of state power, they conserve this logic of classlessness by individualising the portrayal of varying levels of access to mobility. Thus, while *Border Security* and its US spin-off *Homeland Security USA* incorporate what might be described as a pedagogical element insofar as they model proper behaviour for international travel, they also incorporate elements of sovereign power: the subjection of travellers to police procedures of interrogation, invasive search and detention. In this regard, the shows have something in common with reality police formats like *COPS* (1989–) and, in Australia,

The Force (2006), *Highway Patrol* (2009) and *Random Breath Test* (2011), which focus on the spectacle of the exercise of state power. The shows have a somewhat more developed pedagogical side than *COPS*, featuring in-depth instructions for viewers, not just in the protocols for border crossing, but also, in the case of *Border Security*, on the reasons for these protocols.

What is perhaps distinctive about the *Border Security* format is the way in which it operates not just along international boundaries, but also along the border between self-governance and sovereign authority, between normative middle-class existence and an excluded and criminalised underclass. *Border Security* stages those moments when the failure of self-governance crosses over into the realm of criminality – when the very attempt to 'pass' as a member of the mobile classes triggers the direct intervention of state power and the mobilisation of the policing apparatus. What distinguishes the various offenders is, in a sense, eclipsed by what they have in common: the attempt to migrate from the realm of those subject to restrictions on their mobility to the realm of

> those who are both doing the moving and the communicating and who are in some way in a position of control in relation to it … These are the groups who are really in a sense in charge of time–space compression, who can really use it and turn it to advantage, whose power and influence it very definitely increases. (Massey 1993: 62)

These are also the ones with the BlackBerrys and the passports crammed full of visas. They are the ones who are, for the most part, invisible on *Border Security* – perhaps not least because when they do break the rules, they are unlikely to sign the release that allows their transgressions to be publicised. Those who cross the threshold of visibility into reality TV are the ones who ignore the proper travel protocols or who attempt to violate them. The former serve as object lessons in appropriate travel behaviour for members of the mobile classes – what to declare, how to comport oneself – whereas the latter provide the spectacle of what happens when self-discipline is supplemented by the intervention of sovereign power. In this regard, the format combines familiar models of self-management and self-comportment with the direct application of state power. Vignettes of middle-class life characteristic of other self-management formats are interspersed with stories of the desperation of economic refugees and the criminal activity of smugglers. Some of the subplots end with travellers lamenting their failure to declare food items in their carry-on bags, others with suspects led off by police.

This characteristic mix differentiates the *Border Security* format from other subgenres of reality TV and highlights it borderland status. It is also a mix that reflects the psychic landscape of the post-9/11 world in which security threats are perceived as potentially embedded in the mundane details of daily life. The border marks this paradoxical space in which the external threat is internalised. As Sara Ahmed puts it,

> Borders are constructed and indeed policed in the very feeling that they have already been transgressed: the other has to get too close, in order to be recognised as an object of fear, and in order for the object to be displaced. (Ahmed 2004: 133)

This is why borders come to play an important role in the political mobilisation of anxieties in the post-9/11 era: 'the politics of fear as well as hate is narrated as a border anxiety: fear speaks the language of "floods" and "swamps", of being invaded by inappropriate others, against whom the nation must defend itself' (ibid.).

One of Australia's most popular home-grown reality shows, *Border Security* documents the activities of officials tasked with enforcing the country's immigration and customs laws, focusing particularly on airport security and the postal service, the two main (non-industrial) sites of entry for people and goods. The show, reportedly initiated not by the government but by producers, became an immediate hit after its 2004 debut, and has consistently earned high ratings – around 2 million viewers – for its time slot, which has led to its ongoing renewal for a seventh season as of this writing (Price 2006a).

The show's American spin-off, whose title, *Homeland Security USA*, directly invoked the US response to the 9/11 attacks, fared less well in the ratings. Scheduled to run for a season of thirteen episodes starting in January 2009, the show debuted to strong ratings of some 7.8 million viewers, but was pulled by the ABC network after eight episodes when the ratings dropped into the 5 million range (Toff 2009: 1). The different reception of the show in the two countries is an interesting phenomenon in itself, and reflects disparate sensibilities regarding bureaucracy, policing, immigration histories and national identity.[2] There are some significant differences in presentation that likely reflect producers' understanding of their respective audiences. These differences also reflect distinct class sensibilities: Australia's stronger sense of working-class identity allows the political right to mobilise elements of its traditional opposition against the threat of foreign workers, whereas the American Dream of class mobility, combined with its distinct strain of libertarianism, casts the efforts of economic migrants (and the bureaucracy that would thwart them) in a somewhat different light. The US show includes backstory features about security officers, humorous clips of them horsing around and even moments when the policing apparatus seems to break down, as in one episode in which border guards almost allow a drunk driver back to her car because they cannot get local police to respond. Frequently, officers in the US format, including several who are first-generation US citizens, express their empathy for the migrants they investigate, track and deport. In this regard, the US version works hard to humanise the security apparatus, whereas the focus in the Australian version is on the competence and efficiency of the officers, who receive additional camera time only when they are providing a detailed, at times scolding, explanation of the policies they enforce. For the purposes of this chapter, the focus will be on what the shows have in common: their framing of normative mobility and of the threat posed by those who deviate from it.

An Alien Class

One of the results of the supposed demise of class in the neo-liberal era – the notion that 'we' are unmarked by class structures because these have lost their determining power – is that it designates those who do not share a normative 'classlessness' as outsiders. The supposedly unmarked, universal non-class ends up being a version of aspirational middle-class identity, as Skeggs and Wood observe: 'middle-class practices have come increasingly to define the Western social itself' (Skeggs and Wood 2009: 629).

However, a class identity that does not recognise itself as such provides little room for legitimate alternative class identities within the realm of the social: one is either part of the universal class or an outsider of some sort. In this regard, neo-liberalism lends itself to the politics of populism described by Slavoj Žižek: a politics wherein conflicts and contradictions internal to a social forma-tion are expelled to a realm of external threat: 'for a populist, the cause of the troubles is ultimately never the system as such but the intruder who corrupted it' (Žižek 2006: 555). What once might have been construed as a class-based form of politics comes to be portrayed as an attack on the system from the outside – as illustrated by the familiar right-wing rhetoric that accuses those who invoke class of being 'outside agitators' and class warriors: outsiders seeking to create internal con-flicts where there are none. This ascendant form of populism underwrites the resurgent forms of nativism and racism that coincide with the rise of neo-liberal globalisation. As Žižek notes, it is a pol-itics that 'in its very notion … displaces the immanent social antagonism into the antagonism between the unified people and its external enemy' (ibid.: 557).

It is not surprising that conspiracy theory and right-wing populism of the Glenn Beck variety go hand in hand: they both do the work of redirecting internal critique toward a shifting and shadowy borderland of outsiders (always in the process of infiltration). Whether they are communists or ter-rorists, those who pose the threat are always illegitimate outsiders (hence the attempt by right-wing activists in the United States to call into question Barack Obama's citizenship status). This is why con-cerns about communists can readily be redirected toward, say, Muslims, without changing the con-tent of the claims: they are among us but different from us, they are implacable, irrational and they hate our way of life, they have secret sleeper cells devoted to internal infiltration and world domi-nation, and so on.

In its focus on the relationship between the internal enemy and the outside agitator, conspiracy theory displaces class-based critique in the neo-liberal era: hence its appeal to those who are all too palpably aware, first hand, of the depredations of capital. At the same time, it works to reinstitute a social divide: that between insiders and outsiders, those in the know and the 'others' who remain the dupes or accomplices of those who contaminate the system. These outsiders typically come from the Global South and the East – the non-White, non-Western world. In a survey of fifteen sample episodes of *Border Security* reviewed for this chapter, forty-six out of sixty-three people detained were non-white – and of those who were white, many were marked by non-Anglophone accents. Access to mobility capital is marked by race, class and geography.

Terrorists at the Border

Elayne Rapping has demonstrated how the reality show *COPS* models a landscape of outsiders:

> *COPS* is set in a metaphoric border territory, 'out where the buses don't run'. The families and
> neighborhoods that set the standard for 'normality' against which criminal deviance is defined on shows like

Law and Order are gone […] *COPS* is set far from any community in which traditional family life might thrive. This is a landscape of highways, strip malls, trailer parks, and convenience stores, where churches, school, and office buildings – the institutions that make up 'normal' society – have no place. (Rapping 2003: 56)

It is a description that neatly anticipates the arrival of the *Border Security* franchise – set in literal border territories ranging from customs checkpoints at airports and highways to the harsh conditions of the Sonoran desert. In these territories, borders help to highlight the contrast between those with and without access to mobility 'capital'.

Writing well before the September 11 attacks, Rapping presciently identified the figure that haunts the threatening border territories of alien otherness – namely, the terrorist:

an outsider who poses a threat to social order because he does not conform to the psychological and moral norms by which we, in Western society, have learned to live peacefully together … Terrorists are irrational, inscrutable, and inherently violent. They threaten to infiltrate our porous borders, bringing fear, chaos, and disorder. (Rapping 1999: 268)

On *Border Security* as on *COPS*, however, the figure of the terrorist is conspicuous in its absence. To date, the shows have featured plenty of drug couriers, visa breakers and carriers of contraband (both unwitting and deliberate), but no terrorists. Australian host Grant Bowler doubts that the show will ever capture actual terrorists, but he also notes that the threat of terrorism is inseparable from its reception: 'We live in an age of terrorism; we live in frightening times. It's kind of becoming a global village, and along with that you tend to get all the village idiots wandering around freely at will' (Downie 2008; Koch 2006). The show clearly caters to a heightened perception of risk in the post-9/11 era. As one media critic put it, 'There's no question the show taps into growing community fears about immigration, illicit drugs, smugglers, poachers, and even terrorists' (Koch 2006: G3).

The absent but unifying figure of the terrorist highlights the homeland's vulnerability and invokes the alchemy of terror whereby the mundane elements of daily life – drinking water, airplanes, the mail service – can be turned into weapons aimed at the hearts, minds and bodies of the citizenry. In the post-9/11 era, the potentially devastating threat posed to agriculture by an invasive 'non-native' species, or the implicit threat of economic destabilisation associated with economic migration, reminds us of the nation's vulnerability and insecurity.

These may not be the intentional acts of terrorists, but they recall the force-amplifying logic of terror. In the face of the potential devastation posed by a seemingly harmless package of food, the terrifying possibilities are staged for us. The biological threat of pests and non-native species of plants and animals is a recurring theme in the Australian version of the show, highlighting the nation's fragility and recapitulating the logic of weapons of mass destruction in the register of the biosphere. We are reminded, repeatedly, of how destructive the apparently most benign objects can be. A small bag of raw cotton wicks could be carrying mite-sized eggs that will one day devastate Australia's cotton crop, a box of sweets made with cow's milk from India could be a devastating if unwitting Trojan horse threatening the nation's livestock.

The threat of non-indigenous species is aligned with that of smuggling and illegal immigration: all are reflexive risks whose consequences are potentially so great that they threaten national security. In this regard, the figure of the outsider is not simply criminalised through its association with terror – it is 'biologised' as an invasive species threatening the population. This chain of associations echoes Ahmed's description of the way in which fear is amplified through its circulation along a sliding axis of associations (Ahmed 2004). She invokes an example particularly pertinent to *Border Security*:

> The sticking together of the figure of the asylum seeker and the international terrorist, which already
>
> evokes other figures (the burglar, the bogeyman), constructs those who are 'without home' as sources of
>
> 'our fear' and as reasons for new forms of border policing. (Ahmed 2004: 137)

At work in such formulations, she argues, is a productive logic of metonymy that 'works to generate or make likeness: the asylum seeker is "like" the terrorist, an agent of fear, who may destroy "our home"' (ibid.). It is a logic exemplified by Margaret Thatcher's reception of the European Community: 'we joined Europe to have free movement of goods … I did not join Europe to have free movement of terrorists, criminals, drugs, plant and animal diseases and rabies and illegal immigrants' (quoted in Morley 2000: 226).

Classed Mobility

The weaving together of these various threats to the homeland is, in part, a formal element of the subgenre. Every version follows a similar format in which a half-hour episode cuts back and forth between several narrative strands that include passenger searches and interrogations, the apprehension of border crossers or visa violators, and searches through suspicious international mail. In both the US and Australian formats, the security threat is comprised primarily of the smuggling of organic matter, whether inadvertent or not (punctuated by relatively small-scale drug busts), and by those seeking to work illegally. All of these risks are, in a sense, lumped together as the wages of globalisation in a risky world. A network blurb for the Australian show neatly captures this convergence and recalls Thatcher's formulation: 'The stars of the show are the men and women who patrol our airports and coastlines and protect our country from drug runners, illegal immigrants, potential terrorists, harmful pests and disease' (Price 2006a; 2006b: 20). These varied and quite different threats are absorbed into the long shadow of the threat cast by the 9/11 attacks.

In the United States, anti-immigration forces have attempted to recast the immigration debate by blurring the distinction between illegal immigration and terrorism (see Fernandes 2007). By the same token, the ongoing speculation about possible future avenues of terrorist attack helps lump together agricultural and economic threats with assaults on national security. Just as the terrorist attacks of 9/11 had, at least in part, the goal of economic disruption, so too do economic threats carry with them the threat of national vulnerability. In all cases, disruption – whether by biological or economic threat (and the two are assimilated to one another: immigration becomes another form of 'contamination') – falls under the umbrella of national security and hence of anti-terrorism.

The background context of terror that characterises security-oriented reality TV informs and unites the threat of otherness. It is an equation made explicit in one of the posts to the official bulletin board for the US version of the show: 'our country is being destroyed by the flow of illegals crossing every day. THIS IS A FORM OF TERRORISM!!! The US ECONOMY is taking the hit for our stupid watered down laws' (Customs123 2009). It is a rant that echoes the rhetoric of Arizona Governor Jan Brewer, notorious for passing stringent anti-immigration laws that have been criticised for encouraging racial profiling. In an interview on Fox News, Brewer claimed that 'Arizona has been under terrorist attacks, if you will, with all of this illegal immigration that has been taking place on our very porous border' (Armbruster 2010).

The vagaries of the borderlands haunt this rhetoric: it is not entirely clear whether Brewer means that lawbreaking is, in itself, an attack on homeland security, whether she is referring to the drug cartels that she and other immigration hardliners so frequently invoke to spread the fear of the violent crime spilling across the border from Mexico, or to would-be assailants from other parts of the world flocking to the US's allegedly inadequately protected underbelly. This indistinct threat characterised the show's bulletin board and its frequent posts alluding to crimes committed by immigrants – posts that tended to blur the distinction between Mexico and the Middle East, invoking a kind of all-purpose anxiety directed toward people of colour from an indistinctly imagined under-developed other-world. As one post put it:

> what really has me on edge, sometimes, is the fact that a TV station in the Rio Grande Valley in Texas did a segment about 2 years ago where a rancher found all sorts of clothing, passports, and other stuff from people from the Mideast who just left the stuff behind. (JamesW62 2010)

The fact that traces were all that could be found suggested they had already disappeared into the American heartland. The recurring theme of such posts is characteristic of border anxiety: the boundary has already been breached and the populace contaminated – the 'other' walks among us.

In keeping with neo-liberal ideologies of achievement, there is a sense in both versions of the show that the lack of mobility capital represents a moral failure, a failure of responsibility and a potentially dangerous disregard for the rules. The reduction of the social to the individual that is the hallmark of reality TV's narrow-focus style means that accounts of economic relations and histories fall by the wayside (see Wood and Skeggs 2008). The fact that rule breakers and 'queue jumpers' (right-wing Australian rhetoric for would-be immigrants who do not follow the rules) are portrayed as coming disproportionately from particular regions (Africa, Mexico, South Asia) becomes not so much a consequence of economic disparities as an explanation for them. We see suspects attempting to manipulate, stonewall, evade or otherwise dissemble in their interactions with customs officials – they are the dishonest, the crafty, the belligerent, or simply the bewildered and overwhelmed in the face of dispassionate bureaucratic competence. In the absence of any accounting for their desperation, their anxiety and their disregard for the rules, these traits come across as regional personality attributes – a kind of irrational and wilful persistence – rather than the expression of desperation in the face of poverty or oppression.

A Geography of 'Rule Breaking'

It is hard not to respond to the pathos and desperation of many of those featured on the show – especially those fleeing conditions of economic hardship – and the story editors clearly work to manage this response. The US show, in particular, attempts to address the economic plight of the Mexican migrants who play such a central role in its portrayal of immigration enforcement – perhaps as a vestige of the nation's self-identity as a land of opportunity for the 'huddled masses yearning to breathe free'.[3]

As if to address the tension in the show between the promise of the American Dream and the reality of the structural forms of exclusion that thwart it, one episode of *Homeland Security* focused on an officer from the former Yugoslavia who arrived in the US as a refugee and then decided to become a border protection officer 'to repay the US' (according to the show's voiceover). The show portrays him processing the immigration application of a Cuban national: 'I understood her story,' he tells the camera. 'I came here in America looking for protection, now I am honored that I am able to give protection to somebody else.'[4] The show points out, in keeping with one of its recurring refrains, that what differentiates him from those who are apprehended and turned away at the border is that he followed the rules.

This is also the theme of *Border Security: Australia's Front Line*. Those who are turned away, denied visas and banned from re-entry are those who just would not follow the rules: as if the mobility hurdles they face are self-imposed – an appropriate retribution for those portrayed as lawbreakers, whether out of ignorance, arrogance or impatience. Highlighting the contrast between the rule followers and the rule breakers, the US show features border officers of Mexican heritage and the Australian show officers with Asian backgrounds, representing the main source regions for economic migrants in each case. Understanding that the show elicits a certain sympathy for many of those desperate to escape conditions of poverty, oppression or lack of opportunity, the officers frequently observe that they 'feel' for the people they turn away – but that fairness requires the rules be followed. In many cases, of course, the rules serve not to facilitate entry but to exclude – and a certain class of economic migrants knows that getting around the rules is their only way in.

Another effect of framing economic migration in terms of 'the rules' is that it backgrounds the distinction between migrants and tourists: as if the distinguishing factor is a willingness to abide by the rules – and, perhaps, the seriousness of the infringement. Thus, one of the recurring themes in the online forums was the difficulty that travellers seem to have following simple instructions. As one post put it, 'The people coming in should know the rules and laws before they come' (Piker2130 2009). The failure to follow the rules is portrayed as a function of ignorance and, perhaps, a lack of respect for the rule of law in the United States: 'You should familiarize yourself with the rules, if I travelled to another country I would expect to do the same' (TSAPIP 2009). The fact that everyone is a potential security risk – a plane can be brought down by a few contraband fireworks in the bag of an ignorant traveller or by concealed explosives on a terrorist – means that everyone is a target of the new security apparatus.

The shows' vignettes provide clues as to what this apparatus looks for: travellers with too little luggage and too much or too little cash, travellers who are nervous and unfamiliar with the rituals of customs, and those who look like they are living beyond their means. In one episode of *Border Security*, a manicurist from Hong Kong was detained and interrogated, her bags repeatedly swab-tested and searched because she was wearing a $14,000 diamond ring, which officers suspected of being payment for serving as a drug courier. She had to explain in detail how she had acquired the money to buy the ring before she was allowed to enter the country.

The shows also trace a geography of assumed risk: the countries identified over the course of several episodes as source nations for migrants and contraband are predominantly from the Global South and Eastern Europe: India, Indonesia, Malaysia, Vietnam, Mexico, the Philippines, Panama, Kenya, Brazil, Columbia and Argentina, with Romania and Bulgaria making occasional appearances. Within the nation as without, class stratification is spatialised and gated communities develop strategies for keeping the 'undesirables' out, even as fear-mongers claim that the 'neighbourhood' is already under siege. In this regard, *Border Security* highlights the ongoing process of filtering associated with globalisation: the flow of goods, people and capital is crucial to the health of the nation, but these flows must be tightly governed in the name of security and productivity.

Disciplining and Punishing

The Australian version of the show frequently highlights tourists with a bit too much attitude for the Australian bureaucracy: travellers who have failed to fill out their customs declarations cards properly and bristle at the lectures to which they are submitted. The Australian immigrations officials specialise in bureaucratic forms of ritual humiliation such as reducing an exhausted British traveller to tears because she had forgotten about the snack bag of peeled carrots in the bottom of her carry-on bag and then letting her go with a warning to ensure she will not make the same mistake next time. In another episode, a man is reprimanded for an entire segment of the show for not declaring as food the chewing gum he has purchased. The gum is permitted, but that is not the point according to the customs official: anything that can be consumed must be declared. At the same time, the show makes sure to drive home the point that impatience with the inspection and interrogation process is a sign of unsophisticated travellers.

Such scenes form part of the pedagogy of travel conduct provided by the show's voiceover: they are not produced simply to provide some level of emotional tension and conflict, but serve as object lessons in personal responsibility for those invited to identify with the travellers. It is this combination of entertainment and education that host Grant Bowler emphasises, praising the show's pedagogical function in a promotional interview:

> I honestly believe the show has helped educate people. On a small and medium level, it has helped people realise what they can and cannot bring into the country and how to fill out customs forms properly. I think it has helped the officers with the trivial and mundane stuff, and let them concentrate a bit more on the big stuff. (Williams 2007: 7)

Proper conduct does more than ensure friction-free travel – at least for those with the necessary credentials – it also allows the state to offload responsibility for the governance of mobility onto the populace.

The privilege of mobility takes on a certain glow of freedom and desirability when viewed through the eyes of those who are excluded from it. Žižek describes how, with respect to the rise of capitalism in Eastern Europe,

> What ultimately fascinated the political classes, and even the wider public, in the West was the fascinated
> gaze of the East towards the West … out there are still people who look towards us, who admire us and
> would like to become like us. (Žižek and Daly 2004: 139)

This is not to diminish the real, structural, difference between those with access to mobility capital and those without, but rather to highlight the way in which reality TV stages a gaze which highlights the freedoms enabled by the forms of responsibilisation promoted by the pedagogy of travel conduct on *Border Security*.

Global Border Security

The security apparatus portrayed on *Border Security* traces a landscape of risk whose contours take for granted an established set of global social relations and political and economic institutions. In so doing, the shows highlight the international character of classed mobility in the era of globalisation. More specifically and in keeping with Massey's notion of 'power geometry', they highlight the way in which differently situated groups are subject to different regimes of mobility. The work that the so-called war on terror and related notions of homeland and border security do is to erode the particularity of these groups, which include group drug smugglers, people smugglers, thieves (the Australian show has come across credit card skimming technologies on more than one occasion) and economic migrants. As if to highlight the expansive definition of 'border' and 'security', a special episode of *Border Security* featured a visit with Australian troops in Afghanistan. In the era of globalisation, national borders can be expanded indefinitely and homeland security takes on the burden of securing the world. Political rhetoric expresses these developments by recasting the regulation of migration as a security issue and refiguring the migrant as a form of economic terrorist. What gets lost in the version of classlessness that characterises neo-liberal populism is the distinction between the two.

Notes

1. *Border Security: Australia's Front Line.* Channel 7, Season 7, Episode 8, first aired 28 March 2004 (Australian Department of Immigration and Citizenship 2010a).
2. In relative terms, Australia and the United States face similar levels of legal immigration: since 2000, Australia has received about a million migrants and the US about 12 million (Australian Department of Immigration and Citizenship 2010b; United States Department of Homeland Security 2010). As a percentage of the 2010 population of each nation, this amounts to about 4.7 per cent in Australia and

4 per cent in the United States. However, in percentage terms, estimates of illegal immigration are quite different. In Australia, an island nation with tightly controlled borders, an estimated 48,700 people or about one-fifth of 1 per cent of the population are in the country illegally; in the United States, the estimated figure is about 3.5 per cent of the population; more than an order of magnitude greater (Australian Department of Immigration and Citizenship 2010a; Preston 2008).

3. The reference is to the well-known sonnet by Emma Lazarus, 'The New Colossus', which is inscribed on a plaque in the museum at the base of the Statue of Liberty.

4. *Homeland Security USA*, ABC, Season 1, Episode 5, first aired 17 February 2009.

Bibliography

Ahmed, S. (2004) 'Affective Economies', *Social Text*, 22(2): 117–39.

Armbruster, B. (2010) 'Gov. Brewer: "Arizona has been under terrorist attacks" with "all of this illegal immigration"', *ThinkProgress.Org* [online], 30 April 2010. Available at: <http://thinkprogress.org/2010/04/30/brewer-terrorist-attacks/> accessed 2 February 2011.

Australian Department of Immigration and Citizenship (2010a) 'Fact Sheet 87 – Initiatives to Combat Illegal Work in Australia'. Available at: <http://www.immi.gov.au/media/fact-sheets/87illegal.htm> accessed 10 November 2010.

———— (2010b) 'Fact Sheet 2 – Key Facts in Immigration'. Available at: <http://www.immi.gov.au/media/fact-sheets/02key.htm> accessed 10 November 2010.

Customs123 (2009) *Homeland Security USA Forum*, 20 January 2009, posted online at: <site.abc.go.com/primetime/homelandsecurity/> accessed 2 February 2011.

Downie, S. (2008) 'I'm always terrified of going through customs', *Daily Telegraph*, 27 June, p. 6.

———— (2008) 'The hit show with guilt-edged appeal', *Herald-Sun*, 16 January, p. C8.

Fernandes, D. (2007) *Targeted: Homeland Security and the Business of Immigration* (New York: Seven Stories Press).

Haggerty, K. and R. Ericson (2000) 'The Surveillant Assemblage', *British Journal of Sociology*, 51(4): 605–22.

JamesW62 (2010) *Homeland Security USA Forum*, 8 January 2010, posted online at: <site.abc.go.com/primetime/homelandsecurity/> accessed 2 February 2011.

Koch, P. (2006) 'Fear and loathing: how terrorism changed the world and made a surprise hit', *Sunday Mail*, 14 May, p. G3.

Massey, D. (1993) 'Power-Geometry and a Progressive Sense of Place', in J. Bird (ed.), *Mapping the Futures: Local Cultures, Global Change* (London: Routledge), pp. 60–70.

Morley, D. (2000) *Home Territories: Media, Mobility, and Identity* (London: Routledge).

Ouellette, L. (2004) '"Take responsibility for yourself": *Judge Judy* and the Neo-Liberal Citizen', in S. Murray and L. Ouellette (eds), *Reality TV: Remaking Television Culture* (New York: NYU Press), pp. 223–42.

Ouellette, L. and J. Hay (2008) *Better Living through Reality TV: Television and Post-Welfare Citizenship* (Oxford: Wiley-Blackwell).

Palmer, G. (2003) *Discipline and Liberty: Television and Governance* (Manchester: Manchester University Press).

Piker2130 (2009) *Homeland Security USA Forum*, 8 January 2009, posted online at: <site.abc.go.com/primetime/homelandsecurity/> accessed 2 February 2011.

Preston, J. (2008) 'Decline seen in numbers of people here illegally', *The New York Times*, 31 July, p. B1.

Price, M. (2006a) 'Ratings to be afraid of today, *Border Security* and *The Force* are out-rating slick American blockbusters like *Lost* and *Desperate Housewives*', *Sunday Tasmanian*, 3 September, p. 20.

———— (2006b) 'Insecurity now all right', *Sunday Times*, 3 September, p. 56.

Rapping, E. (1999) 'Aliens, Nomads, Mad Dogs, and Road Warriors: Tabloid TV and the New Face of Criminal Violence', in C. Sharrett (ed.), *Mythologies of Violence in Postmodern Media* (Detroit, MI: Wayne State University Press), pp. 249–74.

———— (2003) *Law and Justice as Seen on TV* (New York: NYU Press).

Skeggs, B. and H. Wood (2009) 'The Moral Economy of Person Production: The Class Relations of Self-Performance on "Reality" Television', *The Sociological Review*, 57(4): 626–44.

Toff, B. (2009) 'Hefty returns for biggest loser', *The New York Times*, 8 January, p. C1.

TSAPIP (2009) *Homeland Security USA Forum*, 3 February 2009, posted online at: <site.abc.go.com/prime-time/homelandsecurity/> accessed 2 February 2011.

United States Department of Homeland Security (2010) *Yearbook of Immigration Statistics*. Available at: <http://www.dhs.gov/files/statistics/publications/yearbook.shtm> accessed 10 November 2010.

Williams, G. (2007) 'Grant's reality check', *Sydney Morning Herald*, 6 October, p. 7.

Wood, H. and B. Skeggs (2008) 'Spectacular Morality: "Reality" Television, Individualisation and the Remaking of the Working Class', in D. Hesmondhalgh and J. Toynbee (eds), *The Media and Social Theory* (London: Routledge), pp. 177–93.

Žižek, S. (2006) 'Against the Populist Temptation', *Critical Inquiry*, 32: 551–74.

Žižek, S. and G. Daly (2004) *Conversations with Žižek* (London: Polity).

5/Zala Volčič and Karmen Erjavec

Fame on the Farm: Class and Celebrity on Slovene Reality TV

Introduction

In autumn 2009, the Slovene commercial broadcaster POP TV built on the success of its popular reality format *The Farm* (*Kmetija*) by creating a celebrity version of the show. Like its predecessor, *Celebrity Farm* tapped into a sense of national identity rooted in the values and community of agrarian life, but it plunged into this setting a collection of C-level celebrities including several pop musicians, models and beauty pageant winners, as well as the winner of another reality show (*Big Brother*), a porn star, a journalist, a comedian and a well-known eccentric scientist. The result was a show that subjected a menagerie of contemporary celebrities to the rigours of traditional life, while at the same time transforming the farm into a breeding ground for a new form of economic success. Thanks to the reflexive medium of reality TV, the rapidly disappearing family farm of Slovene folklore was resuscitated as the backdrop for newfound forms of commercial media and celebrity commodification in the post-socialist era. The juxtaposition of traditional forms of labour with contemporary strategies of mediated self-promotion, performance and self-display provided a dramatic demonstration of the ongoing transition from agrarian forms of communal life (filtered through socialist worker solidarity) to the enthusiastic embrace of free-market competition and its commercial spectacles.

Thanks to the show's competitive structure and its modelling of strategies for individual success in the marketplace, it serves as a fruitful site for investigating the relationship between discourses of class and labour in the post-socialist era. Moreover, as we will argue, the viewer reaction to the show demonstrates how discourses of consumer taste come to stand in for class-based distinctions and, simultaneously, disguise them as matters of personal preference and disposition: markers of individual choice and character that help explain why some succeed and others fail in the competitive marketplace. Issues of class, in other words, are both ubiquitous and sublimated in the show and in the responses of viewers.

We draw on an analysis of the show and on focus-group discussions with viewers to argue that *Celebrity Farm* models neo-liberal values of individual competition and enterprise in order to displace those of communal life and worker solidarity invoked by the historical image of the traditional Slovene farm. As many local scholars have shown (Bašić, Kučič and Petković 2004; Splichal 1994), television in Central Europe remains a principal stage on which (national and class) identity is performed, displayed and reconfigured, even though the landscape is being dramatically transformed by the advent of commercial broadcasting and the presence of global economic players. In the post-socialist commercial media, national culture and a middle-class perspective have emerged as dominant frames of reference. In the face of disappearing discourses about class in a nation that has bought into the myth that social mobility renders the category obsolete, the global proliferation of reality shows in the last few decades, and their particular iterations within Slovenia in recent years, presents a challenge and an opportunity for understanding how class operates in this context.

Celebrity Farm was a national phenomenon in many ways: it was not only the most watched television programme, but it also triggered a national moral panic over the 'indecent behaviour represented in the show' (Uršič 2009). There were countless ongoing public debates about decency, morality, the imposition of Western values, the loss of Slovene traditional values, corrupt 'celebrities', the salutary effects of rural life, national identity and the future of the small, newly minted nation. The public debates and critiques centred around four main themes: a) the show's allegedly harmful effects on children; b) its exemplification of lowbrow 'trashy' culture; c) the charge that it promoted immorality; and d) concern about the way in which it sensationalised the intimate/private lives of its cast members in the public sphere.

The show's premise – subjecting a range of media celebrities to the rigours of farm life in a society that identifies with its rural, agrarian past – generated violent reactions. In a way, the show served as a ritual form of humiliation for those who sought to place themselves above their fellow Slovenes: a format that took pleasure in forcing minor celebrities to forsake their sports cars and fancy homes for the rugged but honourable life of the farmer. This provided the paradoxical setting for castigating shallow, Western consumerist celebrity values just as it capitalised upon them.

Participants openly admitted that they were using the platform to promote their public images and careers. *Celebrity Farm* incorporated ethical analysis by three commentators dubbed 'the three musketeers', including television commentator Mark Žitnik, primary school teacher and self-described 'lady of high moral values', Angelca Liković, and the winner of the previous season's *Farm*, Goran Leban. Angelca Liković, in particular, represented a new normative ideal of middle-class values in Slovenia. She remained the harshest critic of the happenings on the farm, ostensibly representing the traditional, middle-class, populist moral majority of Slovene society. She accused most of the participants of 'laziness … they drink too much, swear too much … and I was wondering why they don't pray? In the past, we would always pray. Why not now?' (Episode 7). In this regard, she enacted what Skeggs describes as 'one of the main functions of reality TV':

> to symbolically and morally mark and value persons and to visualise that *value*. We clearly see that what is valuable is the middle-class domestic normative: respectability and the proper are highly valued and fetishised, responsibility for value production is located at the level of the individual. (Skeggs 2004: 14)

This reflexive twist represented by *Celebrity Farm* is characteristic of populist conservatism: the cultural disparagement is presented in the very form it denigrates. The success of *Celebrity Farm* cannot be explained properly without considering local social and political histories of class, gender and nation, which all define structures of identification for audiences (Ang 1996) and which we discuss in the first part of the chapter. In the second part, we will provide a textual and reception analysis. We are particularly interested in the reception of the show by young viewers (female students at Ljubljana and Maribor universities), since the show was most popular among younger female viewers (eighteen to thirty-nine years old) (AGB Nielsen Media Research 2009). We discuss the way the show offers lessons in the enterprising self of neo-liberal discourse and offers advice on how to achieve a 'branded persona' (Hearn 2009).

The Celebrities on the Farm: A Brief Overview

The Farm and *Celebrity Farm* were created by the Swedish production company Strix in 2001 and have been a successful and popular format, selling to more than forty countries. The Slovene show easily outperformed all its reality TV competitors, breaking ratings records, and attracting over half of all TV viewers during its time slot (54 per cent) (*Marketing Magazin* 2009).

In terms of format, *Celebrity Farm* was a hybrid of live and pre-taped footage. Every episode summarised the week's happenings and included interviews with cast members and detailed extracts from their video diaries. The first nine weeks of the show were taped in advance and cast members were eliminated through regular challenges and competitions with one another. Each week, one cast member was selected to be the 'head' of the farm and was responsible for organising the rest of the cast to meet the challenges posed by 'Marjan, the master of the farm, and a real Slovene farmer', such as milking the cows, cutting firewood, building a chicken shed and so on. The head is also responsible for selecting the two cast members who will be servants for the week. These two – one male and one female – are given the traditional titles of *hlapec* and *dekla*, meaning, roughly, groom and maid, and they are not allowed to sleep or eat in the house with the rest of the 'family'. At the end of the week, the rest of the participants vote to decide who did the worst job, the *hlapec* or the *dekla*, and they must take part in an elimination competition with their choice of competitor of the same gender. Whoever loses the duel is eliminated from the show and chooses the head of the family for the next week.

Historical, Political and Media Context

To understand the reception of *Celebrity Farm*, it is necessary to have a basic grasp of the Slovene context in the post-socialist era. Slovenia gained its independence and became a parliamentary democracy in 1991 after the disintegration of the former Yugoslavia. Political independence was followed by numerous economic and political reforms, such as the introduction of a market economy, the denationalisation of public and state-owned property, and the introduction of parliamentary democracy.

The rise of nationalism and neo-liberalism in the 1990s was accompanied by the gospel of individualism. But it was in 2004, when Slovenia entered the EU, and when the country's neo-liberal

right-wing government initiated radical transformations, that neo-liberal governance became a dominant trend. The main goal of the government was to support the state's withdrawal from the economy. One result of the changes to the political and economic systems, and in particular the effect of
rapid and often corrupt privatisation, was the creation, on the one hand, of a new class of wealthy
elite (called *tajkuni* [tycoons] in Slovenia) and, on the other, of an extended working class. This latter
faction consists of a third of the workforce – they receive a minimum salary (roughly €400 per
month) that is well below the Slovene poverty level (€615 per month) (*Minimalna plača* 2010;
Brezposelnost v Sloveniji 2010); around 13.6 per cent of the population is at risk of poverty (Volčič
2007). There is no doubt that in the last twenty years, in the era of neo-liberal politics, Slovene society has become extremely class stratified.

This rapid process of stratification belies the post-socialist ideal of a new 'classless' society – not
one in which all are workers, but one in which everyone is a member of a new, enterprising middle
class. Despite the fact that working-class people have been more and more visible on television
screens, thanks to the introduction of different talk and reality shows, and despite the fact that there
is a huge gap between rich and poor (the winners and losers of the privatisation processes),
class issues no longer receive any critical attention in sociological, cultural and media studies work
in Slovenia.

In many post-communist and post-socialist countries, national identity pushes other relevant
and sometimes even more important criteria of collective identification (including class, gender
and the rural–urban dichotomy) to the background. The ideal of socialist society held that everyone was meant to identify with the same class position (that of the working class – a state of
'classlessness') or, at least, the absence of class distinctions (Bernik 1992). In the post-socialist era,
despite a backlash against this particular model of class identification, much the same result per-
sists, only in neo-liberal socialism everyone is meant to identify with the 'classless' 'unmarked' identity of the middle class. As in socialism, post-socialism claims that society is not riven by class
differences, since everyone is in the same social class (working class, in the former instance, middle
class in the latter).

Perhaps not surprisingly, the end of socialism coincided with the demise of class analysis in both
scholarly and political contexts. Class analysis, which has at its heart a focus on the relationship
among class structures, class mobility, class-based inequalities and class-based social action, has almost
disappeared from the Slovene academic research agenda. Most work on cultural politics privileges
other forms of cultural identity: ethnicity, nationality, race, gender and sexuality. There are many reasons for the shift, including the fact that there is no governmental support for the analysis of class
issues: in the last fifteen years, the grant schema of the Ministry of Education's Research Agency
(ARRS) offered no support for research into class inequality.

The impact of the post-socialist condition, accompanied by the rise of capitalist democracy, is
tellingly illustrated by the fate of media reforms. The economic and the political infuse each other in
the post-socialist media regimes (Sparks and Reading 1994), resulting in what has been defined as a
regulatory regime of paternalistic commercialism (Splichal 1994). Private media investors have
expanded at a fast pace in all Eastern European countries, with the American Central European

Media Enterprises (CME) leading the way. CME now owns the most successful and popular Slovene commercial television station POP TV. To maximise its audiences, POP TV relies on cheap programming typically comprised of light-entertainment programmes, including reality television.

In terms of class representations, the analysis of many Slovene media texts, especially from television (for example, Aleksić 2006; Bašić, Kučič and Petković 2004; Erjavec and Poler Kovačič 2009), show that the programmes produced both by Slovene public broadcaster (RTV Slovenija) and by commercial producers (POP TV and Kanal A) consistently reproduce the myth of a class-free Slovene society.

'Celetoids' on *Celebrity Farm*

The image of *celebrity* plays an important role in media-saturated contemporary commercial cultures. Turner has argued that celebrity is a cultural formation, understood as an ongoing social process rather than some fixed property. He discusses the increasing shift of celebrity to everyday, routine and banal realms as 'the demotic turn':

> a means of referring to the increasing visibility of the 'ordinary person' as they turn themselves into media
> content through celebrity culture, reality TV, DIY websites, talk radio and it represents celebrity's
> colonization of the expectations of everyday life in contemporary western societies. (Turner 2006: 153)

It is important to point out that Slovenia, unlike the West, does not have a long tradition of celebrity and mostly imported foreign celebrities in the 1990s (Vidovič 2006). However, the commercial media in particular have quickly understood the power of making their own celebrities, and in the last ten years or so we have seen the self-conscious creation of local, Slovene celebrities. Most Slovene celebrities are so-called 'celetoids', a term coined by Rojek as:

> the accessories of cultures organized around mass communications and staged authenticity. Examples
> include lottery winners, one-hit wonders, stalkers, whistle-blowers, sports' arena streakers, have-a-go
> heroes, mistresses of public figures and the various other social types who command media attention one
> day, and are forgotten the next. (Rojek 2001: 20–1)

Celebrity Farm's participants fit neatly into the category of celetoids, since most of them became famous because the media apparatus manufactured their celebrity.

It may in part be due to this new form of manufactured and much-hyped celebrity that public debates about the show centred on questions of taste and decency. The show was most commonly described as 'trash' television, or as 'the lowest of the low'. As psychologist Sonja Cotar Konrad argued, the show 'represents a harmful example for the children. Who watches it, I don't know, but surely it affects us all and our moral values' (Cotar Konrad 2009). Slovene newspapers and magazines alike wrote about the appropriateness of the show and outdid one another in 'trashing it' (Uršič 2009). Many state organisations and entities, such as The Council for Telecommunications,

The Agency for Electronic Communication, The Office of Media Oversight, various political parties and civil society groups joined the heated debates (i.e. Group for Better Schools), advocating 'our high moral values' and positioning the show within common-sense moralistic critiques that frame it as corrupting the 'health of Slovene society' and as 'dangerous to the strength of our traditional values' (Uršič 2009).

Dismissing *Celebrity Farm* as emblematic of bad taste, commercialism and vulgarity did not, however, prevent viewers from watching. Here, Bourdieu (1977, 1984) is helpful when he writes about struggles over classifications which help to produce subjectivities, classes and their tastes: '… art and cultural consumption are predisposed, consciously and deliberately or not, to fulfil a social function of legitimating social differences' (Bourdieu 1984: 7). Taste becomes a capacity that one acquires at home and at school, and which helps to define one's position in society. Taste provides the signs with which people try to distinguish themselves as belonging (or aspiring) to a particular class. As Lury points out, distinctions of taste are always accomplished through social practices, so that taste 'is always a variant of class practice' (Lury 1996: 86); furthermore, we would argue that the role of taste in this instance is not simply to reinforce class distinctions but also to mask their structural formation – that is, to individualise class identity by making it a question of one's personal disposition and character.

In the public realm, then, the show recapitulated national high culture–low culture debates. It is important to note that the region of former Yugoslavia has been heavily exposed to Western television programmes over the last thirty years (Vidmar-Horvat 2005) and yet it continues to have a strong binary opposition between high and low culture: if you belong to 'an educated class', you are not to watch 'this cheap, banal programme' (Erjavec 2003).

Narratives of Self-Fashioning and Celebrity Success on the Farm

The show was characterised by two dominant narrative themes. First, the celebrities provided instructions on how to become 'successful', how to 'obtain positive energy' and to 'earn money in this money-obsessed society that we have become' (Goran, Episode 14), as well as how to brand yourself as a celebrity. The show's celebrities would provide each other and the viewers with advice and instructions on what it takes to be famous. Cast member Maja claimed that

> first, you have to know yourself, you have to trust yourself. I always advocate a specific vision, you know … you have to be creative, and innovate, and you must not be scared. You need to learn and in that way … you grow. (Episode 22)

Here, entrepreneurial conduct is articulated in line with neo-liberal political rationality. Furthermore, Aneta (a former Miss Sport) claimed that 'in order for a young woman, such as myself, to succeed, you have to exploit all available means. I need to think only of myself, and sell basically what I have. That's the world we live in' (Episode 26). And Ines (a former Miss Congeniality and an activist for fatter people), during the voting process, openly expressed that this is a game, but every game is a part of real life. I am here to have fun, but we are all here also to win. For me, it's about being pragmatic. I think the socialist days of brotherhood and unity are over. (Episode 29)

The participants would stress notions of choice, autonomy and empowerment while talking about their own success. In these narratives, they would rely upon the principles of individuality and spiritual self-modification. Goran (who frequently shared memories from his 'spiritual' trip to India) pointed out that

our small Slovenia … is becoming too depressed … people feel a lot of stress, exhaustion and anger. We should just relax more, and become more spiritual. We should understand that each individual is responsible for himself only. If you persuade yourself that you are happy and successful, than you'll become happy. (Episode 21)

The tension between solidarity and individualism, or the collective versus the individual, emerges as a dominant narrative through the format of the show. Participants were at first positioned as 'members of the farm family'. When they tried to organise their life and work on the farm, Artur was the first to take on the role of head of the farm, espousing not democratic principles but, as he put it, a sense of 'enlightened anarchy – where everyone is equal, and everyone works as much as one feels' (Episode 2). That immediately triggered a positive reaction among the participants and some of them embraced the idea that the show was about 'relaxing' and 'having holidays'. As cast member La Toya put it (Episode 3), 'this rural life is very simple … you can really relax here. No hardship …'

A moral economy emerged over time in which cast members were criticised for failing to treat the farm as an opportunity for demonstrating their work ethic. Over the course of the show, individuals were portrayed as responsible for their failures as well as their successes, their despair as well as their happiness. Suzana (Episode 3) claimed that 'Look … we should work and clean more. It's so dirty here. I need to live and sleep in a clean space. But the rest of them behave like some stars – and don't work …'. Alenka pointed out that 'life on the farm is not simple … it is hard. One needs to work, and get used to not having any running water … Each of us, individually, should be responsible for a specific task …' (Episode 6).

From early on, the tensions around work started to divide participants. Some of the participants portrayed themselves as 'hard-working individuals' who were 'getting up very early to milk cows and plough the fields … while others sleep until noon …' (Marjan, Episode 23). Marjan, in particular, criticised the laziness of others, claiming that 'the crucial message we are sending out into Slovenia is that if you don't work … if you sit around and play "a star" or if you just work for yourself, as an individual, you know, not for the community … you do the best, you win …'. As part of the show's mobilisation of a nostalgia for rural life, it also celebrates individual work, but work is for the self, not society, and so has acquired alternative meanings, in tune with the post-socialist and neo-liberal context of contemporary Slovenia.

Audience Responses to the Lessons of *Celebrity Farm*

Concerned with class-based patterns of interpretation, we also conducted focus groups with young female viewers of the show. Growing up within the transition from socialism to post-socialism renders young people subject to the development of a unique version of class. We also convened focus groups in order to analyse key themes from our interviews and to explore how group opinions about this show circulated around the popular public debates of the time.

Our research design included six focus groups composed of forty-two Slovene female students aged eighteen to twenty-six. The research was conducted in autumn 2009 and spring 2010 (during the show's broadcast and at the height of its publicity). Our informants were from diverse class backgrounds, coming from both urban and rural areas (including small towns) and different fields of academic study. Each informant was asked to briefly describe if/why they watched the show, and their understanding of class issues. Specifically, informants were asked questions that fitted five main themes:

1. The way they watched *Celebrity Farm* (Where, when and how do you watch the show?);
2. Their perception of class issues in Slovenia (Do you think there are different classes in Slovenia? Do we differ according to which economic class we belong?);
3. Their interpretations of class issues on the show;
4. The main message of the show; and
5. What have they learned from the show? (Following on from the work of Annette Hill 2005, 2007)

Audience Interpretation

Our aim here is to explore what (if any) (class-based) articulations and interpretations were circulating about the show, and specifically, what type of social discourses *Celebrity Farm* produced. One of our main conclusions is that the class positions of viewers did not correlate straightforwardly with different readings of the show. As Morley points out, there is no simple direct determination 'in which audience responses to media materials would be seen as automatically determined by their class position'. He calls for an analysis of 'how structural position, across a range of dimensions ... might set parameters to the acquisition of different cultural codes, the possession of which may then inflect the decoding process in systematically different ways' (Morley 2009: 492). Therefore, we focused on how social, historical and cultural factors influenced our informants' hopes, desires and expectations in a post-socialist, neo-liberal context.

Despite their diverse backgrounds and class positions, the students interpreted the show in a strikingly homogenous manner, constructing a specific neo-liberal discourse about the show that replicated its version of 'classlessness'. The viewers' discourse was characterised by the frequent invocation of the goals that define success in a market-based society: self-realisation, individual happiness, survival, self-esteem, self-knowledge, personal potential and personal responsibility.

Our analysis identified four dominant narratives shared by the informants: *self-initiative*, *independence*, *competition* and *market orientation*.

Self-initiative

One of the crucial messages of the show was that 'everyone has to look after oneself, first, to, as the expression puts it, look out for number one' (Jana, twenty-two-year-old). Individual responsibility for one's well-being and the importance of self-initiative were commonly expressed. A typical example comes from twenty-one-year-old Katarina:

> *Celebrity Farm* actually shows us that everyone has to take care of one's own interests and benefit first.
> No one is out there, you know, to look after me. No government will give me an apartment, as they did to
> my parents in the 1970s … Now, it is basically just about taking care of my own ass.

Respondents would provide various forms of evidence for this argument. Most of them pointed to the fact that the show's participants were not 'so famous', that they had to actively 'look after' their own self-promotion and be involved in their own production of fame. As Sandra, a twenty-one-year-old from Maribor put it:

> Look, most of them were not famous at all. My family members and I … we have never heard before of
> Marjan, Goran, Artur […] Daniel wanted to get famous again … in order for younger generations who
> don't know him yet, to recognise him. For him, this show was a great opportunity for self-promotion.

Respondents observed that alliances in the show were based on self-interest rather than an over-arching sense of solidarity. As Vesna, a twenty-five-year-old student put it:

> Look, they form these friendships on the show, but these are not real friendships … they are more like
> short-term military pacts … that collapse the next day or the next week … then, new connections are
> being made … when the participants vote one of them off each week.

This logic, as we have discussed, is built into the structure of the show, which invoked nostalgia for traditional community while at the same time transposing it into the realm of a commercial competition.

The respondents also evinced their understanding of what is acceptable and unacceptable behaviour according to middle-class norms. For example, they reinforced the notion that nakedness, sex acts and swearing were 'extremely inappropriate'. As twenty-two-year-old Marina put it:

> If I compare this show to other reality shows … this was just too much. It was all very vulgar … it was not
> about who we as Slovenes are. This show was about crude sex … Also the amount of swearing was too
> much. Just too much for the children … This is not appropriate for television. This is a total trash.

In this regard, respondents positioned themselves as moral defenders of children and high culture – in framing sex, nakedness and swearing as 'trash', they classify themselves through the classification. However, the respondents did not describe *all* of the show's contents as trashy. They positively evaluated competitive strategies of intrigue, manipulation and the opportunistic exploitation of information in line with the production of an entrepreneurial self, fully embracing a neo-liberal logic of responsibilisation and self-promotion. For example, twenty-year-old Manca took a realpolitik approach to the necessity of manipulation as a means of winning the game:

> I enjoyed observing different manipulations among participants … you learn a lot. For example, how Artur manipulated all the others on the show. Goran said it well – 'this show is like a chess game' … That was really interesting for me … I did not appreciate all the focus on their sex activities … but I did enjoy listening to their remarks.

The fact that cast member Alenka Sivka, Slovenia's first and most prominent sex columnist, cashed in on the show by publishing a book about it was treated as a sign of her entrepreneurial spirit: 'Sivka has successfully sold internal information and gossip … why not? I don't see anything wrong with it. It's different than using those big artificial breasts that La Toya imposed on all of us,' stated Sara, twenty-one.

  Respondents tended to take the show as a primer for life in a competitive market society, providing them with lessons they could apply to their own lives. As Andreja, twenty, said:

> It was apparent on the show … how each of the participants was after self-promotion and … well, they were all after publicity. They understand that it is only through your own work, and not relying on anyone else … that one can succeed. For example, for me, it's crucial that I get an internship at a PR agency. But I will not wait for the Faculty to arrange this for me – I need to do it myself.

Respondents talk of being self-reliant and not waiting for the help of others, especially not institutions that they deeply mistrust.

Independence

More than half of the respondents claimed that the crucial message of the show was 'independence', observing that famous women, in particular, used their charm for economic advantage and with that, independence, on and off the screen, repeating a logic of aspirational feminism. For example, twenty-four-year-old Mojca said that

> these famous women … Maja M., Maja P., La Toya, Aneta, Salome … exploit their femininity in order to achieve some kind of profit. And they are all financially independent, so they don't need any man to help them to survive. They earn their own money.

Some respondents focused on Suzana, since

> Suzana had such a hard life … she was a single mother … her life full of violence, alcohol … and she lived a
> poor life before she entered show business … being a part of reality shows, the *Big Brother* and *Celebrity Farm*,
> made it possible for her to become economically independent. (Mojca, a twenty-one-year-old from Kranj)

If responsibility and initiative are the ingredients of success, then success becomes not just a measure of character, but a just reward.

Similarly, learning 'life-lessons' from the show was a recurring theme (Hill 2007), as twenty-two-year-old Maja's observation typified:

> What I got out from the show is … what I know already … I have to use my own advantages, either
> physical or psychological in order to make my own way … as participants of the show did. You know …
> wearing tight trousers, mini-skirts, low-cut blouses … That is valued as a marker of success in our society –
> I mean, to be free, to earn your own money, to pay your own bills, to get your own apartment. So, in a way
> … for me … watching the show … despite the fact that these are not my heroes … I still think I kind of
> learned from them … maybe not learned … better said, they made me realise … that I can't count on
> anyone to help me out … in getting a job, in buying an apartment … my parents don't have any money,
> they can't help me … I have to find my own way.

This statement reveals how Maja draws on the pedagogic elements of the show that encourage her to rely upon herself, displaying the complex negotiation of gender in relation to using one's intimate assets to get ahead. Respondents emphasised the exploitation of their own sexuality as a route to independence even as they reinforced traditional and conservative middle-class values.

Competition

Viewers also agreed that one of the crucial mores of the show was the value of competition. As twenty-one-year-old Ana put it: 'In this show, everyone competes against everyone else with all available tricks.' According to many, women in the show relied on beauty and sex appeal, whereas men competed on the basis of physical strength: 'Women compete among themselves in their sex appeal, and furthermore … they want to be seen as good and obedient at the same time … but men compete in working physically …' (Anita, twenty-one).

How to compete and which strategies were used by different participants seemed to be one of the key interests of our respondents. Most enjoyed these aspects of the show as a way of learning about human nature, social relations, and the tricks and tactics that they entail. As twenty-one-year-old Gaja said:

> If I analyse the show from a distance … I see that everyone competes with everyone. There is no honesty
> here. Everyone uses what everyone has … in a way, it's similar to our world at the university. There is no

solidarity, in a sense that my parents talk about it. When they studied, they shared the notes, for example. Now, we sell the notes to each other. We all compete for better grades, for scholarships, internships, for jobs …

This statement shows how both personal and social spheres are interpreted as arenas of struggle and competition, where solidarity is an outdated illusion. Our respondents, like the participants on the show, are eager to network and lobby in order to achieve social power and financial gain. As twenty-one-year-old Tina stated:

Today, I compete for my own bright future … so I will not be a loser … what does that mean? I want to have my own network of important connections, a base that will allow me some financial gains and also social importance.

Focusing mainly on material goods and social power, these respondents did not even pay lip service to those values espoused by previous generations of students, such as social change, solidarity and unity (Roberts 2009).

Market Orientation

The final theme that emerged from the respondents' observations was the marketing of celebrity. These comments tended to focus on the self-commodification of the show's participants. For example, twenty-three-year-old Blanka claimed that 'it's all about the market where fame commands a premium. So these little stars compete in this big market. They sell what they have, usually their own stupidity.'

Respondents frequently described the women on the show as marketing themselves in order to meet someone rich and get married. As twenty-four-year-old Klara put it, 'these young participants, for example Maja P., they want to sell themselves, they want publicity and to further their careers. Look at how Maja P., after the show, got so much money for her modelling work.' And twenty-one-year-old Alenka criticised the show for being a kind of pornography of celebrity:

everyone sells themselves on the porn market. All this is just porn. They should not claim that they are musicians, or models … since they sell their bodies only. La Toya is the only one who is at least honest about it. I of course don't like her, she is really some trashy ugly woman, but the point is that they sell themselves on the market, and that's become a reality for all of us.

Our respondents felt that they were invited to identify not just with the participants, but also with the process whereby specific contestants attempted to turn themselves into a viable brand. Even as they critiqued the cast members, they simultaneously identified the so-called valuable life-lessons and skills of self-promotion they had learned from the show. No longer able to afford the luxury of romanticising talent, achievement and success, instead they need, urgently it seems, to understand the way in which the self can be engineered and constructed as an ongoing process.

The respondents differentiated themselves from the cast members by asserting that they do not sell 'trash' but beauty, knowledge and skills:

> I can tell you what I have learned about my own life, while watching [...] Everyone has a price. Everything is for sale. I am selling myself – first, on the student market, and soon on the job market. I guess we all want to be famous, successful, with lots of money. Let's not pretend – at least one should acknowledge that we are all after money and comfortable lives, and we will do anything it takes to achieve it. (Nina, twenty-one)

Reality shows such as *Celebrity Farm* draw a direct connection between cast members and audiences, highlighting the shared condition of the need to self-brand and promote oneself in the contemporary economy. In the culture of self-promotion, knowing the terms of exchange and what and how to sell is important. Self-promotion is integrated as a generalisable model of normative exchange for all.

Conclusion

In the contemporary Slovene context, the topic of class is studiously avoided by pundits and politicians alike, since class issues are associated with the old system from which most Slovenes want to distance themselves. Thanks to this persistent neglect of class issues, the dramatic forms of class stratification associated with rapid privatisation have been silently normalised. Contemporary public discourses treat class inequality not as a structural issue, nor as the result of wholesale forms of corruption (which accompanied privatisation), but as natural forms of inequality associated with the freedom of the market. The implicit message is that if you do not accept such economic injustice, you do not fully embrace capitalism, and it is striking just how wholeheartedly our respondents endorsed that message.

Reality television shows such as *Celebrity Farm* provide a mechanism whereby viewers learn how to effectively construct public personae and put them to use in the marketplace. For our viewers, *Celebrity Farm* is but one of many glocal sites which allow them to re-imagine their *own* class positions. Narratives of the past as well as social fantasies of the future are naturalised and negotiated as a part of their common sense, popularising the neo-liberal promise that capitalism can be free of class.

In the post-socialist context, the portrayal of a traditional work ethic is updated by *Celebrity Farm* for the exigencies of capitalist competition. The theme of work and cast members' work ethics dominated both the in-show discussions and the responses of our sample audience. In both cases, this served to outline the path to success in a new era of market competition and implicitly to explain the dramatic economic discrepancies of the post-socialist era in terms of individual initiative.

Traditional community is instrumentalised in *Celebrity Farm* as a way of marketing the show and as the backcloth to the competitive narrative. Where work once served as a symbol of unity, in the updated version of the 'traditional Slovene farm' its function is to divide, to distinguish and to serve as the basis for new forms of contrived competition. This seemingly abrupt transition is mitigated by a sense of continuity around work: historically, the notion of 'working hard' remains a cherished value for most Slovenes – a northern-looking form of national identification that often serves as the basis for distinguishing Slovenes (in their own eyes) from their more southerly Slavic neighbours. During the socialist era, a collective work ethic was emphasised and imposed to create a workers' paradise on earth. And today, work emerges as the basis for free-market competition – an alibi for individual differences in wealth and income in a world that has become brutally pragmatic about the promise of enterprise and consumption.

The achievement of this retooled notion of work is evident in our respondents' assertion of the 'classless' character of contemporary Slovene society. In post-socialist Slovenia, talk of inequality reeks of excuse-making and self-pity. It is not considered socially desirable or proper for people to talk about inequality, since this recalls the stale forms of indoctrination of a bygone era. In the case of *Celebrity Farm*, reference to individual work habits becomes a way of explaining the discrepancy in success, as measured by the ability to exchange oneself and consume, effacing older traditions which once bound 'labour' to 'community'.

Acknowledgments

The authors would like first to thank Graeme Turner for his helpful comments. Special thanks also go to Jaka Polutnik from the University of Maribor, Medijske Komunikacije, FERI, for help with recording the show's episodes and collecting some additional research materials.

Bibliography

AGB Nielsen Research (2009). Available at: <http://oldsite.agbnielsen.com/whereweare/dynPage.asp?lang= local&country=Slovenia&id=357> accessed 21 September 2010.

Aleksić, J. (2006) *Medijski mrk: o referendumu o zakonu o Radioteleviziji Slovenija* (Ljubljana: Liberalna akademija).

Ang, I. (1996) *Living Room Wars: Rethinking Media Audiences for a Postmodern World* (London: Routledge).

Bašić Hrvatin, S., L. J. Kučič, B. Petković, (2004) *Media Ownership. Impact on Media Independence and Pluralism in Slovenia and Other Post-Socialist European Countries* (Ljubljana: Peace Institute).

Bernik, I. (1992) *Dominacija in konsenz v socialistični družbi* (Ljubljana: FDV).

Bourdieu, P. (1977) *Outline of a Theory of Practice* (Cambridge: Cambridge University Press).

———— (1984) *Distinction: A Social Critique of the Judgement of Taste* (Cambridge, MA: Harvard University Press).

Brezposelnost v Sloveniji (2010) *Andragoški center Slovenije.* Available at: <http://arhiv.acs.si/InfO-mozaik/2010/ 28.pdf>.

Cotar Konrad, S. (2009) *Dnevnik: Let's Show Something Else to Our Children.* Available at: <http://www.dnevnik.si/ tiskane_izdaje/nika/1042314373> accessed 2 June 2010.

Erjavec, K. (2003) 'Media Construction of Identity through Moral Panics: Discourses of Immigration in Slovenia', *Journal of Ethnic and Migration Studies*, 29(1): 83–101.

Erjavec, K. and Poler M. Kovačič (2009) 'Discursive Approach to Genre', *European Journal of Communication*, 24(2): 147–64.

Hearn, A. (2009) 'Variations of the Branded Self', in D. Hesmondhalgh and J. Toynbee (eds), *Media and Social Theory* (London: Sage), pp. 194–209.

Hill, A. (2005) *Reality TV: Audiences and Popular Factual Television* (London: Routledge).

———— (2007) *Restyling Factual TV: Audiences and News, Documentary and Reality Genres* (London/New York: Routledge).

Lury, C. (1996) *Consumer Culture* (London: Polity).

Marketing Magazin (2009). Available at: <http://www.marketingmagazin.si/novice/rekordni-zakljucek-kmetije-slavnih/> accessed 21 September 2010.

Minimalna plača (2010) *Sindikat-sdpz*. Available at: <http://www.mddsz.gov.si/si/delovna_podrocja/delovna_razmerja_in_pravice_iz_dela/socialno_partnerstvo/minimalna_placa/> accessed 20 September 2010.

Morley, D. (2009) 'Mediated Class-ifications', *European Journal of Cultural Studies*, 12(4): 487–508.

Roberts, K. (2009) *Youth in Transition: Eastern Europe and the West* (Basingstoke, Hants.: Palgrave Macmillan).

Rojek, C. (2001) *Celebrities* (London: Reaktion Books).

Skeggs, B. (2004) *Class, Self, Culture* (London/New York: Routledge).

Sparks, C. and A. Reading (1994) 'Understanding Media Change in East-Central Europe', *Media, Culture and Society*, 16(2): 243–70.

Splichal, S. (1994) *Media Beyond Socialism: Theory and Practice in East-Central Europe* (Boulder, CO: Westview Press).

Turner, G. (2006) 'The Mass Production of Celebrity: "Celetoids", Reality TV and the "Demotic Turn"', *International Journal of Cultural Studies*, 9: 153–65.

Uršič, T. (2009) *Resničnostna televizija* (Ljubljana: FDV).

Vidmar-Horvat, K. (2005) The Globalization of Gender: *Ally McBeal* in Post-Socialist Slovenia', *European Journal of Cultural Studies*, 8(2): 239–55.

Vidovič, N. (2006) *Publiciteta, ustrvarjanje slave in industrija zabave* (Ljubljana: FDV).

Volčič, Z. (2007) 'Yugo-Nostalgia: Cultural Memory and Media in the Former Yugoslavia', *Critical Studies of Mass Communication*, (24) 1: 21–38.

6/Anikó Imre and Annabel Tremlett

Reality TV without Class: The Post-Socialist Anti-Celebrity Docusoap

Reality TV, Class and Post-Socialism[1]

> He [Győzike] is a dumb, primitive animal, who parades around on TV at our expense and all those idiotic Hungarians stare at him with their mouths open. Young people today need normal examples to follow, not a monkey-like freak dancing on stage like him. That stupid RTL suggests that the dumber you are the more famous they'll make you. (*Győzike* TV forum post)[2]

> Győzike [is] the gold playback-award-winner media Roma [...] who hoarded together millions as the lead singer of the band Romantic, as if his family hadn't already owned all of Nógrád County. Of course, the idea is not new. The model is undoubtedly MTV's *The Osbournes*, which depicts the domestic life, complete with rock music and door slamming, of Black Sabbath's former front man. The reality show, which operates with spoiled children and pets who shit on the Persian rug, cannot be transferred directly to Hungary, since we are missing that narrow social layer – not too populous even in the United States – that accumulates castles and yachts while jumping up and down on stage and then escapes with his remaining two dozen brain cells into a marriage, where he creates a bizarre human grouping that resembles a family except they yell a whole lot more.[3]

Watching reality programmes in foreign languages and settings often gives one a jolt of the strangely recognisable. This sense of unfamiliar familiarity has caused minor earthquakes in the case of some post-socialist reality programmes. The Hungarian celebrity docu-sitcom *Győzike* (RTL Klub, 2005–) shook the foundations of national identity by defamiliarising the unspoken bond between the nuclear family and its allegorical extension, the national family. The show adopts the hybrid format established by *The Osbournes* (MTV, 2002–4) to document the daily lives of Roma[4] pop singer Gáspár Győző (nicknamed 'Győzike') and his family. It has been both a massive audience success and, as the comments above indicate, a universally ridiculed object of criticism and overt racism towards Roma minorities.[5] It featured nine times in the top twenty most popular programmes in Hungary in its initial year,[6] with an audience-share average rating of 46.1 per cent (among adults aged eighteen to forty-nine).[7] At the height of its popularity, in May 2009, *Győzike* reached a rating of 50.2 per cent,

DVD cover of *Győzike*, Episodes 1–4

beating the popular soap opera *Between Friends* (*Barátok közt*) out of its long-time leading spot.[8] The emotional outbursts stirred up by the programme, unprecedented in the history of Hungarian television, has brought into discussion the taken-for-granted racial and class parameters of the normative national family in the midst of radical socio-economic transformation.

Reality programming is particularly conducive to making intercultural comparisons. Its worldwide explosion in the 1990s followed large-scale technological shifts in a changing regulatory environment, which favoured 'cheap, common and entertaining' (Murray and Ouellette 2004: 6) programming disseminated around the world. Reality programmes have also come under scrutiny across media, cultural and communication studies as important social texts that attempt to normalise class relations in a global neo-liberal era of technological and economic convergence and increasing state and corporate surveillance.

In 'post-welfare' societies such as the US and the UK, income inequalities have greatly increased since the 1980s. Alongside the well-documented decline of the moral authority of, and economic control by, the state and other traditional institutions, reality TV has taken centre stage as a technology of citizenship in a neo-liberal moral economy that validates the normative practices and choices associated with the middle class. Countless reality formats specialise in identifying good, responsible middle-class subjects and disciplining, transforming, shaming, punishing and teaching those whose refusal to improve their self-care and behaviour incurs costs to the nation (Skeggs, Wood and Thumim 2007). Scholarly analyses of reality television often combine Foucault's emphasis on governmentality with Bourdieu's notions of the habitus and forms of capital. This framework allows one to track how the individual accumulates moral and economic value on reality TV (Skeggs and Wood 2009). Makeover or lifestyle television, in particular, has been argued to showcase how governance has been dispersed into practices of governmentality. It offers a 'decentralized network of entrepreneurial ventures' (Ouellette and Hay 2008: 471) that is supposed to teach personal responsibility, the ethics of good citizenship and demonstrate how to acquire the right kinds of economic and cultural capital necessary for proper middle-class status (Palmer 2004).

Despite calls for studying how reality formats can be both 'culturally specific and globally relevant' (Murray and Ouellette 2004: 9), such studies cannot fully explain the class and race negotiations and citizenship models represented by *Győzike* and the subsequent, explosive responses to shows like it. Reality programmes produced in post-socialist Eastern Europe may derive from the same global economic and cultural flows as their American or Western European counterparts but they solicit very different spectatorial and critical responses, which are overcharged with the local significance of socialist histories and the conditions created by the post-socialist transition. It is true that post-socialist economies have been undergoing (neo)liberalisation in the past three decades. Some of the new European Union member states can even be considered post-welfare societies. Nevertheless, Eastern European countries have followed a modified path to capitalism. Here we use *Győzike* as a lens to highlight two of the interrelated factors that are most relevant to understanding reality TV's stormy visualisation of race and class relations within the national family. The first is the novelty of commercial television after more than forty years of government-controlled media, whose standards of quality have been carefully monitored by a normative intellectual class. The second factor is the historical weakness of a propertied middle class and the resulting confusion as to what counts as normative cultural and social values. A popular reality show about a celebrity Roma foregrounds this confusion of values rather than offering any direct path to self-education or improvement. The media uproar is due precisely to the fact that the show sets off profound anxieties about what constitutes proper class conduct and national citizenship.

First, we reflect on the methodological and ideological difficulties of reading a post-socialist Roma celebrity reality docusoap as a social document. Then we draw on a combination of textual analysis, online audience responses and critical press responses to extract from the *Győzike* phenomenon an understanding of post-socialist class and race relations as they emerge at the interfaces between global neo-liberalism, post-socialist nationalism and reality programming. We discuss the relevant class registers that emerge within the show and its reception: those of the ethnicised underclass on the one hand and the intellectual vanguard of what sociologists János Ladányi and Iván Szelényi (2006) call the 'cultural bourgeoisie' on the other. In the process, we must engage with Anglo-American theories of reality television as a global phenomenon *and* local approaches to post-socialist television, both of which are limited by their own ethnocentrisms.

The Challenges of Studying Post-Socialist Reality TV

Taking reality television seriously in post-socialist Eastern Europe presents unique methodological, disciplinary and ethical obstacles. One reason is that radical media transformation has been characterised by a negotiation between the state and commercial broadcasters over what remain primarily national, rather than segmented, niche markets. State broadcasters first had to compete with and then give up their hegemony of four decades to commercial channels in the years following the fall of socialism in 1989. Since they were launched in Hungary in 1997, RTL Klub and TV2, the two most successful commercial broadcasters, quickly colonised the landscape with their imported and domestically produced entertainment programmes, many of which are reality formats. When finally given the choice, viewers turned away from state television's serious news shows, political discussions, talking heads, art films and other national 'quality' programmes in favour of talk shows, competitive reality programmes and locally produced soap operas.

In response, commercial programming has been universally dismissed by critics for lowering cultural standards and corrupting national citizenship. The programmes are rejected for their affective appeal and debasement of a literature-based national culture in favour of distracting audiovisual infotainment, often blamed on American forms and ideologies. Reality programmes are identified as the trashiest form of television. While the critical outrage about the quality of commercial television is justified on the whole, the refusal to take such programmes seriously as proper objects of analysis also reveals a defensive class position taken by – often formerly dissident – intellectuals. The intellectual elite is in danger of losing the national leadership roles with which it has been historically charged, a role essential to securing its position within the post-socialist 'cultural bourgeoisie'.

The pseudo-documentary display of ordinary people on reality TV and the defensive critical rejection of such spectacles often make these shows all the more raw and unabashed outlets for a variety of views and emotions that were formerly subject to state censorship. Programmes such as *Győzike* constitute a synergy between the objectionable racial and class quality of their protagonists and the objectionable cultural quality of reality TV. The moral disapproval of such shows is due to the fact that they visualise the intimate connection between these two converging kinds of illegitimacy within the national public sphere. *Győzike* presents a special complication in post-socialist class relations because it lifts 'the Gypsy', normally a representative of the racialised underclass, into a celebrity position where the national normative class values of the future are usually modelled and determined.

Another major obstacle to including post-socialist reality television in wider comparative research is the relative obscurity of local national languages and traditions, compared to English- or French-speaking television. As we noted, East European critics, who are the insider experts on these cultures, usually try to distance themselves from a doubly demonised association: forms of commercial television deemed unhealthy for national culture, and ethnic minorities deemed parasitic for the national body. Scholars in Romani studies, who tend to be familiar with local languages and pride themselves in offering an alternative, positive image of Roma minorities, are also dismissive of television. Romani studies, grounded in sociology and folklore, often operates with a somewhat anachronistic and idealised image of the Gypsy as a figure unaffected by contemporary popular culture, and turns its ethnographic attention towards the authentic, folk Gypsy, which is encapsulated in the phrase 'Gypsy way of life' (Tremlett 2009). Popular culture has not significantly entered these discussions and only a smattering of articles deal with the rising popularity of Roma celebrities (Imre 2006, 2008). Roma reality stars and shows constitute inappropriate objects for Romani studies scholars as much as for national critics. Instead of serving as a valuable resource for understanding cultural hybridity, Roma reality TV, then, faces a double stumbling block: a profound investment in a Eurocentric ideal of high cultural value and a commitment to the authentic Roma who is essentially different from national majorities.

The final challenge to taking *Győzike* seriously is that while research in communication studies has begun to map the transformation of post-socialist media industries, it has concentrated on issues of policy and the normative national public sphere at the expense of ideology, identity, programming content, aesthetics, affect and audiences. Since serious studies of East European popular television are scarce, we are also aware of the methodological responsibility of creating precedent. We have tried to translate the separate professional and personal motivations that led us to the same object into a multi-layered methodology which integrates cultural studies with an attention to political economy, studies of nationalism and race, and questions of genre and text.

Love to Hate: Situating Roma Celebrity and Reality TV in Hungary

The rise of racist discrimination against Roma minorities and their continuing poverty have become depressingly familiar themes in the post-socialist region (Stewart 1997; Ladányi and Szelényi 2006; Imre 2006; van Baar 2008). In the most recent instance of government-led xenophobia, in August 2009, Sarkozy's French Government offered €300 to individual Roma people to go back to Romania or face enforced eviction. At the same time, the globalisation and commercialisation of East European media cultures has also enhanced the appeal of Roma popular entertainment, particularly hip hop (Imre 2008). However, the resurgence of anti-Roma violence that accompanies the region's experience of the deepening global economic crisis has shown that the appearance of Roma celebrity has done little to improve the minority's massive deprivation or to challenge the moral majority's perception of Roma people as a problem.

The choice of a Roma family to star in a reality show may therefore seem like an unlikely recipe for success. Nevertheless, shortly after *Győzike* appeared on Hungarian television screens in 2005, it became one of the most watched shows of recent times. Győző Gáspár first came on the media scene in 1999 as the front man of the pop group Romantic, who mixed Roma melodies with rap in their songs. Győzike also appeared as a celebrity contestant on the Hungarian version of *Big Brother* (*Nagy testvér*, TV2, 2003). Already established in public as an affable character, Győzike's Roma identity was played up to generate media interest in the programme. He also took a cameo role in the satirical comedy show *My Big Fat Roma Wedding* (*Bazi nagy roma lagzi*, TV2, 2003). This programme ignited much controversy for its crude Roma stereotypes and resulted in sanctions against TV2 by the state's agency for media regulation (ORTT).[9] It also put Győzike in an ambiguous political position as someone willing to compromise the cause of the minority for national celebrity.

The advertising for the new reality show *Győzike* used this chequered history as an enticement.[10] The weekly 90-minute primetime programme aired on RTL Klub, TV2's rival[11] and Hungary's most successful commercial channel. It began in February 2005 and five years later, in October 2010, the show was on its ninety-seventh episode, with stories about the family's lives appearing consistently on the front pages of the tabloid press. Despite the high ratings, the Hungarian public and media reaction to the show has been a love/hate relationship, or, rather, a love-to-hate relationship. Győzike and his wife Bea were voted favourite TV personalities in 2008 by the readers of the Hungarian celebrity gossip magazine *Hot*. At the same time, the magazine reported a wider survey of fifteen-to sixty-nine-year-olds, in which the couple were voted the least liked celebrities.[12] While this magazine presumes an adult readership (as does the show's later viewing time of 9 p.m.), it appears that there is a children's fan base as well. A survey among 1,500 primary school students in southern Hungary in 2007 revealed that a third of the children considered Győzike as their role model.[13] However, Hungarian cultural critics and Roma activists have widely condemned the show.[14] For example, prominent Roma activist János Daróczi[15] said that Győzike's media celebrity 'brings severe disadvantage to the Hungarian Roma […] I must send a message to everybody: we, the Roma, are not like that' (2006, quoted in Kürti 2008: 16).

The media storm around the show raises the question of whether reality television can help complicate the stereotypical, bifocal lens that invariably produces either the 'noble' or the 'savage' Gypsy. As in other Eastern and Southern European countries, there are scant Roma characters on Hungarian soap operas or dramas,[16] while news and documentary programming tend to focus on the criminality and social exclusion of certain Roma communities (Messing 2008). However, from the start, *Győzike* did not fit into either of these formats. The show opens with a slow pan over

Győzike's large modern house symbolises his status as *nouveau riche* in Hungary

The branding of the zebra-striped pyjamas shows the consumerist, ethnic kitsch style of the programme

snow-covered hills and a panpipe tune on the soundtrack, echoing a romantic documentary style. The camera shows the grey communist blocks of a town, home to Győzike and his family, identified in a subtitle as 'Salgótarján 2005'. The Hungarian audience would know that Salgótarján, an industrial town northeast of Budapest hard hit by recent deindustrialisation and high Roma unemployment, is not romantic at all. But the aesthetic marker of a proper documentary is only evoked to be sharply abandoned for surprise effect as the camera closes in on a large mustard-coloured 'modern' home, whose style is coded in Hungary as *nouveau riche*. This is clearly not a romantic documentary about marginalised Roma people. The sense of comedy amplifies as the camera cuts to a close-up of Győzike's face as he stares into the distance apparently lost in thought. The music speeds up and turns into a fast, popular Gypsy tune. We discover, through a shot of Győzike's legs, that he is sitting on the toilet with his zebra-striped pyjamas around his ankles and his bare toes tapping to the rhythm of the extra-diegetic music. The show's distinctive main title appears as if it were the make of the pyjamas in a cunning marketing strategy that anticipates RTL Klub's consistent branding of the show and its ancillary merchandise as 'ethnic kitsch'.

Bea then appears in a fantastically non-traditional, shiny, red and black kitchen, wearing a fashionable off-the-shoulder top, stirring a mug of coffee and shouting to her husband to come downstairs. Győzike yells back that he is 'thinking'. The camera returns to Győzike's yawning face in several close-up shots, and then cuts to their eldest daughter, Evelyn, who is lying on a zebra-striped bedspread and yells to her father to hurry up in the bathroom or she will kick the door down. The younger daughter, Virág, appears wearing a cowboy hat, rocking back and forth on a hobby horse and waving an American flag. Each of these shots is freeze-framed, with the family members' names flashed onto the screen, evoking *The Osbournes* opening sequence and establishing the show's status as a mix of documentary observation and popular entertainment. These images all point to something other than the 'cultural' or 'poverty-stricken' Roma familiar from documentaries and anthropological texts.

Much like *The Osbournes*, *Győzike* features an 'extraordinarily ordinary' family whose activities are at once banal and excessive (Kompare 2004). They perform their life on the show in an extravagantly decorated house which bears ample evidence of Győzike's well-promoted obsession with zebra stripes and gold. While the programme carefully avoids attaching price tags to the family's consumption habits, it presents an economically upper-class family with lower-class, or specifically ethnic, taste. Like Ozzy Osbourne, in this domestic setting, Győzike is reduced to a bumbling, often sentimental and childish character, whose repeated failures and 'ignominious body' (Kompare 2004: 104) humanise him while providing many comic moments. He and his wife both conform to staple characters of the family sitcom even in the absence of such a generic tradition on East European television.

Many of the episodes focus on the couple's explosive marital tension, which is only occasionally and temporarily resolved. The emotional display that characterises reality shows is generously exploited and clearly racialised. It points to the family's Roma identity, which provides Győzike and Bea with a licence, as well as an expectation, to perform the Roma stereotype of the out-of-control, irrational, corporeally driven racialised minority.[17] These extreme public displays of emotion are still new and rare on East European television and represent a marked departure from the tame (self-censored) and rational aesthetic inherited from state television. The lack of affective self-control is a major explicit reason for critical aversion and, it is safe to speculate, for private viewer fascination. The two Gáspár daughters, teenage Evelyn and pre-schooler Virág, are often brought out to serve as comic relief or as buffers when the couple's confrontations become violent.

Besides domestic affairs that, as John Corner (2002) describes, ambivalently hover between the fictional and the real in reality programming – such as Bea's pregnancy scare, Győzike's infidelity, generational conflicts among family members, disagreements about buying, cooking and decorating, and money matters – the show features two other kinds of prominent storylines. One follows trips abroad taken by Győzike and other family members to locations that range from Istanbul and Paris to Florida and inevitably cast them as representatives of the Hungarian nation. The other kind of narrative depicts events in Győzike's public life as a singer or aspiring politician, such as negotiations over performance gigs and his nomination for Roma community leader. Both kinds of storylines inevitably reflect on the couple's Roma identity and on the family's relationship to both the Roma community and the Hungarian national community.

At first sight, the show would seem to be popular precisely because it delivers a familiar 'Gypsy circus' (Kürti 2008: 17), reproducing racist stereotypes and inviting viewers to laugh at the family's antics.[18] However, Győzike is not an ordinary poor Roma but a media star with considerable power. The intensity of the public's reaction to the show has much to do with specific relations between post-socialist nationalism and budding media celebrity in the region. Győzike's regional accent, frequent use of Roma expressions and references to the family's membership of a wider Roma community repeatedly bring into question their appropriateness as the national middle-class family. The following examples from online forums painfully highlight this perceived threat to the idea of Hungarian nationhood and point to the tortuous position of the Roma media celebrity in post-socialist times.

Online Audience Responses and 'the Roma Underclass'

The fact is that the majority of Gypsies live off crime (committed against Hungarians). They know how to make everyone feel sorry for them, but working hard stinks. All they know is how to crank out all those little mongrels at 14 and then make them do the dirty work of stealing and then collect welfare for them. I did some research about these things even though, believe me, I really don't care, and I still believe that Gypsies are worse than anything else, they are the 'black' plague of the world, the last filth, rotten rats, who spread stealing, cheating, lying ... etc. ... around the world.

They are not humans ... They stink up the whole country. Why don't they get the hell out of here at last? I'd like to drown all the black kids and sterilize all the women to stop them from reproducing. They are like cockroaches. Even their names are disgusting ... I wish they were all killed by cancer, from the smallest newborn to the oldest stinking Gypsy. Death to them!!!!!!!

These are typical selections from the roughly 3,500 postings on the fan forum on one of the show's official websites.[19] For a programme that is so eagerly and universally watched, it appears to have hardly any fans, or at least very few who would defend it in public. Even the self-identified Roma posters tend to dismiss it as a programme about 'show Roma' ('*divatcigány*'), who give the entire minority a bad name. The degree of hatred and fear revealed by the posts, replicated by thousands of other reactions in various similar online discussions, is shocking. The comments reproduce patterns of ethnonationalism successfully erased from the Western vocabulary of politically correct talk about minorities: the Roma are lazy and repugnant parasites who shun work and drain collective resources. Their excessive procreation contaminates the pristine national body and threatens the survival of the rightful majority. These discourses are often encouraged indirectly by the state and directly by the declarations and policies of local politicians, which are often only slightly subtler in their racism than the quotations above (Kürti 2008).

These reflections issue commentary on the uneasy social relations between national and global identities forced to the surface by television. They manifest what Appadurai calls the 'predatory identities' unleashed by globalisation: 'those identities whose social construction and mobilisation require the extinction of other, proximate social categories, defined as threats to the very existence of some group, defined as we' (Appadurai 2006: 51). He elaborates:

Predatory identities emerge, periodically, out of pairs of identities, sometimes sets that are larger than two, which have long histories of close contact, mixture, and some degree of mutual stereotyping. Occasional violence may or may not be parts of these histories, but some degree of contrastive identification is always involved. One of these pairs or sets of identities often turns predatory by mobilizing an understanding of itself as a threatened majority. (Ibid.)

The anxiety displayed by online responses is due to the fact that Győzike and his family evoke *both* the poor, welfare-bound ghost of the enemy within and a rich, transnational threat. Ladányi and

Szelényi (2006) explain this dual class position in terms of a racialised underclass. Their structuralist understanding of the underclass synthesises two sociological theories: Julius Wilson's tracing of the emergence of the underclass to certain features of capitalist deindustrialisation during the last decades of the twentieth century in inner-city black American neighbourhoods, and Oscar Lewis' description of the culture of poverty among the most hopeless in developing countries, where race is linked with the culture of poverty (Ladányi and Szelényi 2006: 1–8). The processes of deindustrialisation, the shift from a Fordist to post-Fordist regime of production that led to the exodus of the black middle class from the ghetto and increasing class differentiation within the African-American minority in the 1970s and 80s, are analogous to those of the post-socialist economic and political liberalisation and the transition from socialist redistribution to a market economy in 1990s. The Roma population paid a disproportionate price in the process, since they were concentrated in industrial sectors with the most severe job losses following the fall of socialism, particularly in the northeastern parts of Hungary, where Győzike and his family live.

The Roma population's post-socialist slide into an underclass position has been worsened by intense racial discrimination. At the same time, the formation of this racialised underclass was complemented by the rise into middle-class status of some upwardly mobile Roma and a subsequent gap between the Roma middle and underclass (Ladányi and Szelényi 2006: 8–10). It is precisely the upward mobility of some Roma that warrants the underclass concept to describe those left behind. In Hungary, an increasingly neo-liberal society, race has taken on growing significance in splitting the Roma population into an underclass and an upwardly mobile middle class.

> Overall, three processes may be complementing and/or reinforcing each other in Hungary: The increasing fuzziness of the ethnic boundaries between Roma and gadjo[20]; an increasing reliance on racial categories in drawing those boundaries; and a process of underclass formation. (Ladányi and Szelényi 2006: 144)

In the case of *Győzike*, the menace of cultural, racial and class hybridity represented by the wealthy celebrity Roma is exacerbated by the fact that this is a television family. It is created by an emasculating media regime of entertainment perceived as the enemy of national culture, at once feminising and racialising. The fascist vehemence of viewer comments, their call for racial purification, is quite out of proportion with the spirit of light entertainment associated with a television show. These comments reveal the majority's profound dependence on maintaining the illusion of the white nation's ethnic homogeneity.

Critical Responses

Reflections in print and online critical journals are invariably outraged about the show's 'quality' and 'values'. However, while online responses by ordinary viewers target the ethnic minority with which Győzike and his family are identified, critics tend to tone down the racist edge of their criticism and focus instead on the show itself as the flagship of an alarming downward trend in national culture in general and television in particular. While worries about commercialising the public sphere are legitimate, a number of assumptions remain, which bind together official criticism and fan responses much more intimately than it would seem. The overt racism of predatory identities and concerns over the rational national culture headed by a literate, national elite class are two sides of the same coin, which differ only in style. Overtly racist 'fan' comments tend to equate Győzike with 'real Gypsies' and personalise their attacks through their own 'experiences' with Roma people. More sophisticated, critical comments – mostly by intellectuals who would reject charges of latent racism or discrimination against minorities – tend to interpret and abstract, while effacing their own personal investment and positioning themselves as the rightful embodiments of collective norms. They defer their indignation from the protagonists and the minority they represent to the medium and the genre.

One well-respected cultural critic, for instance, talks about 'parasite media' in the highbrow literary and cultural journal *Elet és Irodalom* (*Life and Literature*) and cites the *Győzike* show as his chief example.[21] Critics' unanimous dismissal of commercial television derives from the special rights and responsibilities historically bestowed upon intellectuals in small Eastern European nations. While the bourgeoisie was central to building capitalist institutions in Western Europe, in Eastern Europe, *cultural* capital has dominated the history of nation-building and remains the main source of power, prestige and privilege in post-socialism (Eyal, Szelényi and Townsley 1998: 6). The socialist regime further stalled the development of an economic middle class. The major actors of building civil society and capitalism during the post-socialist transformation have been intellectuals, many of them former dissidents. They formed an uneasy alliance with those segments of the former socialist technocracy that were able to convert their skills and cultural capital to remain in the new managerial elite. The alliance is based on the shared ideology of civil society and economic rationalism, or managerialism: a governmentality that unites diverse fractions of the post-socialist elite within a hegemonic power bloc. The post-socialist intelligentsia has thus formed a neo-liberal alliance with the technocratic managerial elite in the interest of developing capitalist and democratic liberal institutions under the notion of 'civil society'. As a result, intellectuals have long carried a special ethical responsibility for society as a whole as 'the searchlight into the future, the soul of the nation' (Eyal, Szelényi and Townsley 1998: 56).

Intellectuals' hold on special class status has become tenuous in the course of post-socialist transformations, which have brought about the disintegration of an idealised, homogeneous national public and initiated a subsequent crisis of authority for cultural and political leaders. *Győzike* sets off especially intense anxieties because the show threatens to expose the implicit racial and gendered parameters of intellectual exceptionalism. Whiteness and masculinity are also two of the central pillars of the rational, national public sphere (Morley 2007). The liberal sympathy that public intellectuals have long displayed for the single visible racial minority has helped efface the racialised quality of this one-directional, hierarchical relationship. The repressed returns in *Győzike*'s frequent, unfavourable comparisons in the reviews with 'proper' ways of representing Gypsies: filmic documentaries about victimised, poor Roma (Örkény 2005; Bori 2005). The implication is that the true Roma is a victim, a member of the ethnicised underclass, whose social position is fixed and can only be sympathetically revealed through the hard work of those who are able to see, understand and show. This attitude is not essentially different from the racism of those who openly blame Gypsies for being backward and unwilling to assimilate. Gypsies are tolerable on reality shows as long as they are the passive victims of media exploitation (Kolozsi 2005; Fáy 2001; Varró 2005; Darab 2008).

While traditionally, intellectuals have been expected to speak for and down to a unified national public, that same public is now being directly addressed by ratings-driven media – most evidently in reality shows. In this context, Lajos Császi rightly calls the top-down intellectual tradition of judgment exercised by teachers, politicians and cultural experts profoundly paternalistic (quoted in Jenei 2006). Such a position seems to be animated less by an activist sense of responsibility than by a desire to increase the distance between the 'rabble' public and the shrinking number of intellectuals blessed with reliable aesthetic and moral sense, a way of 'reclaiming authority in the re-drawing of class relations' (Skeggs 2005: 968). This class disgust with low-class celebrity culture is somewhat hypocritical, 'simultaneously about *desire and* revulsion' (ibid.: 971; italics in original). Such a position also forfeits the possibility of building pedagogical bridges between highbrow and popular cultural forms.

Conclusion: Class and Post-Socialist Neo-Liberal (Ir)responsibility

As we can glimpse from the public reactions to the show, the class implications associated with reality programming are embedded in a specific historical trajectory and political context in the post-socialist arena. Existing analyses of the class configurations of reality television are useful but only partially applicable to the specific conditions of post-socialism. The anxiety about, and the fascination with, the *Győzike* show are both due to the sense of profound transformation signalled by the very existence of the Roma celebrity docusoap. In class terms, *Győzike* is a threat to national culture because it represents an emerging middle-class cultural and economic value that is inherently mixed. The economic middle class has long been a missing element in Soviet-controlled, allegedly egalitarian societies. *Győzike* causes heightened anxiety because the show dares to represent the nuclear Roma family as the national middle-class family. They are media stars who are without a hint of victim mentality – although some critics are eager to construct them as miserable victims of the media, or of the format. Győzike and his wife revel in displays of emotion, irresponsibility and excess. They are generous with money, go on foreign trips and shopping sprees, and throw lavish parties for hundreds of guests without showing any guilt. Győzike uncomfortably evokes the figure of the excessive Balkan or East European man, a national and regional icon, the opposite of the (imagined) money-saving Western Puritan.

Győzike's unapologetic celebration of irresponsibility duly causes national concern along with secret admiration. In fact, the show associates irresponsibility with respectability. This respectability does not require the kind of cultural capital derived from Eurocentric national values represented either by an Eastern intellectual class or a Western economic middle class. Győzike does not need education, does not need to control his emotions and does not even need to speak proper Hungarian to be successful and therefore respectable. The schizophrenic value schema behind this reality show is specific to the transition from cultures where intellectuals constituted a normative class to a form of neo-liberalism where the space occupied by the middle class in Western neo-liberal democracies is up for grabs.

RTL Klub successfully placed a controversial hero, Győzike, in this no man's land. Győzike performs both Gypsiness and national whiteness to both constituencies' great unease, suspicion and fascination – but perhaps not to the untapped opinions of those 'ordinary' viewers who delight in the show. Unlike the self-censored views of adult viewers' responses cited above, the reactions of children and other fans to the show point to more fuzzy boundaries between the Roma and the mainstream white public. Therefore, we argue that audience studies are fundamental both to understanding the broad cultural shifts occurring in post-socialist landscapes and to recognising other 'ordinary' viewers, such as children, women, lower-class groups and/or Roma minorities, as avid participants in Hungary's growing media industry, who often remain undervalued and under-researched (see Bernáth and Messing 2002).

Whereas in the West, the middle-class viewer addressed by reality shows easily distances oneself from the abject spectacle of traumatised individuals in need of televisual charity and self-help, in Eastern European national cultures the class distance between viewer and viewed spectacle, even of stars, is reduced and occluded. It can only be recrystallised in racial terms, by foregrounding Győzike's Roma difference – a difference constructed and performed on the show for commercial purposes. In turn, however, such efforts at distancing are undermined by Győzike's demonstrated class success. *Győzike* celebrates the entrepreneurial individual who makes the best of the wild post-socialist neo-liberal conditions, registering seismic shifts in the nation's self-definition.

Notes

1. We use 'post-socialist' here to mean a period of economic, cultural and political transition and transformation across countries that were, in the mid- to late twentieth century, part of a socialist regime. We prefer 'post-socialist' to 'post-communist', as the former was the self-designation used by Soviet-controlled governments and citizens while the latter is a homogenising term imposed by Western powers and steeped in the divisive logic of the Cold War.

2. 'GyőzikeTv Fórum'. Available at: <http://forum.sg.hu/forum.php3?azonosito=gyozike> accessed 4 October 2010.

3. SzabóZ, 'Cigányok ideje', *Index*, a Hungarian-language online news source, 8 February 2005. Available at: <http://index.hu/kultur/media/gyozi594/> accessed 4 October 2010.

4. The term 'Roma' is mostly used in this chapter in recognition of its acceptance in pan-European discourse as a substitute for the previous term 'Gypsy', which has been considered pejorative. However, it is contested as an umbrella term for minority groups that may more strongly identify themselves separately from 'Roma' and use terms such as Gypsies, travellers, Sinti, Vlach Rom, Ashkali, etc.

5. Roma minorities are considered the largest minority in Europe today. The expansion of the European Union (EU) to include post-socialist states can be seen as a turning point in the history of the EU and its attitude towards Roma minority groups. The process of EU expansion has highlighted Roma as the largest and poorest minority group in Central and Eastern Europe, with calls for individual governments to deal with poverty and discrimination prior to European accession. Numbers of Roma in the recent post-socialist accession countries range from approximately 8,000 in Latvia to 600,000 in Hungary and

about 2 million in Romania. (Source: *European Union Support for Roma Communities in Central and Eastern Europe* [Brussels: European Commission, 2003, p. 4]).

6. RTL Group Annual Report 2005, available via RTL Group web page at: <http://www.rtlgroup.com/www/htm/annualreport.aspx> accessed 4 October 2010.

7. 'RTL Group Announces Its Audited Results for the Year Ended 31 December 2005', available via RTL Group web page at: <http://www.rtlgroup.com/www/htm/pressrelease_5FF713CD29834E139F376 B89E1E0BA22.aspx> accessed 4 October 2010.

8. 'Szenzáció! Győzike lekörözte a Barátokat', 22 May 2007. Available at: <http://www.est.hu/cikk/47650/ szenzacio_gyozike_lekorozte_a_baratokat/ro409> accessed 4 October 2010.

9. P. György, 'Gáspár Győző szerepei', *Népszabadság Online*, 6 January 2006. Available at: <http://www.nol.hu/archivum/archiv-389740> accessed 4 October 2010.

10. 'Ugyanakkor megtudhatjuk azt is, milyen egy "bazi nagy roma buli" Győzike módra', from the *Győzike* show, 27 January 2005. Available at: <http://www.rtlklub.hu/musorok/gyozike/cikk/238742> accessed 4 October 2010.

11. RTL Klub and TV2 both began broadcasting in 1997 and have dominated the Hungarian television market ever since. They both specialise in producing reality formats and broadcasting American fictional programming. RTL Klub is owned by the RTL Group, Europe's largest content producer for television and radio, majority-owned by German media conglomerate Bertelsmann.

12. See *Hot Top 100 sztár: a száz legfontosabb magyar híresség*, 2008/1 (Budapest: Euromedia BT).

13. 'Hmmm … – Győzike a példaképe minden harmadik somogyi általános iskolásnak', 9 February 2007. Available at: <http://www.mtv.hu/modernkepmesek/cikk.php?id=183025> accessed 4 October 2010.

14. György, 'Gáspár Győző szerepei'.

15. János Daróczi is a member of a family well known for their Roma activism. He is editor of the *Roma Magazin* weekly TV show devoted to Roma issues on MTV (Hungarian National Television).

16. The exception is the mixed-race (Roma/Hungarian) character of Nóra on the popular primetime soap opera *Barátok közt* (*Between Friends*), which marks the first Roma presence on fictional programming (Bernáth and Messing 2001).

17. Depicting ethnic minorities as essentially emotional – rather than rational – beings is a recognisable racist discourse, and one that has been attributed to Gypsies even as far back as the nineteenth century ('They were said to live by nature's clock and react instinctively to external impulses', Willems 1997: 50).

18. Indeed, after some complaints about the show's Gypsy stereotyping, RTL Klub issued a statement insisting that it was not a 'Roma show' but a 'comedy reality show': 'The *Győzike* show is not Roma, but is rather an entertainment programme, which, if it is influential in any way, certainly doesn't deepen, but rather reduces discrimination.' Péter Kolosi, the RTL Klub programme manager, quoted in György, 'Gáspár Győző szerepei'.

19. Győzike Tv Fórum'.

20. 'Gadjo' is a Romani term used for non-Roma people.

21. Péter György, *Élet és Irodalom*, 49(22), 3 June 2006. Available at: <http://www.es.hu/pd/ display.asp?channel=MUBIRALAT0522&article=2005-0605-2241-12PHRS> accessed 4 October 2010.

Bibliography

Appadurai, A. (2006) *Fear of Small Numbers: An Essay on the Geography of Anger* (Durham, NC: Duke University Press).

Bernáth, G. and V. Messing (2001) 'Roma szappan-opera karakter a *Barátok közt*-ben: az első fecske', *Médiakutató*, 2: 1–6.

——— (2002) 'The Neglected Public: On the Media Consumption of the Hungarian Roma', in E. Kállai (ed.), *The Gypsies/The Roma in Hungarian Society* (Budapest: Regio), pp. 107–25.

Bori, E. (2005) 'Cigányutak. Roma dokumentumfilm', *Filmvilág*, 6. Available at: <http://www.filmvilag.hu/xista_frame.php?cikk_id=8270> accessed 4 October 2010.

Corner, J. (2002) 'Performing the Real: Documentary Diversions', *Television and New Media*, 3(3): 255–69.

Darab, Zs. (2008) 'Pop, tabu, satöbbi: a hét föbün a televízióban', *Filmvilág*, 2. Available at: <http://www.filmvilag.hu/xista_frame.php?cikk_id=9262> accessed 4 October 2010.

Eyal, G., I. Szelényi and E. Townsley (1998) *Making Capitalism without Capitalists* (New York: Verso).

Fáy, A. (2001) 'Mónika, avagy a buta ország', *Élet és Irodalom*, 45(23). Available at: <http://www.es.hu/index.php?view=doc;3445> accessed 4 October 2010.

Imre, A. (2006) 'Global Entertainment and the European "Roma Problem"', *Third Text*, 20(6): 659–70.

——— (2008) 'Roma Music and Transnational Homelessness', *Third Text*, 22(3): 325–36.

Jenei, Á. (2006) 'Neotelevízió: válság vagy megújulás?' (interjú Császi Lajossal és Síklaki Istvánnal), *Médiakutató*, 2.

Kolozsi, L. (2005) 'Smink nélkül: kultúra a képernyőn', *Filmvilág*, 5. Available at: <http://www.filmvilag.hu/xista_frame.php?cikk_id=8258> accessed 4 October 2010.

Kompare, D. (2004) 'Extraordinarily Ordinary: *The Osbournes* as "an American Family"', in S. Murray and L. Ouellette (eds), *Reality TV: Remaking Television Culture* (New York: NYU Press), pp. 97–118.

Kürti, L. (2008) 'Media Wars: Cultural Dialogue and Conflict in Hungarian Popular Broadcasting', SUSDIV paper 8, January, from the Fondazione Eni Enrico Mattei Series Index. Available at: <http://www.susdiv.org/uploadfiles/SD2008-008.pdf> accessed 4 October 2010.

Ladányi, J. and I. Szelényi (2006) *Patterns of Exclusion: Constructing Gypsy Ethnicity and the Making of an Underclass in Transitional Societies of Europe* (New York: Columbia University Press).

Messing, V. (2008) *'In a White Framework': The Representation of Roma in the Hungarian Press* (Frankfurt: VDM Verlag).

Morley, D. (2007) *Home Territories: Media, Mobility, Identity* (London: Routledge).

Murray, S. and L. Ouellette (2004) 'Introduction', in Murray and Ouellette (eds), *Reality TV*, pp. 1–18.

Örkény, A. (2005) 'Cigány film vagy roma film? A Dallastól a Nyóckerig', *Filmvilág*, 6. Available at: <http://www.filmvilag.hu/xista_frame.php?cikk_id=8271> accessed 4 October 2010.

Ouellette, L. and J. Hay (2008) *Better Living through Reality Television* (Oxford: Blackwell).

Palmer, G. (2004) '"The New You": Class and Transformation on Lifestyle Television', in S. Holmes and D. Jermyn (eds), *Understanding Reality Television* (London: Routledge).

Skeggs, B. (2005) 'The Making of Class and Gender through Visualising Moral Subject Formation', *Sociology*, 39(5): 965–82.

Skeggs, B. and H. Wood (2009) 'The Moral Economy of Person Production: The Class Relations of Self-Performance on Reality TV', *Sociological Review*, 57(4): 626–44.

Skeggs, B., H. Wood and N. Thumim (2007) 'Making Class through Moral Extension on Reality TV'. Available at: <http://www.sprak.umu.se/digitalAssets/29/29326_workshop_intimacy_ahorarkop.pdf> accessed 4 October 2010.

Stewart, M. (1997) *The Time of the Gypsies* (Oxford: Westview Press).

Tremlett, A. (2009) 'Bringing Hybridity to Heterogeneity in Romani Studies', *Romani Studies*, 19(2): 147–68.

van Baar, Huub (2008) 'The Way out of Amnesia?', *Third Text*, 22(3): 373–85.

Varró, Sz. (2005) 'Romák a képernyön. Sötét hírek', *Filmvilág*, 6. Available at: <http://www.filmvilag.hu/xista_frame.php?cikk_id=8272> accessed 4 October 2010.

Willems, W. (1997) *In Search of the True Gypsy: From Enlightenment to Final Solution* (London: Frank Cass).

7/Tania Lewis

'You've put yourselves on a plate': The Labours of Selfhood on *MasterChef Australia*

On 27 April 2009, the Australian commercial free-to-air channel Network Ten, a channel that usually plays poor cousin to the two major commercial broadcasters Nine and Seven, debuted a television show that was to go on to make Australian television history. The premise of the show – a group of 'ordinary' Australians are brought together from around the country to live in a shared house in Sydney while vying to become Australia's leading amateur cook – hardly promised to be audience-grabbing programming. The accepted wisdom among Australian producers of reality and lifestyle programming is that primetime cooking shows are not usually popular fare with Australian audiences. *MasterChef Australia* (as the originally British format was titled and rebranded for Aussie audiences), however, proved this particular truism to be spectacularly wrong. More popular than *Big Brother* (2001–8) and *Australian Idol* (2003–9), both major successes in Australia, the show has had extraordinary appeal across a wide audience. The third-highest-rating programme in Australia (the other two highest-rating programmes were sporting events) since OzTAM began collecting ratings figures in 2001 (2010: 632), it was watched at least once by over 11 million Australians – 75 per cent of people in the five mainland cities (Meade 2010).[1]

There has been much debate in the local press about why '*MasterChef* has brought us, as a nation, together over the table celebrating food' (Hardy 2009). Described as 'accessible', 'family-friendly' and 'comforting', the show's success has been put down to its being a relatively non-conflictual 'feel-good' variant of reality television at a time when, faced with a global financial crisis, audiences are staying home and cooking more (Kalina 2009). In this chapter, I want to interrogate the show's national appeal in the face of global economic pressures, focusing in particular on the way *MasterChef Australia* negotiates class, labour and social identity.

Jonathan Bignell suggests that the transnational mobility of reality television may indicate the growing universalisation of a 'Western' preoccupation with 'personal confession, modification, testing and the perfectibility of the self' (Bignell 2005: 40). Certainly, the widespread uptake of reality formats around the world and across different cultures – from Chinese/Singaporean reality-based home renovation shows like *Home Décor Survivor* to the Panamanian version of *Extreme Makeover* (*Cambio Radical*) – point to the global currency of consumerist and neo-liberal models of selfhood and citizenship. However, as Bignell also notes, while the embrace of reality television and its associated

modes of selfhood and lifestyle consumption might be an increasingly global phenomenon, the failure of some formats in certain countries and the popularity of indigenised versions of imported formats indicate that this mode of programming is still strongly shaped by local conditions.

My argument here is that *MasterChef Australia* (henceforth *MCA*) is characterised by a complex
negotiation between globalising forces and domestic concerns. This is especially the case in relation
to questions of class and the valuing of different forms of capital. Much scholarship on lifestyle-
oriented reality television has noted the way in which some shows operate as sites of popular pedagogy, promoting middle-class taste preferences, lifestyles and consumption, with British shows (and
the often moralising lifestyle experts that front them) in particular often equating good forms of selfhood and citizenship with the acquisition of bourgeois forms of cultural capital (Palmer 2004; Wood
and Skeggs 2004; Lewis 2008). While *MCA* is concerned with teaching audiences culinary taste, in
the Australian format, class and aspirationalism are also enacted through rather more pragmatic
mechanisms such as the acquisition of labour skills and social capital. Part of the show's success in
the Australian context lies in the way the rejigged *MCA* format manages to democratise its mode of
address and uncouple issues of cultural capital and taste from classed identity through a focus on
ethnicity, labour and economics.

Nationalism, Entertainment Media and 'the Real'

In common with vocational/career-oriented reality formats such as *The Apprentice* (2005–),
MasterChef is a competitive cooking game-show format that blends elements of lifestyle programming – with its focus on transmitting various life skills and forms of taste to the audience – with reality game-doc conventions. Originally made for the BBC as a rather sedate game show, the Australian
version significantly reworked the *MasterChef* format. In Australia, the show aired on primetime commercial television six nights a week and was a glossy, more theatrical and faster-paced take on the
BBC concept. In series two, the format saw Australians from around the country audition for fifty
semi-final places, undergoing various 'challenges' over a week before being whittled down to twenty-
four contestants. The 'top twenty-four' were then put through various individual and team-based contests, with each week structured around a regular cycle of nightly challenges (mystery box and
invention test, pressure test, celebrity chef challenge, off-site challenge, elimination and then a
masterclass with the remaining contestants), culminating in a finals week and the 'crowning' of
the winning *MasterChef*, whose prize includes work experience in leading restaurants, chef training
from professional chefs, the publication of their own cookbook and $100,000 to support their
'food dream'.

Along with a revamped narrative structure, the show has also been strongly indigenised at the
level of cultural content and rebranded along strongly nationalistic lines. This has involved the usual
replacement of foreign hosts and judges with local talent (the show features three Australian judges
– chefs Gary Mehigan and George Calombaris and food critic Matt Preston), alongside a particularly
self-conscious embrace of national tropes. Drawn from a variety of backgrounds, the top twenty-
four contestants on the show stand in for a kind of idealised, cross-class multicultural Australia.

Various iconic markers of Australian national identity are also a feature, from 'classic' Aussie foods such as the 'chiko roll'[2] to the frequent insertion of panoramic shots of Sydney, the location of the *MasterChef* house and kitchen. The format has also been tailored to reflect Australian national myths of social egalitarianism, with the competitive aspects relatively downplayed and rather more emphasis given to the social bonds that have developed between contestants.

Graeme Turner foregrounds 'the construction of cultural identity as one of [the media's] primary spheres of activity' (Turner 2009: 3). Discussing reality television, he emphasises the commercial logics that drive media imperatives, pointing in particular to the limitations of claims about the (much vaunted) democratising nature of reality television as a 'participatory' medium. In emphasising economics, Turner's argument is that media industries today need to be understood as having moved beyond a purely mediatory role to one of considerably more authorial power and centrality – where *their* interests rather than those of just the state or nation are being served through processes of representation. Given that these interests are structured by regimes of value that are distinct from those of the social or the political sphere, participatory television is thus a very different animal from participatory democracy.

I want to stress, however, that at the same time, such media interests are clearly not served in complete autonomy from those of the state or nation; rather, they are in complex articulation. Indeed, Turner's concern is to understand the increasingly central role played by the media at a point where crucial social institutions are stepping back from processes of identity-shaping, leaving media players to fill the gap. The utility of Turner's argument for understanding the status of shows like *MCA* is that such media phenomena need to be understood not simply as a devolved technique of state governance that mediates the social (see Palmer 2003; Ouellette and Hay 2008), but rather as the (somewhat serendipitous) outcome of certain social tendencies. These include the privatisation of once structural social processes, the increasingly central role of the media in making and shaping cultural identities, and the growing merger between culture and economics. In a Gramscian turn, instead of figuring the relations between media culture and broader socio-political and ideological structures in determinist terms, these processes, as per the theory of articulation, are both semi-autonomous and mutually constitutive. As Turner argues, 'we are now entering an age in which *entertainment* has become increasingly important' (Turner 2009: 10; my emphasis).

Such a shift dovetails with arguments related to the growing centrality of performance – of self-conscious enactments of community and personhood in contemporary social relations (Skeggs and Wood 2009a). While shows like *MCA* do of course function, at an ideological and informational level, as important sites of popular pedagogy that teach the optimal management of social identity, they do so in a way that is not purely textual but which is also *productive* of the social itself. While the immediate interests of the reality television industry may seem to be economistic, the broader implications of the populist media logic of the reality turn is to produce 'a direct and sustained intervention into the construction of people's desires, cultural identities and expectations of the real' (Turner 2009: 24). This chapter examines what kind of social imaginary is enacted inside the *MasterChef* kitchen.

'One nation, united, under a colourful oven mitt'[3]: Ordinariness, Cosmopolitanism and Ethnicity

Media commentators have put the success of *MCA* down to the 'feel-good' nature of the show as opposed to the more conflictual narrative logics often associated with US and British reality television. Australian television producers are often reluctant to overly emphasise aspirationalism or competitiveness on local versions of lifestyle and reality television (Lewis 2009: 302–3). On the surface at least, *MCA* embraces and performs a kind of non-hierarchical, democratic version of Australian 'ordinariness' through shoring up 'a cultural mythos of "mateship" and social egalitarianism' (ibid.: 303). The winner of the first series of *MCA*, Julie Goodwin, a homely Anglo woman concerned with cooking 'honest food' 'using ingredients everyone cooks', is perhaps the epitome of (a certain normative model of) Australian ordinariness. Julie represented herself (and was likewise presented in the media) as an ordinary 'home cook' and (despite running an IT business) 'stay at home mum', while her *MasterChef* web profile describes her favourite cuisine as 'Aussie!' and her favourite dish as 'baked dinner', positioning her values and taste as that of an 'average' white Australian free of class pretensions.

MCA, however, is also concerned with promoting thoroughly bourgeois and cosmopolitan forms of taste as well as modelling entrepreneurial models of selfhood. The runner-up in series one, South Australian Ling Yeow Poh (who has subsequently gone on to host her own cooking show on the public channel, the Australian Broadcasting Corporation or ABC), is a highly articulate artist whom the judges consistently praised for her far-from-ordinary, cosmopolitan cuisine. Given Poh's high-end culinary prowess, there was much controversy over Julie's victory, with many audience members claiming the final vote had been rigged. The heated nature of the debate reflected tensions around *MCA*'s attempts to speak to a very broad Australian audience, from commercial viewers to the more bourgeois audiences normally devoted to the ABC. What the glib media byline 'one nation, united'[4] intimates but glosses over is the show's efforts to negotiate the rather rocky terrain of Australian social identity.

As Greig, Lewins and White (2003) point out, while notions of social egalitarianism lie at the core of Australian self-identity, this national perception has been built on rather shaky foundations, with claims to a coherent Australian nationhood glossing over major historical and political exclusions around citizenship and identity.[5] Australian national culture is founded on the notion of the 'fair go', reflected in the pervasive belief that it is a classless society, in direct contrast to its British colonial origins. Myths of social equity and mobility abound, but while Australia is one of the most ethnically diverse nations in the world, its national identity is still centred around a hegemonic Anglocentrism in which ethnic multiculturalism and indigeneity feature as forms of strategic economic branding for Australia on the world stage.[6] Migrants are often popularly depicted as socially mobile, with prominent successful figures held up as markers of Australian egalitarianism. But as Greig *et al.* (2003) point out, new migrants coming to Australia often enter into the working class, with many finding themselves downwardly mobile, while recent events such as the Tampa affair[7] and the Cronulla riots[8] have put paid to the perception that Australia is some kind of multicultural haven, receiving migrants and refugees alike with open arms.

In light of this more complicated picture, such apparently bland statements about *MCA* uniting Australia as 'one nation' start to take on a rather different complexion. *MCA*, in its attempts to negotiate a sense of national ordinariness and inclusiveness, represents an intervention into a complex cultural field marked by considerable struggle. Class differences tend to be largely disavowed in Australian culture or displaced onto other social categories. *MCA* is somewhat unusual here in its broad demographic reach and its attempt to speak to a range of classed identities – though the programme is marked by anxieties around the bourgeois connotations of the culinary and fine-dining culture promoted on the show. *MCA* thus uses various strategies to manage the class issues raised by its focus on distinction, taste and value. One central way in which class is negotiated on the show is via ethnicity.

The contestants on reality shows – particularly at the more tabloid end of the television spectrum – are often drawn from lower-middle-class or working-class backgrounds. With its relatively bourgeois cultural focus and high production values, *MCA* has attracted contestants from all walks of life, with a number of more upper-middle-class, professional-managerial contestants featuring on the show. It has also sought a roughly equal balance of men and women, although the contestants to date have been largely in their twenties and thirties. While the producers have clearly striven to include a broad range of participants, questions of class and gender are not necessarily highlighted. Where *MCA* is rather more self-conscious in its claims to 'diversity' and national representativeness is in its focus on ethnicity and multiculturalism.

Newman and Gibson note that Australian food media is often divided along distinct class lines. Food magazines such as *Vogue Entertaining* and the *Australian Women's Weekly* speak to very different social groups, with the latter type of publication 'quite resistant to strong implications of ethnic difference' (Newman and Gibson 2005: 90). In contrast, food television is rather more inclusive in its demographic reach and mode of address because 'television has the capacity to domesticate and reassure, to erase the more obtrusive markers of difference' (ibid.: 91). *MCA* is overtly cosmopolitan, embracing and championing Australian multiculturalism. Throughout the show, much is made of the Greek background of chef and judge George Calombaris, a highly successful chef and restaurateur (who plays up his role of ordinary Aussie Greek boy 'made good'). The ethnic backgrounds of contestants on the show are also often foregrounded as part of their personal cooking 'journey' and 'style', though race and indigeneity is noticeably absent from *MCA*'s purview. Ethnicity largely seems to stand in or act as a (relatively safe) site for the negotiation of social diversity more broadly – in particular, class difference.

Such points of 'difference', though, are quite literally 'domesticated' – with the show's house and kitchen (the strangely familiar hybridised 'non-places' that we have come to associate with reality television) acting as stages for performing (and containing) a rather unchallenging version of multiculturalism. This 'safe' multiculturalism is heightened by the fact that the 'ethnically' marked contestants (particularly those who make it to the final twenty-four) are largely second- or third-generation migrants complete with Australian accents and habitus. It is fair to say that cultural difference is celebrated on the show but only to the point where it adds a degree of cultural colour or gives a contestant that extra edge in terms of personal branding or culinary know-how, with the performance of ethnic skills or knowledge often conflated with 'inventiveness'. At times, though, this is a double-edged sword. When a Greek contestant is encouraged to make baklava, the gambit fails when they are then chastised for not making a dish innovative enough to be served at a high-end restaurant. The object on *MCA* is to aim for a particular model of savvy, cosmopolitan, bourgeois food culture – a point illustrated by the winner of *MCA*'s second series, Adam Liaw. Liaw, an Australian-born, Japanese-based lawyer with a Chinese Malaysian background, offered up cuisine that was a fusion of international and various Asian influences (such as prawn scotch eggs with coconut and chilli sambal). Likewise, Liaw performed a kind of trans-Asian identity on the show, speaking Japanese to 'Iron Chef Sakai' from the famous eponymous Japanese cooking show while often linking his 'innovation' dishes to family narratives or to Asian mythology (as reflected in his high-scoring dish based on the seven lucky gods of Japan). Ethnicity functions on the show as a kind of cultural capital, one that only 'works' when it is flexible enough to be articulated into certain forms of (globalised bourgeois) taste.

If ethnicity stands in for class, enabling an embrace of middle-class cosmopolitanism, the kind of food cooked on *MCA* moves between the extremes of cutting-edge cuisines such as molecular gastronomy and food that is self-consciously marked out as ordinary and 'Aussie'. *MCA* is clearly concerned with educating audiences about food (and there has been much positive media commentary on the educational value of the show) and, in the process, about certain kinds of middle-class taste and cultural capital. However, it also seeks to distance itself from excessively bourgeois forms of taste, with the show's producers clearly aware of steering a careful course between its aspirational values and the values of so-called 'ordinary' Australians. For instance, the contestants have to master Country Women's Association[9] favourites such as scones and participate in a team cook-off on a P&O cruise ship. In one particular episode, teams are challenged to create vegetarian dishes for a panel of Australian men of the 'Aussie bloke' variety – notably blue-collar workers and a farmer, all somewhat oddly, given the studio setting, wearing their work clothes – with much made of their unfamiliarity with the main ingredient used in the show, goat's cheese, and their general disdain for meatless meals. While the episode caricatured Australian working-class men and their perceived lack of taste, it also evidenced a discomfort with class pretensions. These broader concerns with the class connotations of the show were laid out on the table, as it were, by FremantleMedia chief executive Ian Hogg. Commenting on the top recipe downloads on the *MCA* website – pavlova, spare ribs, crème brulée, beef wellington and sausage rolls – he argued: 'It's not Parisian food. It's very Australian working class. It's very comforting. People are hungry in winter and they want something accessible to watch and to eat' (Meade 2010).

Overlooking the dubious definition of crème brulée as Australian working-class food, such comments indicate the way in which the embrace of culinary multiculturalism is perhaps not as blandly apolitical a manoeuvre as it might at first seem. Newman and Gibson (2005) note that Australian food culture since the 1970s has been characterised by a growing 'multiculinarianism', becoming internationally renowned for its fusion food. Australia's shift away from a progressive policy of multiculturalism with the election of the Conservative Government under John Howard in 1996 saw the rise of both anti-race and anti-class discourse, with multiculturalism increasingly associated with a perceived intellectual elite characterised by 'cosmopolitan values' (Newman and Gibson 2005).

In the context of growing wage inequity in Australia and a declining industrial base, Howard re-directed fears about a struggling labour market to this imagined 'new class' of the cultural left who are often dismissed in Australian media and political circles (strikingly, as Newman and Gibson note, in culinary terms) as the 'latte set' and 'chardonnay socialists' (ibid.: 90).

The choice of Matt Preston as a judge on *MCA* is an interesting one, marking the show's complex engagement with both middle-class and working-class audiences. An eloquent and, at times, somewhat pompous food critic for the Melbourne newspaper *The Age*, with a rather plummy British accent, Preston is a fully signed-up member of the 'latte belt'. Before the airing of *MCA*, Preston would have been little known to audiences outside of Melbourne's foodie middle class, but he has since become a huge favourite with audiences, even winning a Best New Talent award at the Australian annual television awards, the Logies, a distinctly lowbrow cultural event. While this is per-haps surprising given that commercial Australian television presenters tend to work hard at being seen as ordinary, it reflects Newman and Gibson's point about food television's broader scope in relation to cultural representations and its role in democratising culturally exotic and bourgeois forms of taste for a broad audience. Preston's posh food critic is balanced out by George Calombaris' working-class Greek chef made good and by chef Gary Mehigan's more middle-of-the-road television host persona (both of whom, as successful working chefs, also anchor the show in questions of labour, craft and vocationalism). While not a chef, Preston plays to a tradition of televi-sion chefdom through flamboyant displays of camp and cultural capital. Such overt displays of 'per-sonality' are also central to the economic logics of reality television, where Preston's larger-than-life and highly performative persona as an overweight Oscar Wildish dandy has seen him positioned as a 'branded expert' characterised by certain trademarks, from his cravat to his rotundness (Lewis 2010).

Economies of Personhood: Work, Mobility and Insecurity on *MCA*

Matt Preston's status as a highly marketable food personality leads us into another key dimension of *MCA*'s mode of sociality – its embeddedness, as 'a master stroke of branding' (Cauchi 2010), in eco-nomic logics.[10] Linked to this logic, a crucial aspect of the way *MCA* navigates the politics of class is through its focus on labour and job mobility. It is here that the show perhaps speaks most overtly to the pressures of global neo-liberalism. As Skeggs and Wood argue, such logics have seen the grow-ing centrality of a culture of performed selfhood in which we see the naturalisation of 'an economy of personhood' (Skeggs and Wood 2009a: 632).

Clearly, one way in which this performative, economised self is realised on *MCA* is through the focus on contestants as entrepreneurial subjects and as sites of potential branding. Here *MCA*'s extensive branding franchise embraces not just the celebrity chefs and judges featured on the show but also the participants. Like the various celebrity chefs who appear as guests, the contestants are presented to the audience as 'personalities' and as sites of (potential) economic and brand value (Hearn 2009) – from the glossy opening titles where contestants are individually introduced to the audience (via 'glamour' shots set to American popster Katy Perry's top 40 hit 'Hot N Cold'), to the recurrent use of pop-up text identifying them (and often their age and current occupation/work status), to the names embroidered on their uniforms (along with the *MasterChef* logo) and the focus on their particular 'food styles'.

What is distinctive about the kind of 'foodie lifestyle' (de Solier 2008) promoted on *MCA* is its focus on production, with the skilled, labouring self figured as a marketable product. The model of economic selfhood promoted on *MCA* is one that speaks to Australian class mores and in particular Australian conceptions of social mobility, which compared to the UK, for example, are often more overtly tied to material rather than symbolic resources. As Emmison, Bennett and Frow (1999) argue, while cultural capital and regimes of taste clearly play a role in social identity formation and class distinction in Australia, for many Australians, social status is also strongly linked to the acquisition of social and economic forms of capital. Class concerns are also therefore played out on the show through a focus on the acquisition of work skills, knowledge and relevant work 'connections' as well as on forms of entrepreneurialism. There is a strong emphasis on the importance of industry networks, with the judges and contestants often commenting on the potential benefits of being connected with and mentored by the various celebrity chefs featured on the show. Fitting in with this utilitarian approach, cultural capital is treated as a social advantage or utility that can be 'cashed in' in the marketplace: for instance, Melbourne lawyer Claire's ability to speak and read French is depicted as a skill that gave her (and her team) a distinct advantage in various challenges. While Matt Preston's surfeit of bourgeois cultural capital as a cravat-wearing, educated Briton is acceptable on Australian television in part because it ties neatly into the economics of *MCA* – functioning as a persuasive and highly likeable branded personality.

Self-branding is of course central to the logics of reality television more broadly (see Palmer in this volume). But what is distinctive about the narratives of success and social mobility promoted on *MCA* is the rather pragmatic focus on work skills and career development within the food industry. One cross-promotion on the show's website entitled 'If you're no *MasterChef* get the skills with Guy Grossi [a well-known Melbourne chef]' was linked, for instance, to an Australian state government website for 'skills Victoria' with information on 'education and training options' for Victorian workers. In contrast to the instant success aspired to on other reality formats, the focus of the *MCA* narrative instead is on rather more realistic and achievable career pathways, with many of the contestants having relatively modest expectations (usually to run their own business in the form of a small restaurant or café). Rather than seeking fame, Alvin, a scientist, and Matthew, an accountant, both speak of escaping the boredom of their desk jobs for the 'creativity' of cooking, reflecting the show's broader emphasis on job satisfaction and finding one's vocation. And while publicly prominent figures like Julie and Poh are represented as *MCA* success stories, so too are 'evictees' such as Fiona who, as we are told in one media report, 'landed her dream role as a kitchen garden teacher' at a primary school. Here the show again plays out its egalitarian credentials – anyone can achieve some degree of success. The 'dreams' of mobility promoted on the show are not just those of fame and status but are often the more ordinary aspirations of contestants and viewers. And here labour itself is the equaliser on *MCA* – if one is prepared to work at one's vocation and on oneself, then achieving life goals is guaranteed.

While much of the scripted rhetoric of *MCA* is about the 'journeys' of contestants as they work towards their vocational goals, the flipside to 'the dream' – reflected in the show's pressure tests, challenges and eliminations – is the reality of life and work under late-modern conditions: risk, stress, insecurity, with the potential for downward mobility or 'elimination' from the labour market for the worker who is unable to be flexible or entrepreneurial enough to make the grade (Hearn 2009). The broader social, political and economic backdrop to a show that dramatises work processes and the acquisition of vocational skills is one common to most developed neo-liberal states. While many Australians identify themselves as middle class (McGregor 2001), the Australian labour market has become an increasingly insecure, risky place marked by a growing gap between the 'work rich' and the 'work poor', with increasing numbers of workers clocking up longer hours and holding down multiple jobs (Broomhill and Sharp 2007: 93). In contrast to the image of the laid-back Australian lifestyle, the evidence is that 'middle Australia' has been experiencing growing work stress and insecurity, with many expressing a sense of dissatisfaction with their quality of life (Greig, Lewins and White 2003: 98). These recent shifts come off the back of longer global trends since the 1970s towards relative deindustrialisation and the growth of an informational economy with increasing numbers of people employed in the service sector. Alongside the deregulation of the Australian labour market in the 1980s and the replacement of protections around wage equality with the 'flexibility' of enterprise bargaining, the rise of the informational economy has heralded an era of insecure employment.

This culture of flexible labour is reflected and normalised in the narrative logic of *MCA* itself, with contestants depicted as often being prepared to give up highly paid jobs in order to pursue their vocational 'dream' even if that dream comes at significant personal risk. In this context, 'mobility' has now become a growing part of life but not necessarily in a positive way; rather, contemporary workers find themselves forced to be mobile and flexible in order to fit into the changing needs of capital. Such shifts have resulted in some paradoxical developments around the nature of work. On the one hand, the rise of informational capitalism has seen a growing proportion of professional-managerial workers with an associated increased focus on the need for education, qualifications and for continual upskilling (Greig, Lewins and Frow 2003: 101). On the other hand, a hollowing out of the middle sector of the job market has resulted in a relatively small core of highly educated workers possessing symbolic-analytic skills, while the majority of workers find themselves increasingly in low-skilled, insecure, part-time employment.

This is the backdrop to *MCA*'s focus on work – a global marketplace in which mobility and flexibility are twinned with risk and insecurity and by a complex set of tensions between 'immaterial' symbolic work and skilled/unskilled labour (Hardt and Negri 2000). The show's mode of address attempts to be broadly inclusive, addressing the concerns of a wide range of Australians from the professional-managerial class to blue-collar workers, something it manages partly through the kinds of labour it chooses to focus on. Unlike reality shows like *The Apprentice*, which use the narrow frame of business and managerialism, the focus on cooking and the twinned figure of the amateur cook/professional chef enables *MCA* to straddle a much wider range of classed and gendered concerns and to embrace a more romantic work ethic, linked to notions of creative labour. Viewers witness the show's contestants labouring in a range of settings and under a variety of (often pressured) conditions, from the Fordist factory-like scenario of cooking on a cruise liner, to preparing meals in an army kitchen out in 'the bush', to working in the kitchens of high-end restaurants in Sydney and in London.

Contestants also move between participating as members of a collaborative team, working as individuals against each other and against the clock, and also at times playing a supervisory role as 'team leader'. The kind of labour they are asked to perform crosses a broad spectrum, from relatively unskilled supervised work through to the exhibition of leadership skills and to highly creative, analytic forms of labour, as evidenced in the example of the 'invention' tests where contestants have to create new dishes, often from ingredients they haven't chosen themselves. The focus on creative labour and the blurring of the lines between productive leisure and labour is reinforced by the apparently permeable boundary between amateur cooks and professional chefs and by the way the show encourages viewers to engage in restaurant-level cooking ('you too can be a *MasterChef* at home'). The emphasis on communal enterprise is extended here to the audience, who are called upon to identify with and participate in the creative endeavours of the contestants. This focus on both creative and skilled labour thus allows *MCA* to embrace the interests not only of a wide range of contestants from a variety of backgrounds but also to connect with a broadly diversified audience.

Conclusion

As Graeme Turner suggests (2009), successful reality TV shows work not just as textual mediations of the social but rather produce active interventions into social space, shaping normative conceptions of identity and, perhaps more importantly, framing people's social expectations and their imagined life trajectories. Much scholarship on reality and lifestyle formats sees them as vehicles for globalising models of social identity articulated, in particular, to individualised, consumerist conceptions of selfhood, which are, in turn, often tied to cosmopolitan middle-class forms of taste and cultural value. In its attempts to democratise high-end culinary taste for a broad audience while simultaneously promoting an enterprising, branded conception of selfhood, *MCA* can certainly be read in this vein. But while inflected by an enterprise model of selfhood (Rose 1999), the show also offers a distinctive engagement with the economic and cultural pressures around transnational cosmopolitanism, linked to the way in which the format has been Australianised. The show's appeal across a large audience reflects the way in which it manages to re-articulate questions of taste and cultural capital, as well as the competitive individualist elements of the global reality television format, to a variety of Australian social, cultural and economic concerns, as well as to local industry and commercial interests.

While *MCA*'s narrative trajectory is ostensibly focused on social mobility and the acquisition of cultural, social and economic capital, the show's producers have been careful to strive for an inclusive cross-class mode of address, portraying the *MasterChef* kitchen as a space of egalitarianism. As Skeggs and Wood's work on UK reality programming has shown, such formats often set up a moral hierarchy between middle-class lifestyles and cultural values and working-class subjects, with the latter often positioned as socially deficient and in need of reform (Skeggs and Wood 2009b). *MCA* in contrast, by reflecting Australian anxieties about overt displays of class distinction, works hard to pave over class difference. And the show is somewhat unusual in bringing together contestants from a broad range of class backgrounds in the same (highly artificial) social space. Paradoxically, though, while MCA embraces social diversity, at the same time it works to deny class hierarchies – the MasterChef kitchen is portrayed as a level playing field where crème brulée is 'working-class food' and where labourers and lawyers alike can aspire to the same goals.

This sleight of hand is enabled on the show by an emphasis on economics and labour. The focus on work and personal drive, rather than on cultural capital and taste, works as a kind of equaliser. While middle-class forms of cultural capital and habitus are valued on MCA, they are depicted as personality traits and life skills that can be used to add value to the branded, economised self. MCA's focus on ethnicity, for instance, is framed in terms of economic capital; representing cultural identity as a potentially useful form of personal branding enables the show to negotiate and embrace middle-class cosmopolitanism without having to foreground the role of class in social mobility.

Likewise, the show speaks to a range of classed experiences through its focus on a variety of forms of labour and recognition of the pressures of the labour market. However, while the show acknowledges such pressures through its narrativisation of risk and insecurity, the 'solutions' it offers largely involve the contestants learning to see themselves as risk-bearing entrepreneurial subjects. Part of the huge success of the format in Australia has been the way the producers have managed to personalise and humanise these issues for a broad cross-demographic audience, tying questions of enterprise, mobility and self-fulfilment to the often modest personal aspirations of a range of Australians. MCA's underlying concern with viewing contestants as sites of enterprise and capacity-building in the end leads to an overemphasis on the possibilities of individual mobility and on the self as a value-added economic entity, glossing over the realities of a labour market structured by class-based inequities and by a growing gap between the rich and the poor.

Acknowledgments

I'd like to thank Alison Huber, Beverley Skeggs, Graeme Turner and Helen Wood for their helpful critical comments on this chapter.

Notes

1. Its national import was recently further highlighted by the fact that the federal election leaders' debate for the 2010 Australian election, traditionally aired in the time slot of 7.30 p.m. on Sunday, was moved to an earlier time to avoid a clash with the finale of Series 2 of the show. On being questioned about why he wasn't invited to be part of the TV debate, Greens leader Bob Brown quipped, 'I've as much chance of making the debate as I have of making the finals of MasterChef' (Curtis 2010).

2. Invented in Australia in the 1950s as a snack for outdoor events, the chiko roll is essentially a larger, more robust version of the Chinese spring roll.

3. This phrase is taken from a byline of an article on MCA in the Melbourne broadsheet The Age (Quinn 2009).

4. The byline also conjures up some presumably unintended resonances with the far right nationalist One Nation Party.

5. For instance, the myth of 'terra nullias', of Australia as unpopulated when it was first colonised by British settlers, was only overturned in the late 1990s.

6. The *Immigration Restriction Act* of 1901, known as the white Australian Policy, prohibited entry to Australia of non-whites. Most migrants who came to Australia before World War II were of Anglo stock, while more than half of postwar migrants came from non-English-speaking backgrounds. These migrants faced a strongly assimilationist culture.

7. The Tampa affair occurred in August 2001 when the Howard Government refused permission for the Norwegian freighter MV *Tampa*, carrying 438 rescued Afghans from a distressed fishing vessel, to enter Australian waters, leading to controversy locally and internationally over Australia's breach of international human rights.

8. What became known as 'the Cronulla riots' began in December 2005 with reports of clashes between volunteer lifesavers at Cronulla (a beachside suburb of Sydney) and a group of youths of 'Middle Eastern appearance'. This was followed by a period of race-based violent confrontations and incidents commonly depicted in the press as 'race riots'.

9. The CWA is Australia's largest voluntary women's organisation whose primary remit is to make life better for families, especially those living in rural Australia.

10. Commercial interests lie at the core of the *MCA* franchise, which includes a magazine, cookbooks, two spin-off shows, *Celebrity MasterChef* and *Junior MasterChef*, estimated to bring in $65 million in revenue (Cauchi 2010).

Bibliography

Bignell, J. (2005) *Big Brother: Reality TV in the Twenty-First Century* (Basingstoke, Hants.: Palgrave Macmillan).

Broomhill, R. and R. Sharp (2007) 'The Problem of Social Reproduction under Neo-Liberalism: Reconfiguring the Male-Breadwinner Model in Australia', in M. Griffin-Cohen and J. Brodie (eds), *Remapping Gender in the New Global Order* (London: Routledge), pp. 85–108.

Cauchi, S. (2010) 'Food, glorious food, and magazine, and books, and …', *Sunday Age*, 20 June, p. 3.

Curtis, L. (2010) 'Debate to Avoid *MasterChef* Cook-Off', *ABC News*, 20 July. Available at: <http://www.abc.net.au/news/stories/2010/07/20/2958424.htm> accessed 30 July 2010.

de Solier, I. (2008) 'Foodie Makeovers: Public Service Television and Lifestyle Guidance', in G. Palmer (ed.), *Exposing Lifestyle Television: The Big Reveal* (Aldershot, Hants.: Ashgate), pp. 65–81.

Emmison, M., T. Bennett and J. Frow (1999) *Accounting for Tastes: Australian Everyday Cultures* (Cambridge: Cambridge University Press).

Greig, A., F. W. Lewins and K. White (2003) *Inequality in Australia* (New York: Cambridge University Press).

Hardt, M. and A. Negri (2000) *Empire* (Cambridge, MA/London: Harvard University Press).

Hardy, M. (2009) 'Why we united over mystery boxes', *The Age*, 23 July, p. 7.

Hearn, A. (2009) 'Insecure: Narratives and Economies of the Branded Self in Transformation Television', in T. Lewis (ed.), *TV Transformations: Revealing the Makeover Show* (London: Routledge), pp. 55–63.

Kalina, P. (2009) '*MasterChef* sets ratings on fire', *The Age*, 17 July, p. 3.

Lewis, T. (2008) *Smart Living: Lifestyle Media and Popular Expertise* (New York: Peter Lang).

———— (2009) 'From Global to Glocal: Australianising the Makeover Format', in A. Moran (ed.), *TV Formats Worldwide: Localizing Global Programs* (Bristol: Intellect), pp. 293–305.

———— (2010) 'Branding, Celebritization and the Lifestyle Expert', *Cultural Studies*, 24(4): 580–98.

McGregor, C. (2001) *Class in Australia* (Ringwood, Victoria: Penguin Australia).

Meade, A. (2010) 'Wildly popular *MasterChef* goes live', *Weekend Australian*, 12 June, p. 3.

Newman, F. and M. Gibson (2005) 'Monoculture Versus Multiculinarianism: Trouble in the Aussie Kitchen', in D. Bell and J. Hollows (eds), *Ordinary Lifestyles: Popular Media, Consumption and Taste* (Maidenhead, Berks.: Open University Press).

Ouellette, L. and J. Hay (2008) *Better Living through Television* (Malden, MA/Oxford: Blackwell).

Palmer, G. (2003) *Discipline and Liberty: Television and Governance* (Manchester/New York: Manchester University Press).

———— (2004) ' "The New You": Class and Transformation in Lifestyle Television', in S. Holmes and D. Jermyn (eds), *Understanding Reality Television* (London/New York: Routledge), pp. 173–90.

Quinn, K. (2009) 'One nation, united, under a colourful oven mitt', *The Age*, 21 July, p. 16.

Rose, N. (1999) *Powers of Freedom: Reframing Political Thought* (Cambridge/New York: Cambridge University Press).

Skeggs, B. and H. Wood (2009a) 'The Moral Economy of Person Production: The Class Relations of Self-Performance on Reality Television', *Sociological Review*, 57(4): 626–44.

———— (2009b) 'The Labour of Transformation and Circuits of Value "around" Reality Television', in T. Lewis, *TV Transformations: Revealing the Makeover Show* (London: Routledge), pp. 119–32.

Turner, G. (2009) *Ordinary People and the Media: The Demotic Turn* (London: Sage).

Wood, H. and B. Skeggs (2004) 'Notes on Ethical Scenarios of Self on British Reality TV', *Feminist Media Studies*, 4(2): 205–8.

PART TWO

Normalisation, Aspiration and Its Limits

8/Lisa Taylor

'I'm a girl, I should be a princess': Gender, Class Entitlement and Denial in *The Hills*

Introduction

The Hills (MTV, 2006–) is a semi-scripted reality programme which tracks the 'real lives' of Lauren Conrad, Heidi, Audrina and Whitney – four twenty-something female friends who live and work in the glamorous culture industries of Los Angeles. The show is a by-product of MTV's *Laguna Beach* (MTV, 2004–), which charted the lives of a group of upper-middle-class,[1] white high-school students in California's Laguna Beach.

Whereas UK reality programming has been conceived as cheap trash television, its low production values delivering a gritty type of 'verisimilitude', *Laguna Beach* and *The Hills* have made a break with the 'real', replacing it with high production values, which render it with a more sumptuous, cinematic aesthetic (Schlotterbeck 2009). When I first viewed *The Hills*, I was jarred by a visual style with which I felt quite unaccustomed. Indeed, critics commented on the 'strange' yet 'lush' look of *Laguna Beach* on initial viewings (Rochlin 2005). Stylistically, *The Hills* draws on the films of Michael Mann (Gay 2008: 44). Generically curious and labelled by some as a 'hybrid-reality series' (Hearn 2010), these shows register a formally interesting and pleasurable television aesthetic, arguably marking a moment of 'genrefication' (Altman 1999) of the reality format.

Undergirding the analysis which follows is my own understanding of the seductive pleasure of glamour[2] coupled with a concern about the ideological meanings provided by a television series like *The Hills* for young viewers. It is an especially alluring text in that it uses a glossy cinematic form to carry new modes of product placement as a means to sell other desirable goods and services in what Deery (2004) has called 'advertainment', thereby generating income streams which extend well beyond the series.[3] What Alison Hearn suggests is common to reality programming, but uniquely effective in *The Hills*, is that it provides: 'the means for individuals to produce their own image personae, or "branded selves"' (Hearn 2010: 233) (see also Palmer in this volume). This is a strategy which has proved extremely lucrative for Lauren Conrad and her friends. Indeed, Hearn argues that *The Hills* is a narrative about self-branding, which, in an age of what Giddens (1991) calls the reflexive project of the self, is a key phenomenon.

A distinct form of labour in post-Fordist capitalist culture, self-branding draws on the narrative and visual codes of the media and cultural industries to accumulate profit across a range of locations, from the corporate workplace to online social networking sites such as Facebook.com. Hearn (2008) argues that self-branding is always ultimately a cynical product, corralled and circumscribed by the interests of global capitalism (see also Palmer in this volume). So that while the girls on *The Hills* live out their real lives for the MTV cameras, 'being' is a form of labour in a chain of value accumulation for the cast, the MTV producers and the network. This chapter is concerned with the representational strategies of class and gender employed by *The Hills*. What do the female promotional selves of contemporary MTV look like and how are they 'made good' in a moral sense beyond their own corporate image? How is self-branding desirably coded as a means to attract a young, mainly female audience?

A generic hybrid which appropriates soap opera conventions and moments of melodrama, *The Hills*, I would argue, acts as a pedagogical tool for young women. If as Annette Hill (2005) reveals in her qualitative research that audiences become intrigued by adjudicating, decoding and *learning from* the 'people-watching' element of reality television, *The Hills* offers valuable guidance, drawn from popular feminism, about how to make and keep close female friends, choose a good boyfriend and make an impression when you first climb onto the career ladder.

However, while *The Hills* is concerned with providing subtle lessons in moral self-management, it does so not by visualising a failure of personhood or pathologising its (working-class) subjects, as critics have argued in relation to reality television in the UK (McRobbie 2004; Taylor 2005; Wood and Skeggs 2008; see also Walkerdine in this volume). Rather, it presents its dilemmas of ordinary life within a class milieu of privilege. The 'person-characters' (Bellafante 2009) living *The Hills* life enact its narrative against a backcloth of entitlement. Exclusive luxury resources (palatial accommodation, 'high-end' cars, designer clothes, employment opportunities) are at hand at every turn of these young women's lives. They are so privileged they do not even recognise their entitlements as such. Just as the 'real person' celebrity enjoyed by the cast members – the histrionic magazine gossip, the fashion lines, the press interviews – are absolutely denied in the diegesis of the text, so too is any reference to where the cultural or economic resources come from to support their glamorous lifestyles. While class works through material distinctions to construct the background to the show, it is continually effaced as a category. They are afforded, using soap conventions, the reflexivity to evaluate ordinary 'dilemmas of existence'[4] and they are sufficiently resourced – both culturally and economically – to self-govern in ways which enable them to learn from their mistakes and live successful and potentially interesting lives. Yet its bid to 'level down' these upper-middle-class subjects by rendering them ordinary, and to deny the particular circumstances which provide the resources to access such entitlements, acts to construct these attractive young women universalistically, as though such selves are available to all in a classless society. In this way, *The Hills* perpetuates the neo-liberal notion that individuals have equal access to social mobility. Moreover, I argue that the innovative genrefication of the MTV series around the construction of a monied upper-middle-class world is part of a project to re-legitimate and re-establish middle-class values, as a means to set the standard of how we live and interact in everyday life (hooks 2000).

A Note on Researching and Writing about Third-Wave Reality Television

The Hills belongs to what Annette Hill (2005) has termed 'third-wave' reality television (*c*. 2000), a shift characterised by 'a discernible intensification of the histrionic commentaries in magazines, tabloids and websites with which reality forms are now interdependent' (Piper 2006: 133). There are time-lag consequences for such 'interdependence', which is especially germane in reality formats where 'person-characters' play themselves. Moreover, there is a troubling dimension to the research process. While *The Hills* television series was originally screened on MTV in the US in 2006, I viewed it using DVD box sets, releasing the text from its original historical context. These kinds of issues raise particular questions for the scholar working on reality television: the third-wave reception context is akin to holding wet soap; textual readings about Heidi Montag in Season 1 become slippery and open to change in the light of recent magazine coverage about her extensive plastic surgery.

The difficulty for the media scholar 'is what can be said meaningfully about the exhilarating kaleidoscope of simultaneously accessible material' (Brunsdon 2009: 30). While access to materials is rendered easier, the work of historically sensitive interpretative analysis is rendered far more difficult. However, I want to argue for a reading of *The Hills* as television series without looking through the prism of contemporary gossip, and for the need to focus on the question of representation in what might be thought of as 'old-school' analysis. This is especially pertinent for scholars interested in tracing how class is made for viewers. For example, class may well be made invisible for audience members as they become embroiled in the labyrinth of stories which enter a broader sociality spawned by an extended text. And while old-school analysis which relies on representation is critiqued for ignoring the broader sociality, to refuse to fix the meaning of reality television because the text is constantly on the move would be to further contribute to the invisibility of class.

Living on Camera: Marketing the 'Branded Self'

Hearn (2010) argues that reality television is itself a belt-tightening response to the global economic struggle of broadcast television from the late 1980s. The high fees – especially in North America – of media celebrities, deregulation, audience fragmentation and increased competition across media markets, along with the debilitation of public broadcasting, have all contributed to the lowering of production costs by cutting the labour time required to make television. Capital's will to cut loose its dependence on labour is realised by requiring actors to 'play themselves' at no cost, which circumvents the need for unionised actors and writers. In the process, 'being themselves' on television serves to mythologise 'processes of creative, innovative and virtuosic self-performance' (Hearn 2010: 237) while underscoring television's key role in these practices.

Largely uninterested in making any claim to be documentary,[5] *The Hills* is actually dedicated to making Lauren, Heidi, Audrina and Whitney into promotional mannequins in ways which market the values of consumption. For Hearn, the narrative of the show is beside the point. For her, the 'real story' of *The Hills* is to showcase 'the spectacularised lives' of the girls in a way which is akin to the showroom spaces on display at Ikea: 'The directive to viewers is simple,' she argues, 'insert your "self" here' (Hearn 2010: 238). For Hearn, the notion of the branded self is totally subsumed into the market; yet the branded self is in no sense a neutral project. It is directly tied to the pleasures offered by the unfolding of the narrative in ways which offer gendered lessons in reflexivity that are resourced by class.

How to Be a Good Princess: Gendered Lessons in *The Hills*

One of the tensions in *The Hills* is that it presents its main person-character as something of a paradox. Alice Leppert and June Wilson (2008) argue that *The Hills* mixes 'high' cinematic aesthetics with 'low' soap opera conventions: the former enables Lauren to produce the distance required to make her extraordinary, the latter renders her ordinary enough to garner viewer identification. These features make Lauren the first reality television star, as distinct from 'trashy' celebrity marked in new hierarchies of fame (see Weber in this volume). Leppert and Wilson argue that in this way, Lauren provides what they call 'a profoundly gendered solution to some of the economic limits of previous forms of reality television celebrity' (Leppert and Wilson 2008: 1). This kind of generic melding means that young audiences may aspire to the glamorous consumer lifestyle brand relayed by the show while identifying with Lauren as a 'soap opera heroine'.

The branded 'gender solution' offered in *The Hills* is formulated around the aspiration to be a 'princess'. While being a princess has literal connotations around the idea of royal sovereignty, in *The Hills* it is used as a colloquialism to signify an upper-middle-class or elite version of femininity in contemporary California. It is also configured as an aspiration to be treated like a princess by any potential suitor, who is expected to dote on their desires. The girls are pretty and consistently well-dressed. They have a look of understated glamour, produced by feminine labour, but which it strives to conceal by recourse to a 'natural' modest feminine look. The girls are carefully observant about the proprieties of female dress in ways which tie in with the moral pedagogy of how life ought to be lived by decent young women making their way in life. In this way, the branded feminine self of *The Hills* conveniently extends another arm of capitalist accumulation: the 'feminine' products of clothing, accessories and cosmetics. As Leppert and Wilson assert:

> The products that populate *The Hills* … are not simply discreet entities articulated to or 'placed' in a reality
> television platform to create 'branded content'; they appear as firmly embedded within and already
> belonging to the generalized, glamorous lifestyle represented in the show. (Leppert and Wilson 2008: 15)

Indeed, as I argue later, modest femininity is achieved in *The Hills* by resources and material privilege via the unstated presence of designer boutiques and exclusive labels.

While Helen Piper argues that reality television reminds scholars that there is 'no consensus as to what "it" actually is', she concedes that a key component of the aesthetic of reality television, 'owes much to [...] forty-odd years of *Coronation Street*' (Piper 2006: 134). While *The Hills* is aesthetically a generic hybrid utilising elements of cinematic drama, it can also be said to draw on elements of docusoap. I want to argue that along the viewing journey, the young female audience navigates using soap conventions and melodrama across particular sites – work and relationships – which the cast must negotiate. In their work on UK reality television, Helen Wood and Beverley Skeggs argue that melodrama is 'one of the main dramatic devices for making moral values visible across many domains of social life' (Wood and Skeggs 2008: 183). Fastened on to the aspirational branded self regaled by a version of modest, natural femininity, the show pulls the viewer into the intimate corners of the lives of the cast while weaving its subtle pedagogic agenda.

Lauren operates as the moral centre in *The Hills*. Historically, she brings a good persona from her role in *Laguna Beach*, where the plot is centred around a love triangle between Lauren, her friend Stephen and his sometimes girlfriend Kristin. Lauren's authority is emphasised by her omniscient voiceover at the start of each show, and it is here that the challenges of balancing work, college, friendship and relationships are relayed across an edited history of significant scenes from the previous episode. The subsequent episode visualises the 'working through' of the pleasures and pitfalls of life in LA. In the opening episode from Season 1, 'New City New Drama', Lauren faces her first important assignment as an intern at *Teen Vogue*: to help host a big Hollywood fashion party. She is charged with the responsibility of protecting the VIP seats by the pool of the prestigious Roosevelt Hotel, and the viewer identifies with Lauren's frustration as her friends Heidi, Audrina and their boyfriends compromise her debut assignment by crashing the party and disobediently sitting in the protected area. Lauren is scolded by *Teen Vogue* editor Lisa Love and the final shots focus on the minute detail of Lauren's face: she blows sighs, gesticulating anxiety and disappointment – the cliffhanger is in place as the cameras leave the scene.

Reaction shots, which have a long-standing history within lifestyle and reality television, are part of the visual grammar of melodrama (Moseley 2000; Brunsdon 2003). The lingering pause on the reaction often allows the viewer to adjudicate the morality of 'what is right or wrong' in relation to what Wood and Skeggs have called 'the judgement shot' (Wood and Skeggs 2008: 182). It is Lauren's facial expressions which carry the most weight in *The Hills*; she is the pivotal character position from which the viewer calibrates moral judgments about other cast members. At the start of the next episode, 'A Change of Plans', Lauren reminds the audience about where the narrative has been:

> My first assignment was to work a huge Hollywood party. It was a pretty amazing party, which is probably why Heidi decided to crash it. Heidi did what she wanted, when she wanted and of course she didn't do it quietly, and now I was going to have to answer to my boss …

In the opening scene, it is the day after the party and Lauren and Heidi are mooching about in Heidi's bedroom. This is a humdrum day of ordinary clothes, no make-up and visible pimples. It is the type of day when issues need to be tackled: 'You can't keep crashing in on my work things,' she tells Heidi. In a healthy move to avoid passive/aggressive behaviour, Lauren bravely broaches Heidi's unacceptable behaviour from the previous evening by discursively presenting the fact that she was scolded by *Teen Vogue*. In a bid to give her friend an opportunity to change, Lauren communicates her needs in a clear way.

Lauren is made good through her contrast with Heidi, whose characteristics make her a question-able friend. Heidi's susceptibility to less desirable traits of passivity, self-centredness and poor judgment lead her in Season 2 to get involved with new boyfriend Spencer, in a relationship that ultimately splits the friendship between Lauren and Heidi apart. Recognising Lauren as a person who judges his behav-iour as a 'player' (he attempts to woo Audrina, and invites a group of 'playmates' out to a nightclub – behaviours which fall short of treating Heidi like a princess), Spencer sees Lauren as a difficult force who needs to be managed into isolation. Time and again during the course of Season 2, Heidi is subject to the controlling masculine behaviour of Spencer. Across multiple scenes, Lauren attempts to make Heidi question the move away from her friends towards the conventions of settling down with a boyfriend. Over and again, Lauren questions the mores of 'compulsory heterosexuality' that Spencer insists must be in place for the continuation of the relationship. 'Do you want to live with Spencer?' Lauren asks Heidi. 'I know that you once told me that you would want to date a guy for at least two years before you moved in with him.' In these intimate scenes, we see these young women, who by definition as imma-ture adults have scant life experience, trying to help each other by working through their mistakes. The point is that they have the depth and the educational competence to articulate and manage their feelings, enabling them to reflexively question the positions in which they find themselves. Indeed, as the series progresses, Lauren moves into a position of omnicompetence, as she further develops her moral evaluations of the situations she finds herself in. The text addresses the viewer by illustrating the possi-ble pathways that are available to young women to help them navigate through social space.

While the pedagogical project of *The Hills* might be seen as both morally and ethically admirable, it shouldn't surprise us; indeed, it extends the corporate interests and the branded self marketed in the television series. *The Hills* is preceded by an already established history of American television where moral lessons can be extremely corporately lucrative. Eva Illouz (2007) explores how Oprah's 'failed self' works alongside the show's focus on working through case studies of 'therapeutic biog-raphy' and 'psychic pain and self-help' as a means of building Oprah's identity as a moral entrepre-neur. By continually casting herself as morally rather than financially motivated – she refused to pay her guests and famously stopped her book club in 2002 because she felt uninspired by the books she was reading – she built further financial wealth 'from the trust she generates, which is in turn a direct outcome of the moral framing of her enterprise' (Illouz 2007: 59). I would argue that the moral pedagogical project of *The Hills* precisely extends the corporate interests of the MTV brand.

In these ways, *The Hills* acts to foreground what scholars in gender studies have argued lies at the very centre of feminist politics: the idea that women have a choice. Yet choices are class bound: they can be realised only by those privileged enough to have the cultural and economic resources to support them. *The Hills* is different to the governmental model offered by comparable UK reality formats which represent young women. Programmes such as *Ladette to Lady* (RDF Television, 2005) or *From Asbo Teen to Beauty Queen* (North One Television, 2006) are based on a Pygmalion model, where access to making a feminine self is predicated on the removal of grotesque working-class mores, such as sexual lasciviousness, spitting or swearing, and on rebuilding a feminine self through modes of feminine bodily deportment, elocutioned speech and middle-class manners (see Walkerdine in this volume). Wood and Skeggs (2008) argue that at the heart of these programmes is a refusal to sociologically contextualise working-class subjects, so that when these subjects are placed in situations and are unable to cope, their failure – the result of bad choices, vulgar taste or 'life lived at the surface' – is signposted as individual failure where the working class are represented as refusing to make the responsible moves required for self-governance. In *The Hills*, we see learning modes which are similarly insufficiently contextualised as the programme draws on textual techniques which work to disavow the class location of the cast members. So that these young, wealthy white women who are seen to be living (but never struggling), learning (yet never having to cope) and ultimately spiralling to success through the development of self-reflexivity are also individualised within the context of a class milieu which is portrayed as a norm. In this way, both UK and US reality programmes are two halves of the same coin: both uphold neo-liberal myths about the mobility of the 'individual' while effacing reference to structural inequalities. It is to the class dimension of *The Hills* that I would now like to turn.

The Thing That Does Not Speak Its Name: Class in *The Hills*

In class terms, *The Hills* is paradoxical. On the one hand, it is precisely about class entitlement and aspiration: upper middle classness is felt and practised by the cast and they have seamless and unbridled access to luxury assets and resources. On the other, *The Hills* belongs to a brand of American reality television which uses textual strategies which work to deny the existence of class.

From a UK standpoint, there has been a long-held anecdotal conception that the US is a classless society. It would seem that a notion of America as classless and as a nation which offers almost unbounded class mobility to its citizens is also shared by American people,[6] as the blurb on the back of a journalistic collection of essays below testifies:

> We Americans have long thought of ourselves as unburdened by class distinctions. We have no hereditary aristocracy or landed gentry, and even the poorest among us feel that they can become rich through education, hard work or sheer gumption. (Back cover of *Class Matters* by correspondents of *The New York Times* 2005)

Indeed, this conception also finds some support in academic quarters. Kingston (2000) argues that when Americans were asked to complete a survey, the results demonstrate a weak link between objective and subjective class positions, with most respondents – including the working class – identifying broadly with the middle class. Similarly, Keller states that the US is 'a country where the overwhelming majority identify themselves as "middle-class"' (Keller 2005: ix). This kind of data seems to imply that class has become less significant; indeed it leads Kingston (2000) to argue that America is a classless society. Yet, class in the West is becoming more not less significant for those at the extreme ends of the social scale. 'Classlessness' is a social myth used to deny the inequalities which structural class relations actively produce. It is the myth that supports the idea that the self or individual floats free of class. As Skeggs reminds us, when people think of the term 'self', it is regarded as a neutral concept, when in fact the self is always a classed concept. She goes on, 'denial of the class-based nature of the self is continually produced and authorised, thereby making, constituting and producing difference and inequality, not challenging it' (Skeggs 2004: 134). Classlessness as a category is a method by which the resources and techniques needed to produce privileged, classed selves is masked. *The Hills* serves to re-produce these popularly held conceptions by denying the class-based nature of the idea of the branded self.

Paradoxically, one can be in no doubt that the cast members of *The Hills* are represented as occupying the upper-middle-class echelons of California society. Lauren and her friends are essentially narcissistic. They each share a *raison d'être*: to begin a biography of a successful self. As the lyrics by Natasha Beddingfield proclaimed over the opening credits: 'put yourself in words unspoken/live your life with arms wide open/today is where your book begins/the rest is still unwritten'. Working as interns in the glamorous media and culture industries in LA, these selves are made in a context of extraordinary privilege. The social mores and practices of the upper middle class run through the cast like Brighton rock.[7] Lauren, Heidi, Audrina and Whitney have an aversion to servile forms of labour, even though their internships are 'entry level' (Leppert and Wilson 2008): for example, the camera zooms in on Heidi's sullen face when she is asked to stuff letters into envelopes at Bolthouse Productions. Similarly, the labour required to make a feminine self is passed on to hairdressers and beauticians: 'Are you getting your nails done too, Heids?' remarks Lauren as they sit talking while getting a blow dry in preparation for Heidi's birthday party. 'Of course,' replies Heidi, 'I'm not lifting a hand. I'm an American Princess.' Moreover, Lauren and her friends have seamless access to all the assets and resources they could ever want. They drive luxury cars and 4x4s, they rent well-appointed apartments in Hollywood, they shop for clothes in expensive boutiques, they freely consume in the most desirable cafés, bars and clubs, and they work in dream positions in the glamorous media and culture industries. But what is shockingly noticeable, especially for a British audience, is that just as the first viewing of the aesthetic style of *The Hills* looks strangely jarring, there is absolutely no reference in the text's diegesis either to the idea that it is somehow worthy of note that such lavish resources are available to these young people, or any reference to where such resources come from. Objects are simply there to be utilised: the BMW that Spencer drives, or the Chanel handbag that sits on Lauren's shoulder, or the supply of money required to finance *The Hills* lifestyle are simply entitlements that are never reflexively signposted. In similar vein, the semi-scripted dialogue between the person-characters never strays into a discussion of class background – neither parental occupation nor financial support is ever talked about. In these ways, class privilege is disavowed.

It is precisely this textual strategy which makes any attempt to exactly locate the class faction of its person-characters quite difficult. Michelle Lamont's (1992) empirical work on the differences between the French and American upper middle class is germane here. Lamont asked managers, professionals and businessmen about the symbolic boundaries used to define their own identities and their relationship with others regarding questions about moral character. She found that socio-economic categories were 'considerably more salient in America than they are in France' (Lamont 1992: 64). The American men were attracted to success, money was central to their sense of 'ability and desirability', and consumer goods acted as 'indices of success' (ibid.). Their French counterparts were more interested in distinguishing themselves through culture and moral boundaries. Interestingly, Lamont also found that American men were keen to disclaim their elite statuses by describing themselves as, '"ordinary Joes", despite their sometimes extraordinary professional power and success' (Lamont 1992: 79). Lamont's work offers insight into the paradoxical sense in which people in the US aspire to material wealth, while harbouring a weak identification with a corresponding upper-middle-class identity. What writers on class in the US (Kingston 2000; Keller 2005) seem to concur on is that American people are more comfortable with a more amorphous, all-embracing middle class, a feature which may go some way to explaining why the textual world of The Hills is represented as materially privileged, while eschewing key measuring devices for precisely identifying class location. What can be safely claimed is that The Hills serves a function as 'advertainment'; it showcases an aestheticised aspirational lifestyle through the use of hip cultural goods. Its milieu would seem to be one which is constructed from the bricolage of consumerism – a kind of class which can be bought and which might therefore be accessible to all. Most identifiable is the money required to support the consumerist branded objects and aesthetics of The Hills. The effect is one in which a sealed-off world of upper-middle-class entitlement – which is never spoken of and where there is no friction with others from other class fractions – is simply delivered up as the 'norm', where the young female cast are free to make the appropriate (invisibly classed) choices that any 'decent' person might make.

Why does class both exist and simultaneously disappear in texts like The Hills? Mike Savage (2003) argues that new kinds of contemporary class relations make class no less significant, but increasingly more difficult to trace. Historically in the UK, for example, for much of the twentieth century the middle and working classes were clearly demarcated and visibly identifiable by powerful oppositions around cultural tastes, financial differences and living space. By contrast in the late twentieth century, factors such as the decline of trade unions and the labour movement and modes of deindustrialisation meant that the working class had ceased to be a visible key presence in Britain. The middle class then acted to fill the remaining sociocultural void, becoming in the process, 'the "particular universal class" … around which an increasing range of practices are regarded as universally "normal", "good" and "appropriate"' (Savage 2003: 536). Savage argues that this had a radical impact on British politics and recent social theory (Giddens 1991), where class friction is explained away by individualising identities. Those who concur with unacknowledged middle-class values are regarded as normal, while the rest are admonished as individual failures. While Savage describes social change in the UK, the unmentioned universality of middle-class values he outlines is an apt description of the class world evoked in programmes like The Hills.

Yet one thing is certain: America, like the UK, is not classless. Fiona Devine found that middle-class Americans do draw on the language of class: they use the notion of 'being' a class and people's life histories were 'told through the lens of class' (Devine 2004: 142), though they were often uncomfortable doing so. Moreover, recent statistics about the 'regressive redistribution' (Savage and Williams 2009: 1) of wealth and resources in contemporary society show that class is more significant than ever for understanding the social dynamics of the West. As Savage and Williams argue:

> By any account, the last twenty years of the 20th century have seen the most rapid and dramatic shift of income, assets and resources in favour of the very rich that has ever taken place in human history.
> (Savage and Williams 2009: 1)

The 'super-rich' have grown in 'old' capitalist nations like the US and the UK, where neo-liberalism has been eagerly adopted (Savage and Williams 2009: 1). Johnston (2005: 182) notes that the top 0.1 per cent of income earners in the US took home an average of $3 million per year in 2002; in the UK, the top 1–5 per cent of income earners have seen their salaries double since the 1980s, while in both the UK and the US, income inequality has almost returned to prewar standards (Savage and Williams 2009: 1).

One of the key causal factors in these processes in the last thirty years is financialisation, a term which Savage and Williams use to describe the innovation and mobility of contemporary capitalism. New financial elites, driven by profit-sharing incentives, act as highly paid intermediaries in corporate finance and banking, playing a key role in global financial centres. This new group has been responsible for 'innovation in the wholesale financial markets and in the mass consumption of retail financial services' (Savage and Williams 2009: 10), which has afforded them new markets and increased influence at industry and household level. It is now axiomatic that finance makes money and that financialisation acts to increase elite financial intermediaries. Savage and Williams argue that 'money itself' needs to be seen as a 'key social device and technology' (ibid.: 9), because those who manage money are finding a voice as important socio-political actors in wider fields of power. What these kinds of statistics and processes show is that the rich have retreated to live within increasingly privileged worlds: small wonder, then, that the lifestyle signifiers of the super-rich form the backcloth to a whole tranche of reality television texts besides *The Hills*, such as, to name but a few: *My Super Sweet Sixteen* (MTV, 2005–), *Teen Cribs* (MTV, 2010–) and *Keeping up with the Kardashians* (Bunim-Murray Productions, 2007–).

Conclusion

The enthusiastic promotion of neo-liberal values in both the US and the UK since the early 1980s must go some way to explaining the successful export of these reality television formats. In a world of glamour and consumerism, *The Hills* is like a modern fairytale, showcasing through a series of learning tableaux what it means to be a contemporary Californian good 'princess'. Along the journey, the person-characters display a distinct brand of femininity which proffers particular pleasures for female viewers: they cultivate a modest, natural and well-dressed look as they move through the hip social space of Hollywood. Viewers witness how Lauren, negotiating work and relationships, acquires self-reflexivity: she makes mistakes, weighs them up and is an active agent in constructing a bright future. These narratives, which weave a subtle moral pedagogic agenda while tracing the gendered pleasures associated with being a princess, contribute to the occlusion of class. Sociological literature on the individual in post-industrial society (Giddens 1991) argues that the shift to the privatised self weakens the link to structural inequalities, making both gender and class redundant concepts in late modernity. Yet it is precisely the entitlement of occupying a privileged class location which enables the self-reflexivity and choice enjoyed by the young female cast. In neo-liberal political discourse, class differences appear to melt away, leaving individualised identities to continuously reinvent themselves in new social circumstances. At the centre of neo-liberalism is the self-governing, self-branding entrepreneurial subject, which 'is made in the image of the middle-class' (Walkerdine 2003: 239). In this way, *The Hills* perfectly acculturates neo-liberal values: class as a demarcated category is heavily repressed, as the spectacular promotional branded selves of *The Hills* spiral to success. Mike Savage argues that 'the innocence, the kind of unacknowledged normality of the middle class needs to be carefully unpicked and exposed' (Savage 2003: 537). It may, he cautions, require a kind of 'forensic, detective work, which involves tracing the print of class in areas where it is faintly written' (ibid.: 536–7). The worry, even for those of us interested in the complexities of audience engagements (Wood and Taylor 2008), is that young viewers just might not quite be able to trace the thing in *The Hills* that does not speak its name.

Notes

1. As I show later, when placed in a US context, the girls could arguably be identified as either upper middle class or as an elite 'over' class, which may be hard to measure sociologically. For that reason, I classify the cast of *The Hills* as upper middle class.

2. Beverley Skeggs finds that glamour serves a particular function for the working-class women of her study in *Formations of Class and Gender* (1997).

3. *The Hills*' product synergy is a phenomenon. For example, the show embeds its corporate partnerships with companies like Bolthouse Productions and *Teen Vogue* into the narrative by locating Lauren and her friends as employees within them. It also labels all its on-screen locations, so that viewers are given a tour guide to mimic the experience. The women have used *The Hills* as a launch pad to promote their celebrity self-brands: Lauren, Heidi and Whitney have personal fashion lines, Whitney has her own MTV reality show *The City* (MTV, 2009–), and so on.

4. Wood and Skeggs (2004) use this term to describe how the white working class were positioned by UK reality television in the early 2000s. Such dilemmas are rather different for the cast in *The Hills*.

5. For interesting discussions of the production of *The Hills*, see Schlotterbeck (2009) and Hearn (2010).

6. Devine documents how both the US and the UK enjoyed 'high rates of absolute social mobility in the twentieth century' (Devine 2004: 147). However, social mobility in the US is currently said to be in decline; see Keller (2005).

7. My ethnographic work on gardening and taste in the UK revealed classed practices (Taylor, 2008).

Bibliography

Altman, R. (1999) *Film/Genre* (Berkeley, CA: University of California Press).

Bellafante, G. (2009) 'West Coast fashionista takes on Manhattan, Manolos in tow', *The New York Times* [online]. Available at: <http://www.nytimes.com/2009/01/05/arts/television/05city.html> accessed 22 August 2010.

Brunsdon, C. (2003) 'Lifestyling Britain: The 8–9 Slot on British Television', *International Journal of Cultural Studies*, 4(1): 29–62.

———— (2009) 'Television Criticism and the Transformation of the Archive', *Television and New Media*, 10(1): 29–30.

Correspondents of *The New York Times* (2005) *Class Matters* (New York: Times Books).

Deery, J. (2004) 'Reality TV as Advertainment', *Popular Communication*, 2(1): 1–20.

Devine, F. (2004) 'Middle-Class Identities in the United States', in F. Devine *et al.* (eds), *Rethinking Class: Culture, Identities and Lifestyles* (Basingstoke, Hants.: Palgrave Macmillan).

Gay, J. (2008) 'Are they for real?!', *Rolling Stone*, 15 May, pp. 40–8.

Giddens, A. (1991) *Modernity and Self-Identity: Self and Society in the Late Modern Age* (Cambridge: Polity).

Hearn, A. (2008) 'Variations on the Branded Self: Theme, Invention, Improvisation and Inventory', in D. Hesmondhalgh and J. Toynbee (eds), *The Media and Social Theory* (London: Routledge), pp. 194–210.

——— (2010) '"Lightening in a bottle": Reality Television, *The Hills*, and the Limits of the Immaterial Labour Thesis', in L. Baruh and J. Hoon Park (eds), *Reel Politics: Reality Television as a Platform for Political Discourse* (Cambridge: Cambridge Scholars Press), pp. 232–49.

Hill, A. (2005) *Reality TV – Audiences and Popular Factual Television* (Abingdon, Oxon.: Routledge).

hooks, b. (2000) *Where We Stand: Class Matters* (London: Routledge).

Illouz, E. (2007) *Oprah Winfrey and the Glamour of Misery: An Essay on Popular Culture* (New York: Columbia University Press).

Johnston, D. C. (2005) 'Richest are leaving even the rich far behind', in Correspondents of *The New York Times*, *Class Matters*.

Keller, B. (2005) 'Introduction', in Correspondents of *The New York Times*, *Class Matters*.

Kingston, P. W. (2000) *The Classless Society* (Stanford CA: Stanford University Press).

Lamont, M. (1992) *Money, Morals, and Manners: The Culture of the French and the American Upper-Middle Class* (Chicago: University of Chicago Press).

Leppert, J. and A. Wilson (2008) 'Living *The Hills* Life: Lauren Conrad as Reality Star, Soap Opera Heroine, and Brand', *Genders Online Journal*, 48. Available at: <http://www.genders.org/g48/g48_leppertwilson.html> accessed 23 August 2009.

McRobbie, A. (2004) Notes on *'What Not to Wear'* and Post-Feminist Symbolic Violence', *Sociological Review*, 52(2): 97–109.

Moseley, R. (2000) 'Makeover Takeover on British Television', *Screen*, 41(3): 299–314.

Piper, H. (2006) 'Understanding Reality Television', *Screen*, 47(1): 133–8.

Rochlin, M. (2005) 'An MTV coming of age that went far on charm', *The New York Times* [online]. Available at: <http://www.nytimes.com/2005/08/30/arts/television/30lagu.html> accessed 21 April 2008.

Savage, M. (2003) 'A New Class Paradigm?', *British Journal of Sociology of Education*, 24(4): 535–41.

Savage, M. and K. Williams (eds) (2009) *Remembering Elites* (Oxford: Blackwell).

Schlotterbeck, J. (2009) 'What Happens When Real People Start Getting Cinematic: *Laguna Beach* and Contemporary TV Aesthetics', *Scope* [online], 12. Available at: <http://www. scope.nottingham.ac.uk/article.php?issue=12&=1081> accessed 24 September 2009.

Skeggs, B. (1997) *Formations of Class and Gender: Becoming Respectable* (London: Sage).

——— (2004) *Class, Self, Culture* (London: Routledge).

Taylor, L. (2005) '"It was beautiful before you changed it all": Class and the Transformative Aesthetics of the Garden Lifestyle Media', in D. Bell and J. Hollows (eds), *Ordinary Lifestyles: Popular Media, Consumption and Taste* (Maidenhead, Berks.: Open University Press), pp. 113–27.

——— (2008) *A Taste for Gardening: Classed and Gendered Practices* (Aldershot, Hants.: Ashgate).

Walkerdine, V. (2003) 'Reclassifying Upward Mobility: Femininity and the Neo-Liberal Subject', *Gender and Education*, 15(3): 237–48.

Wood, H. and B. Skeggs (2004) 'Notes on Ethical Scenarios of Self on British Reality TV', *Feminist Media Studies*, 4(2): 205–7.

———— (2008) 'Spectacular Morality: "Reality" Television, Individualisation and the Remaking of the Working Class', in D. Hesmondhalgh and J. Toynbee (eds), *The Media and Social Theory* (London: Routledge), pp. 177–93.

Wood, H. and L. Taylor (2008) 'Feeling Sentimental about Television and Audiences', *Cinema Journal*, 47(3): 144–51.

9/Gareth Palmer

Organic Branding: The Self, Advertising and Life-Experience Formats

Just like any other artificially imaged commodity, then, the resultant construct – a persona constructed for public consumption – is marked by the transformative effects of the promotional supplement. The outcome … is a self which continually produces itself for competitive circulation: an enacted projection. (Wernick cited in McFall 2006: 42)

Now you look like you participate in modern society. (*WNTW*, Season 7 [US])

In 'The New You' (Palmer 2004), I argued that lifestyle television formats could be understood as invitations to change the self aided by experts as a blend of empowerment and public service. My aim here is to develop this work by looking more specifically at the ways in which life-experience formats articulate a developing trend in consumer culture, offering an invitation to brand the self. To illustrate this I will consider the makeover programmes *10 Years Younger* (2003–) and *What Not to Wear* (2001–) (hereafter *10YY* and *WNTW*, respectively). These formats offer often graphic experiences which work inasmuch as the transformations achieved in skin, body and character serve to prove the value of developing an ever more pliable self. *WNTW* and *10YY* prove the value of the process of branding by promoting a supposedly positive self-transformation. While the 'realistic' components of the shows – non-scripted documentary elements and to-camera moments given over to the participants – give the impression of autonomy and choice, the structure of the programmes is powered by the dominance of brand objectives and renders the individual as little more than a dramatic cog in the consumerist machine.

I begin by defining brands and branding as increasingly important forces in contemporary life. I then consider branding as a force within television at both macro and micro levels. I follow this by looking at the close stylistic links between reality lifestyle programming and advertising. The similarities between these two formerly discrete programming strands are notable and instructive. Both *WNTW* and *10YY* take the promise of branding to the next level by making it appear organic and floating free of the commercial base that is obvious in advertising. I substantiate this claim by offering a close analysis of *WNTW* and *10YY* and in particular their relationship to gender and class. I will suggest that both formats offer branded solutions to working-class individuals – who historically have not had the cultural capital or the leisure time to work on the incited project of the self.

Organic Branding

Brands first developed as a solution to the problem of choice. In a world in which products are still often indistinguishable, brands sell difference with a guarantee of regularity and predictability in a world of potentially confusing choice. Myers (1999) maintains that brand identity is produced by investing in all elements of the marketing mix including Product, Promotion, Price and Placement. Past, Position, Practices and Paradigms can be added to this list – all of which share the same basic function of attaching meaning to what are otherwise characterless products. Therefore, a brand is not just a named product, service or trademark. Customers or users develop relationships with brands, which in turn become part of their value. A brand then comes to mean a set of beliefs and expectations held by the customer about goods or services sold under the trademark: 'Brands have strong emotional appeal because they are signs standing for ideas that have great emotional appeal [...] they are perceived subconsciously as a means for attaining things that are beyond our reach (Danesi 2006: 137). As information streams multiply and more data is generated, the most advanced brands can be thought of as organisms that seem to be self-modifying and have memory. As a result, Celia Lury has suggested that the brand is not fixed in time but has a fluid mode, 'it is a platform for the patterning of activity, a mode of organizing activities in time and space – it implicates social relations [...] it is an object of possibility' (Lury 2004: 1).

The brand has gained greater significance in our time as it takes over work previously undertaken by agencies of the state. For example, the shift from national health systems to privatised medical solutions could only have been accomplished because consumers were prepared to make new investments in brands whose commercial bases are hidden in rhetorics of concern. Allied to this is the rise of the therapeutic ethos. The increasing amount of media showcasing emotional vulnerability is valuable for the caring brands. For example, Sears and Disney became involved in *Extreme Makeover: Home Edition* (2003). The programme gives people who have experienced particular hardships, often through the loss of relatives and spouses, a spectacular home and extras like a college education or a new business. This was notoriously visible in New Orleans in the aftermath of Hurricane Katrina, as the brands reaped value through association.[1]

While broadcast regulators consider the possibility of increased sponsorship and product placement, the move into programming might be seen as a consequence of the shared rationale of advertisers and producers to reach consumers. Lifestyle-programming environments are stimulating showcases for better ways of living in which the physical products – be they clothes or shoes or conditioners – are secondary to the foregrounding of the branded self in service to an idea of malleability. What prevents this from being too threatening a commercial message is the style of programming, which shows contestants engaging in a playful embrace, or even gesturing towards a refusal of the brand, which gets incorporated into the drama.

Brands play a crucial role in contemporary life as sign-values that have to be maintained, because the source of their power for consumers is belief in their core meanings as a safe place for (self) investment. The wearing of a certain T-shirt or the use of a particular bag is understood by others as bestowing meaning on the wearer. But this is the most obvious way the brand actualises itself –

in products – as the lingua franca of consumerism. To choose a brand is to make an investment which must be visible to others. A branded self is calculable and as such inclined to measure itself, indeed to find measurement the equivalent of understanding. This, then, is a self without depth, one happily discounting the psycho-dynamic depth models of old in celebration of a surface change that works because everyone else can see that it does. The brand shows us that to be *seen* to be OK *is* to be OK.

Brands represent solutions to our culture's uncertainties. The individual we see submitting to the processes of branding on screen is a model for the ideal self acquiescing to the entreaties of a culture fixated on the potential of change. We see this process enacted in advertising campaigns for the British businesses Abbey and B&Q, in which individuals do the work of selling the goods from their position as branded employees. This is the brand instantiating itself – humans humanise the brand. This style of brand recommendation would only be possible in a promotional culture where it is understood that brands have power (Moor 2007).

The malleability of selves is now the stuff of popular debate. While identity politics holds out the promise of empowerment, powerful commercial forces offer us the power to redefine ourselves (through surgery etc.) as our vital elements become opportunities for branding. Nikolas Rose (2007) writes of how we are offered new ways of thinking about the body via genetic engineering and other technologies. Our new vulnerability before a world of risk is contained and harmonised by brands that rescue and remould us. Lifestyle formats such as *WNTW* and *10YY* are only possible because promotional culture has helped fashion a structure of feeling that has enabled brands to speak directly to the human experience. In *WNTW* and *10YY*, the subject/participant is the human product – it is (usually) she who is seen working (i) for their own emerging guided identity, (ii) in and for the brand, (iii) for the production company and advertisers who reap benefits from their labour, (iv) to please those others who submitted the subject for treatment in the first place. The fact that this 'individual' style is to be found in any high street matters less than the inevitability of subjectivity mediated through brand consumption.

Television and the Brand

International reality television formats become established by proving their value both as products (for the media marketplace) and as processes (that help fashion people for the wider marketplace): there is a symbiotic relationship between the two. Their success as TV brands stems from their artful mixing of advertising technique and the persuasiveness of the contestants' performances. The result is all the more convincing, because it calls forth levels of emotional investment.

The television industry is constantly in the process of marketing itself, and its particular virtues as a medium (liveness, immediacy and reflexivity) mean that it can embed branding and enliven it in ways few other media can. Brands represent signposts for viewers and a successful brand incorporates comfort, originality and awareness of its fit in the broader media environment. This is for the simple reason that in a commercial environment, each programme has to communicate the brand values of the channel (Eastman 2000: 128). It is the job of commissioning editors and channel bosses to see that each of the programmes broadcasting under its auspices 'speaks' the brand in a way that underlines it and extends it. Thus, Fox News represents the core identity of the station, while broadcasting *The Simpsons* illustrates a brand-personality that is able to laugh at itself. In the UK (in America on TLC), *WNTW* represents an interesting variant on the public service imperative core to the BBC's brand identity. The relationship of the programme to the station is important and does not come about by chance.

If it is sufficiently developed, a brand can become a supple mechanism able to monitor itself and effect changes at high speed. Thus, while the *Big Brother* scandal in 2007 about the racist taunting of Shilpa Shetty may have made the news headlines from a commercial perspective (see Tolson in this collection), the problem was one of how a reaction could be calculated that did not harm Channel 4's brand. In one example of a swift response, Carphone Warehouse pulled its sponsorship because they did not like the changed 'brand environment'. This was a telling example of a brand in crisis and points ahead to the dilemma of lifestyle television where a brand's survival value is played out in the reactions of participants. When the latter behave in unpredictable ways, they go beyond the control of brand managers, which is the unspoken role adopted by producers. The business of maintaining the brand identity that will distinguish their show from others becomes a matter of professional survival.

Brands travel. In importing new formats, lessons can be learned from the past. Economies can be made by knowing how the model operates without much testing. Furthermore, the proof that a format has worked elsewhere may be comforting for advertisers in other countries. Demographic analysis showing how a format has operated with target groups in its country of origin may sweeten the pill for those advertisers and sponsors cautious to invest in an imported version. All of these conditions make for a very conservative approach to successful formats (Moran 2005).

Reality television brands are at the forefront of those forms advocating a new orientation to the self achieved through branded goods. For example, *You Are What You Eat* (2004) articulates the shifting emphasis from the role of the state in social care to the individual's responsibility for his or herself (Ouellette and Hay 2008). The ingestion of what turn out to be branded foods is a telling illustration of branding which literally, if we ingest, reconfigures us.

Alison Hearn wrote that 'reality television programs are, for the most part, stories about television itself, its modes of production, its commercial and promotional logic, its specific privations and rigour and its mechanisms for celebrity-making and work' (Hearn 2009: 165). It may be useful to extend this and consider how certain lifestyle formats reveal the *mechanisms* of branding the self. They reveal how much labour goes into looking good, not to shock us with the amount of labour necessary, but to celebrate the effort. Mark Andrejevic (2004) claims that some reality TV formats represent a kind of unpaid labour. Not only are production costs kept low, but we are shown models of working on the self and become involved in delivering intimate knowledge of ourselves to be used by the market. Participants are doing the work of being watched and they go through the stages of submission, participation and acceptance. Such labour showcases the participation of consumers in the rationalisation of their own consumption, which is promoted in the lifestyle experience as 'empowerment' but which is in service to the programme-brand. As Susan Bordo wrote in

reference to dietary regimes: 'These are practices which train the female body in docility and obe-
dience to cultural demands while at the same time being "experienced" in terms of power and control' (Bordo 1993: 192).

The reflexivity of reality television, the apparent exposure of its processes, is also illustrative of the
way in which the brand can reflect on itself and make adjustments so that potential users can feel more
comfortable within its boundaries. Thus, lifestyle-experience formats can be read as brands in action.

Life-experience formats from *Wife Swap* (2004) to *Ladette to Lady* (2005) to *The Biggest Loser*
(2004) operate in a very regular and disciplined way. Although on the surface they appear stylistically related to the random fragments of reality television's immediacy, nothing is left to chance.
The precise nature of each segment and the way in which, however wild and whacky the contestants might be, these segments follow careful, repeated sequestration makes it evident that the programme is a machine-like process and the individuals within it merely interchangeable elements.
In each format, the subject is placed into the machinery before surrendering to the panoply of
experts arraigned to engineer the necessary changes which serve the brand.

The surrender of the individual is a precondition of treatment and the pliable flexibility of the
self is made evident at each step. By adhering to the format, the point is drummed home that however truculent or even class-bound the individual, change can happen and, in all cases, is much appre-
ciated. The drama of life-experience formats lies in the fact that the audience knows the lifestyle
brand and can safely predict the sort of work that it will do. The brand strategies that the show is
known for (strict discipline, cruel-but-fair judges, hygienic policing, etc.) will inform television participants' and viewers' expectations.

Each episode is also about brand management inasmuch as every personal interaction, every
sign of an unruly personality, threatens to destabilise the brand and its transformative power. But just
like the happy ending promised by mainstream entertainment, we know the brand will always win
in the end. What is significant for our purpose is that what is at stake here is a self, a self that has
trusted the brand to develop it and has surrendered to its processes. Casting is significant inasmuch
as what we are privy to are the ways the old/before self emerges only via its immersion into the
brand's processes. The individual becomes 'empowered' not for an autonomous self but for one
designed by the brand's processes, in which we celebrate surrender to the bourgeois normative
(Palmer 2004) and to the belief that submitting oneself to selling oneself is actually good and proper.

Lifestyle Experiences and Advertising – Form and Style

When Kellner (1995: 251) wrote that advertising 'magically offers self-transformation and a new
identity, associating changes in consumer behaviour, fashion and appearance with metamorphosis
into a new person', he might have been describing lifestyle formats. What I want to illustrate here
are the close formal and stylistic connections between *10YY, WNTW* and the techniques and methods of persuasion adopted by the advertising industry. I will go through these techniques and compare them to the shows, paying particular attention to the way representations of class, physicality
and gender work within them. At the core of both programmes is this notion that 'our bodies have

become ourselves, become central to our expectations, hopes, our individual and collective identities, and our biological responsibilities in this emergent form of life' (Rose 2007: 105).

Interiority is represented on lifestyle television formats by a focus on the body. The frequent declaration from participants on both *10YY* and *WNTW* is that they now, for the first time, 'feel truly themselves'. As Kathy Davis' research on women who had plastic surgery has revealed: 'They had cosmetic surgery because they did not feel at home in their bodies; their bodies did not fit their sense of who they were. Cosmetic surgery was an intervention in identity' (Davis 1999: 455).

The principal target of these programmes is the female body. Although men have featured in some of these shows, they are for the most part aimed at women. As we have seen, at the crux of such presentations is the notion of choice, but as Cronin points out, 'Consumerism paradoxically offers women the opportunity to act in consuming goods and image while framing these actions in terms which deny any specificity of female identity' (Cronin 2000: 4).

Lifestyle formats traditionally define the working class by their physicality and this, in the flashy, aggressive style of the formats, means that they have to be seen to eat to excess/often/in a haphazard way, etc. (Wood and Skeggs 2008). Thus, the camera closes in on detail, mastications are heard, or scenes of excess are lingered upon. The working-class participant is seen to take pleasure in physicality, and the pleasures of excess and disorder are signed in close-fitting clothes or an indelicate mixing of colours (McRobbie 2004; Taylor 2005; Palmer 2004). All of this is joyfully contrasted with the finished and measured performance of middle-class presenters. Makeovers work to eliminate signs of working class-ness from female bodies represented through ignorance, decay or neglect, and in the 'process a white middle-class subjectivity is privileged ... middle-class style codes (are) unmarked by an excess of indicators of race or ethnicity' (Weber 2009: 128–9).

In both British and American versions of the shows, working class-ness is presented as something bad to be escaped from:

> Class based messages and their implications about cultural legitimacy are rampant on US-based makeover
> television yet these messages are generally tacitly uttered only barely obscuring the makeovers' investment
> in a deeper tie between normativity, gender and socioeconomic status. (Weber 2009: 139)

In order to persuade viewers of the merits of change, it makes sense to utilise the most effective techniques. Both *WNTW* and *10YY* can be read as forms of extended advertising that are effective because they borrow precisely the model adopted by the advertising industry of the self as a problem to be solved. What *WNTW* and *10YY* offer is what all women should experience – a youthful appeal to others.

Overt messages about the failings of a class might offend, but the skill of lifestyle media producers is to evoke the individual's background through visual and audio signifiers in ways that entertain as well as underscoring difference. The key verb is to transcend. To rise above one's station serves both to celebrate individuality and to disprove the value of class affiliation or socio-economic positioning. When a contestant in *WNTW* complains that a dress costs the same as six weeks' worth of electricity, she is listened to with apparent concern before being directed to the market. The message is that authenticity is not to be found in one's class position (which is a restrictive force holding one back in shackles) but in realising oneself in the real world of the market coded as 'putting myself first' or 'giving myself permission'. This, in the rhetoric of television, is a dream anyone can aspire to. Ideally we are all to be entrepreneurs of the self (Miller and Rose 2008).

How then do WNTW and 10YY borrow advertising strategies to generate persuasive strategies for self-transformation? The style, techniques and procedures of the advertising industry have a long history that has involved integrating extensive psychological research. These insights have come at considerable cost, but they can and have been utilised by lifestyle producers to maximum effect in order to mobilise consumers and sell belonging by integrating people into brands and brand-stories. The core baseline of advertising is to present problems – often to invent them – and then offer solutions. But unlike advertising, which is openly in the business of selling a specific product or service, the programmes discussed here showcase the fragility of real people to demonstrate how a self can be changed. The programmes represent the sound economic sense of advertisers and programme-makers moving in the same direction. The result is formats that integrate people as elements in commercial stories in which no hope goes unrealised, in which consumerism is always the answer.

(i) Before and After

Perhaps the defining trope of the makeover is the 'before and after' (Moseley 2000). Both WNTW and 10YY start with a 'before' and the narrative is designed to get us to the hoped-for 'after'. The American version of WNTW even begins with a sequence in which presenters Stacy and Clinton transform people with a mere touch. In both formats, the 'before' is a self defined by neglect. In one edition of WNTW, the contestant spoke tearfully of profound 'body issues' in a manner more reminiscent of a sober investigation, yet this moment offers only emotional colour rather than a pause for thought. The participants are presented as hapless victims with whom we are encouraged to identify.

At the beginning and end of both WNTW and 10YY, the individual is subjected to the gaze – in the 'before', they have to remain objective, to take a cold scientific view of the material (self) to be changed in the eyes of the other. For example, in an American edition of 10YY, 'Norma Jean' is placed in a Perspex box to endure the open humiliation of public reckoning in the hope of reformation. Her past is of value only inasmuch as she proves worthy of change. It is of no interest to the brand beyond this: the future potential of the individual is what matters, in the words of Stacey and Clinton, 'to realise her net value in the marketplace'.

(ii) Presenters

WNTW and 10YY both have narrators whom we have come to identify with the brand. Nicki Hambleton-Jones (10YY) and Trinny and Susannah/Stacy and Clinton/ (WNTW UK, WNTW US) are representative of the brand and what it can do. Their weekly presence endures for the brand and as such they become guarantors of quality – more than spokespeople, they are the living representations of value that exceed the temporary promise of an advertisement. Indeed, Trinny and

Susannah have become very successful brands for themselves and other commercial organisations. In advertisements, the presenter/spokesperson often serves as a magical helpful friend who has already learned the values of the product. In *WNTW* and *10YY*, the presenters can act in ways that go beyond the expectations of everyday advice and civil interaction – like ripping up clothes and speaking in a confrontational fashion. This merely exaggerates the latent drive for change in advertising. The presenters are those who have the cultural capital and the education to gracefully craft their own project of the self. They are the 'finished' product who can also speak to the ongoing project as they discuss themselves, their own failings and how they have overcome their 'skinny legs', for example, giving them the authority from which they offer advice.

It is important also to note the tone of the narrators. *WNTW* echoes the fabled bitchiness of the fashion industry with its theatrical gestures, and in so doing calls to mind so much advertising (McRobbie 2004). *10YY* features narrators who comment acidly, humiliating and shaming the participants, speaking with dramatic emphasis, again recalling the work that narrators do in advertising to catch the drifting viewers. But they also do this through moving between acid judgment and intimations of care and familiarity. They can ask 'How Do You Feel?' because feeling is important evidence for brand-effect. Brenda Weber (2009) calls this 'affective domination' in makeover programmes, where care must come before pedagogy.

Both *WNTW* and *10YY* offer middle-class conceptions of femininity dependent upon a contrast between the presenters and the contestants. In place of overt sexuality, they offer models of discretion and taste. They will teach at most an artful sensuality rather than blunt sexuality. One contestant on *WNTW* openly asked for help, saying 'sexy comes off as slutty for me'. As Weber suggests, 'makeovers draw a harsh line with those women considered excessive and out of control, usually in a highly sexualised way' (Weber 2009: 83). What humbles the individual is being unveiled to 'finished' presenters who represent, in highly focused form, the critical others they now need to please. When confronted by them and getting star treatment, the programme enters the same magical transformative space of advertising.

(iii) The Use of Evidence – 'the Science Bit'

In few places does the profound sexism of the advertising industry stand so exposed as in the treatment of science. It is here that men in white coats speak and women react, because science is supposedly beyond the understanding of women. While *WNTW* hints at the sisterhood of women, *10YY* presents women dependent on principally male expertise. In the UK version, Nicki Hambleton-Jones introduces the participant to the male surgeon, dentist and hairdresser, all of whom consider her in the cold objective hallmark of ad-science. The participant is barely permitted to speak until the programme process ends. Here we can see how

cosmetic surgeons make use of new visualization technologies to exercise a high-tech version of Foucault's scientific bio-power that effects first the objectification of the material body and, second, the subjection of the body to the discipline of the normative gaze. (Balsamo 1999: 281)

Flashy graphics and fast cutting all convey the image of an up-to-date industry put in service of the participant. Again this is reminiscent of advertising's blunt but visually arresting use of science to sell cosmetics etc. *10YY* makes much of what science can do by presenting potentials on screen and then letting them develop with the attendant gestures of surprise and gratitude. The subordinate role of these female participants is reinforced when they are seen marvelling at the results rather than broaching any form of negotiation. In short, it is an old cliché we are used to seeing in advertising – men act, women react (Berger 1990).

As many writers have pointed out, cosmetic surgery is a complex dilemma. It is both problem and solution, 'symptom of oppression and act of empowerment, all in one' (Davis 1999: 455). However, what we see in *10YY* articulates only a form of empowerment under the strict terms and conditions of the brand. No negotiation takes place. The new identity has been arrived at in which the woman's role has been principally one of submission. Just like advertising, you can be free to be what you want to be – as long as it's 'this'.

(iv) Rhetoric and Voice

Advertising works by making grandiose claims and this is very much the technique adapted by *WNTW* and *10YY*. When we see those selected, we find ourselves wondering how changes can possibly be made. Language, like an advertising tag line, plays its affirmative and anchoring role: 'I've reclaimed myself', 'I'm gonna worship you like a god', 'I've put together an all-star team', all of which reveals the intensity of the process for the participants and how both they and the experts have learned to speak the rhetoric of branding.

This is further reinforced by the ways in which family and friends use emotional language to underline the power of the experience and the 'worthiness' of the participant. Words like 'sacrifice' and 'life-changing' all provide the quality of intensity we expect from advertising, especially in their excited delight at the emotional reveal. At the same time, the narrators' use of puns – 'If it looks like your number's up when you should be in your prime ...' and (of a comedienne) 'Her appearance is no laughing matter' (*10YY*) – recall the jokey brevity of the industry, the repetition of which intensifies the humiliation.

In advertising, the hyperbolic use of language is necessary to distinguish indistinguishable products from one another. In such a climate, the catchphrase or slogan becomes crucial. In *WNTW* and *10YY*, exaggerated claims such 'You look like a film star' are used not so much to convey a judgment, but to contrast with an earlier version of the self that was openly mocked. The phrase becomes part of the brand-identity.

Powerful rhetoric underscores the emotionalism of these formats. Thus, while it might be amusing to hear talk of 'gnashers being turned into a winning smile', we are more likely to be moved by the responses of all involved, echoing current emphases upon 'emotional branding' in advertising (Gobe 2001). The participants are only one of the parties being swept away by the sheer force of the emotions, and the more unrestrained a performance the better. Furthermore, it is in emphasising these poignant high points that lifestyle connects with advertising in its concentration on emotional outpouring. What we see here is the fragility of people exposed to the workings of the brand as they are also seemingly refreshed by it. This return to the real 'me' that was always hidden 'deep down' draws on pseudo-psychological techniques and discourses.

(v) Testimony

One of the oldest techniques adopted in advertising is that of the testimonial, which remains a staple of the industry to help establish trust in a brand. In both *WNTW* and *10YY*, the testimonials work to recommend the necessity of change to others and to signify a belief in submitting oneself completely ('body, soul and wardrobe') to the process. Testimony is a starting point for both programmes. In *WNTW*, friends submit the individual for treatment, who is then secretly filmed – a process we are now so familiar with that it has completely lost its sinister surveillant potential. In *10YY*, the individual stands mute while passers-by guess their age. What is clear is that each participant is to subject themselves to the look of the other, which is actualised in spectators and experts. The 'middle-class gaze' (Lyle 2008) is here extended to everyone. Their testimony provides an overwhelming rationale for change – this is what most people think – therefore you should act.

In *10YY*, the hosts ask Jennifer, a comedienne, 'Who are you?' She replies, 'I'm becoming a new me.' Even this exchange has the rhythm and cadence of advertising. When a former rocker is asked to comment on her change, she remarks, 'I can't believe it's me. I'm like a completely different person' – again the sound bite is a perfect anchorage for the virtues of the show/process. The 'slice of life' that helps guarantee the virtues of a product is of real value here. The retrospective analysis from the participants provides testimony for what they have been through and shows how they come to share the view expressed by the presenters who opened the show: change is necessary.

What we see played out in both shows is an immersive experience in which even the gestures of rebellion are incorporated by the format as part of its brand-value. The testimony of friends, presenters and finally the subject all serve to underline the value of harsh judgments to evoke change.

(iv) Editing

Finally, I note that the editing style of these programmes borrows a great deal from advertising. Micro-moments of emotional intensity condense the time and pain of change into shorter narratives of transformation. Throughout both shows, short segments are offered that illustrate the progress that has been made, and are often used as mini-trailers for the larger show. It is the busy rhetoric of advertising style that drives these programmes, as if it were all in a rush, but it combines to provide an intense effect that underscores the magic of the process.

Conclusion

In this chapter, I have considered the various ways in which reality lifestyle brands such as *WNTW* and *10YY* work to rectify and correct certain class-based practices. The working classes are made to feel honoured to be selected for treatment. They are agog and compliant in the glittery world from which the presenters and experts originate. Their class basis is something to be escaped from (Lawler 2005), and their bodies are a sign of that materiality from which the brand is designed to rescue us. Although it is to be discarded in the programme, it is worth dwelling on the 'before' body.

We can view the 'before' moment as a representation of the working body. We see the scars of labour, the neglect of dental care, the effects of environmental damage, the distortions left by high-fat low-cost meals, and the other exigencies of consumer culture that leave their marks on the individual. These marks serve to classify. No value can be found in the body that has to be left behind; no scars of a working life can be worn with pride in this arena. Consumer culture encourages the individual to reflect on that body as an abortive organ. It has failed, no matter that the standards are set elsewhere and are both expensive and impossible to manage. The 'before' moment of each programme is only dwelt upon as the moment when crisis has been reached, its history has been erased (Wood and Skeggs 2008), and it is referred to throughout as the starting point. However, it is eminently possible to see this 'before' as the 'after', since it is the result of the pressures on a working life. But, of course, according to the dictates of consumer culture, articulated in the brand, there is no opportunity to celebrate this body as a class-honouring labouring achievement, no opportunity to see it other than through the lens of a promotional consumer culture fixated on potential.

My approach has been to consider these two reality television formats as extensions of advertising which use human participants to guarantee the efficacy of branding. The reality of working life is gradually effaced in the drive to a classless branded future. Similarly, the anxieties and uncertainties of modern life are to be banished – as if real economically grounded human susceptibilities were merely blemishes to be swept away. I chose *WNTW* and *10YY* because these international formats have a porous boundary with advertising. It is not simply that the programmes are sponsored and have a range of merchandising, but that they incorporate the techniques of advertising to persuade the individual and the viewer. While certain regulatory controls may keep both formally separate for now, what informs each programme is of course the ideology of consumerism. The brand is what it has always been – an antidote to risk. What has changed is the reach and scale of the platforms demonstrating the virtues of brand obedience.

Note

1. See <http://www.extremeneworleans.com/> accessed 28 January 2011.

Bibliography

Andrejevic, M. (2004) *The Work of Being Watched* (Lanham, MD: Rowman and Littlefield Publishing Group).

Balsamo, A. (1999) 'Forms of Technological Embodiment: Reading the Body in Contemporary Culture', in J. Price and M. Shildrick (eds), *Feminist Theory and the Body: A Reader* (Edinburgh: Edinburgh University Press), pp. 278–89.

Berger, J. (1990) *Ways of Seeing* (London: Penguin).

Bordo, S. (1993) 'Feminism, Foucault and the Politics of the Body', in C. Ramazanoglu (ed.), *Up against Foucault* (London: Routledge), pp. 179–202.

Cronin, A. (2000) *Advertising and Consumer Citizenship: Gender, Images and Rights* (London: Routledge).

Danesi, M. (2006) *Brands* (London: Routledge).

Davis, K. (1999) '"My body is my art": Cosmetic Surgery as Feminist Utopia', in J. Price and M. Shildrick (eds), *Feminist Theory and the Body: A Reader* (Edinburgh: Edinburgh University Press), pp. 454–65.

Eastman, S. T. (2000) *Research in Brand Promotion* (Mahwah, NJ: Lawrence Erlbaum).

Gobe, M. (2001) *Emotional Branding: The New Paradigm for Connecting Brands to People* (New York: Allworth Press).

Hearn, A. (2009) 'Hoaxing the Real: On the Meta-Narrative of Reality Television', in S. Murray and L. Ouellette (eds), *Reality TV: Remaking Television Culture* (New York: NYU Press), pp. 165–78.

Heller, D. (ed.) (2007) *Makeover Television: Realities Remodelled* (London: I.B. Tauris).

Kellner, D. (1995) *Media Culture* (London: Routledge).

Lawler, S. (2005) 'Introduction: Class, Culture and Identity', *Sociology*, 39(5): 797–806.

Lury, C. (2004) *Brands: The Logos of the Global Economy* (London: Routledge).

Lyle, S. (2008) '(Mis)recognition and the Middle Class/Bourgeois Gaze: A Case Study of *Wife Swap*', *Critical Discourse Studies*, 5(4): 319–30.

McFall, L. (2004) *Advertising: A Cultural Economy* (London: Sage).

McRobbie, A. (2004) 'Notes on "*What Not to Wear*" and Post-Feminist Symbolic Violence', *Sociological Review*, 52(2): 97–109.

Miller, P. and N. Rose (2008) *Governing the Present* (London: Polity).

Moor, L. (2007) *The Rise of Brands* (Oxford: Berg).

Moran, A. (2005) 'Configurations of the New Television Landscape', in J. Wasko (ed.), *A Companion to Television* (Maldon/London/Victoria: Blackwell), pp. 291–307.

Moseley, R. (2000) 'Makeover Takeover on British Television', *Screen*, 41(3): 299–314.

Myers, G. (1999) *Ad Worlds: Brands, Media, Audiences* (London: Arnold).

Ouellette, L. and J. Hay (2008) *Better Living through Reality TV* (London: Blackwell).

Palmer, G. (2004) '"The New You": Class and Transformation in Lifestyle Television', in S. Holmes and D. Jermyn (eds), *Understanding Reality Television* (London/New York: Routledge), pp. 173–90.

———— (ed.) (2008) *Exposing Lifestyle Television* (Aldershot, Hants.: Ashgate).

Rose, N. (2007) *The Politics of Life Itself: Biomedicine, Power and Subjectivity in the Twenty-First Century* (Princeton, NJ: Princeton University Press).

Taylor, L. (2005) '"It was beautiful before you changed it all": Class and the Transformative Aesthetics of the Garden Lifestyle Media', in D. Bell and J. Hollows (eds), *Ordinary Lifestyles: Popular Media, Consumption and Taste* (Maidenhead, Berks.: Open University Press), pp. 113–27.

Weber, B. (2009) *Makeover TV: Selfhood, Citizenship and Celebrity* (Durham, NC/London: Duke University Press).

Wood, H. and B. Skeggs (2008) 'Spectacular Morality: Reality Television, Individualisation and the Re-Making of the Working Class', in D. Hesmondhalgh and J. Toynbee (eds), *The Media and Social Theory* (London: Routledge), pp. 177–93.

10/Anita Biressi

'The Virtuous Circle': Social Entrepreneurship and Welfare Programming in the UK

Reality TV: From Business Enterprise to Social Entrepreneurship

As Anna McCarthy observes, rather than being dismissed as a 'debased piece of mass cultural detritus', reality television should, in fact, be viewed as a privileged site working across the three discursive apparatuses of family, state and cultural text to 'annotate' already dominant current transformations of the individual (McCarthy 2007: 19). This chapter focuses on one such transformation-in-progress: that is, the transformation of the British welfare 'dependent' into a self-reliant, self-supporting 'citizen'. In doing so, it examines the ways in which reality TV, and especially the makeover show, annotates this ideal by interpreting, glossing and promoting the neo-liberal project and its enterprises in accessible and entertaining ways. This examination will begin by exploring how programming works to reinforce dominant political ideologies of entrepreneurship through its links to mainstream political communication and policy. Using the example of the British series *Benefit Busters* (hereafter *BB*) (Channel 4, 2010), it will then go on to consider the ways in which the format of the reality makeover sometimes struggles to maintain the integrity of the transformation it aims to show and in doing so reveals the precariousness of self-reliance and social enterprise as the motors of social progress and security.

It could be argued that programming based around business, enterprise and the world of paid employment offers a simple illustration of the discursive and pragmatic alliance between government, economics and entertainment television's (see Boyle and Magor 2008) endorsing of enterprising *qualities* or characteristics as prerequisites of the proactive, self-reliant and productive individual. As Nick Couldry and Jo Littler observe, in the business competition show *The Apprentice* (BBC 2, 2005–), this programming 'transforms the norms of the neo-liberal workplace into taken-for-granted "common sense"' and offers a 'popular education in what it means to be a contemporary entrepreneurial worker' (Couldry and Littler 2008: 259–60). In addition, the tutorial and governmental dimensions of the show were further authorised in 2009 when its protagonist, Sir Alan Sugar, was appointed the British Government's Enterprise Tsar. Also Channel 5's 2010 series *The Business Inspector* was sponsored by HM Revenue and Customs (HMRC), which drew on tax payers' money to promote both small businesses and proper accounting through popular factual programming. The cross-fertilisation of television with politics and commerce is evident on *The Business*

Inspector website, which includes links to Lord Sugar's 'Business Basics' advice, to the HMRC website and to the Government's Business Link initiative.

As a counterpoint to the reality-world of ambitious, politically sanctioned would-be entrepreneurs, seen in *Dragons' Den* (BBC 2, 2005–), *Junior Apprentice* (BBC 1, 2010) and so on, are shows depicting less sanctioned lifestyles, focusing on the socially marginal (or even 'antisocial'), such as *Pramface Babies* (Channel 4, 2008, see Tyler in this volume), *How the Other Half Live* (hereafter *HOHL*) (Channel 4, 2009/10) and *Benefit Busters*. Taken together, these observational documentaries, life intervention or makeover series arguably help to establish the ground on which judgments are formed about the deserving and undeserving poor, about entrepreneurs, good citizens and bad welfare beneficiaries in the context of a philosophy of individual self-reliance as the motor of social mobility. These and many others, including *Mary Queen of Charity Shops* (BBC 2, 2009), *The Secret Millionaire* (Channel 4, 2006), *7 Days on the Breadline* (ITV 1, 2009), *Tower Block of Commons* (Channel 4, 2010) and *Famous, Rich and Homeless* (BBC 1, 2009), arguably act as a popular endorsement of the social enterprise message in which citizens can be helped towards social mobility and self-reliance via private non-state intervention.

Most, if not all, of these series are explicitly evaluative, asking viewers to form their own judgments of 'problem' cases alongside the experts or qualified amateurs who decide who is eligible for practical help, financial assistance or future investment to improve their own lives. In *HOHL*, for example, the aim is 'to show just what it means to grow up in poverty in twenty-first-century Britain'. In order for this to be achieved, 'each episode follows the story of two families as a wealthy family decides to assist one that is living below the poverty line'.[1] In *HOHL*, the donating family review the progress of the family they sponsor, debating on screen whether the money given over was wisely spent and whether further investment was merited. The narratives which appear to make explicit the processes by which these decisions are made also produce accessible and diverting stories about citizenship, individual responsibility and welfare dependency in an era of restricted resources and limited sympathy for those who consistently draw on them. As such, their ideological load is far weightier than implied by their formatting as popular factual programming.

This chapter will focus on these counterpoint shows, which might loosely be called 'welfare programming', by situating a discussion of the TV series *Benefit Busters* in the context of British political thinking on social entrepreneurship and its intersection with notions of social capital, self-help and civic virtue. This context is important, because *Benefit Busters* depicts the work of 'third-sector' agencies contracted to implement New Labour's welfare-to-work scheme (designed to help the long-term sick and unemployed into paid work). With the blessing of the Department of Work and Pensions (DWP), the series focused on 'real people' in the welfare system, the implementation of the Government's 'New Deal' and its commitment to delivering this by contracting out to business and charity. In doing so, it followed the work of the Shaw Trust (a charity) and of the global training and enterprise agency A4e (Action 4 Employment) whose function is to motivate its clients and make them 'work ready'. A4e's director Emma Harrison, a politically influential business woman with ambitions to promote her own brand of entrepreneurial philosophy, features strongly in the first two episodes, and the company would have appeared in all three episodes if the DWP had not intervened to request that other service providers be included.[2] As will be seen, Harrison's media persona and her brand of social enterprise offer a model of social entrepreneurship which fits well with reality television's already established transformative narratives, in which individuals are motivated to change their lives despite the strictures of social background or current disadvantage.

The Social Entrepreneur and Reality TV

In the year that New Labour came to power, the political think tank Demos published a booklet by Charles Leadbeater called *The Rise of the Social Entrepreneur* (1997) which was credited with popularising the notion of social entrepreneurship in Britain and ushering it into the mainstream of social policy debate. Leadbeater offered a solution for a country struggling under the burden of an outmoded welfare state ill-equipped to tackle modern social problems: the promotion of new-style philanthropic initiatives. The leaders of these initiatives, dubbed 'social entrepreneurs', would drive forward social innovation through the creative use of underused and undervalued resources: buildings, equipment and people. In other words, the principles and practices of enterprise would be deployed to initiate and manage projects which would effect positive social change but which could also bring profit to project managers. So while some social entrepreneurs would work within not-for-profit and citizen groups, many might also work in private and governmental fields, most typically through the establishment of private agencies contracted to the public sector as the result of a growing 'contract culture' (Leadbeater 1997: 12). The success of many of these initiatives would be judged on their ability to effectively blend social values with market values for the benefit of all parties.

At the time, Leadbeater's call was underpinned by commonly held pragmatic and philosophical assumptions: that as old hierarchies of class, church and family crumbled away, the active, self-shaping, *choosing* individual, someone 'free within their private sphere', must now be the 'central character of our times' (Leadbeater 1997: 14) and the model of contemporary citizenship. Diversity, scepticism and individualism are all indelibly inscribed into this model, to the extent that new social initiatives need to speak this character's language and understand its moral positioning if a more inclusive and progressive society is to be achieved. 'We will only create a sense of "community"', notes Leadbeater, 'if it is avowedly liberal, voluntaristic, de-centralised, self-governing, anti-statist and anti-hierarchical' (ibid.: 15). Social entrepreneurs then would seem to be the perfect, if rather contradictory, agents of change in this post-welfare, post-hierarchical vision, because they could be individualistic innovators and social adventurers, market players and community leaders, doers and communicators, pragmatists and idealists. As such, they would be the outliers, attracting like-minded citizen-collaborators, and forging new instruments to tackle the unmet needs of the socially marginalised, the disenfranchised and the disaffected.

Leadbeater's proposals were explicitly driven by a concern to address social problems such as long-term joblessness under a welfare state experiencing increasing financial pressure. His opening Executive Summary called for 'social innovation to develop a new philosophy, practice and organisation of welfare ... to develop a problem solving welfare system ... designed to create social capital by encouraging people to take greater control of their lives' (Leadbeater 1997: 1–2).

This challenge brought together two, soon to be voguish, phrases: 'social entrepreneur' and 'social capital'. These phrases were increasingly deployed by New Labour thinkers (1997–2010) and their advisors seeking a philosophical underpinning and practical approach to welfare. Social capital, created by social entrepreneurs and drawn on by citizens, would help establish 'para-welfare provision', an increasingly privatised, community-based resource for repairing a tattered and increasingly threadbare social fabric.

As the term suggests, social capital, although rooted in human relationships and often tied through bonds of trust, shared values and goodwill, is explicitly *economistic*, with Leadbeater (1997: 67) describing a 'virtuous circle' for the development of entrepreneurial social organisations in which social capital is inherited, invested (together with other forms such as financial and human capital) and made to pay 'dividends'. Also, as Halpern (2005) and others have pointed out, not everyone has access to the right networks, nor is everyone equally well equipped to draw on their benefits, and these inequalities of access and advantage are drawn along classed and other lines of social difference; what Putnam refers to as 'the dark side of social capital' (Putnam 2000: 350). In other words, some people have far lower stocks of social capital and lack the skills to build on those they do have, or else they are excluded through intolerance or prejudice. This original lack or exclusion results in a cycle of disadvantage, preventing them from accessing the employment, educational, medical or social benefits which would make social mobility more achievable. As Leadbeater (1997) makes clear, then, in his Executive Summary, the aims of the effective social entrepreneur must be not only to lift the dependent citizen out of welfare but also to integrate them more effectively into the networks of social capital which will go on to both support and direct them and to which they should also actively contribute.

This promotion of social enterprise was, from the start, strongly associated with New Labour's 'third way' (see Giddens 1998) and was regarded as marking a shift from Thatcherism's 'enterprise culture' (in which notions of community and society seemed to play little part) to a hybridisation of business and social responsibility, drawing cross-party support and quickly attracting resources, policies and media attention (Grenier 2009: 175). But it is arguable that the rhetoric and practice of social enterprise – its adoption of moralistic language, its acceptance of an individualist ethos, its faith in the market, in enterprising values and its promotion of entrepreneurs as charismatic heroes – also drew on the legacy of Thatcherism. For Thatcherism had banked on the 'natural justice of the market and the citizen's right and obligation to care for him or herself with only a minimal welfare safety net' (Nunn 2002: 57), and Thatcher always asserted that economics had a moral dimension, that individuals have the choice about whether to depend on the 'bounty of the state' or earn their own living (ibid.: 88). As Leadbeater makes plain, the new social entrepreneur also occupies a *moral* position as well as a market position: 'their language is caring, compassionate and moral', they communicate their aims 'in moral terms' in order to contribute to the social good (Leadbeater 2007: 55–6). In sum, we might say the notion of the social entrepreneur reinscribes the moral significance attributed to entrepreneurship via what was once referred to as the 'spirit of capitalism' through activity which takes on an explicitly social agenda (see Weber 2001). Its function is to revitalise the voluntaristic, non-statist tradition that Leadbeater argues originally paved the way for the welfare state; a move which critics might view as both nostalgic and anachronistic. Nonetheless, by 2007, Leadbeater could confidently claim that the idea and the movement had flourished in the 'shadow of the state' (which Thatcherism aimed to dismantle) and that globally, where state provision was weak, social entrepreneurs had made up the shortfall in the fields of care and community action. For Leadbeater, everything from the US-based venture philanthropy of the super-rich to third-sector services bore the hallmarks of social entrepreneurial zeal and, if taken on face value, these claims would further reinforce arguments that state support rather than market-based philanthropy is both unproductive and outmoded.

Some aspects of the social entrepreneur philosophy have been popularised (and distorted) in reality TV through the depiction of the venture capitalist or self-made individual as philanthropist, social interventionist or life coach. In these series, the qualifications for 'presenter' or advisor include not only the accumulation of wealth, resources (financial capital) and contacts (social capital), but also personal experience and expertise (human capital) (Halpern 2005). This experience and expertise is best forged in the heat of straitened circumstances earlier in life, thus branding the entrepreneur as someone in touch with the real world. The drive in these programmes is to make over the failing, struggling or marginalised project, whether a small business, a charity, a community, family or an individual. Sometimes the project in need of rescue is presented as suffering from outmoded practices or convictions, apathy or unreasonable expectations, while others present as a deserving case for assistance precisely because they have struggled on, without complaint, in difficult circumstances. The brisk, exhortatory tone employed by the TV social entrepreneur is nicely encapsulated in the titles of books written by *Dragons' Den* star and philanthropist Duncan Bannatyne, *Anyone Can Do It* (2007) and *Wake up and Change Your Life* (2009). Bannatyne, whose concerns have included health clubs and care homes for the elderly (both businesses), and more lately a substantial charity trust, is exemplary here as someone whose success story was forged in the school of hard knocks; a narrative trajectory which also supports many of the entrepreneurs featured in shows such as *The Secret Millionaire*.

As Leadbeater suggests, the social entrepreneur adopts a caring but *moral* position, often based on the conviction that it is possible to overcome the disadvantages of social class (for example) through drive, planning, personal endeavour and self-belief. This conviction and its moral attachments are obviously played out in a huge range of reality shows featuring ordinary people or experts who make over others (e.g. *Wife Swap*, Channel 4, 2003–9, and *The World's Strictest Parents*, BBC 3, 2010), but it is the business and social-insight programming that most explicitly marries enterprise, moral ascriptions and social intervention to the politics of what is generally referred to as neo-liberalism. This move in reality TV is referred to by Anna McCarthy (2007: 18), glossing Nikolas Rose, as 'responsibilisation' and is evident in the moral judgments made when the books are balanced and the secret millionaire decides how much money, time and resources to allocate to each cause or individual.

If we take the 'social entrepreneur' more specifically as someone who applies business practices to solve social problems, then these figures also populate reality TV. In addition to *The Secret Millionaire* and *Benefit Busters*, these have included Mary Portas importing business acumen into high street charity shops, John Bird[3] (founder of the *Big Issue*) mentoring celebrities roughing it in *Famous, Rich and*

Homeless and Jamie Oliver training disadvantaged youngsters to work in the restaurant industry, in *Jamie's Kitchen* (Channel 4, 2002).[4] Game formats have also engendered competitive philanthropy, such as Oprah Winfrey's *The Big Give* (US, ABC, 2008) and *Millionaire's Mission* (Channel 4, 2010) in which eight self-made millionaires were given three weeks to familiarise themselves with the needs of a remote farming village near the Rwandan border before competing to deliver a charitable project worth £120,000. Here, more traditional charitable interventions (the new school, water wells) were weighed up against explicitly profit-making proposals such as the launch of eco-tourism.

Clumsy and distorting as these shows are in their depiction of the social entrepreneurial agenda, they do capture something of its peculiar hybridity and brassy confidence, a formulation nicely encapsulated in a definition offered by David Puttnam (2004):

> Broadly speaking, social entrepreneurs are what you get when you cross Richard Branson with Mother Teresa. They do their most effective work at the fringes of the market place, where both the public sector and the market itself have failed to deliver important goods and services, particularly to those who can pay little. The organisations they create defy the boundaries that traditionally separate welfare and business.

In sum, as Leadbeater suggests, social entrepreneurs are 'constitutionally uncomfortable; there is always a tension between their social goals and their commitment to commercial operation' (Leadbeater 2002: iii). What better subject matter then for reality television, a format whose own constituents are so often in tension between social intervention and sheer entertainment.

Faring Well in the Reality TV Economy? A4e and *Benefit Busters*

> The British government wants to revolutionize the welfare system and it's targeting lone parents, the long-term unemployed and the sick. This major documentary series looks at the radical idea of awarding large contracts to private sector companies and charities and rewarding them for getting claimants into work. (Studio Lambert website[5])

Benefit Busters, which was made by Studio Lambert (Chief Executive Stephen Lambert was previously responsible for *The Secret Millionaire* and *Wife Swap*), attracted above-average audience figures of 2.3 million.[6] The series, consisting of three 60-minute episodes (including commercials), was flagged by Lambert as observational documentary but referred to by reviewers as reality TV. It made for riveting viewing, with its scrutiny of ordinary people in difficult circumstances (single mothers, unskilled long-term unemployed and those too sick to work) leading, more often than not, to intense moments of acute embarrassment, shame and distress as well as humour. The vulnerability of those involved was starkly exposed as clients were confronted on camera about their poor attitude, lack of discipline, low self-esteem, financial laxity or hidden alcoholism. As one reviewer wryly noted,

> It was powerful, incendiary even, but most of all it was a comic masterpiece, darkly lit due […] to the Catch-22 circuit in which both clients and advisors were trapped; attempting to, on the one hand,

implement the Government's back to work policy and on the other, to exit welfare dependency without becoming even poorer. (Rumbelow 2009)

For the people on both sides of the divide, financial incentives (and penalties) were at stake. The third-sector agencies involved – A4e (Episodes 1 and 2) and the Shaw Trust (Episode 3) – were motivated by results not action, a directive already in place for some years and known as the 'New Deal' (DWP 2006: 15, para. 36). By January 2008, this was redesignated the 'Flexible New Deal' (DWP 2008) signalling further reform and an increasing emphasis on 'tailor-made' back-to-work packages delivered by public/private partnerships. Surprisingly perhaps, at the heart of the recession, the message of the *new* New Deal was that the major challenge was not lack of paid employment but the 'employability' of those who remained on welfare. Then Prime Minister Gordon Brown's preface to the revised programme declared: 'In the old days the problem may have been unemployment, but in the next decades it will be employability. If in the old days lack of jobs demanded priority action, in the new world it is lack of skills' (DWP 2008: 2). Both A4e and the Shaw Trust were stakeholders in this reformed welfare landscape, with the Trust delivering the Pathways to Work programme to help those on incapacity benefit back to work and A4e operating in Britain and overseas as a multimillion-pound training and enterprise company.

For A4e, in particular, not a charity but a global company, participation in *Benefit Busters* was not only desirable but part of a broader project of media visibility. In interview, Harrison declared that she was happy to appear as 'TV's face of social and welfare reform' and that her involvement in television extended her sphere of influence: 'Politicians, even Prime Ministers do watch these programmes' (Davison 2010).[7] The A4e website is a model of self-marketing and is especially acute at drawing on the experiences of its clients, whose success stories are evident in quotations, case studies and on its own A4eTV video channel. The story of its founder is the classic tale of a determined entrepreneur whose small business, set up in response to redundancies in the Sheffield steel industry, grew into a powerful global company. Harrison, a self-styled welfare reformer, had already appeared in two Lambert productions, *Make Me a Million* (Channel 4, 2005) and *The Secret Millionaire* (Episode 5, Series 1, 2007), and following *BB* was to feature as an expert in *Famous, Rich and Jobless* (BBC 1, 2010) and *Who Knows Best: Getting a Job* (Channel 4, 2010), the latter a Pygmalion format in which she transforms the life of a young unemployed man called John, 'the hardest study the researchers could find' (Davison 2010). The challenge here is typical of makeover programming, which frequently attends to the extreme or hard case when effecting life transformations, welcoming the ultimate test of the 'problem family' (Biressi and Nunn 2008; Ferguson 2010), the difficult teenager (*The Unteachables*, Channel 5, 2005) and even the substance abuser (*The Intervention* [US], A&E, 2005). By the end of *Who Knows Best*, and only six weeks later, John is transformed from hopeless case into a 'handsome young man in a sharp city suit' earning £17,500 a year.[8]

The clients in *BB* are also presented as difficult cases and, in advance of the series, as essentially undeserving of sympathy. A controversial Channel 4 advert featured an overweight young man (not in the actual series) wearing leisure clothes, slumped on a large leather sofa and clutching his TV remote control: 'Nice work if you can get it' was the tag line. Although the films themselves do point to the pitfalls of automatically condemning welfare recipients or rushing them into unsuitable work, the introductory montage puts them in a very bad light: composed of six, less than flattering vignettes taken from the three episodes, and intercut with woeful statistics detailing the costs to the taxpayer of supporting welfare claimants. It launches, for example, with tutor Hayley Taylor asking shame-faced 'lone mothers': 'Why aren't you all queuing up outside McDonald's, KFC and Burger King then, why aren't you queuing up at their door if you want a job so badly?' Other scenes include a young man with a back injury groaning in pain, followed by an advisor expressing suspicion about the extent of claimants' ill-health and Taylor declaiming: 'benefit scrounger, loan parent, blah, blah, blah, blah, sapping off the system, can't be bothered to work, staying at home and using the kids as an excuse, you've heard it all before, haven't you'. In the final scene, Taylor again declares that there's nothing to stop her group getting work that very day. Although there is more to the series than this, nothing suggests that it will be anything but an exercise in shaming and humiliation for those taking part.

As this summary suggests, Taylor is the star 'character' here, predominant in the trailer and featuring in the launch episode, which resembles reality television rather more closely than documentary.[9] Episode 1 follows the progress of an A4e pilot course called 'Elevate', devised and run by Taylor and aimed at helping lone mothers get jobs once their children turn seven years old. The stated goal is to boost confidence; 'positivity is the key to everything', declares Taylor. Jaunty music and intertitles mark out the stages of the course and signpost the direction the women will be taking: 'caterpillars to butterflies', 'confidence', 'tough love', 'job ready', 'employment versus unemployment' and finally 'butterflies'. Paid by results, in reality A4e is given six weeks to make a difference, allowing the film-maker to follow clients from their first daunting day with Taylor through to either employment or return to welfare support. The phrase 'caterpillars to butterflies' is Taylor's, making an analogy between the journey to job readiness and the transformation from dull grub to beautiful butterfly. Taylor leads a process of transformation which includes banning casual clothing (her 'bible' is *What Not to Wear*), negativity and excuses. She introduces herself while holding a large box of tissues to signal, perhaps, both the toughness and the love to come, which will include confronting the women about their own personal obstacles to employment and taking them to the job centre to remind them how low they have fallen on the social ladder.

Some of Elevate's clients, referred to by their first names only, also speak to camera from their own homes, explaining their circumstances and the importance of getting properly paid work. None refuse to entertain the idea that paid work is better than benefits and several concede that life is a little too comfortable on state support. But they also explain their entrenchment in a system whose security outweighs the uncertainty of low-paid work, especially when burdened by debt (frozen while on benefits) or the cost of bringing up children. In Episode 1, the dramaturgy of transformation works well enough, even managing to produce a big 'reveal' in which five of the ten women discover that they have been given a two-week unpaid placement at the discount store Poundland. Even Taylor has a fairytale moment when she is visited on site by Harrison and then invited to return the call at Harrison's mansion for an ideas session called 'tea with Emma'. Even this 50 per cent success rate is challenged when Donah (*sic.*), a woman with alcohol problems, puts her new job at risk and Yvette, a mother of four, and one of the keenest to leave benefits behind, finds that she will be poorer working at Poundland and has to withdraw her labour, leaving Taylor dismayed at the problems inherent in the 'system'.

Taken in isolation, Episode 1 seems replete with 'success' stories detailing Taylor's, her unemployed mums' and even Harrison's achievements as the wealthy head of A4e, although, in fact, the five women who do not find work are barely visible in the film. In this way, it incorporates the features of the reality makeover show within an observational documentary format and through its success stories also supports the case for the Flexible New Deal and public/private partnerships as the solution to unsustainable social problems. The five women were demonstrably employable and the work, albeit poorly paid, seemed to be there for the taking. The dimensions of social class and gender (they were all white) which must have structured these women's lives were not only absent and unaddressed but patently irrelevant, overcome by Taylor's dedication, the incentives and sanctions attached to the course, and a common-sense conviction that every obstacle was an opportunity.

However, this was not the whole picture, as evidenced by both the structure and content of the second and third episodes. These retained a docusoap style (ensemble casting, extra-diegetic music, voiceover, direct interviews and an emphasis on the experience of ordinary people) but lost the slightly comic tone, emphasis on success stories and the intertitles which signalled the makeover transformation. Focusing on the long-term unemployed and those too sick to work, it revealed more plainly the true extent of the risk threatening those who move off benefits and into paid work. For example, Episode 2 followed Mark, a former soldier who, unemployed for a decade and apparently resistant to the A4e course, proved to be overjoyed on gaining employment as a landscape gardener. The significance of the improvement in his situation was marked by the modest treats which he could give his wife – some hair dye, a takeaway meal – but in less than a month he was laid off as the company downsized. Mark's anger was palpable and the film revealed the precariousness of a job market that seemed both exploitative and risky. While A4e advisors pushed 'vacancies' and agency work to apparently disaffected young men, the film revealed that these were mostly temporary, part-time, low-paid and even 'zero-hours' contracts (i.e. employees would sign a contract which guaranteed them no minimum number of hours). Anyone taking a job might suddenly find themselves with no work and no state support, slipping into debt while waiting for welfare to come back on line. The course itself featured very little on screen and the scenes presenting it seemed to include rather a lot of non-productive time-filling activities. In this episode, when Harrison was challenged directly by the film-maker about the poor and precarious placements which clients are pushed to accept, she seemed impervious to criticism. Episode 2 placed government policy and A4e's involvement in such a poor light that it was even rumoured that these negative outcomes led to the pulling of the show from various watch-again platforms.[10]

Episode 3 painted an equally dismal picture. It focused on the government's initiative to reassess long-term sickness status, with a voiceover announcing that 2.7 million people 'are on the sick … they are paid more than the unemployed and they don't have to look for a job but that's about to change …' The film focused on advisors at the Shaw Trust who received financial bonuses for reaching their target number of 'customers' going back into employment. Sherrie Jepson, a former saleswoman and the most successful in meeting her targets, is a key figure here, challenging and persuading her clients that they would be better off in work and that there is work available despite their poor health. All the clients are in difficult situations: disabled and nearing retirement, struggling with severe mental health problems, unable to do physical work or too poorly educated to do office work. Speaking to camera, they confide that in an 'ideal world' they would work and that paid work is their goal, although it is sadly apparent to the viewer that several of these are unlikely ever to be employable. As Jepson observes, 'it's a cruel world' and little wonder perhaps that at the end of the film no one has met their target.

Conclusion

In the reality TV makeover show, the markers of class origins, class distinction and social difference are paradoxically invoked and erased via the insistence that self-respect, personal responsibility, choice and initiative are the primary (class-free) traits of the socially successful (see Palmer in this volume). In both *The Secret Millionaire* and *HOHL*, for example, the recipients of donated time, money and expertise are often heard to comment on the surprising ordinariness of their wealthy benefactors and the shows stress the self-made nature of their own success; the point hammered home is that modest or disadvantaged social origins need not impede the progress of the industrious and the ambitious. Here, social entrepreneurs are characterised as figures who have moved beyond class-based or ideological politics to become 'ideological chameleons': intellectually 'agile' and 'ideologically adaptable' (Leadbeater 1997: 56).

In these formats, those less likely to be seen and heard in the public sphere (volunteers, health service users, welfare recipients, the socially marginal, etc.) become the subject of social intervention and life-changing transformations. Clearly, these formats and their ideological freight fit well with the broader neo-liberal message of self-fashioning, entrepreneurship and 'responsibilisation' promoted by New Labour and reiterated by the new administration's commitment to 'the big society', amplifying that message and naturalising it as common sense.[11] Social sponsorship, individual mentoring, philanthropy or business experience is provided to the most deserving cases in order to produce pro-social results (socialised children, self-reliant communities, responsible citizens), results which, it seems, state intervention could not achieve. For those project-subjects who resist, do not comply or simply fail to stay the course, a dramatic and entertaining lesson is nonetheless presented to viewers, who perceive that an opportunity to change has been wasted. In these stories of potential social mobility, state support is relegated to the margins as irrelevant, unhelpful or even socially and morally corrosive, while social entrepreneurs, innovators and business leaders are presented as the obvious solution.

In this context, the second and third episodes of *Benefit Busters* inevitably moved a little further away from the reality format established in the launch programme (although they were very far from constituting investigative documentary), their judgmental tone as signalled in the advert and opening shots giving way as the series progressed to scepticism about the New Deal. *Benefit Busters'* shift in both format and tone demonstrates how the social entrepreneurial messages and the Pygmalion trajectory of the various reality series discussed above are only sustainable when things go mostly according to plan: that is, when participants are successfully made over. Hence, the moral ground which supports these transformations is gradually undermined when we see the clients, no matter how hard they try, failing to escape welfare. In Episode 1, the 'constitutionally uncomfortable' position of the social entrepreneur, who works for both profit and social goals, is swiftly dealt with, as Taylor refuses to entertain the suggestion that there is a problem with her boss becoming rich from welfare work which seems to deliver to everyone's advantage. But by the third episode, we learn that the makeover project, in life if not in reality television, cannot guarantee results after all, no matter how compliant, deserving or industrious its subjects.

Notes

1. <http://www.channel4.com/programmes/how-the-other-half-live> accessed 4 August 2011.

2. Harrison's blog <http://www.a4eblog.co.uk/Articles/000321.aspx> accessed 27 June 2010. It should also be noted that charities are not usually regarded as social enterprises, presumably because as not-for-profit organisations they cannot draw on a business framework to generate social benefit.

3. Bird also featured in an episode of the documentary series *The Insider* (2006, 2007) called 'Getting Tough with the Homeless' (Channel 4, 2007) where he outlined his 'radical programme of tough love'. For Leadbeater, the *Big Issue* is the ideal exemplar of the potential of social enterprise (Leadbeater 2003: 3).

4. In 2010, it was also reported that Oliver would present a new reality show in which he sets up a school for children struggling in mainstream education (Topping 2010). The first episode of the seven-part series *Jamie's Dream School* aired on 2 March 2011.

5. <http://www.studiolambert.com/benefitbusters.html> accessed 12 July 2011.

6. Source: <http://www.studiolambert.com/benefitbustersnews2.html> accessed 12 July 2011.

7. The influence of A4e is certainly not understated and the inclusion of a manifesto on its website is testament to the seriousness with which it approaches its role in welfare reform. *Ending Poverty: Solutions from the Front Line* is available at: <http://www.mya4e.com/4-Governments/A4e-Manifesto> accessed 12 July 2011.

8. The quotation is from Jo Davison, 'A4e boss Emma Harrison's road to success', *Sheffield Telegraph*, 28 May 2010. At the time of the interview, the programme's working title was *The Wager*, arguably underlining the Pygmalion challenge at the heart of the show.

9. Taylor, a colourful and assertive personality, went on to perform in a new Studio Lambert series for Channel 4 called *The Fairy Jobmother*.

10. Discussed at <http://www.flexible-new-deal.co.uk/2009/08/29/did-a4e-get-benefit-busters-2-pulled-from-on-demand/> accessed 12 July 2011.

11. A key speech on the big society and the role of social enterprise was delivered by David Cameron at the Young Foundation on 10 November 2009 and can be accessed at: <http://www.conservatives.com/News/Speeches/2009/11/David_Cameron_The_Big_Society.aspx> accessed 12 July 2011. For a key text on the new 'civic Conservatism', see Blond (2010).

Bibliography

Biressi, A. and H. Nunn (2008) 'Bad Citizens: The Class Politics of Lifestyle Television', in G. Palmer (ed.), *Exposing Lifestyle Television: The Big Reveal* (Aldershot, Hants.: Ashgate), pp. 15–24.

———— (2010) 'Shameless?: Picturing the "Underclass" after Thatcherism', in L. Hadley and E. Ho (eds), *Thatcher and After: Margaret Thatcher and Her Afterlife in Contemporary Culture* (Basingstoke, Hants.: Palgrave Macmillan), pp. 137–57.

Blond, P. (2010) *Red Tory: How Left and Right Have Broken Britain and How We Can Fix It* (London: Faber and Faber).

Boyle, R. and M. Magor (2008) 'A Nation of Entrepreneurs? Television, Social Change and the Rise of the Entrepreneur', *International Journal of Media and Cultural Politics*, 4(2): 125–44.

Couldry, N. and J. Littler (2008) 'The Work of Work: Reality TV and the Negotiation of Neo-Liberal Labour in *The Apprentice*', in T. Austin and W. de Jong (eds), *Rethinking Documentary: New Perspectives, New Practices* (Maidenhead, Berks.: Open University Press), pp. 258–67.

Davison, J. (2010) 'A4e boss Emma Harrison's road to success', *The Star*, 18 May. Available at: <http://www.thestar.co.uk/news/a4e_boss_emma_harrison_s_road_to_success_1_855455> accessed 12 July 2011.

Department of Work and Pensions (2006) *A New Deal for Welfare Empowering People to Work* (Norwich, Norfolk: HMSO).

———— (2008) *Transforming Britain's Labour Market: 10 Years of the New Deal* (Norwich, Norfolk: HMSO).

Ferguson, G. (2010) 'The Family on Television: Who's Shaming Whom?', *Television and New Media*, 11(2): 87–104.

Giddens, A. (1998) *The Third Way: The Renewal of Social Democracy* (Cambridge: Polity).

Grenier, P. (2009) 'Social Entrepreneurship in the UK: From Rhetoric to Reality', in R. Ziegler (ed.), *An Introduction to Social Entrepreneurship: Voices, Preconditions, Contexts* (Cheltenham, Glos.: Edward Elgar), pp. 174–206.

Halpern, D. (2005) *Social Capital* (Cambridge: Polity).

Leadbeater, C. (1997) *The Rise of the Social Entrepreneur* (London: Demos).

———— (2002) 'Life in no man's land', *The New Statesman*, Social Enterprise Supplement, 3 June, pp. 2–4.

———— (2007) 'Mainstreaming of the mavericks: the social entrepreneurship movement has come of age', *Observer*, 25 March.

McCarthy, A. (2007) 'Reality TV: A Neo-Liberal Theatre of Suffering', *Social Text*, 25(4): 17–41.

Nunn, H. (2002) *Thatcher, Politics and Fantasy* (London: Lawrence and Wishart).

Putnam, R. (2000) *Bowling Alone: The Collapse and Revival of American Community* (New York: Simon and Schuster).

Puttnam, D. (2004) 'Social enterprise – hearts before pockets', *The New Statesman*, 9 February, p. 26.

Rumbelow, H. (2009) 'Benefit Busters', *The Times* [online], 21 August. Available at: <http://entertainment.timesonline.co.uk/tol/arts_and_entertainment/tv_and_radio/article6804313.ece> accessed 28 January 2011.

Topping, A. (2010) 'Jamie Oliver to set up school for reality show', *Guardian*, 15 June. Available at: <http://www.guardian.co.uk/lifeandstyle/2010/jun/15/jamie-oliver-school-reality-tv-show> accessed 12 July 2011.

Weber, M. (2001) *The Protestant Ethic and the Spirit of Capitalism* (London: Routledge Classics).

11/Brenda R. Weber

From All-American Mom to Super Bitch from Hell: Kate Gosselin and the Classed and Gendered Politics of Reality Celebrity

'You are called plain Kate,

And bonny Kate and sometimes Kate the curst;' (William Shakespeare, *The Taming of the Shrew*, Act 2, Scene i)

'You don't even have to call her Kate Gosselin now. You can just call her Kate and people know who you're talking about.' (Meredith Vieira, 'Inside Kate's World', *Kate Plus 8*)

In many ways, the reality television star Kate Gosselin epitomises the American Dream. Born in rural Pennsylvania in 1975 and raised in working-class circumstances, she has through hard work, cunning and determination achieved not only a comfortable life but also entered a field of public visibility. In 2003, the twenty-eight-year-old Kate was mother of twins and a registered nurse; by 2004, she had given birth to sextuplets and become a television personality; as of this writing in 2011, she is a verifiable celebrity with a net worth in the millions of dollars. One fact to evidence her celebrity: she has appeared on or in countless issues of tabloid magazines such as *People*, *US Weekly*, *In Touch Weekly*, *Star* and the *National Inquirer* (*People* alone has published 211 articles). As such, this reality celebrity helps make clear a new imperative in the meanings of the American Dream: that to achieve the promise of upward mobility, it is not enough to work for education, a modest career and a home. Now one must also be famous.

Kate has certainly made good on this mandate. Not only is she one of the most sought-after and paparazzi-stalked figures in America, she is a best-selling author and automatic ratings magnet. She is also the continual butt of late-night comedians' jokes and the favoured target of irate fan blogs. Yet, rather than being perceived as an entertainer – someone who performs labour within an industry and knowingly barters anonymity for celebrity – her status as a mother on television means she is typically regarded as, by turns, a 'professional mother', a 'fame-crazed narcissist', and 'sickly obsessed' with 'money, freebies, and her appearance' (Reinstein and Souter 2009: 64–70). By all accounts, it is Kate Gosselin's avarice for celebrity, combined with her willingness to commodify her private life for television audiences, that turned her from an all-American mom to a super bitch from hell.

But why should this be the case? If fame is the new evidence that one has reached the apogee of American achievement, then should not the aspiration toward fame be as highly regarded as the effort to earn college educations or shiny new cars, the markers of success that have until now announced commitments to upward mobility? Why has there been such rage directed at this fame-seeking, ambitious and by all accounts harsh woman? Why do media tabloids and the blogosphere register such a sense of injustice at both Kate Gosselin's newly loaded bank accounts and her rise to celebrity? In the value put on meritocratic achievement that is part and parcel of the American Dream, is Kate not simply taking full advantage of the cornucopia of opportunities presented to her in this particular historical moment?

It seems she does not deserve and should not desire the celebrity she possesses. Like the par-venue in the domains of the wealthy upper-crust, Kate Gosselin exposes the fallacy that undergirds a class hierarchy structured on achievement, since her particular situation as a reality TV celebrity so graphically demonstrates how celebrity can be the result of a flukey combination of cunning and arti-fice rather than the reward for hard work and determination. In this case, she is like an anti-Horatio Alger signboard, undermining the values of the American Dream even as she lives out its promise.[1] Importantly, web postings, tabloid headlines and late-night comedians do not suggest that the values by which we understand 'making it' are themselves bankrupt (in other words, famous people really are, and deserve to be, living the American Dream) but that the bartering of a private life for a public career is somehow false and wrong, particularly for mothers.[2]

Moreover, as Kate's case indicates, those who rise to the top through deliberate fame-seeking more often incite wrath than approval, thereby underscoring the degree to which certain celebrities, as Imogen Tyler and Bruce Bennett argue, elicit not 'desire, admiration or benign interest' but a 'blend of contempt, envy, scepticism and prurience' (Tyler and Bennett 2010: 375). Tyler argues that 'chav' is a new term of abuse and widespread disrespect in Britain for what in the United States is often an amalgam between 'poor white trash' and the 'welfare mom', those who flout the conventions of the middle class through a lifestyle and demeanour often deemed 'bad' or 'vulgar' (Tyler 2008: 21). Chavs seem to merit punishment, Tyler explains, because they, like the nineteenth-century 'wretched poor' or 'ignorant savage', so fully personify cultural disgust, thus allowing race and class to function as categories of critical importance even while going unnamed in the seeming universal hatred of 'social vermin', no one more fully vilified than the chav mother (ibid.: 25, and see Tyler in this volume).

Although Kate Gosselin was herself raised in modest circumstances, I am reluctant to term her working class. Indeed, I would argue that the particular form of disgust directed at her differs from the type identified by Tyler and Bennett (2010), where working-class women are despised for vio-lating a larger set of middle-class values. The logic of the representation in the shows on which Kate appears does not press on working-class identity in the way, for instance, that *Ladette to Lady* or *Jersey Shore* might, but instead underscores Kate's insistent middle-class residency. As such, Kate is a middle-class mother, dissatisfied with her social standing, and this, it seems, constitutes an alarming crime that merits social punishment. It is Kate's desire for fame, combined with being the mother of eight children, that puts the finishing touches to her infamy, since the children alone (the logic goes) should offer the satisfaction she seeks.

The aggregate conversation around Kate Gosselin indicates that she is guilty of two crimes: she cheated in her climb to upward mobility by wanting celebrity too much and she has defied a dearly held (if not always overtly uttered) belief that middle-class motherhood should be fully consummating for a woman. E. Ann Kaplan (1992) demonstrated two decades ago that the mother's idealised place within the private realm of the home made her public representation difficult. The controversial figure of Kate Gosselin further demonstrates that a larger ambivalence about the role of the mother has not been resolved.

'It might be a crazy life, but it's our life'

What occasioned this meteoric rise to both fame and infamy? Kate, with her husband Jon Gosselin, used reproductive technologies (intrauterine inception) to conceive children, first leading to twins and later resulting in sextuplets. They then used their large family to attract a series of reality programmes that captured the imagination and crystallised the fears of the viewing public: starting in reality TV with *Surviving Sextuplets and Twins* (Discovery, 2006), following with *Twins, One Year Later* (Discovery, 2007) and moving on to renown in *Jon and Kate Plus 8* (TLC, Advanced Medical Productions, 2007–9). Kate struck out on her own in *Dancing with the Stars* (ABC, 2010), *Kate Plus 8* (TLC, Advanced Medical Productions, 2010) and *Twist of Kate* (TLC, 2010). She is now equally vilified and validated in celebrity tabloids, entertainment news features and internet blogs, her image so instantly recognisable that her hairstyle was turned into a highly popular Halloween wig, her body so fully exposed that fan sites discuss the length of her tummy-tuck scars, her image so much in demand that she is hounded by the paparazzi wherever she goes.

On *Jon and Kate Plus 8*, Kate was the controlling, shrewish wife and Jon the meek, henpecked husband. Like Lady Macbeth, Kate's rule of her husband and ambitions for greatness made her an unsympathetic character who thrived in the limelight, while Jon's retiring ways made him the sympathetic and beset everyman who shrinks in the spotlight. The story changed, however, when Jon decided to 'assert his manhood', publicly dumping Kate for a much younger woman (and then a series of much younger women) and giving the country one of its more public divorces. Jon's status as good father and tortured husband suddenly plummeted as his series of brief relationships and increasingly juvenile behaviour put his semi-midlife crisis into stark relief against Kate's domestic commitments and celebrity aspirations. Though she was still a controversial figure whom people loved to hate, more people found themselves sympathetic to the spurned Kate, even while Jon fell into a PR nightmare that culminated in him being sued for breach of contract on a morals clause, thus 'necessitating' Kate's participation in *Dancing with the Stars* (ABC, BBC Worldwide Americas, 2005–) and the premiere of two new shows in which she was the main star, *Kate Plus 8* and *Twist of Kate*. Kate's resiliency in the face of her divorce and ensuing custody woes has not bought her much slack in the blogosphere. Though she complains of being a single mom making it on her own, postings are almost entirely unsympathetic, regarding her as a disingenuous parasite who has put her private life in the public gaze and is therefore making money 'riding the shirt tails of her children. GET HER OUT OF HERE!' (Donna Snarkfood, 6 May 2010). In the words of one poster, Beatrix:

> I am sick and tired from somebody who is using kids for making money. Her statement like I am single
> mother (but with $20,000 monthly support and made half million from Dancing with Stars). She doesn't

spend time with her kids. Has 3 nannies and person for maintaining the household. Do people watch because they are fascinating with her arrogance and narcissistic behavior. She is so pathetic. (Beatrix Snarkfood, 4 June 2010)[3]

Even before the controversy brought by Jon's infidelity and their divorce, *Jon and Kate Plus 8* was the most popular series on The Learning Channel (TLC) network, but the rift in the house of Gosselin increased viewer interest and their consequent celebrity to phenomenal proportions. When Jon and Kate announced on air in June 2009 their decision to separate and divorce, 9.8 million people tuned in (generally, reality TV that draws 1 million viewers is considered strong programming). Ratings for Kate's go-it-alone episodes of *Kate Plus 8* have not achieved those heights, but have still topped TLC's programming. Episodes 1 and 2 (airing 6 June 2010) garnered 3.4 million viewers, constituting triple-digit gains over TLC's second-quarter averages (Sperling and Rice 2010). Equally strong has been the level of fascination and frustration that has riveted the nation in this family's perpetuation of a governing cast of characters – the controlling, narcissistic mother who will prostitute her children for fame and money; the feckless, irresponsible (and mixed-race) father who allows it all to happen and may actually be more dangerous than his hyper-ambitious spouse; the eight innocent and terrifically cute children, exploited by our interest and the intrusion of television cameras that have turned their home into a studio, now all seeing a therapist (also being filmed and aired on TLC). Is this the American Dream or an American nightmare?

All-American Dreams of Fame

I hope we'll both rise, Dick; we've got well started now, and there've been other boys, worse off than we are, who have worked hard and risen to FAME AND FORTUNE. (Horatio Alger, Jr, *Fame and Fortune*, 1868)

The American Dream is a concept that most people have heard of, but few have a clear understanding of its meaning. The haziness about the term is not due to some highly complex or excessively intellectualised definition but rather because the American Dream has always represented a plurality of possibilities, even though references to 'the Dream' position it as a single, inviolable concept. When we try to define the American Dream, we discover that, much like mercury, it is an incoherently coherent entity that can be both solid and fluid. James Truslow Adams first coined the term in 1931 as 'that dream of a land in which life should be better and richer and fuller for everyone, with opportunity for each according to ability or achievement' (Adams 1931: 150). Writing for *Vanity Fair* in a more contemporary mode, John Kamp (2009) opines that the American Dream is unique to America. 'There is no correspondingly stirring Canadian Dream or Slovakian Dream', he notes, praising the egalitarian call of an ideology that posits realistic success as an 'invigorating possibility' for those willing to work hard. Such ideas of meritocracy and reward have fuelled the notion that the United States is a class-free society, unhindered by the social class conflicts that have divided Britain and Europe.

It is a difficult dream for the European upper classes to interpret adequately, and too many of us ourselves have grown weary and mistrustful of it. It is not a dream of motor cars and high wages merely, but a dream of social order in which each man and each woman shall be able to attain to the fullest stature of which they are innately capable, and be recognized by others for what they are, regardless of the fortuitous circumstances of birth or position. (Adams 1931: 151)

The American Dream has been code for talking about class in the United States. Contained in its meanings is a twofold guarantee: that a man (almost always literally a white, heterosexual male) could rise in status simply due to his efforts and that children in each generation could expect to live a better life than their parents. It is Adams' assertion that they 'shall be able to attain to the fullest stature of which they are innately capable' that throws the whole notion of equality-based meritocracy out of kilter, since on the ground and in the real world such notions of a work-based class-free culture do not pan out.

Perhaps due to the simultaneous promise and myth of meritocracy, the appeal of the dream prevails and its larger influence pervades an imagined sense of class in America. Governing narratives about class have historically worked to tacitly shore up the 'average guy', the common man invested in living comfortably and non-ostentatiously within the middle class. The achievable and more typical way of conceptualising success in America has since World War II indicated the upward mobility denoted by college education, home-ownership (and mortgages), heteronormative families, and an expression of taste and deportment that constitute the bourgeois. In essence, the American Dream has come to indicate the aspirational fantasy of the everyman, he who does not desire to rule the world but simply wishes for his modest house and happy family. This myth of egalitarian upward mobility attaches not just to the United States but to an abstract concept of Americanness bigger than the nation state itself. Inderpal Grewal (2005) has noted, for instance, that the meanings of the American Dream circulate around the world and serve as signifiers not just of the United States but of an imagined America.

Over the last several decades, the American Dream as expressed through appliances (such as washers, dryers and refrigerators), diplomas and egalitarian achievement has been trumped by a new form of class mandate, fame. In the mediated spaces of postmodernity where image functions as an index to identity, one has not really succeeded until she breathes the rarefied air of the glamorous celebrity, thus turning the achievable possibility of success American-style into a much more elusive proposition.[4] This is not to say that fame's role in marking success is new: just take a look at Alger's *Fame and Fortune* to witness a nineteenth-century co-articulation of financial success and public visibility as aspirational targets. Indeed, Joseph DeVitis and John Martin Rich have argued that '[S]uccess in America has usually meant making money and translating it into fame and status' (DeVitis and Rich 1996: 1). What is new may be the way that celebrity itself contains multiple meanings. Leo Braudy (1986) has argued that there is an important difference between the terms fame and celebrity, since he considers fame to be the reward offered to those who perform great and wonderful deeds (like walking on the moon or becoming president); celebrity, by contrast, indicates the flash-in-the-pan personalities who entertain us for a short period of time but ultimately sink into obscurity (see also

Turner 2010). In this nomenclature, fame stands for the high, celebrity for the low. Fame marks aspiration, celebrity brands ambition. Fame is for the aristocrat, celebrity is for the proletariat (see Grindstaff in this volume). Fame rewards valour, celebrity stains scandal. And clearly, these binaries convey both classed and gendered distinctions, since the machinery of fame is often the elite masculinist theatre of politics, war and heroism; whereas the workings of celebrity often reside in the feminised domains of rumour and innuendo.

Reality Stars Flaunt Lives; Real Stars Guard Privacy

Celetoids are the accessories of cultures organized around mass communications and staged authenticity. Examples include lottery winners, one-hit wonders, stalkers, whistle-blowers, sports' arena streakers, have-a-go-heroes, mistresses of public figures and the various other social types who command media attention one day, and are forgotten the next. (Rojek 2001: 20–1)

In the land of reality TV, where everyone can be (or at least look like) a star, success carries more registers than either hot (you're a star!) or cold (you're a nobody). Heidi Klum may tell us on *Project Runway* that one day you are in and the next you are out, but fame itself has become a striated and fluid category indicating many things and people besides those we regard as great or talented. As *USA Today* rather derisively put it, on reality TV, 'nobodies [can] walk the path to stardom, no talent required' (Oldenburg 2009: D1). In the reality TV world, extra-diegetic visibility constitutes the reward for labour, where meritocracy is defined as those who can survive on an island longest, those who can sing pop songs best or those who look spiffiest after ten plastic surgery procedures and a style makeover.[5] But the reality celebrity won as a consequence of such shows as *Survivor, American Idol* and *The Swan* is fleeting and often stained by stigma. If enduring public memory is one of the factors that make being famous matter, it seems that reality celebrity is a form of public recognition, important as a phenomenon, but more about the hierarchical nature of fame itself rather than the unique personhood of the individuals who cycle in and out of recognition and remembrance.

Celebrity culture indexes ideological information about a specific historical moment's investment in glamour, uniqueness and transcendence, particularly in relation to the self: 'Stars articulate what it is to be a human being in contemporary society' (Dyer 2004: 7). In other words, stars help us make sense of identity by offering coherent and concrete models of the 'unique individual', thus allowing the somewhat abstract category of 'personhood' to become more salient (ibid.: 8–9). This is accomplished through the discursive contrast that takes place between a star's varying roles in films where they perform a self, as distinct from their 'real selves', which are presumably not performed, offering the promise of a sincere, authentic being that, through the actor's talent, fuels the star persona (Dyer 2004).

It is worth asking what happens when we turn our gaze to the smaller screen of television. John Langer (1981) argues that due to its emphasis on the familiar and intimate, television can only create personalities not stars, and P. David Marshall explains, 'whereas the film celebrity plays with aura through the construction of distance, the television celebrity is configured around conceptions of familiarity' (Marshall 1997: 119). Reality TV extends the notions of the intimate and the 'authentic' but in its depiction of ordinary people, reality TV is anything but real. Even in the context of reality TV's obvious construction, 'realness' functions as a commodity of value.

What kind of class information might be embedded in what are often coded as the experiences of 'actual' working-class people, who barter a shameful story, a personal tragedy or a gaggle of children for the visibility that reality TV confers. If as Dyer (2004) and Gamson (1994) have told us, celebrity functions as a brand that must be produced, packaged, commodified and circulated, in turn fostering consumer recognition and loyalty, can reality celebrity, with its ties to real people, possibly contribute to and be enmeshed within star culture? Further, what might it mean for the 'ordinary person' to claim what has been coded as a middle-class right to privacy within the identity-as-commodity economy of celebrity?

Mother or Monster?

> She doesn't understand, perhaps, the protocol of the entertainment industry, but she doesn't need to. She's not an entertainer, she's a mom. (Jim Moret, *Inside Edition*[6])

> If Kate shut off the cameras and stayed home with her kids, the problems would be solved. (Virginia Forrestall 2010)

Kate Gosselin helps answer some of these questions about the shifting meanings of identity, class and gender within reality celebrity. As is evident from the epigraphs that start this section, Kate is simultaneously a public and private figure, who must guard access to her home and family and fight off the paparazzi. Several episodes of *Jon and Kate Plus 8* that aired during the couple's marital rift made much of the jackal-like paparazzi waiting at the edges of their property line or in the trees at the sextuplets' fifth birthday party celebration, as if to underscore the benevolent gaze of TLC cameras and the threatening voyeurism of the tabloid press. On an outing to a party supply store, Kate instructs her children to refer to the paparazzi as 'P-people'; on a trip to the supermarket, she turns the tabloids around so that her kids will not see their own faces (or their mother's) on the covers. In a 2009 episode of *Jon and Kate Plus 8*, Kate took her boys on a tour of the USS *North Carolina* battleship during a trip to North Carolina. On deck, the boys had an opportunity to play with the cannons, and Kate encouraged them to aim at the band of marauding photographers across the bay. She recounts in narrative direct address: 'We had a really good target. I told them, "Aim at the paparazzi!" I figured they were shooting us with their cameras, we could shoot them with our "guns".' In spite of public outcry that the publicity surrounding their reality show was exploitative to her children (and suits being brought in Pennsylvania by Child Protective Services), Kate argued that the true exploitation of her kids came not from the show but from the tabloid press. 'If we stop filming, we're missing the paycheck but not the frenzy [of paparazzi]. You've still got the negative' (Tauber 2010: 76). But Kate has had a difficult time maintaining her protective mother stance given that she seems to actively court the very menace she claims to hate. If movie stars can be accorded a degree of sympathy for the loss of their private lives or even the exploitation of their children in exchange for the nurturance of their careers, reality TV stars can claim no such quarter, since they have elided the lines between public and private by selling the quotidian details of their lives.

With a headline in yellow capitals declaring 'Mom to Monster', a 2009 *US Weekly* cover depicted before and after pictures of Kate. The before image showed a dark-haired, chubby-faced and unglamorous Kate pre-television show; the after image displayed the bleach-blonde, trim and uber-stylish (to the point of being a bit cartoonish in her ultra-mod haircut and over-large sunglasses) Kate, now 'infatuated with fame' (Reinstein and Souter 2009: 64). The magazine offers a pointed critique of the makeover celebrity, suggesting that glamorous motherhood is a contradiction in terms so dangerous that it in fact betokens megalomania, obsession and narcissism. 'Real' celebrities might put their children on display as part of the necessary publicity contract that goes with the job of being a star, but only a monster, the logic indicates, becomes famous through her children.

Kate's sins are compounded by what is considered to be her eager desire for celebrity. The website Gosselins without Pity is fond of calling her 'fake 'n bake Kate' and several conversation threads are headed by 'She's Such a Phony'. One website, which goes by the name of JibberJabbers and cleverly references TLC as The Lying Channel, berated Kate as ambitious and vain. 'Kate is a narcissistic tool bag. And main reason she is doing what she's doing is to remain in the spotlight. It has NOTHING to do with her kids. She loves the attention' (26 May 2010). This website, in particular, often makes note of what it terms Kate's disingenuous smiles, posting pictures of her with her children, while superimposed dialogue bubbles say, 'I'd rather be in Hollywood'. In one discussion, the invective quickly turns misogynistic when an anonymous poster slams Kate's friend Jamie, as 'just like Katie Kreider [Kate Gosselin's maiden name], an abusive attention seeking whore' (3 June 2010). Gotti Girl, a respondent to the *US Weekly* 'Mom to Monster' issue on Kate, posted a similarly misogynistic dismissal:

> at first my impression was that she signed up 2 do the reality show & perhaps the fame and fortune went straight 2 her head. but the more i read about her, the more i realize … she's always been an arrogant, superialistic, self-centered biotch. i feel bad 4 anyone that has 2 deal with her, but mostly 4 her kids. and 2 all u ppl squawking about how she mite b really nice & we don't know her … well, i don't c any of her family or friends jumping up 2 defend her integrity! (does she even have friends?). (22 May 2009)

Adding to this frenzy, Kate was the brunt of much criticism when in early 2010 she agreed to participate in the highly popular *Dancing with the Stars*. Critiques were largely centred on the fact that the show, with its demanding rehearsal schedule, takes place in Los Angeles, and Kate's young children were in Pennsylvania. People wondered how – after the disastrous and public ruin of her marriage and the cessation of *Jon and Kate Plus 8* – she could possibly be so cavalier (or fame-obsessed) as to leave her eight children in order to take part in a new reality programme. After her particularly ghastly performance on week three of *Dancing with the Stars*, in which she and partner Tony Dovolani danced a paso doble that featured Kate as a celebrity hounded by Tony's insistent paparazzi, the judges slammed her for being wooden and awkward. The only thing she got right, said one judge, was a glowering face that said she was a 'super bitch from hell'.

Kate buttressed herself against these blistering critiques by explaining that her decision to appear on the show was 'a career move. It was a job, essentially. It was work' ('Inside Kate's World', *Kate Plus 8*). These statements fit with her broader rationales for her original decision to put her family on television at all – it is a matter of expediency and economics. Quite simply, reality TV offers the quickest and most reliable way to provide college educations and financial stability for her large family. But the 'doing it for the children' rationale clearly loses its persuasive appeal when the family lives in a $1.1 million mansion and the matriarch is a polarising celebrity figure who continues to repurpose domestic life for public consumption. Most people now seem fairly well convinced that Kate is 'doing it' for herself, and this is an unpardonable sin in the gender politics of both motherhood and celebrity. As Shari Thurer observed about motherhood and work more generally:

> Motherhood and ambition are still largely seen as opposing forces. More strongly expressed, a lack of ambition – or a professed lack of ambition, a sacrificial willingness to set personal ambition aside – is still the virtuous proof of good mothering. For many women, perhaps most, motherhood versus personal ambition represents the heart of the feminine dilemma. (Thurer 1994: 287)

As a public mom, Kate fully exemplifies the degree to which motherhood functions as both institution and social discourse (Kaplan 1992). Kaplan demonstrates the degree to which the injunction against ambitious mothers can often bespeak nation-based anxieties about values and aspirations. She argues, 'North American culture seems ready to critique its drive for more markets, for aggressive, ambitious pursuits and often uses the figure of the mother to localise this critique' (Kaplan 1992: 198). At this point, gender scholars have to step back and ask, 'What's going on here?' Why is it permissible to label a mother who courts fame a hypocrite, a bitch or a whore? Should we not praise those women who have been resourcefulness enough to achieve what the land of milk and honey has to offer rather than degrading them on both classed and gendered grounds?

In my book on transatlantic gender and fame in the nineteenth century (Weber forthcoming), I have theorised that ideological and structural injunctions of the period made it nearly impossible for a woman to proudly claim either her desire for, or possession of, fame. After the publication of *Uncle Tom's Cabin* (1853), Harriet Beecher Stowe travelled to Great Britain and the European continent to take part in a speaking tour. But due to injunctions that marked a middle-class woman as immodest if she spoke in public, the famous Harriet sat in the back of the gallery as her husband, Calvin Stowe, and brother, Charles Beecher, spoke for her. Surely now, some 160 years later, these gendered injunctions that make women's desire for fame a gender crime have abated? But that hardly seems the case in the example of Kate Gosselin, where the coupling of fame with motherhood produces such violent reactions.

Somewhat ironically, when she defends herself, Kate often reinforces the terms of value for which she is critiqued, since she endlessly argues that she is in the public eye 'only for the kids', that she is incapable of artifice and that being famous is her job not her desire. 'I lack the ability to pull myself out and be someone else,' she confesses on *Dancing with the Stars*. 'If I'm thinking about cooking dinner, that's what you're going to see on my face.' Reinforcing this bid to an authentic inner self that cannot perform the actor's artifice, *Dancing with the Stars* devotes scene after scene to Kate as she struggles with dance steps and expression. She learns to emote as a dancer not by taking acting lessons but by working with a therapist who teaches her how to better access and express her own emotions. These lessons are too little too late, however, and when she is voted off the show, she is told it is because her dancing has been dispassionate. In the first episode of *Kate Plus 8*, airing roughly two months after her elimination, Kate ruminates on being cut from the show in terms that, again, reinforce her bid to authenticity. When she danced in front of the camera, she admits in direct address to the viewer, 'I literally went blank. I had no idea where I was. Honestly, the whole experience to me was very humbling.' Here, Kate's words buttress her separation from 'real' celebrity; she is not an actress skilled in the arts of deception, 'really, in my heart, I'm a mom to my eight kids'.

'I'm not choosing fame over my kids'

Q: What are opinions about if Kate Gosselin failed in her marriage?
A: She insisted in being the center of attention. Everything was about her and no one else mattered. She estranged herself from her relatives and those that wanted to help. She was controlling and actually abused Jon, constantly hitting him and belittling him. It seems that she has exploited her children. (Wiki Answers)

If Kate Gosselin is not a 'real' celebrity but a mom with eight kids, can we then expect reality celebrity to fulfil the same sort of cultural work as that performed by the more traditionally theorised star system? No, for in reality celebrity there is a unique amalgam of public and private that ups the ante on the front-stage/backstage machinations of the movie star. Indeed, if part of the fascination with fame can be credited to our efforts to identify the 'real' person behind the façade of stardom, much of our contempt for reality celebrity stems from a sense of falseness, that reality celebrities betray us because they do not reveal their 'true selves' on television. Consider, for instance, *US Weekly*'s damning indictment of Kate, 'Often portrayed as a brusque presence on screen, Kate off screen has morphed into something far beyond the snippy supermom … [Kate] has fallen in love with fame and fortune at the expense of almost all else' (Reinstein and Souter 2009: 66). This article reminds readers of Kate's more 'authentic' identity and social class: a 'stay-at-home mom', and before that a 'modest nurse', who grew up in a trailer park. But it is not her working-class status that earns invective but her overt desire for fame. Her aspirations toward celebrity verge on the 'vain' and the 'obsessed' (ibid.: 68). It is worth noting that both Sarah Jessica Parker and Hilary Swank, among many other 'real' celebrities, grew up in humble surroundings that included working-class trailer parks, but the discourse surrounding these stars praises their meritocratic rise to fame. Kate Gosselin, by contrast, is depicted as disingenuous and delusional precisely because the nature of her reality celebrity makes her bid for celebrity obvious. In this case, her celebrity stands as a gross miscarriage of justice rather than the apogee of the American Dream.

The implications for the classed and gendered meanings of the American Dream in the context of reality celebrity and motherhood become all the more heated when the spectacle of Kate's (sexy motherly) body is included in the mix, since the body is so often relied upon as a marker for maternalism, class residency and aspiration. One of the perks of Kate's celebrity has been the hyper-glamorisation of her appearance. She received plastic surgery free of charge, including a tummy tuck to reclaim a body stretched by bearing eight children, as a dividend of her reality celebrity (one of her fans was married to the surgeon). Through these procedures, both surgical and cosmetic, Kate has joined the ranks of 'normal' women seeking a 'mom job' to erase the physical effects that ageing, pregnancy and childbirth have wrought on the body. But paying for it with and through her celebrity has also raised what Debra Gimlin (2002) identifies as the 'taint of inauthenticity', or a sense that she has not earned and so does not deserve the beautiful body within which she resides, since it was achieved via the surgeon's scalpel or celebrity stylists rather than her own blood, sweat and tears. Ironically, such critiques help suture Kate Gosselin's reality celebrity to 'real' celebrity, since they put her in league with the bevy of starlettes who are featured each week on the covers of magazines, their cellulite highlighted with arrows, their body-based shame on display at every supermarket and newsstand in the country.

In the midst of her marital trials with Jon, Kate threw the spectatorial surveillance of her body back on the gazer. Knowing that the paparazzi were watching, she donned a bright orange bikini and headed to the beach. In response, web postings quickly turned misogynistic. Writes 'trainer' to the Just Jared website (2009): 'Undefined legs. No muscle tone. Cankles. Start running Kate and don't stop till I tell you. No wonder Jon is off to greener and younger pastures.' Responds another poster named 'It's all for the kids', '4 plastic surgery procedures and one chemical face lift. I'd say it's the best child labor can buy' (31 May). These remarks were capped by a poster to the site named 'Kate Gosselin – publicity whore!' who wrote, 'SHE says she doesn't like publicity, yet everyday she has her kids, they're on display. She LOVES the publicity. Hey Kate, you ain't looking that good, is that the ugli-est bikini you could find?' (ibid.). Kate's efforts to use her body as a weapon of defiance clearly did not overturn an angry blogosphere bent on punishing the mother who desires fame.

The case study offered by Kate Gosselin reveals a depressingly familiar misogynistic backlash toward ambitious women, particularly since, in Kate's case, she actively defies norms of idealised moth-erhood even as she defines herself according to those same normative codes. That Kate appears to have sold her private life in order to finance her celebrity makes her public persona all the more rep-rehensible, particularly since her public image has been solely fostered under the auspices of reality TV rather than Hollywood. If fame constitutes a new class marker to indicate achievement of the American Dream, reality celebrity functions as degradation of the dream in what *USA Today* termed a 'cheapening of stardom' (Oldenburg 2009: D2). To paraphrase Graeme Turner, the demotic turn in celebrity is not producing democracy (Turner 2010: 19). The case of Kate Gosselin quite bleakly sug-gests that all of the rights, entitlements, upward mobility and even citizenship that the American Dream stands for are not offered to fame-seeking mothers within the representative domain of reality TV.

Notes

1. Bev Skeggs and Helen Wood's (2008) reception studies with British viewers suggest that middle-class audiences felt disdain for reality TV participants who got something for nothing without 'proper' labour, whereas their working-class participants saw reality TV as a realistic opportunity to 'make good'.

2. This in itself is an ironic critique, since the cachet of celebrity is so often predicated on that very balance (or conflict) between the public and the private.

3. Blog posts appear as they do online and have not been 'corrected' for grammar.

4. Graeme Turner (2010) sees aspirational fantasies as not moving out of reach but appearing closer due to the seemingly achievable goal of fame. Turner and I both agree that 'celebrity still remains a systematically hierarchical and exclusive category, no matter how much it proliferates' (Turner 2010: 16).

5. As I note in *Makeover TV*, reality programmes rarely guarantee their participants celebrity; if fame comes, it is as a consequence of public attention to the show rather than as an element of the diegesis (Weber 2009).

6. Talking head on entertainment documentary *Inside Edition* (King World Productions).

Bibliography

Adams, J. T. (1931) *The Epic of America* (Boston: Little Brown and Company).

Braudy, L. (1986) *The Frenzy of Renown: Fame and Its History* (New York: Oxford University Press).

DeVitis, J. and J. M. Rich (1996) *The Success Ethic, Education, and the American Dream* (Albany: SUNY Press).

Dyer, R. (2004) *Heavenly Bodies: Film Stars and Society*, 2nd edn. (New York/London: Routledge).

Forrestall, V. (2010) 'Mailbag', *People*, 28 June, p. 12.

Gamson, J. (1994) *Claims to Fame: Celebrity in Contemporary America* (Berkeley: University of California Press).

Gimlin, D. (2002) *Body Work: Beauty and Self-Image in American Culture* (Berkeley: University of California Press).

Gosselins without Pity website (2010) Available at: <http://gosselinswithoutpity.blogspot.com/2010/05/free-discussion-52964.html?showComment=1275627608503#c3046951473081031723> accessed 20 June 2010.

Grewal, I. (2005) *Transnational America: Feminisms, Diasporas, Neoliberalisms* (Durham, NC: Duke University Press).

JibberJabbers (2010) Available at: <http://thelyingchannel.blogspot.com/2010/05/kate-gosselin-ratings-goldmine.html> accessed 20 June 2010.

Just Jared (2009) 'Kate Gosselin Is a Bikini Mama'. Available at: <http://justjared.buzznet.com/2009/05/31/kate-gosselin-bikini/> accessed 17 June 2010.

Kamp, J. (2009) 'Rethinking the American dream', *Vanity Fair*, April.

Kaplan, E. A. (1992) *Motherhood and Representation: The Mother in Popular Culture and Melodrama* (New York: Routledge).

Langer, J. (1981) 'Television's Personality System', *Media, Culture and Society*, 4: 351–65.

Marshall, P. D. (1997) *Celebrity and Power: Fame in Contemporary Culture* (Minneapolis: University of Minnesota Press).

Nudd, T. (2010) 'Kate Gosselin: "I'm not choosing fame over my kids"', *People* [online], 13 April 2010. Available at: <http://www.people.com/people/article/0,,20360412,00.html> accessed 2 June 2010.

Oldenburg, A. (2009) 'Decade in celebrities: nobodies walk the path to stardom', *USA Today*, 31 January, p. D2.

Reinstein, M. and E. Souter (2009) 'Mom to monster', *US Weekly*, 20 May, pp. 64–70.

Rojek, C. (2001) *Celebrity* (London: Reaktion).

Skeggs, B. and H. Wood (2008) 'The Labour of Transformation and Circuits of Value "around" reality TV', *Continuum*, 22(4): 559–72.

Snarkfood (2010) Available at: <http://snarkfood.com/kate-gosselin-new-show-on-tlc-makes-us-nauseous/37750/> accessed 20 May 2010.

Sperling, N. and L. Rice (2010) 'Hollywood insider', *Entertainment Weekly* [online], 7 June 2010. Available at: <http://hollywoodinsider.ew.com/2010/06/07/kate-plus-8-ratings/> accessed 7 June 2010.

Tauber, M. (2010) 'Kate Gosselin and her kids: our year of change', *People*, 7 June, pp. 72–6.

Thurer, S. L. (1994) *The Myths of Motherhood: How Culture Reinvents the Good Mother* (Boston, MA: Houghton Mifflin).

Turner, G. (2010) *Ordinary People and the Media: The Demotic Turn* (Los Angeles/London: Sage).

Tyler, I. (2008) '"Chav mum, chav scum": Class Disgust in Contemporary Britain', *Feminist Media Studies*, 8(1): 17–34.

Tyler, I. and B. Bennett (2010) 'Celebrity Chav: Fame, Femininity and Social Class', *European Journal of Cultural Studies*, 13(3): 375–93.

Weber, B. R. (2009) *Makeover TV: Selfhood, Citizenship, and Celebrity* (Durham, NC: Duke University Press).

——— (forthcoming) *Women and Literary Celebrity in the Nineteenth Century: The Transatlantic Production of Fame and Gender* (Burlington, VT: Ashgate).

Wiki Answers, available at: <http://wiki.answers.com/Q/FAQ/5570-5>.

12/Heather Nunn

Investing in the 'Forever Home': From Property Programming to 'Retreat TV'

> Home is where the heart is. You can get inside and slam the door. We dream of the big, beautiful, sensate commodity-to-live-in, the bathroom done in textures of stone and precious metals, a utopia of colourful décor. But the synaesthesia of being at home is always already afloat in the circuits of the prevailing public winds – privatization, sensible accumulation, family values, or some kind of identity or lifestyle or something. (Stewart 2007: 2–3)

Home is where the heart is. But the contemporary home is inextricable from material culture and market forces. In British culture, the emotional experiences of home are often bound to broader social expectations and values, status anxiety, financial (in)security and notions of futurity. Many in the relatively affluent West have embraced the fantasy of sensual, well-designed comfort that Kathleen Stewart invokes in her account of the affective nature of everyday life in America. This image of insured, secure, well-coordinated comfort has been promulgated over the past twenty-odd years in British political discourse, as well as in lifestyle programmes and journalism. It encapsulates the aspirant working or, more often middle-class, domestic space, the assumed experience of successful home-ownership and attendant values of responsibility and care, bound together with consumerist investment. My concern is with the deployment of house and home in popular factual television to perpetuate and to an extent naturalise some of these broader cultural associations that link dwelling, space, property and classed identity. This chapter will reflect upon lifestyle television's mobilisation of property and of home, and its recent transformation in format and message as it negotiates and adapts to the changing landscape of social class, national prosperity and the financial squeeze.

I suggest that there are three components which support the cultural imagining, political mobilisation and material importance of domestic property in general, and property and home programming in particular: capital investment, subsistence and security, and emotional investment. These are often interconnected and, as we will see below, inform representations of familial and national well-being.

First, capital investment in domestic property in Britain is forged by Thatcher's brand of neoliberal popular capitalism which prevailed in the 1980s. By the late 1990s (a period when two-thirds of British households were home-owners), the privately owned home as marker of familial collateral, domestic security and national well-being was firmly embedded in the national psyche. Under consecutive Conservative and New Labour governments since Margaret Thatcher, owner-occupation was strongly associated with being securely middle class, with sensible investment and financial accumulation, social mobility and lifestyle success. Thus for many British people, the owned (rather than rented or squatted or parental) home is the keystone of security and social success. Similarly in the United States, President Bush's model of the 'ownership society', which gained ground in the early 2000s, amplified an existing 'cultural repertoire centred on personal responsibility, possessive individualism and self-reliance' seen as analogous to Thatcher's neo-liberal popular capitalism (Béland 2007: 95–6).[1] Until recently, this confidence in home-ownership as a touchstone of security and social achievement, both individually *and for the national good*, prevailed.

Second, security and subsistence: the occupation of a property which provides privacy, basic amenities and a space for domestic retreat is central to late-modern notions of comfort and self-respect. In a recent study of social exclusion, a representative sample of the British population listed heated accommodation, a bed and damp-free living space as the top three necessities of subsistence (Burrows 2003: 1225).[2] In other words, the warm, safe home is the material ground upon which the good life might thrive or a difficult life be made tolerable, and that material well-being supports our sense of personal value and a place of value in the social world.

Third, the emotional, powerfully affective landscape of the domestic dwelling is central to contemporary understandings of aspiration, responsibility, well-being and self-development. The symbolism of the home is central to our mapping of the outer world, and research into the meaning of the home repeatedly throws up the same key emotionally laden terms: 'security, family, intimacy, comfort, control' (Putnam, in Morley 2000: 24). Social theorists have long scrutinised the modern notion of status for the middle classes. Money, they argued, was a key component of the cultural imagination of late capitalism; possession of financial wealth enabled one to acquire property, and the secluded home became the standard benchmark of reputation, status and social standing, which ensured the middle classes could ward off the unpleasant emotions associated with censure and contempt. Property and financial security also bolstered against self-reprimand and a sense of personal failure.

Bearing these three components in mind, this chapter falls into two parts. First, it explores the political backdrop of Thatcherism and the ongoing promotion of a market populism that underpinned widely circulated notions of home-ownership as responsible and aspirational citizenship. The popularisation of this ideology informed lifestyle TV programming in the 1990s and early 2000s which endorsed the image of the home as primarily a capital investment firmly attached to lifestyle choices. The second part of the chapter will move to home and property lifestyle programming from the late 2000s to consider the impact of the downturn, a middle-class exhaustion with consumerism and stressful work/life imbalance, and the shift towards more affective registers of the home.

A Private Home for All: Politics and Lifestyle Television since Thatcherism

Recent housing research demonstrates a contradiction. In the current economic downturn, 'house buyers are positive about replacing the prevailing philosophy of home-ownership with other, more sustainable and socially just models of house occupancy', but nonetheless, the dominant model of housing occupancy stalwartly remains private home-ownership (ESRC, 2008: 73).[3] The association between responsible adulthood, individual responsibility and the mortgage is nationally specific, and in the UK, home-ownership has been particularly reified since Margaret Thatcher's long decade of government.[4]

In 1975, the Conservative Party elected Margaret Thatcher as leader and ushered in a new era in which class was subsumed under widespread conversations about identity, social mobility and entrepreneurial responsibility. From 1979 onwards, its modernisation of Britain entailed a reworking of neo-liberalism and Conservatism. This redefined the socio-political realm: the virtues of the market would displace the dependencies of state welfarism and an entrepreneurial spirit would enliven and drive forward both public and private life creating independence and consumer choice. Thatcherism contained profound disjunctions. On the one hand, it endorsed a neo-liberal vision of a deregulated, freewheeling enterprise culture represented by the stock market, financial 'big bangs', deregulated shares and competitive business frontiers to conquer.[5] On the other, it maintained older Conservative mores through the language of moral discipline, law and order, family values and the national hearth. Put simply, Thatcher negotiated the inherent contradictions of her populist agenda through the repeated image of the home (Nunn 2002). Thatcher's 'property owning democracy' extended the Conservative tradition because she saw property as an indelible right and an asset: a symbol of paternal responsibility and the core of generational transmission of wealth. She declared, assuming perhaps a level of fiscal responsibility that many would struggle to undertake, that home-ownership 'will give more of our people ... that prospect of handing something on to their children and grandchildren' (Adonis and Pollard 1997: 207).

The British 1980 Housing Act which enshrined the council tenant's 'right to buy' their property was a potent feature of the expression of consumer choice (Clarke et al. 2007) and the instrument of the decline of social housing as a viable and *respectable* option. In Britain, the opportunity to buy one's council home signified the attempted widespread dissolution of public sector provision of homes in favour of private home-ownership.

Neo-liberal politics of the late twentieth century have involved liberating the market from state-imposed forms of regulation and enabling a more flexible labour force, freeing up 'individual choice' (Harvey 2005; Rosenthal 2005; Schwartz 2005; Salecl 2010). The ethos of consumer choice and the mortgage which effected a transition to a new, apparently middle-class lifestyle seemed to have occurred quickly, inadvertently and without a conscious drive towards social mobility. In *Surviving the Blues* (Scanlon 1990), published at the tail end of Thatcher's era, young women recount what it meant to come of age under Thatcher's government. Mandy Nichol (cited in Scanlon 1990: 48) wryly observed that she lived her teenage years and early married life under Thatcherism in 'a climate where you think of yourself and your bank balance first and care about others second'; where the only government she had ever known had been blue (the colour of Conservatism). She charted her movement from her working-class origins via marriage, property and the labour of fixing up the house with a watchful eye on the rise and fall of interest rates. Nichols recalls: 'There I was, I had become a product of Thatcher's Britain. I had the good husband, the house, the twenty-five-year mortgage and all the trappings … it took to be acceptable and respected … I'd become a nasty shade of blue' (cited in Scanlon 1990: 48).

Post-Thatcher Conservative and subsequent New Labour policy continued to emphasise the privately owned home as central to individual success and responsibility. In 1997, New Labour promoted the citizen-consumer as the emblem of modernising public reform (Clarke *et al.* 2007: 37). Indeed, New Labour extended the promotion of social mobility into its imperative form and consequently signifiers of success were intimately bound up with public displays of power, consumer affluence or entrepreneurial achievement (Dench 2006: 12–13; Nunn and Biressi 2008). Since the late 1970s, then, and thanks to the accession of neo-liberalist ideologies, the privately owned house has overridden any other notions of domestic dwelling – rented, communally owned, charity or social housing, drop-off space, travelling home, and so on – to become the prime symbol of security and success (and by implication vulnerability) in modern Britain.

Just over a decade ago, the Institute of Fiscal Studies (1996: 2) argued that 'Being a council or Housing Association tenant is now one of the best available indicators of being poor.' Council homes are now frequently seen as 'the ghetto' of the 'underclass', an image frequently underscored in reality programmes such *Tower Block of Commons* (Channel 4, 2010) in which MPs 'live' with working-class constituents and experience their cash-strapped lifestyle and deprived physical environment. The neglected tower block or litter-strewn council estate has become shorthand for communal apathy and moral decline. And, until recently, social and housing policy research tended to reflect dominant associations of home-ownership with financial success by ignoring the growth of low-income home-ownership and corresponding rise in coincidence between unemployment, home-ownership and poverty in the latter years of the twentieth century (Burrows 2003: 1224).

In Britain, lifestyle formats helped boost the tradition of the factual home-improvement programming which was established during the 1980s and proliferated in the 90s[6] underlining 'the consolidation and proliferation of everyday discourses of value and investment associated with the purchase of housing' (Brunsdon 2003: 8). Images of aspirational home-making translated easily across advanced capitalist Anglophone nations (Rosenberg 2008). From the 2000s, lifestyle television colonised the mid-evening slots on terrestrial channels and there was an observable spike in the number of lifestyle-home, property and gardening programmes. Home/property lifestyle programming also became a key component of dedicated lifestyle cable channels, and relatively low production costs, accessibility as a platform for commercial sponsorship and spin-off products, and generic flexibility ensure its continuation.

In the 2000s, new home location programmes such as *Relocation, Relocation* (2009–) (Channel 4's more ambitious updating of *Location, Location, Location*, 2001–) and *A Place in the Sun: Home or Away* (which looked at property home and abroad), along with personal finance and makeover shows, helped normalise the (implicitly middle-class) processes of self-improvement required in both the public and private spheres, domains whose distinctions have become increasingly blurred (Palmer 2008; Ouellette and Hay 2008). Tensions between a drive for investment and emotional responses to property were played out as property experts invoked the affective language of 'gut feeling', 'instincts', 'the wow factor' to register home-hunters' emotional responses to property while frequently, in asides to camera and in staged pragmatic advice sessions with their clients, reminding them and those at home of the need for business acumen and a firm rational hold on purchasing decisions. In *Homes under the Hammer* (BBC 1, 2003–), the hard-headed business side of buying for investment was emphasised as viewers were invited into frequently shabby, half-renovated or derelict properties that have been put under auction. Here, the underside of the property market was present as cameras entered repossessed homes. But the emphasis on property as financial investment prevailed as the viewer watched punters bidding at the auction house and their subsequent transformation of a cheaply purchased property into a viable rentable or resale property. Purchasers (of whom there were many) who bought without viewing a property or miscalculated costs for renovation were judged by the experts, assessed by estate agent evaluations and held to financial account.

In 2003, *Guardian* journalist Claire Cozens affirmed property as the 'new reality TV', while her *Guardian* colleague Zad Rogers, creative director of IWP, an independent TV company, asked, 'How many property programmes can we watch on TV?', observing that on a single night just two programmes (*Relocation, Relocation* and *Escape to the Country* [BBC 2, 2002–]) attracted nearly 8 million viewers. TV production company promotional material tapped into a general expectation that amateur property investors could generate easy money. Prospective participants for new series *House Auction* were asked, 'Do you want to try and get rich quick? Ever wondered if you've got what it takes to make a small fortune on the property market?' (Cozens 2003). Property programmes tapped into the ongoing aspirational-consumer zeitgeist: 'our need for change; our sense that we deserve better' (Rogers 2003).

Anglo-American property, personal finance and makeover shows normalised the processes of self-improvement required to brand oneself in the spheres of both work and personal identity as part of the broader shift to an 'enterprising self' (see Palmer in this volume). The reality of these 'lifestyle choices' was a continually renewed exchange of money for goods, services and experiences often fuelled by credit/debt, one of the dirty secrets of contemporary consumer capitalism. In lifestyle programming, debt has appeared fleetingly in individual makeover programmes, where it is depicted as irresponsible individual money management capable of reform with expert guidance on downsizing. In programmes like *Bank of Mum and Dad* (BBC 2, 2000–) and *Your Money or Your Life* (BBC 2, 1999–2003), stern but slightly ironic bantering experts help debt-ridden 'consumer-addicts' follow 'spendaholic' development plans or counselling to appraise and manage their consumption (Palmer 2008: 9). Debt here becomes another indicator of the mismanaged life which refuses future investment.

By 2007, the financial systems were on the verge of dramatically unravelling. Private property became a prime sign of the vulnerability of the private individual in the face of unstoppable global economic systems. In 2007, expansion of housing provision was one of the key objectives of British Prime Minister Gordon Brown's new government, with an ambitious target for delivering 240,000 homes per year (Lloyd 2009: 19). Within six months, the credit crunch and financial downturn had weakened dominant fiscal models for private residential development and drastically diminished the availability of loans and secure mortgages. As Toby Lloyd commented, the home is the point 'where the financial economy meets the real, where ephemeral debt instruments meet solid bricks and mortar, and where the evaporation of investor confidence impacts directly onto people's lives and jobs' (Lloyd 2009: 19). And while all classes and social economic groups encountered the effects of the recession, the middle classes recognised themselves as betrayed, besieged and embattled.

The global market downturn was, of course, triggered in part by irresponsible lending to 'sub-prime' borrowers who could ill afford to take on the financing which they needed to buy housing. One consequence was a fall in the market value of housing which affected the more 'responsible' but actually higher-consuming middle class. The irony of this situation was not lost on media critics, who had already observed with consternation the disproportionate number of property programmes in the schedules. Even lifestyle property presenters such as Sarah Beeny (*Property Ladder* [Channel 4, 2001–]) conceded that TV schedules were replete with property programming and the downturn might weed out weaker programmes, but as Kirstie Allsop (*Location, Location, Location*) predicted in the longer term, property programming would simply adapt to the new environment (Henley 2008, see also Nunn 2009).

The Recession and 'Retreat TV'

At the outset of the recession, economic news reports relaying the story of home-ownership and domestic security under threat stood in stark contrast to many of the lifestyle programmes still running on terrestrial and cable channels. Media critics, and no doubt some viewers, felt increasingly queasy when confronted with discourses of excessive consumption and risk-related investment at a time of rising unemployment and fiscal gloom.

In fact, the TV industry recognised that its programming must reflect, adapt and even to a certain degree clarify the impact on home-owners and buyers of the economic downturn. First, in the immediate aftermath of the financial downturn, established programming acknowledged the unstable market, but without radically altering their tone or format. They downplayed 'fast buck' property investments and house moves were presented as strategies for longer-term affective investment. Newer programming adapted familiar formats with a modified register of emotional and financial appreciation for current dwellings. For example, in *The Home Show* (Channel 4, 2009), architect George Clark stressed home-owners' emotional investment in their neglected home. *Property Ladder* was renamed *Property Snakes and Ladders* in the UK in 2009 (after the board game where players can win by ascending ladders or lose by falling down a snake) to indicate that not all property investments ensured winners. The updated version of *Location, Location, Location* responded to new, unstable market conditions by presenting property as bulwark against risk and discontent and as the place where the family can retrench until better times return.

Audiences were offered escapist fantasies with narratives of possible flight from economic gloom in programmes such as *Phil Down Under* (Channel 4, 2010), a series in which property expert Phil Spencer explored properties, jobs and culture in Australia. Similarly, property series *Relocation, Relocation* perpetuated visions of middle-class flight from urban stress as couples aimed to relocate to the country or coast to enable the restoration of a family life, integration into a smaller community or comfortable downsizing after retirement. The series rested each week on the sale of a substantial inner-city or large suburban property to release equity for the purchase of two properties – one the idealised rural or coast location and the other a small inner-city property near to the main wage earner's employment. The programme accentuated homes with 'added value', room for development or renovation in riskier times. Property experts Allsop and Spencer promised house-hunters that problems with space, location and fraught lifestyles might be remedied by an informed purchase of the 'forever home': 'the forever home' (a new catchphrase that appeared as financial times become straitened in the late 2000s). While such programmes point in the direction of 'retreat TV's' revision of consumerist dreams, they nonetheless cling to the image of property as site of endless strategic investment amid the vagaries of the market. As Lyn Thomas notes, such programmes do not neatly resolve the complex dissatisfaction of affluent upper-middle-class lives. Frequently, for example, in *Relocation, Relocation*, 'affluent consumers are caught in a double bind, where their desires for peace and pleasure require ever more complex deployments of their labour and property if they are even to be half satisfied' (Thomas 2008: 688).

More explicitly, recession-based shows aimed to instruct the newly embattled middle classes how to consume, save and invest responsibly for a more secure future. As such, they also joined a raft of lifestyle journalism which had been quick to address the condition of the middle classes under financial pressure: the 'rump' of 'middle England' which seemed in danger of being swept away in the economic tide of declining house values, over-borrowing and dwindling investments.[7] In 2009, BBC 2 in particular confronted the recession head on with a new season of factual programming instructing putative middle-class viewers on how to adjust spending behaviours (more caution when investing in property), how to enjoy the home and make it comfortable (home as sanctuary), and even how to learn economies from the already poor who shop for budget brands and mend rather than spend (home as subsistence). The latter included *Mary Queen of Charity Shops* (usually *Mary Queen of Shops*), which aimed to make charity shop shopping as desirable (and profitable) an experience as boutique shopping; *Economy Gastronomy*, which showed people how to eat well for less money; and *Brand New Home* (how to make your old home look like new). *Propertywatch* (May 2009), which ran over four nights and examined how changes in the market affected people's lives, was promoted as the first show to thoroughly address the recession's impact on homes and their residents and adopted a more sceptical attitude towards the market while still retaining a populist emphasis on the lived experiences of ordinary people.

The other strand of post-financial downturn lifestyle programming is what I have termed 'retreat TV'. This strand again prioritises home/property as a space of comfort and emotional succour; it affords its subjects (primarily middle class) the privilege of self-reflexivity with, and often without, expert advice. The performers in many of these programmes are 'educated', culturally competent individuals who articulate a current disenchantment with consumerism, 24/7 work, fast-time capitalism and so on. Positively, they speak the disillusionment of the white-collar and professional classes with the dictates of late capitalism. Negatively, they address this disenchantment in programmes that mainly require money, mobility and cultural competences to escape, resources that are unavailable to many viewers who are also probably excluded from consumerist narratives and therapeutic disciplines of work/life success.

Programmes developed from the green lifestyle agenda and non-secular philosophies have paved the way for a more ethical relation to the home through expressions of 'downshifting', 'upcycling', 'downsizing' in a retreat from the pressures of consumer-led society to a more ethical, sustainable life (Thomas 2008). Drawing on Soper's notion of 'alternative hedonism', Thomas explains how these desires were refracted through series such as *It's Not Easy Being Green* and I suggest are also explored in series such as *How to Live a Simple Life* (a modern update of St Francis of Assisi [BBC 2, 2010]) and *The Edible Garden* (in which a gardener lives the good life in a small urban space). These programmes span a spectrum of interests including cookery, property, gardening and farming, and home-making crafts, and while some are about being 'green', many are more concerned with a new kind of individualist work upon the self. The programmes tap into a new zeitgeist for lifestyle simplification that was already beginning in popular culture just before the recession, when downsizing blogs, vintage and second-hand guidebooks and chick-lit-style budgeting books signalled dissatisfaction with consumption, demanding professional work regimes and the predicament of fast capitalism.

The dominant models of self-improvement and fulfilment through consumption prevalent in much lifestyle programming are challenged and partly resisted by the cultural imagination of new routes to a good life which re-prioritise ethical and thoughtful modern living. The abnegation of consumption and its accompanying self-immersion in paid work are the new middle-class mantra (so far so good and so far so understandable). But a retrogressive slippage can occur. Retreat TV sometimes succumbs to and reworks older models of the mechanically self-perfected self from which the programmes' central subjects are often desperately trying to escape. Retreat TV offers a new model of 'being all you can be' but does so by once again individualising the problem and solution: the rectification via personal struggle of a faulty lifestyle and/or belief system.

This ethos is delivered in *How to Lead a Simple Life*, where the Reverend Peter Owen-Jones, last seen in the series *Round the World in 80 Faiths* (BBC 2, 2009), turns his back on consumerism and swaps his stressful, superficial life for one which follows some of the ground rules of St Francis of Assisi. He hands over his cheque book and credit cards to the BBC and attempts to live without money, trading work for food, petrol and the occasional beer, and foraging for food in the South Downs around his parish. The series presents the haphazard and sometimes unsuccessful attempt at humility and reliance on the goodwill of others. The formula is paralleled in *My Dream Farm* (Channel 4, 2010), as a working farm or commercial garden offer a form of therapeutic retreat where affluent participants leave high-flying professional careers and sell their homes to fund new businesses farming sheep, keeping chickens and working the land. In one episode, young professional Kierti Vaidya draws upon a parental loan to begin life as a lone farmer raising alpacas in Warwickshire for their lucrative wool. Guided by the weathered experience of gardening celebrity presenter Monty Don, the viewers are invited to assess their commitment and ability to learn new entrepreneurial skills and become part of the local community. Here, the rhetoric of good business practice, financial acumen and hard-headed decision-making sit with the respect for the land and pleasure in rural life extolled by experienced farmer and gardener Don.

There is a deeply gendered nostalgic undertone to many of these programmes. The implied retrogressive return to a fantasised era when women made do within the home was writ large in Sally

Hewitt's half-hour documentary *Time Warp Wives* (Channel 4, 2008), which recorded the lives of four women who had chosen to return to a pre-feminist era of domesticity. The publicity for the series showed a mid-twentieth-century woman in vintage clothing smiling in a 1950s-style kitchen. Property expert Kirstie Allsop, host of *Location, Location, Location* and *Relocation, Relocation*, mentioned above, fronted a new post-recession series, *Kirstie's Homemade Home* (Channel 4, 2009), which charted her transformation of her five-bedroom home via charity shop buys, sewing and making her own candles with the expert guidance of local craftspeople. Here, she melded her business expertise about home renovation with creative home-making crafts to disclose how these were pleasurable work that could enhance a home interior adding both emotional succour and, implicitly, financial value.

The *Edible Garden* followed the current trend of 'retreat TV' as it charted ex-*Gardener's World* presenter Alys Fowler's year-long attempt to opt out of consumption and grow edible crops amid the ornamental plants and flowers in her West Midlands terraced garden. The series takes viewers through the trials and tribulations of attempted self-sufficiency as Fowler encounters tomato blight and torrential rain. The camera lingers on close-ups of Swiss chard and demonstrates in soft focus the visual pleasures of courgettes and climbing beans. The narrative is interspersed with Fowler's small social gatherings as twenty–thirty-somethings in quirky vintage-style clothes share home-made wine or swap home-grown produce. The pleasures on offer are quite seductive as the programme cultivates an attitude of life simplification. It presents everyday living as a modest philosophy in which one resolves to reduce superficial consumption and to accept that crops will fail, produce will be blighted and that hens will not always lay an egg on demand. This retreat is rendered as an aesthetic pleasure rather than money saving or political strategy. Fowler is captured in slow camera takes as she consumes her hens' eggs (the hens are named after early twentieth-century modernist writers Alice B. Toklas and Gertrude Stein). Employing soft focus, the camera follows Fowler as she picks home-grown herbs or forages for berries or elderflowers. There is a profound nostalgic quality here that emphasises the visual pleasures of the home as sanctuary: shots of flowers or fruits, old enamel plates, willow frames for beans (foraged from the local park and made with the help of a friend). This is coupled with a new version of individualised choice: here, individual superficial consumption can be modified and one can make, repair or selectively purchase locally grown or ethically produced products.

In the six-part series *The Delicious Miss Dahl* (BBC 2, 2010), model and children's writer Sophie Dahl retreats into the kitchen. Her setting is a contemporary-rustic kitchen complete with enamel kitchenware, vintage scales, battered old pots, heavy preserving jars and pastel-coloured tableware. Each episode was shaped to an emotional state: Melancholy, Romance, Escapism, Nostalgia and so on. For instance, in 'Selfishness', Dahl left the kitchen for small local shops to buy an art-deco cocktail shaker with which to later make herself a dirty martini. Close-ups of Dahl preparing food or mixing her martini accentuate the solipsism of the kitchen and the simple delight of the found object. The retreat Dahl signifies is one of comfortable upper-middle-class domesticity; the camera lingers on kitchen surfaces strewn with vintage-shabby feminine objects: a tiny bone-china teacup; some faded silk flowers; a worn enamel ladle; a set of simple old bowls. Like *The Edible Garden*, this series accentuates the synaesthetic pleasures of food, aroma, warmth, the rhythm of poetry or literature, and the visual and tactile pleasure of the found object celebrated by modernists such as Proust and

Virginia Woolf but here overlaid with a contemporary sensibility that rewrites this affluent security as a delight in selective consumption, the joyful retreat into a domestic femininity in which cooking is not about work or budgeting or the grind of the supermarket after a day at the office, but indulging the senses.

To return to Stewart with whom we began this chapter: she speaks of instability at the heart of the fantasy cocooned home, suggesting a state of 'jumpy', vital vulnerability. Particularly for women, in the early twenty-first century, the ideology of the domestic property as safe retreat is presented as 'a practiced possibility, emergent in projects like home remodelling, shopping, straightening up the house, rearranging furniture, making lists' and so on (Stewart 2007: 56). Property magazines such as *Elle Deco, Living Etc, Homes and Gardens* or *Period Living* present household objects as still life and even 'a small wooden table arranged by a window holds the promise of a profoundly secluded interior' (ibid.).

As in numerous lifestyle property programmes and property journalism of the 2000s, buying and working on the home is presented as an amalgam of crafts, business and design skills – never overtly about just consumption or investment. Renovating 'know-how' is combined with painterly skills in discerning light and shade, and buying from antique or flea markets is now presented as 'sourcing'. A hybrid urban collector-consumer is addressed; aware that the home is an economic resource but reminded that an upbeat, assertive mindset aids the bargain hunt. Here, capital investment is recast as emotional labour, as exemplified by the editor of *Period Living* who described the rescue of an old property and installation of authentic interior fittings and distressed furniture as a new kind of (implicitly fiscal) gratification: the serendipity of the found treasure is combined with a new street-aware planning: 'upcycling with attitude' the 'hidden treasures of the salvage yard' (*Period Living*, July 2010: 7).

It is important not to write pleasure out of such processes. The pleasure in such media narratives derives partly from the promise of transformation, the enjoyment of a bargain, the nostalgic retrieval of history in a lovingly restored object and the mindfulness of one's budget. This vocabulary is a novel inflection of older forms of discourse which fused work and leisure to consumption. The fascination with property and its fetish status is not new, but bears the inheritance of late-nineteenth-century expansion: as capitalism surged into its advanced swaggering stage, we, in the affluent West, inherited the drives, anxieties and inequities of the period, albeit styled and trimmed to contemporary times and stitched through with class inflections. Does the shift towards a reflexive criticism of this whole way of life entail a troubling refiguration of consumption, lifestyle and working-on-the-self which perpetuates distinctions between economic and culturally competent classes? Or does it also offer an emergent new praxis which partially renders visible the strata of society for which 'making-do', working the land/allotment/garden and refusal of/inability to participate in the neo-liberal models of fast capitalism have been a longer-term way of life?

Conclusion: Emotional Capitalism

The ghost of our recent past and the spectre of both present and future is finance capitalism. For many an abstract, disconnected system, it weaves through our lives in invisible but powerful ways and shapes the hopes and the material practices of everyday life. Cultural critics contend that we now inhabit an intensely emotional culture – one in which the signifiers of finance capitalism (of bargaining, exchange, investment and good return) have informed our current close, intimate relationships and the cherished spaces of our private lives (Illouz 2007).

One aspect of the new millennial zeitgeist has been an enhanced sense of risk with attendant anxiety. As subjects in the affluent nations increasingly recognise our disempowerment in the public world, our immediate environment takes on fraught extra psychological burdens. Consumption humanises, distracts and individualises the broader structures of capitalism. How we enact our lives in the private space of home subtends contemporary lifestyle advice about conduct and mechanisms of self-improvement: what we eat, what we furnish our property with, how we garden, how we add value to our property, regulate the day-to-day behaviour of ourselves and family within its walls.

Domestic property is seen simultaneously as 'the mirror of the self' and 'its incubator' (Salecl 2010: 35). The 'you are your home' mindset is captured in prevailing platitudes found across lifestyle media in the idea that 'your inner self will find fulfilment as long as you create the right environment for it'. Here, the art of interior design meshes with prevailing economic rationalist models of expectation that invite us to mould our inner self and our intimate domestic surroundings within the arena of market choice available to the discerning consumer. Even in new versions of lifestyle media such as retreat TV, the home and the self are to be worked on and developed to fulfil our potential as human subjects. In the current (perhaps temporary) downplaying of property as foremost a secure financial investment, the affective and emotional register has been elevated to offer a rebranded vision of home as futurity in times of financial risk.

But 'choice', the motor of neo-liberal ideologies, is still a crucial term in the post-recession imagination. Paradoxically, prohibitions continue to accompany many contemporary 'mantras' that mesh promises of psychological and subjective well-being to the abandonment of consumerism, the search for rural living or the grow/cook-your-own urban or suburban home. Of course, choice to engage in the make-do and mend culture is as always shot through with the inequities of class identity. For some, this way of living is pure necessity that will become greater as the downturn, job insecurity and governmental revisions to the welfare state dig in; for others, the embracing of domestic skills marks a choice that distinguishes the thrifty deserving classes from the debt-ridden undeserving poor visible in other reality television shows discussed in this volume. Whatever the inflection, the backdrop to popular TV depictions of the home indicates that in the early twenty-first century, capitalism is endlessly capable of revision and is firmly embedded in the most intimate of spaces.

Notes

1. At the end of 2006, American home-ownership peaked at 69 per cent before sliding down in response to the recent 2008 financial meltdown and collapsing sub-prime market, in which the risk to the lower-waged mortgage recipients was exposed (Martin 2010).

2. The comfortable home was ranked higher as a necessity than two meals a day, the ability to visit friends or relatives in hospital, or to access prescribed medicines. Roger Burrows' (2003) research

draws upon the data-set from the Joseph Rowntree Foundation Poverty and Social Exclusion Survey of Britain (2000).

3. An ESRC report charts the immediate impacts on British life following the recent recession. It notes that in 'June 2009, the British economy was about 5.5 per cent below its peak in the first quarter of 2008, when the recession began'. The report notes that British social attitudes to home-ownership were shaken by the summer of 2008 and 40 per cent of respondents to a British Social Attitudes survey indicated that they viewed house-buying as a 'risky investment' (see Vaitilingam 2010: 5, 26).

4. The acute ties between personhood, self and property have a long history intimately related to capitalism, as key cultural thinkers have outlined in detail, tracking this back to the rise of developed industrial society and the symbolic as well as literal distinctions gauged by personal property (for a succinct overview of how this relates to the making of classed identities, see Skeggs 2004: 1–26.)

5. As Harvey indicates, 'Neoliberalism is in the first instance a theory of political economic practices that proposes that human well-being can best be advanced by liberating individual entrepreneurial freedom and skills within a framework characterized by strong private property rights, free markets and free trade' (Harvey 2005: 2–3).

6. As I have argued elsewhere (Nunn 2009), the proliferation of British home transformation and property investment shows during the 1990s such as *Changing Rooms* (1996–2004), *Ground Force* (1997–2005) and *Home Front* (1992–7), and the successful distribution of many of these in the USA and Australia, can be attributed to at least four factors. First, at an industry level, they met the demand for cheap, easily reproducible programming. Second, they benefited from the globalisation of taste and universalised models of social mobility which would underpin their international reception and ultimately underwrite their popularity. Third, they prioritised the experiences of ordinary people as much as the contribution of lifestyle experts and hence chimed with reality TV's allegedly democratic turn. Fourth, they chimed with and accentuated a broader political ethos which has promoted a concerted shift from rented accommodation to a prioritisation of home-ownership as a measure of self-worth and social citizenship.

7. See, for example, the front-page headline 'Goodbye to all that: is the middle class extinct?', *Guardian Weekend Supplement*, 24 July 2010, or the *Observer*'s 'Housing crisis forces couples to postpone having babies' (Doward 2010).

Bibliography

Adonis, A. and S. Pollard (1997) *A Class Act: The Myth of Britain's Classless Society* (London: Penguin).

Béland, D. (2007) 'Neo-Liberalism and Social Policy: The Politics of Ownership', *Policy Studies*, 28(2): 91–107.

Biressi, A. and H. Nunn (2008) 'Bad Citizens: The Class Politics of Lifestyle Television', in G. Palmer (ed.), *Exposing Lifestyle Television: The Big Reveal* (Aldershot, Hants.: Ashgate), pp. 15–24.

Brunsdon, C. (2003) 'Lifestyling Britain: The 8–9 Slot on British Television', *International Journal of Cultural Studies*, 6(1): 5–23.

Burrows, R. (2003) 'How the Other Half Lives: An Exploratory Analysis of the Relationship between Poverty and Home-Ownership in Britain', *Urban Studies*, 40(7): 1223–42.

Clarke, J., J. Newman, N. Smith, E. Vidler and L. Westmarland (2007) *Creating Citizen-Consumers: Changing Publics and Changing Public Services* (London: Sage).

Cozens, C. (2003) 'Home sweet home for Channel 4', *Guardian* [online], 21 February. Available at:
    <http.//www.guardian.co.uk/media/2003/feb/21/broadcasting.channel4> accessed 28 January 2011.

Dench, G. (2006) 'Introduction: Reviewing Meritocracy', in G. Dench (ed.), *The Rise and Rise of Meritocracy*
    (Oxford: Wiley-Blackwell), pp. 1–14.

Doward, J. (2010) 'Housing crisis forces couples to postpone having babies', *Observer*, 4 April, p. 3.

ESRC (2008) *Britain in 2008* (Swindon, Wilts.: Economic and Social Research Council).

Harvey, D. (2005) *A Brief History of Neoliberalism* (Oxford: Oxford University Press).

Henley, J. (2008) '"Repossession, repossession": what will happen to all of those TV shows that have
    succeeded on the back of the property boom?', *Guardian* [online], 10 April. Available at:
    <http.//www.guardian.co.uk/media/2008/apr/10/television.realitytv/print> accessed 28 January 2011.

Illouz, E. (2007) *Cold Intimacies: The Making of Emotional Capitalism* (Cambridge: Polity).

Institute of Fiscal Studies (1996) *Living with the State: The Incomes and Work Incentives of Tenants in the Social
    Rented Sector* (London: Institute of Fiscal Studies).

Lloyd, T. (2009) 'The Housing Disaster', *Soundings: A Journal of Politics and Culture*, Special Issue, 'Recession Blues',
    41, Spring: 19–29.

Martin, R. (2010) 'The Good, the Bad, and the Ugly. Economies of Parable', *Cultural Studies*, 24(3):
    418–30.

Morley, D. (2000) *Home Territories. Media, Mobility and Identity* (London/New York: Routledge).

Nichol, M. (1990) 'Shades of Blue', in Scanlon (ed.), *Surviving the Blues*, pp. 45–54.

Nunn, H. (2002) *Thatcher, Politics and Fantasy: The Political Culture of Gender and Nation* (London: Lawrence and
    Wishart).

———— (2009) '*Programas voltados para o lar e para a propriedade: transformando a TV factual popular*', in
    J. F. Filho (ed.), *A TV em transição. Tendências de programção no Brasil e no mundo* (Porto Alegre: Editora
    Sulina and Globouniversidade), pp. 89–110.

Nunn, H. and A. Biressi (2009) 'The Undeserving Poor', *Soundings: A Journal of Politics and Culture*, Special Issue,
    'Recession Blues', 41, Spring: 107–16.

Ouellette, L. and J. Hay (2008) *Better Living through Reality TV* (Malden, MA/Oxford: Blackwell).

Palmer, G. (2008) 'Introduction – the Habit of Scrutiny', in G. Palmer (ed.), *Exposing Lifestyle Television: The Big
    Reveal* (Aldershot, Hants./Burlington, VT: Ashgate), pp. 1–14.

Rogers, Zad (2003) 'Television as it is lived', *Guardian* [online], 31 March. Available at:
    <http.//www.guardian.co.uk/media/2003/mar/31/mondaymediasection6> accessed 28 January 2011.

Rosenberg, B. C. (2008) 'Property and Home-Makeover Television: Risk, Thrift and Taste', *Continuum: Journal of
    Media and Cultural Studies*, 22(4): 505–13.

Rosenthal, E. C. (2005) *The Era of Choice: The Ability to Choose and Its Transformation of Contemporary Life*
    (Cambridge, MA: MIT Press).

Salecl, R. (2010) *Choice* (London: Profile Books).

Scanlon, J. (ed.) (1990) *Surviving the Blues: Growing up in the Thatcher Decade* (London: Virago).

Schwartz, B. (2005) *The Paradox of Choice: Why More Is Less* (New York: Harper Perennial).

Skeggs, B. (2004) *Class, Self, Culture* (London: Routledge).

Stewart, K. (2007) *Ordinary Affects* (Durham, NC/London: Duke University Press).

Thomas, L. (2008) 'Alternative Realities: Downshifting Narratives in Contemporary Lifestyle Television', *Cultural Studies*, 22(5): 680–99.

Vaitilingam, R. (2010) *Recession Britain*: *Findings from Economic and Social Research*, Economic and Social Research Council Report. Available at: <http://www.esrc.ac.uk/ESRCInfoCentre/about/CI/CP/Our_Society_Today/economists/RecessionBritainPublication.aspx> accessed 28 January 2011.

PART THREE

Performing and Feeling Class

13/ Vicki Mayer

Reality Television's 'Classrooms': Knowing, Showing and Telling about Social Class in Reality Casting and the College Classroom

Sociologist C. Wright Mills (1951) expressed the vagaries of defining class in the United States more than half a century ago with the paradox of who is middle class. On the one hand, most mid-century Americans defined themselves as 'middle class'. On the other hand, the lack of a material basis for this self-definition would make people anxious, if not paranoid, to find measures of status that reinforced their position inside the amorphous boundaries of this class. The result is not a group that can be described either as a class in itself or for itself: that is, a class of people that necessarily shares objective measures of wealth or property nor a consciousness of sharing any objective conditions. Class, as individuals understand it in the United States, is a relative term that expresses both one's membership in the nation and uniqueness as individuals who are doing better than some and worse than others with regards to status. At the same time, class identities seem less easily detected or transgressed relative to more visible identities, such as race or gender. Racial and gendered performances frequently supplement class calculi, in that they seem to provide visible confirmation of assumptions about one's status in society. In this chapter, I will discuss the shifting places of college education and television industry employment as ways of establishing one's class through these relative terms, the ways they engage gender and race, and as a feature of the relationships through which they are articulated, most obviously between my interviewees and myself.

From 2004 to 2008, I conducted research into the labour of reality television casters, the people who scout, select and promote participants for reality television programmes.[1] I was interested in the ways casters do much of the sales and marketing work involved in reality television. Through casting calls and events, casters are often the first people to introduce programmes to the public. They sell the programme to the public and then sell the people they select to programme producers as the best cast members. All the while, casters collect copious data on the types of people who may be part of the reality audience, data that they can use in future casting gigs and that studios and advertisers need in assessing the value of their investment in the programme. At the centre of these acts of sponsorship, the caster and those she casts are both workers and products; their bodies condense labour power and exchange value, as they represent either brands or audiences. These representations privilege identities already associated with creative labour and quality audiences: namely, young adults, gay urbanites and other middle-class niches that television industries desire. It so happens that these demographics are in abundance in private, liberal arts universities, such as the one where I work.

I realised these homologies as I talked with my media studies students about my research experiences with casting and they began to tell me about theirs. Inevitably, a few students revealed that they had tried out for a reality programme or worked in casting and would be happy to share their experiences. Four of them gave interviews lasting more than an hour each; two of them checked in with me regularly, as they had had different experiences with the casting process. One of these students had assisted me in observing casting calls and conducting interviews, blurring the line between a co-investigator and an informant. Admittedly, this is a very small sample group, but I believe the intimate nature of our relationship, as well as the sustained contact with the students, makes these valuable sites for understanding social class in the new economy. Students demonstrated their class knowledge in the ways they emphasised their expertise about reality television, all the while playing within the rules of the game for preserving and mobilising class privilege. Rather than generalising this sample to all reality workers, what interests me is the way that these particular individuals, all subjects of elite university training, attempted to reconcile the contradictory status of reality television with their education, while trying to secure an increasingly unstable position in the middle class.

In these negotiations, students talked about their education less in terms of guaranteeing middle-class jobs than in terms of bolstering class knowledge that could be put to use in getting work in the media industry, even if breaking in at the lowest entry levels. Researchers have long realised that television talk is a way to establish social class differences and cultural capital (Seiter 1990; Press 1991; Thomas 1995). In these calculi, speakers often reference reality television in general as a body of programmes that sits at the low end of television hierarchies. Like soap operas, talk shows and infotainment genres that preceded the proliferation of reality television genres, reality programmes are often grouped as the latest manifestation of what Laura Grindstaff (2002) called 'trash TV', a way of equating the quality of television production values with their supposed audiences. On the other hand, college students have been raised practically in a reality-saturated television environment. Students watched reality programmes, had their favourites and thus made distinctions between what they saw as higher-quality reality shows and lower-quality programmes. These more specific delineations guided their approaches to the industry and, more importantly, the ways they talked about reality as a path to preserving middle-class lifestyles, respectability and possible careers. What their talk about casting revealed is that enterprising students in the new economy feel they have to juggle various kinds of class competencies just to establish their proper symbolic place in social class hierarchies, even if this place is only a projection of their future material potential.

College and Class Futures in a Middle-Class Nation

Even as Mills stressed the paradoxes of being middle class in the United States, a college education has been a standard signpost on the way to articulating one's middle-class status. The development and expansion of land-grant colleges at the turn of the last century and the passage of the GI Bill just before the end of World War II promised the democratisation of post-secondary educational access and middle-class entry for a large proportion of the (Anglo) American population (US Code, Title VII, Subchapter I, § 304; *Servicemen's Readjustment Act of 1944*, P.L. 78-346, 58 Stat. 284m). In the post-civil rights era, college has also been a tool of racial integration, supplementing the belief in class mobility with faith that the system is colour-blind (Harriford and Thompson 2008: 29–30). The expectation of college entry as a prerequisite for career success and upward class mobility continues to figure into middle-class ideology. The vast majority of students, white and of colour, and their parents I have encountered in my fifteen years as a professor would find it unthinkable that young people forgo college in order to enter the workforce directly and reproduce their class status.

Meanwhile, changes in the economy have at the very least destabilised the objective bases that supported the promise aligning a university degree with class maintenance. The shift in the US economy from an industrial model based on contained and sustained production and consumption to a post-industrial model based on globalised and fragmented production and consumption has led to boom and bust cycles that have made class conflict more visible as the US middle class jockeys with others in emerging markets worldwide. Professionalism, once the province of a few members of the bourgeoisie who could claim specialised training, has become the primary way to justify wages above a minimum scale across a wide variety of jobs dealing with knowledge, information or entertainment. The 'professionalisation' of work has not led to stable wages, however, as globalisation facilitates outsourcing and subcontracting, and contingent labour arrangements subvert place-based professional organisations and unions. These real changes in the new economy make past calculi of class position and future potential all the more indeterminable and devalue the symbolic weight of a college education. As political economist Donald Clark Hodges explains:

> Contrary to preconceived notions, the class struggle begins in America's colleges and universities. It goes by many names: careerism, professionalism, ambition, pursuit of happiness, being a good student, excelling, making something of oneself [...] Increasingly, the class struggle means the struggle for 'class', for specialized knowledge, for the soft job that goes with expertise, and for the fat paycheck that goes with both.
> (Hodges 2000: 7)

College students thus contend with the residual value of their educational investment at the same time as they face modest career prospects and an uncertain class future.

These contradictory pulls are present on US college campuses. Students act as both consumers and workers in their universities. The exploding costs of tuition in both public and private schools mean that the average US student accrues $23,000 in loan debt (Chaker 2009). More than half of college students hold jobs, often as part of 'work-study' requirements linked to loan availability ('College Enrollment and Work Activity of 2009 High School Graduates' 2010). These jobs tend to be low-paid service-sector positions, providing the university with a steady and nearly free workforce that drives down its own labour expenditures. At the same time, anxiety that debts outpace earnings after college has promoted clientelistic relationships in which students are educational 'consumers'. Students and their parents expect universities to offer a wide array of internship opportunities to build their résumés and establish networks as symbolic chits for future success. Free and nearly free labour experiences provide the illusion of control over the uncertain job market they will soon face.

In this environment, reality television production jobs are paradigmatic of the new economy while offering the illusion of class security. Like internships, reality television jobs tend to be unpaid or underpaid short-term gigs that guarantee only entry-level work experience. University departments such as my own often support these positions as a means for students to work their way up through the industry. Entertainment companies, which target young people as a preferred labour and consumer base, often promote these as ways to break in. The imbrications of college education and reality television are most apparent when companies require universities to give college credit in exchange for a free work opportunity in the business – a deal that universities can hardly afford to turn down. Especially in the liberal arts, professors and students face a conundrum in teaching critical thinking skills while also preparing for the realities of the job market. At these moments, the seemingly democratic college experience openly reinforces the class boundaries encoded in reality programmes and the industry that creates them.

Knowing about Class

Whether or not they studied media, students' shared class knowledge with producers formed the basis of their expertise in reality casting. Students demonstrated their knowledge of social class in the US in the ways they identified programmes, their networks and storylines as classy or trashy, educational or exploitative. These subtle determinations, based on their own experiences as viewers, were useful in guiding which shows they might apply to as a worker.

In general classroom discussions, media studies students favoured reality programmes that showcased participants' affluent lifestyles and adventures over daily life and its routines. For example, students preferred MTV's *The Real World* (1992–) or *The Hills* (2006–) (see Taylor in this volume), which assembles its cast in luxury accommodations in high-rent, cosmopolitan neighbourhoods, over programmes which took place in the participants' own home or community. Students also wanted to be part of programmes that would show off their own skills or knowledge, rather than educate or lead them to self-improvement. Students favoured contests that emphasised their abilities, such as CBS's *Survivor* (2000–) or Bravo's *Top Chef* (2006–), over those in which they might benefit from experts, such as makeover programmes like TLC's *What Not to Wear* (2003–). While they might have watched all of these programmes, the decision to participate in one revealed class-based considerations. Students not only sought programmes geared to their younger and more privileged demographics, but also looked for ones that would feature their good training and taste: in other words, their habitus and cultural capital.

The interviewees had to rationalise these distinctions further when casters used their applications for multiple casting pools – a standard practice that fills cast slots more effectively. For example, 'George', then twenty-one years old, told me that he chose *Survivor* (a competition to be the last person who survives in the wild) as his first pick of programmes to solicit for a casting interview. Although he did not make the initial cut, George said casters wanted to use his application materials for another network programme, *The Amazing Race* (2001–), a contest-cum-travelogue format in which people, in this case families, compete in a variety of athletic and intellectual tasks across multiple foreign and 'exotic' locales. Although George knew his family would not be competitive in the selection, he still maintained interest in what he regarded as a quality reality programme that would put his extensive travel experiences to good use.

The idea of quality reality television might be seen as an oxymoron in most societies with a public service tradition, but for US college students, the concept is related to degrees of authenticity and their own personal identification. 'Mary', my assistant who became a reality caster shortly after graduating from college, ranked desirable casting jobs based on the programmes with which she identified. She guessed that programmes such as *The Real World* would hire fun and intelligent people who understand the college-age person's experience. Although she ended up working on another programme on the same network, Mary said she could relate to the people she scouted because, like her, the good cast member would be 'very driven'. She also confirmed her suspicion that she would identify with fellow members of staff:

> The associate casting director and I got along really well [in our phone interview]; we have very similar
> goals for our careers. She's just a few years older than me, and whenever we talked about what we liked in
> the industry, or what we wanted to do in it, we always seemed to be on the same page … Then, when I
> finally met her, it was crazy, we were both wearing almost exactly the same outfit.

Condensed here in her comment about matching wardrobes, Mary noted the homologies between authentic representations, college experience and career aspirations, all ways of indirectly discussing class.

In the classroom and in interviews, students made class distinctions in choosing which programmes they preferred and might apply to themselves as a worker. These choices replicated casters' knowledge about class divisions as articulated through a shared language of generational niches and lifestyle consumerism. Noting the ways other people dressed, walked and talked were integral parts of students' knowledge base about reality worlds and how to enter them. Knowing class, then, assisted the interviewees in showing class in casting situations.

Showing Class

Job applicants had to demonstrate that they did not simply know class divisions in a casting pool, but that they could embody them as well. My experience with the reality casting process revealed its emphasis on embodied performances. Casters search not only for people within certain demographics, but also for those who act appropriately to the demographic. Viewers witness these class-appropriate performances in reality narratives, even when the goal of the programme is to remake the cast member by prescribing (usually middle-class) behaviours for members of the working class (Redden 2008). Understanding the producers' needs almost instinctively as reality viewers, Mary and George strove to appear as though they 'belonged' in middle-class roles, whether doing a videotaped audition or applying expertise and taste in selecting good cast members. The ambiguity between

being oneself and playing a desirable role for others is central to the emotional labour of reality production. As Grindstaff writes on her own observations of reality productions, producers seek 'ordinary' people, meaning non-professionals 'willing to play themselves with a maximum of emotional
and physical expressiveness in ways that reinforced prevailing class-based cultural stereotypes'
(Grindstaff 2009: 71–2). For the already class-aware students, the need to show one's class in particular ways led to a fair amount of negotiation with casters, who shared their class-based language
but might read racial or gender cues differently.

In the case of 'Robin' and her attempt to be accepted by one of the quality reality programmes, she
said class was something she could demonstrate to casters simply through her clothing. Over the
course of several months of call-backs and cuts, casters told her whether she should look 'dressy' or
'casual' for photo shoots and videotaped auditions, words that communicate differently across class lines.

> V: So the casters never asked directly about your social class?
> R: They never asked, 'What does your mom do? What does your dad do?' None of those kind of
>   questions.
> V: What about in terms of consumption?
> R: They definitely commented about the name brand of my jeans, knowing that they cost more. I mean
>   it was an obscene amount to spend on jeans, $150. They just knew from the information I gave them
>   in my application … which led them to ask those questions about consumption. They really weren't
>   like, 'What kind of car do you drive?' or anything like that. But we did get into conversations about
>   money at school.

While never explicitly discussing Robin's family income, casters spoke about class status in other, less
formal ways, such as what her peer group did at weekends and how much money they wasted on
leisure. By suggesting taste in an outfit or commenting on consumption, casters tried to position
applicants in ways that ensured class status was both evident and represented in the final cast decisions. In turn, Robin, a young white woman attending an affluent college, had no problem living up
to the cultural script that casters envisioned her playing.

In another case, however, casters did not recognise my interviewee's class status, at least not at
first. 'Shellond', an African-American woman studying and working full time, seemed to present an
anomaly for the casters on a campy African-American reality programme because she was neither
poor nor uneducated. Like Robin, she was involved in a lengthy casting process, but, unlike her, casters initially struggled to categorise Shellond into a class- and race-based character type. I asked about
her initial interview with the casting team.

> S: Some of the questions were really ridiculous. They would ask me, 'Have you ever been to the ghetto?
>   Do you have any home girls who are on welfare?' I just looked at them and would ask questions like,
>   'What does that have to do with me? How does that have any influence on what I do? Even if I have
>   friends on welfare doesn't mean that I am on welfare.' And they will be like, 'Oh yeah.' And brush it off
>   and change the topic.

V: Yeah, even asking you a question like, 'Did you grow up in the projects?'

S: Yeah, they asked me if I grew up in the projects and I said no, so they were like, 'Oh you didn't grow up in the projects, then do you live in an apartment?' And I was like, 'No.' And then they would be like, 'Oh where did you live?' And I would be like, 'I grew up in a house.' And they would be like, 'Oh, was it a rented house?' I would be like, 'No, my mother and father paid for it.' And it was like, 'What neighbourhood do you live in?' and I told them the neighbourhood. So they asked, 'What is the demographic there?' and I said, 'It's mainly … it's a mix. It is a lot of Caucasians. It is very diverse. You have Indians, you have Spanish people. It is a well-off neighbourhood.' And he was like, 'OK.' And they would get to, 'So what does your father do for a living?' 'He works for the state.' 'What does your mother do for a living?' 'She also works for the state.' And he said, 'OK, what types of job does your father do? Is it with sanitation? Is it NYPD? It is firefighting?' and I said, 'No, he works for New York State Insurance Department.' And they were like, 'Oh really. Is he an accountant?' 'No, he is one of the executive board members.' And they were like, 'Oh really. That is very interesting.'

V: It seemed like they low-balled you every time.

S: They were expecting me to be this young … this impoverished girl who didn't have much.

As she retells the interview experience, class and race were central themes in the casting questions, creating increasing layers of dissonance between her and the casters, all of whom were white. In this case, the lack of shared assumptions had to be discussed at length to determine what kind of character Shellond might ultimately play on the programme, which put contestants in competition to date a hip-hop celebrity. According to Shellond, casters finally recognised her when they asked if she thought she would make more money from doing the programme. She said her response – 'Well, honestly, I don't need the money because if I need more money, I just ask my father' – seemed to enliven the caster, who reportedly said, 'Oh, then you are kind of upper middle class.'

Shellond's class designation influenced the ways casters tried to convince her to become part of the programme. As a member of the 'upper middle class', she received more generous incentives than the other women to return to auditions. Whereas other applicants who said they had travelled in from a poor neighbourhood received bus money and a Burger King certificate, Shellond began with paid parking and petrol for her car. From there, the cash value and the cultural status of gifts increased, from $400 gift certificates for an upmarket make-up line to Broadway theatre tickets. Over the course of the months, Shellond revealed how no one else among the winnowing group of applicants received such lavish treatment. When the producers told her she had been selected, the crew made some final, special appeals as she tried to decide what to do.

S: They tried several times to persuade me, saying that if I come to the show I will get this amount. Some of these girls get paid to do the show because they tend to back out, so they actually offered me a stipend and told me what they will do based on what my parents told me [about not doing the show]. They said that they could pay my car loan, pay for my lease for the next year or so, and pay for the rest of your school if I do the show. I stood firm. And every day […] I got a better offer. Every single day someone else would call me to offer me something better and more. Even to the day

> before they started taping they offered me more and said what they will do is fly me first class and I
> wouldn't even have to pick up any clothes. They will have a driver come and pick up my clothes or
> they can take me shopping and do all of this stuff as long as I get on a plane by such and such time.

Even as producers establish the conditions to encourage good performances from ordinary people, they shape the expectations for different classes of 'ordinary' people. In this case, Shellond's visible race seemed to imply a lower class status. Had she not established her class status, casters would have probably given her the same fast-food certificate as other applicants and played down the monetary rewards of the programme. Instead, their concerns that she might be doing the programme for money transformed into a concern that she might not understand how the show would exceed her current financial abilities. As with Robin's experience, the casting process could talk about class implicitly by offering a lifestyle that would fit her presumed aspirations, one in which she was independent of her parents, college debts and consumer constraints. In other words, when Shellond became middle class in the eyes of casters, they became 'colour-blind' in their entreaties.

The promise of autonomy in both Robin and Shellond's cases also countered what casters read as the Achilles heel of the middle-class, female applicant. The give and take between casters and applicants for reality programmes centred on these associations between class, objectives, taste and, ultimately, morals. This focus on money displaced other presumed concerns that casters associated with Shellond and Robin, namely respectability. Casters try to dig into the psyches of their applicants, asking questions about sex and sexuality, childhood experiences, embarrassing moments and psychological traumas. Much like Robin, Shellond's interactions with casters involved discussions of parental approval and respectable behaviours. When she assented, casters changed their line of questions around money to ones of respectability and parental consent:

> S: They asked, 'How do your parents feel about you doing the show?' I told them, 'They don't really
>   know yet until I tell them.' So then they asked how my mother would feel if I told her. I said, 'Most
>   likely they would tell me not to do the show, because they refuse to have someone like him in my
>   life. Not to embarrass myself like that. It's not worth it.'

With these moral connotations around class and marriage, casters reinforced middle-class associations between gender, sexuality and respectability (Skeggs 1997). Shellond conceded that these associations ultimately persuaded her to not participate in the reality programme. In the end, love would trump money, or, as she told me, she would *never* be interested in marrying the celebrity singer, because, in her words, 'he is not my type'.

Telling about Class

I was initially surprised at my interviewees' candid and detailed revelations about their experiences trying to get work in reality television. After all, my classes stress critiques of media representations, industrial hierarchies and audience commodification. Without exception, though, the four students

remained optimistically enthusiastic in their reflections, even when it was clear that the private information they shared might be embarrassing or reflect badly on them. What seemed most important
in these interviews was that the students were using their knowledge about the industry to assist
me with my research and to help themselves assert class status. Telling me about their experiences,
in other words, afforded a place and a time to perform a class identity (Wood 2009) that bridged
the contradictions between their elite college education and their free labour in the lowly genre.

In one sense, self-reflexivity about the television industry worked to create clear distinctions
between 'educated' people, such as the students and me, and the 'uneducated' who would enter reality television naively or for the wrong reasons. Speaking as if they could regard the industry at a distance, they tended to downplay the times they felt upset or emotionally disturbed by the
experience. Initially applying for a programme as a drunken dare, Shellond, for example, said she continued the two-month casting process of repeated call-backs, videotapings and phone conversations
because she was simply 'curious'. At the same time, she told me she consulted a lawyer whenever
casters presented her with a contractual obligation, suggesting that she took the dare increasingly
seriously. Occupying a typical middle-class disposition (Skeggs 1997), Shellond maintained a distanced
bemusement, while mobilising class resources to protect her identity. In discussing the other casting
applicants, she was careful to distance herself and her status from the rest.

V: How could you tell many of them didn't go to college?
S: Based on the conversations they had. *Like, if you were a girl who was in college, you talk about how many
      people are going to recognise you or how much fame you are going to have. Just the way they talk and
      carry themselves makes you realise.* I asked some of them and they are just like, 'No, I've never been to
      college. I didn't have the money.' But the majority of the girls … were like dancers who've done stuff
      in strip clubs, like have done X-rated videos, and they never had a problem with it and could hold
      their heads high to the point that a couple of the girls actually did a porno film. […] So that's what
      the girls were doing when they were inspired to be a singer or an actress. *They wanted to get their
      faces out there so they can start making money.* (My emphasis)

Shellond's use of 'you' and 'they' in the above quote references the class status of 'us', the college-
educated interviewer and interviewee, and 'them', the strippers and the one who 'actually did' a porn
film. Whereas the former group might aspire to be famous on a reality programme, Shellond denigrated the latter group's instrumental aim of just making money. The expectation that I would share
her attitudes as an academic speak to the interview situation itself as a setting in which she could
display her cultural capital (Skeggs, Thumim and Wood 2008), validating the former over the latter,
the middle-class disposition over those of lower status. Shellond seemed determined that I would
not make the same inferences between blackness and low-class status that the casters had inferred.

Beyond these alliances that students tried to forge in the interview process, however, the students' self-reflexivity also highlighted the obvious gap between their belief in a college education and
their anxiety around their future class status. Working in reality television seems to contradict the
taken-for-grantedness of a college degree as a first step to a profession and the reproduction of

middle-class status. Yet, as Kaufman (2005) also shows in interviews with college students, subjects frequently stressed their agency, straying from perceived class norms as part of a personal success story. For Robin and Mary, the conscious choice to work in reality television was, as they told the story, a strategic step from the classroom to a career. Mary said she became interested in working in reality casting after doing an independent study with me on the topic. 'When I started going on casting calls for reality shows [with you], I really saw that I loved it and it was something I really wanted to explore,' she said. Positioning my research as her job training, Mary said the project gave her the knowledge to succeed as a caster; her initial contacts with my subjects would later be her references. Similarly, Robin described herself as plotting a path towards a permanent job in the television industry, consciously auditioning for the most prestigious reality programme among young people to better her chances of building a career with the parent network. Although her father was a cable industry executive, Robin felt she had to mobilise her own knowledge and resources to 'do it for herself', even though she might work for her father's business later.

Far from undermining the value of their college educations, the interviewees who spoke to me tried to reconcile their academic education with the legitimacy of reality television work. Reality television for them was a site for knowledge application, skill development and career potential. Promoting their own agency in pursuing a class-conscious strategy, all four of the students fashioned themselves as the kinds of individuals who could control their destinies in the new economy. To do this, however, they had to recreate other hierarchies that would not deny that exploitation or class stereotypes were part of the format, and, by implication, its production workers. Indeed, they all ended up working for media companies during my time with them, suggesting that their knowledge, both learned and part of their habitus, *did* help them to get jobs. Yet, none of them expressed to me the downsides of these jobs: the long hours, short contracts and poor compensation. Further, by emphasising the individuality of their class strategies, the students failed to acknowledge how they produced exactly the kinds of individuated and malleable working selves that television industries desire for their flexible labour force (Mayer 2011). What this suggests is that these subjects may have been highly self-reflexive but in ways that conformed to media industries' definitions of labour value. Much like the narratives in makeover reality programmes themselves, students framed their choices as ones that achieved both 'personal satisfaction and [...] their enhanced worth to others', affirming, in the words of Guy Redden, 'an economic logic that works through the moralization of options for living, binding the subject into regimes of status-value that operate through the acquisition of cultural capital' (Redden 2008: 488). The motivations to know, show and tell about class in reality television, and then embody these divisions through industry work, thus may have demonstrated the students' own attempts to take some of the uncertainty out of the new economy, but they also reinforced the exploitative features of the new economy itself.

Conclusion

Most people in the United States understand social class differences hazily at best, and disregard them altogether when they claim that they, and everyone else they know, is middle class. Despite the mass appeal of this claim, however, the hyper-vigilance paid to distinctions in work and consumption suggests that classes exist in the United States, but Americans know them through another lexicon. For a generation raised on reality television, class-effacing discourses and class-based dispositions are not only formative, but become performative when those viewers then enter the workforce. My interviews with college students gave them an opportunity to perform class identities once again by allowing them to display their own confidence in their industrial knowledge and class dispositions. If their quest to reproduce their class status through reality work revealed their complicity with the new economy, the interviews revealed my own complicities as well. Our shared belief in the value of a degree which has become unaffordable to the majority of Americans and our failure to critique a job market that survives on young people's free labour unwittingly supported the entanglement of political economies and cultural capitals, making reality television work seem like a good experience for the future. In fact, though, neither the degree nor the television contract can ensure middle-class stability, much less mobility. Of the four interviewees, none of them work in the television industry in 2010. Their experiences should stand as lessons for the media studies professor and her students alike in the realities of reality TV labour and class labours beyond the college classroom.

Note

1. This research has been published in Mayer (2009, 2011).

Bibliography

Chaker, A. M. (2009) 'Students borrow more than ever for college', *Wall Street Journal* [online], 4 September. Available at: <http://online.wsj.com/article/SB10001424052970204731804574388682129316614.html> accessed 17 May 2010.

'College Enrollment and Work Activity of 2009 High School Graduates' (2010) Bureau of Labor Statistics. Available at <http://www.bls.gov/news.release/hsgec.nr0.htm> accessed 17 May 2010.

Grindstaff, L. (2002) *The Money Shot: Trash, Class, and the Making of TV Talk Shows* (Chicago: University of Chicago Press).

———— (2009) 'Self-Serve Celebrity: The Production of Ordinariness and the Ordinariness of Production in Reality Television', in V. Mayer, M. Banks and J. Caldwell (eds), *Production Studies: Cultural Studies of Media Industries* (New York: Routledge), pp. 71–86.

Harriford, D. and B. Thompson (2008) *When the Center Is on Fire: Passionate Social Theory for Our Times* (Austin: University of Texas Press).

Hodges, D. C. (2000) *Class Politics in the Information Age* (Urbana: University of Illinois Press).

Kaufman, P. (2005) 'Middle-Class Social Reproduction: The Activation and Negotiation of Structural Advantages', *Sociological Forum*, 20(2): 245–70.

Mayer, V. (2009) 'Bringing the Social Back in: Studies of Production Cultures and Social Theory', in V. Mayer, M. Banks and J. Caldwell (eds), *Production Studies: Cultural Studies of Media Industries* (New York: Routledge), pp. 15–24.

———— (2011) *Below the Line: Producers and Production Studies in the New Television Economy* (Durham, NC: Duke University Press).

Mills, C. Wright (1951) *White Collar: The American Middle Classes* (New York: Oxford University Press).

Press, A. (1991) *Women Watching Television* (Philadelphia: University of Pennsylvania Press).

Redden, G. (2008) 'Economy and Reflexivity in Makeover Television', *Continuum: Journal of Media and Cultural Studies*, 22(4): 485–94.

Seiter, E. (1990) 'Making Distinctions in TV Audience Research: Case Study of a Troubling Interview', *Cultural Studies*, 4: 61–84.

Skeggs, B. (1997) *Formations of Class and Gender: Becoming Respectable* (London: Sage).

Skeggs, B., N. Thumim and H. Wood (2008) '"Oh goodness, I am watching reality TV": How Methods Make Class in Audience Research', *European Journal of Cultural Studies*, 11(1): 5–24.

Thomas, L. (1995) 'In Love with *Inspector Morse*: Feminist Subculture and Quality Television', *Feminist Review*, 51: 1–25.

Wood, H. (2009) *Talking with Television: Women, Talk Shows and Modern Self-Reflexivity* (Urbana: University of Illinois Press).

14/Laura Grindstaff

From *Jerry Springer* to *Jersey Shore*: The Cultural Politics of Class in/on US Reality Programming

Scholarly research on reality TV has grown apace with the genre itself, exploring many critical dimensions of its production, reception and political-economic context.[1] This essay explores what might be considered the 'performance logic' of reality programming as it relates to the cultural politics of class. Having conducted ethnographic research on two different genres of reality television in the US (daytime talk shows in the 1990s and, more recently, the MTV docusoap *Sorority Life*, 2002–4), I am interested in the tensions between class as an embodied phenomenon and class as a discursive phenomenon as parlayed by social institutions such as the media. As many scholars have noted, the 'therapeutic turn' in contemporary Western societies from the 1970s onward signals a new middle-class sensibility rooted in the reflexive performance of individual subjectivity (see Rieff 1966; Foucault 1979; Lasch 1979; Giddens 1991; Beck 1992), a sensibility that the new media environment amplifies in particular ways. The investment in and performance of the self have become moral imperatives, serving as measures of both individual worth and cultural value (capital) and constituting what Skeggs and Wood (2009) call a 'labour theory of person-production'.

The emphasis on public intimacy and emotional expressivity in reality TV – which clearly rejects the bourgeois edict to conceal rather than reveal private life – would seem an especially hospitable environment for both women and the working classes, who are, after all, presumed to lack emotional and physical reserve. But while reality TV as a cultural discourse may be moving us farther away from bourgeois uptightness toward a more 'popular' (and feminised) aesthetic, this does not herald the demise of class inequality but arguably makes it more difficult to 'see'. This balancing act – preserving class hierarchies within an overall environment that appears to deny them – is partly why reality programming 'works' as well as it does, particularly in the US where discussions of class are either ignored or subsumed under discussions of race. Further complicating the picture is the critical response on the part of journalists and political pundits to reality programming, which, much like the critical response to daytime talk shows in previous decades, helps feed the perception that the 'real' class politics at play are not within the genre but between reality TV (characterised as low, vulgar, tasteless) and more 'respectable' media. This tends to render invisible the distinctively middle-class influences within reality programming and deny the larger trend toward performativity of which reality TV is only one part.

A Tale of Two Talk Shows

My own interest in the cultural dimensions of social class – more specifically, in the performance of class identities in the media – developed out of my research on US daytime talk shows in the 1990s, a period when the format was as ubiquitous on television as reality programming is today (see Grindstaff 2002). Few media scholars were writing specifically about class in connection with the genre; not surprisingly, class issues tended to be overshadowed by the focus on daytime talk as a 'women's genre' that brought into public discourse issues, concerns and modes of expressivity typically associated with the private (= feminine) sphere. Class analysis crept in primarily through discussions of 'ordinariness', both in relation to guests' social location as 'just folks' and to their expertise, which was inevitably rooted in personal experience rather than formal educational or professional credentials. Talk shows, some argued, democratised the public sphere by showcasing people and issues formerly excluded from media discourse even as they also opened up new ways of governing bodies through a confessional, self-help mode of discipline that encourages an individualistic rather than structural approach to knowledge-production (see Livingstone and Lunt 1994; Priest 1995; Shattuc 1997; Lowney 1999).

Because it is much easier to see class when its symbolic codes are stereotypical and exaggerated (in either an upwards or downwards direction), the emergence and success of *Jerry Springer* within the talk-show arena prompted a different kind of analysis, my own scholarship included. After having already spent a year working as a production assistant at a 'nice' middle-class show that I call *Diana* (a pseudonym, after Princess Di, this being several years before her death), I relocated to Chicago in order to work at a show that I call *Randy* (also a pseudonym). Fifteen years later, this show is still on the air: I tell my students it is '*Jerry Springer*-like' and leave it at that. During the heyday of talk shows, *Randy* was to *Diana* what, today, *Jersey Shore* is to *The Real World*: the bottom rung on the ladder of class distinction, a cultural cartoon for embodying a decidedly lowbrow aesthetic. By design, the two shows I studied represented the anchoring points on a class continuum: at the 'high' end, *Diana* explored social issues through personal experience and was relatively restrained in style and execution. Confessional rather than confrontational, soft-core rather than hard-core, it was a forum largely for, and about, middle-class white women, aiming for a feminine 'money shot' based on heartache or joy rather than conflict and anger (Grindstaff 2002). While branded embarrassing or melodramatic compared to more distanced or 'rational' discussion, the soft-core performances of *Diana*'s guests nevertheless tapped into (indeed were a product of) an increasingly legitimate contemporary discourse about the therapeutic benefits of emotional expressiveness.

At the 'low' end, *Randy* harnessed, and continues to harness, people's interpersonal conflicts in the service of orchestrating dramatic (often physical) on-air confrontation. *Randy* makes no pretence of rational discussion and eschews the participation of even token experts; more often than not, brawling guests have to be pried apart by well-muscled bouncers. It is hard-core (and 'masculine') compared to other daytime talk shows, with an ethnically diverse array of lower-class guests and a viewing audience that skews young. Even in its tamer moments, 'talk' on *Randy* has consisted almost entirely of body language, its emotional expressiveness a breach of taken-for-granted norms that transgresses acceptable therapeutic limits. It occupies the far outpost of the genre, the 'bad object' against which other shows can construct their legitimacy, notwithstanding the genre's overall slide toward sensationalism in the latter half of the 1990s as the number of shows proliferated and the competition for ratings grew fierce.

In the current spate of reality shows, the corresponding bad object is arguably *Jersey Shore*, an MTV docusoap production featuring a group of young, self-identified Italian Americans who live together in a seedy resort town on the New Jersey coastline. Renewed for a fourth season, the show recently set an all-time ratings record for the network with 8.6 million viewers.[2] *Jersey Shore*, like its model and predecessor, *The Real World*, is a carefully crafted human experiment in which we observe eight colourful personalities (apparently not all of Italian descent and only one of whom actually comes from the Shore) drink, party and bicker their way in and out of various 'situations'.[3] Promotional videos for the show promise viewers 'a whole new crazy' and characterise the cast as the hottest, tannest 'Guidos' you've ever seen – kids who 'keep their hair high, their muscles juiced, and their fists pumping'. The opening credits of every episode feature a memorable quote from Snooki, one of the more theatrical housemates: comparing herself to a praying mantis, she quips, 'after I have sex with a guy I will rip their [*sic*] heads off'. (Snooki also has the dubious distinction of being punched in the face by a drunken guy at a bar.) Not surprisingly, the show has been the subject of protest by several Italian-American groups and the target of countless spoofs and parodies on YouTube. *Jersey Shore* is excessive and quite clearly markets itself that way. Only on *Jerry Springer* can one find a more clichéd illustration of the binary construction of class difference as outlined by Bourdieu: 'the antithesis between culture and bodily pleasure (or nature) is rooted in the opposition between the cultivated bourgeoisie and "the people", the imaginary site of uncultivated nature, barbarously wallowing in pure enjoyment' (Bourdieu 1984: 490). Both the men and women on the show express their 'uncultivated natures' by having a lot of sex and showing a lot of skin, usually after consuming vast quantities of alcohol.

Precisely because they are so cartoonish, *Jerry Springer* and *Jersey Shore* illustrate in no uncertain terms that class-as-culture stands in for, but is not reducible to, class-as-socio-economic status. Class is more than one's relation to the site of economic production. Especially in the context of television, class is also a performance, a social script involving, among other things, language use, mannerisms, deportment and dress. To quote Julie Bettie, 'class can be conceptualized as performative in that there is no [innate or] interior difference that is being expressed; rather, institutionalized class inequality creates class subjects who perform, or display, differences in cultural capital' (Bettie 2000: 11; see also Bourdieu 1984; Skeggs 2004). In the US, the working classes are said to be unrefined, indiscreet and visceral in their pleasures and tastes. These attributes are doubly stigmatising for working-class women, since they violate not only the codes of bourgeois respectability but also the codes of hegemonic femininity. Despite the fact that women as a group have tended to occupy the nature side of the nature/culture divide, gender and class intersect such that the 'higher' standards of refinement and restraint (particularly sexual restraint) associated with cultural elites partly define the standards of 'ideal' femininity as well – an ideal that working-class women by definition fail to attain.

Racial meanings coexist and interact with class meanings in more analogous ways, as Western discourses on race have constructed Africa as a sign of savagery, and dark skin more generally as a sign of nature and physicality (see Torgovnik 1991; Goldberg 1993; Omi and Winant 1995). Race and class distinctions thus reflect and reinforce one another, their intersection seemingly 'naturalised' by the over-representation of people of colour among the poor and working classes. The favoured term for describing *Randy* guests – 'white trash' – underscores the race/class nexus through its use of the racial qualifier: when white folks act like trash, their whiteness needs to be named, because it is understood as exceptional to the 'normal' way of being white. Indeed, Wray and Newitz (1997) argue that the construction of 'white trash' helps mediate white guilt and animosity toward racial minorities by substituting a 'safe' (i.e. white) target believed to embody many of the same racist assumptions (see also Hartigan Jr 1999; Wray 2006).

Class-as-culture is more wide-ranging and mobile than class-as-socio-economic status, because it connotes an interlocking set of aesthetic qualities and moral/behavioural dispositions that can be enacted by and attributed to different groups regardless of actual material circumstance. Any talk-show guest or reality TV participant who looks, talks and behaves a certain way can be labelled 'white trash' (or 'trailer trash') whether or not they are poor, white and/or living in a trailer park, because the term contains such an excess of meaning, functioning to mark symbolic boundaries between groups rather than simply differences of race or class per se. Of course, most *Randy* guests are in fact poor or working-class whites, as I found out, but in and of itself, this is not what makes them 'trashy' nor is it why critics deride their performances. The popularity/familiarity of the white-trash performance, in combination with its unidimensionality, makes it readily adoptable as a television per-sona by virtually anyone willing to embody its codes. *Jerry Springer* and *Jersey Shore* are like modern-day minstrelsy, with participants performing in 'trash face'. On the one hand, such performances help to unmoor the stereotype from its historical base, widening the gap between the media image and the people it supposedly references. The more exaggerated and cartoonish the performance, the more free-floating the stereotype seems to be. On the other hand, the referent is still there and its recirculation functions to reinforce constitutive boundaries of exclusion and inclusion around notions of 'worth' and 'respectability' – not only between the middle classes and those 'below' but also among the poor and working classes themselves.

Jerry Springer and *Jersey Shore* are clearly caricatures; what is less obvious is that caricature has become necessary to mark the difference between 'excessive' and 'normative' performances within a broader media landscape in which 'letting it all hang out' is the order of the day – that is, within a broader media landscape in which the very qualities historically attributed to the working classes and other Others are increasingly normalised. To say that differences of cultural capital organise around norms of physical and emotional expressiveness does not tell us enough: how have these norms changed? What sorts of expressiveness 'count' in the reality TV arena, and for whom?

Economically speaking, reality programming is an outgrowth of both the rapid development of new media technologies and a changing industrial context characterised by deregulation, increasing competition and financial scarcity. Culturally speaking, it is consistent with the seepage of perform-ance demands into everyday life (see McKenzie 2001) and a preponderance of social and psychic spaces for externalising the self – for watching others 'play themselves' and for being watched in turn. Once the province of marginalised groups, emotional expressiveness is now expected and highly prized, and this state of affairs suggests a general cultural drift across many different spheres, including, especially, the media. The US website *Reality TV World*, which provides news and episode summaries for a broad range of reality programming, currently lists 917 reality shows. When one eliminates the repetition within a given series (for example, counting *Survivor* only once, instead of twenty-two times for each thirteen-week instalment), then the number of shows is 660. The vast majority are not as caricatured as *Jerry Springer* and *Jersey Shore*, popular as these shows are. Indeed, as noted above, caricature is constitutive, marking the difference between 'normative' and 'excessive' emotional expression in reality programming.

Class Dismissed?

Some reality programmes signal class indirectly, via proxy codes such as 'lifestyle' and 'health' – especially in the specific subgenre of makeover television where people's bodies, wardrobes, homes and even pets are perpetually in need of transformation. The class dimensions of transformation shows are seemingly more oblique in the US compared to the UK, the latter having a longer history of documentary lifestyle programming within a more class-conscious national context. According to Skeggs and Wood (2009) in their analysis of class relations in British reality programming, working-class participants are not only over-represented on transformational-style shows (*Ladette to Lady*, *What the Butler Saw*, *What Not to Wear*, *Wife Swap*, *Supernanny*, etc.), they inevitably possess the 'wrong' kind of culture, body, clothing, speech and/or disposition for achieving happiness/social success and hence are used to display the need for expert intervention. The so-called lifestyle experts on the programmes legitimate normative middle-class aspirations through instruction in psychological and physical self-management. Gareth Palmer summarises the general category of UK lifestyle television, of which makeover shows are part, this way: 'From public-service documentary with its patrician elite to new forms of reality television fashioned by rising middle-class fractions, the bourgeoisie are still there recommending courses of action to modify the behavior of the lower orders' (Palmer 2010: 76).

   Perhaps the closest US counterpart is *The Biggest Loser* (2004–), in which fatness could be said to relay class in a metonymic chain of associations that are never explicitly addressed. The show, which features large people struggling to lose weight via a series of competitive physical challenges, focuses on bodies (and minds) in transformation and not the social conditions that produce a positive correlation between income and health or an inverse correlation between income and weight. Thus, class is figured only indirectly, less through individual narratives and more through the broader sociocultural meanings attached to fatness. As Kipnis (1996) so eloquently argues in her essay 'Life in the Fat Lane', body type is linked both factually and stereotypically to social class. Fat people – especially fat women – are less likely to be hired when competing for jobs, less likely to be promoted in their jobs and less likely to 'marry up' socially or economically. According to Kipnis, psychological studies of body image demonstrate that fat is linked to a range of attributes that people fear and despise, including loss of control, infantile regression, failure, self-loathing, laziness, sloth and passivity. She writes, 'substitute "welfare class" for "fat" here and you start to see that the phobia of fat and the phobia of the poor are heavily cross-coded' (Kipnis 1996: 102). The few real-ity shows in the US more obviously 'about' the socio-economics of class depict either hyper-masculine blue-collar heroes – consider the Discovery Channel's *Deadliest Catch* (2005–), about the real-life adventures of Alaskan crab fisherman – or morally upright, 'deserving' folks who just need a helping hand. *Extreme Makeover: Home Edition* (2003–), for example, helps low-income families experiencing heartache or tragedy (the death of a child, a natural disaster) get a leg up on their circumstances, compliments of the magical makeover team at ABC, who effectively stand in for the (ever-diminishing) safety net of the welfare state – but only for those who truly deserve it (as judged by producers).

By and large, American reality programming works hard to ignore class as a structuring force in everyday life. This is not to say that class relations disappear from reality programming, but that class-as-socio-economic status is *systematically displaced*. When media scholars point out the 'flattening' of social inequalities in reality TV, they are typically referring to the fact that social-identity categories such class, race and gender are reduced to individualised performances divorced from structural forces and historical contexts and subject to reconceptualisation within neo-liberal media institu-tions. This is an important insight, and a necessary frame of reference for understanding the per-formance logic of reality programming.

To elaborate, television takes differences in cultural capital and reinvents them as the property (and choice) of individual subjects who could presumably act differently if they chose. Individualising social-identity categories in this way ignores both the socio-economic dimensions of class distinc-tion and the power of media organisations to determine the parameters of performance through their own priorities and production practices. Indeed, I saw first hand the deployment of these pro-duction practices when working behind the scenes of *Diana* and *Randy*. The media mediate, and this is as true (albeit differently true) of talk shows and reality programming as it is of fictional or narrative television. Otherwise, producers would be out of a job. Moreover, mediation is systemic and not idiosyncratic. Reality TV re-presents social relations in predictable ways; in the case of class, it glosses over the connections and disjunctures between the cultural performances enacted by individual bodies and the institutional power arrangements that the bodies encode. In this, reality TV feeds neatly into the class-unconsciousness of US society more generally insofar as most Americans, save for the very rich or very poor, tend not to think of themselves as occupying par-ticular class locations outside of a vague, amorphous middle (see DeMott 1990; Pakulski and Waters 1996). More significantly, the correspondences between the cultural/performative and socio-economic dimensions of class are far from straightforward in the US – which is why a wealthy Connecticut blue blood like former president George W. Bush can pass himself off as an ordinary Texas cowboy, champion of 'the people', all the while working to reinstate nineteenth-century levels of income disparity. Or why presidential hopeful Sarah Palin can star in her own reality show (*Sarah Palin's Alaska*, 2010–11) presuming that the 'ordinariness' it cultivates will abet her professional polit-ical career.

Express Yourself: Reflexivity and Performativity

The performance logic of reality television – in which class-coded performances are disassociated from the socio-economic bases of class inequality in the service of 'class-less' self-expression – is commensurate with and predicted by certain features of late modernity: the rise of therapeutic discourse (Rieff 1966; Lasch 1979; Foucault 1979), the positioning of the self as a 'reflexive project' (Giddens 1991) and the heightened emphasis on performance in everyday life (Alexander 2004). These are, of course, interrelated phenomena. Writing in the 1970s, Lasch (1979) noted the 'pathological narcissism' of the 'performing self' that he saw as an increasingly pervasive aspect of social life fuelled by the 'therapeutic mindset' of an information-based (rather than manufacturing-based) economy. The therapeutic turn requires the exteriorisation of interior life and the blurring of public/private distinctions, organised and legitimated through the language of psychology. As Eva Illouz observes: 'like no other cultural language, the language of psychology mixes together private emotionality and public norms. [It] has codified the private self and made this private self ready for public scrutiny and exposure' (Illouz 2008: 184). Of course, the exteriorisation of interior life works differently in different spheres. Illouz (1997) shows how, in the 1970s, 'speaking emotion' became both a management technique for controlling/increasing worker productivity and a strategy employed by second-wave feminists to address gender inequality. Foucault (1977, 1979) and Rose (1990, 1998) see the shift in regulatory power from 'outside' to 'inside' as producing certain technologies of self-management necessary to modern forms of governmentality and neo-liberal marketisation, respectively.

The historic rise of therapeutic culture is generally taken to be a white, middle-class phenomenon (Rieff 1966; Lears 1981; Kovel 1988). According to Pfister (1997), inventing a therapeutic culture enabled the white middle-class to embrace and value psychic (internal) labour over physical (external) labour and to demonstrate its superiority over subordinate groups. This is consistent with Bennett's (2003) observation that the working classes are assumed to lack the psychological depth necessary for self-governance, hence their association with the 'masses' and their supposed 'need' for expert guidance (cited in Skeggs and Wood 2009). At the same time, the moral imperative to narrate the self through the revelation and performance of one's inner life pervades the entire class structure, and such self-performances are, arguably, more readily mastered than categorical changes in wealth or social status. If middle-class presumptions about the 'failures' of working-class interiority are more about safeguarding power than about 'objective' class differences in psychological depth, then it seems plausible that at least some participants who are not white and/or middle class are nevertheless quite capable of delivering a middle-class performance. This is not to suggest an even playing field; the middle class constitutes what Savage *et al.* (1992) calls the 'particular-universal class' because of its ability to set the rules of the game for everyone despite its own specific investments in the game's outcome.

Enter Giddens' notion of reflexivity, which is related to but not synonymous with the ascendancy of therapeutic culture. Like other scholars, Giddens describes 'an increasing interconnection between the two extremes of extensionality and intentionality: globalising influences on the one hand and personal dispositions on the other' (Giddens 1991: 1). His assessment of this interconnection is more optimistic, however. He sees in 'the reflexive project of the self' a kind of politics of everyday life in which people actively construct a coherent self-identity. For Giddens, post-industrial societies position the individual as an ever-changing work in progress, despite the standardising influences wrought by commodification; people navigate a plethora of lifestyle choices in pursuit of a consistent biography or self-narrative that expresses an 'authentic', inner being. The politics of self-actualisation in a reflexively ordered environment are what he calls 'life politics', in contrast to 'emancipatory politics'. Whereas emancipatory politics is primarily concerned with liberating individuals from the constraints adversely affecting their life chances in order for them to make choices, life politics is 'the politics of choice' – it presumes a certain level of emancipation from the rigidities of tradition and from conditions of domination (Giddens 1991: 210–14). The notion of 'lifestyle' is not the exclusive purview of the middle and upper classes but also includes the decisions and actions taken by less affluent groups. Lifestyles are inevitable, Giddens insists, because 'they give material form to … particular narrative[s] of self-identity' (ibid.: 81).

To say that the notion of 'lifestyle' operates across class strata is not to say that all lifestyles are the same or that all lifestyle choices – including those dramatised on television – are equally valued. But it does point toward performance as an accepted strategy for giving material form to narratives of self-identity. Reality TV heightens performativity for viewers and participants alike. As Skeggs and Wood observe, reality TV offers:

> the performance of heightened existence and a more interesting psychic engagement of the ordinary transactions in which we are daily often implicated … [it] uses the unknown capacity of affect to great effect … we see affect-in-action, people out and in control, relationships visualised, broken-down and opened-out, amplified in intimate detail. (Skeggs and Wood 2009: 634)

If this reflects the imposition of a white, middle-class standard, it is a standard that, in its performative register, seems to borrow from 'below' – which helps explain the deployment of middle-class framing techniques to 'elevate' and contain narrative meaning (hosts, experts, voiceover, etc.). The rise of reality programming invites us to rethink what is and is not acceptable public conduct, and not simply because of the 'Guidos' (and 'Guidettes') on *Jersey Shore*. But emotionality is difficult to regulate, and, as empirical audience research shows, how people actually respond and relate to reality television is often unpredictable (Skeggs and Wood 2008).

The gendered valence of the 'ideal' performance cultivated by reality TV is no less evident, not only in the 'intimate publics' (Berlant 1997) created by the narratives enacted or the 'psychological excess' (Brooks 1976) of their melodramatic codes, but also in the 'emotional labour' (Hochschild 1983) required of those in front of and behind the camera. As I have written elsewhere, reality TV is a saturated emotional environment in which producers as well as below-the-line technical crew members have little choice but to become emotional labourers par excellence, just as character-participants must engage in plenty of 'feeling-work' too (see Grindstaff 2009, 2010). Reality shows may not 'androgynise' emotional labour in an expressly political way, but they increasingly expect men to perform in an emotional register, both as character-participants delivering on-air performances and production staffers cultivating/shaping those performances behind the scenes.

The specific contours of late-modern performativity may be informed by the 'reflexive project of the self' along with a therapeutic sensibility, but the broader cultural trend toward performance has a longer history. According to Alexander (2004), the development of the social role of actor, as distinct from ritual performer, was tied to a shift in ritual content from the sacred to the mundane in the context of early state-formation and the transition from religious to secular authority; the incorporation of secular concerns into the sacred realm via performance introduced symbolic dynamics into everyday life and reconfigured culture in a more socially oriented and dramaturgical way. Throughout the Western world, Alexander tells us, ritual moved toward theatre in tandem with growing social complexity and the reconfiguration of power; as power became more pluralised, the means of making and distributing cultural representations became more accessible. Today, perform-ance is a key mode of cultural expression, so much so that we may be better served by the concept of a public stage (Alexander 2004) or a public screen (DeLuca and Peeples 2002) than a public sphere (Habermas 1989). Self-mediation via blogs, video-logs, webcams, reality programmes and social networking sites such as Facebook and Twitter suggest that, in contemporary, complex soci-eties, the means of making and distributing cultural representations have not only become more accessible but have become overtly and self-consciously performative.

Conclusion

Although Alexander does not write about reality programming, the participation of 'ordinary' people in reality TV could be viewed as yet another iteration in the gradual process whereby performance moves from the sacred to the mundane. This is, at least in part, a class-based shift in a cultural if not strictly socio-economic sense. 'Ordinary' typically means untrained or non-professional (as an actor/expert) rather than 'average' or 'typical'; it often also operates as a euphemism for 'working class' (Bromley 2000). Just as 'profane' actors entered the 'sacred' space of ritual performance in the development of early social drama, so are 'ordinary' people who are not trained actors infiltrating the 'sacred' spaces of professional media production. And although the infiltration reflects specific economic developments – the ascendance of flexible modes of production in which the unpaid, non-union, widely available labour of ordinary people generates new avenues of profitability and control for media institutions (Raphael 1997; Turner 2006) – it also reflects the pluralisation of a key arena for the cultivation of American elites: celebrity.

In constructing an 'ordinary' version of celebrity, reality programming is 'democratising', in the sense that constructions of ordinariness now join constructions of religious, political, economic and/or cultural authority as the basis for celebrity. Certainly none of the talk-show guests or reality partici-pants I interviewed would have appeared as characters on national (and international) television had it not been for the rise of reality programming. For better or worse, the genre represents a shift in the structure of opportunity in the pursuit of celebrity status. At the same time, the exchange value of cheaply produced 'ordinary celebrity' is inherently limited, because the vast majority of reality TV participants lack the accumulated intertextual capital that 'real' (professionally networked) actors have (see Collins 2008). As Collins argues, the increasing visibility of ordinariness on television reinforces the value-hierarchy separating ordinary from celebrity categories in the first place by upholding the higher value of 'real' celebrity, protecting it from clutter. 'Ordinary celebrity' marks the individual as special but not categorically 'outside' or 'beyond' the everyday; it ensures that television exposure is both an escape from and an affirmation of ordinary status, with 'ordinariness' rooted, as always, in the expressive performance of everyday life. Critics continually remind us of this value-hierarchy when they denigrate reality shows and their participants in class-coded ways.

As a lower (the lowest?) order of celebrity, ordinary celebrity is made possible by what I call the 'self-serve' nature of reality television, in which producers construct the conditions of possibility for specific performances out of particular narrative contexts so that participants can serve themselves, cafeteria-style, to ready-made roles without the bother of extensive training, scripts, rehearsals or even talent (Grindstaff 2009, 2010). This helps explain the preponderance of cultural clichés in reality shows, including caricatures of 'white trash': because participants must take up their roles quickly and confidently in the absence of the infrastructure that professional actors take for granted, the roles have to be easily recognised and readily assumed. That some portion of the clichés are organised around social class speaks to the continued salience of class difference in American culture even when (or perhaps especially because) class difference is so frequently denied.

None of this is to argue that reality TV reduces class inequality or democratises the media. To paraphrase Turner, semiotic participation is not political self-determination (Turner 2006: 497). Rather, it is to stress that the class politics of reality programming are expressed through cultural discourse (the therapeutic turn, the reflexive project of the self, an increasing emphasis on performance) as well as on and through individual, performing bodies (which are, to be sure, themselves part of discourse), and the two levels are not always neatly aligned. The discourse or cultural formation may signal one class register, while the body signals another; this is because culture works on and through bodies, but is not reducible to them. It is also to stress that however they are expressed, the class politics of reality programming articulate a complex relationship between class-as-culture and class-as-socio-economic status. The performance logic of reality TV, in which social-identity formations are flattened beneath the weight of individualised performances of selfhood, can foreground (e.g. through caricature) or obscure the relationship between culture and socio-economic status but never position the relationship itself – or the material inequalities it references – as beyond individual control. Since reality programming is part and parcel of the larger political-economic project described by many as neo-liberalism, it is perhaps unsurprising, even predictable, that we see an increasing obfuscation of class difference on television at the precise historical moment when actual differences of wealth, income, education and opportunity loom so large.

Notes

1. Although the scholarly literature on reality programming is too vast to list comprehensively, book-length contributions include Friedman (2002), Brenton and Cohen (2003), Kilborn (2003), Smith and Wood

(2003), Andrejevic (2004), Murray and Ouellette (2004), Mathijs and Jones (2004), Holmes and Jermyn (2004), Hill (2005), Biressi and Nunn (2005), Lewis (2008), Kraidy and Sender (2010).

2.　See <http://insidetv.ew.com/2011/01/14/jersey-shore-ratings-new-record/> accessed 26 July 2011.

3.　The fact that not all of the members of the cast are of Italian descent and only one is from the Jersey Shore is reported by Franklin (2010) in her *New Yorker* article about the series.

Bibliography

Alexander, J. (2004) 'Cultural Pragmatics: Social Performance between Ritual and Strategy', *Sociological Theory*, 22(4): 527–73.

Andrejevic, M. (2004) *Reality TV: The Work of Being Watched* (New York/London: Rowman and Littlefield).

Beck, U. (1992) *Risk Society: Toward a New Modernity* (London: Sage).

Bennett, T. (2003) 'The Invention of the Modern Cultural Fact: Toward a Critique of the Critique of Everyday Life', in E. B. Silva and T. Bennett (eds), *Contemporary Culture and Everyday Life* (Durham, NC: Sociology Press), pp. 21–36.

Berlant, L. (1997) *The Queen of America Goes to Washington City: Essays on Sex and Citizenship* (Durham, NC/London: Duke University Press).

Bettie, J. (2000) *Women without Class: Girls, Race, and Identity* (Berkeley: University of California Press).

Biressi, A. and H. Nunn (2005) *Reality TV: Realism and Revelation* (London: Wallflower Press).

Bourdieu, P. (1984) *Distinction: A Social Critique of the Judgement of Taste* (Cambridge, MA: Harvard University Press).

Brenton, S. and R. Cohen (2003) *Shooting People: Adventures in Reality TV* (London/New York: Verso).

Bromley, R. (2000) 'The Theme That Dare Not Speak Its Name: Class and Recent British Film', in S. Munt (ed.), *Cultural Studies and the Working Class: Subject to Change* (London: Cassell), pp. 51–68.

Brooks, P. (1976) *The Melodramatic Imagination: Balzac, Henry James, Melodrama and the Mode of Excess* (New Haven, CT/London: Yale University Press).

Collins, S. (2008) 'Making the Most out of 15 Minutes: Reality TV's Dispensable Celebrity', *Television and New Media*, 9(2): 87–110.

DeLuca, K. and J. Peeples (2002) 'From Public Sphere to Public Screen: Democracy, Activism, and the "Violence" of Seattle', *Critical Studies in Media Communication*, 19(2): 125–51.

DeMott, B. (1990) *The Imperial Middle: Why Americans Can't Think Straight about Class* (New York: Morrow).

Foucault, M. (1977) *Discipline and Punish: The Birth of the Prison* (London: Allen Lane/Penguin).

———— (1979) *The History of Sexuality: Volume One, an Introduction* (London: Penguin).

Franklin, N. (2010) 'Jersey jetsam: MTV goes to the beach', *The New Yorker*, 18 January, p. 70.

Friedman, J. (ed.) (2002) *Reality Squared: Televisual Discourse of the Real* (Brunswick, NJ: Rutgers University Press).

Giddens, A. (1991) *Modernity and Self-Identity: Self and Society in the Late Modern Age* (Cambridge: Polity).

Goldberg, D. T. (1993) *Racist Culture: Philosophy and the Politics of Meaning* (Oxford: Blackwell).

Grindstaff, L. (2002) *The Money Shot: Trash, Class, and the Making of TV Talk Shows* (Chicago: University of Chicago Press).

———— (2009) 'Self-Serve Celebrity: The Production of Ordinariness and the Ordinariness of Production in Reality Television', in V. Mayer, A. Lotz and J.T. Caldwell (eds), *Production Studies: Cultural Studies of Media Industries* (London/New York: Routledge), pp. 71–86.

———— (2010) 'Just Be Yourself – Only More So: Ordinary Celebrity in the Era of Self-Service Television', in Kraidy and Sender (eds), *The Politics of Reality Television*, pp. 44–57.

Habermas, J. (1989) *The Structural Transformation of the Public Sphere: An Inquiry into a Category of Bourgeois Society*, translated by Thomas Burger (Cambridge, MA: MIT Press).

Hartigan, J. Jr (1999) *Racial Situations: Class Predicaments of Whiteness in Detroit* (Princeton, NJ: Princeton University Press).

Hill, A. (2005) *Reality TV: Audiences and Factual Television* (London/New York: Routledge).

Hochschild, A. R. (1983) *The Managed Heart: The Commercialization of Human Feeling* (Chicago: University of Chicago Press).

Holmes, S. and D. Jermyn (eds) (2004) *Understanding Reality Television* (London/New York: Routledge).

Illouz, E. (1997) 'Who Will Care for the Caretaker's Daughter? Towards a Sociology of Happiness in the Era of Reflexive Modernity', *Theory Culture and Society*, 14(4): 31–66.

———— (2008) *Saving the Modern Soul: Therapy, Emotions, and the Culture of Self-Help* (Berkeley: University of California Press).

Kilborn, R. (2003) *Staging the Real: Factual TV Programming in the Age of Big Brother* (Manchester: Manchester University Press).

Kipnis, L. (1996) *Bound and Gagged: Pornography and the Politics of Fantasy in America* (New York: Grove).

Kovel, J. (1988) *The Radical Spirit: Essays on Psychoanalysis and Society* (London: Free Association Books).

Kraidy, M. and K. Sender (eds) (2010) *The Politics of Reality Television: Global Perspectives* (London/New York: Routledge).

Lasch, C. (1979) *The Culture of Narcissism: American Life in the Age of Diminishing Expectations* (New York: Norton Press).

Lears, T. J. (1981) *No Place of Grace: Antimodernism and the Transformation of American Culture 1880–1920* (New York: Pantheon).

Lewis, T. (2008) *Smart Living: Lifestyle Media and Popular Expertise* (New York: Peter Lang).

Livingstone, S. and P. Lunt (1994) *Talk on Television: Audience Participation and Public Debate* (London: Routledge).

Lowney, K. (1999) *Baring Our Souls: TV Talk Shows and the Religion of Recovery* (New York: Aldine de Gruyter).

McKenzie, J. (2001) *Perform or Else: From Discipline to Performance* (London/New York: Routledge).

Mathijs, E. and J. Jones (eds) (2004) *Big Brother International: Formats, Critics, and Publics* (London/New York: Wallflower Press).

Murray, S. and L. Ouellette (eds) (2004) *Reality TV: Remaking Television Culture* (New York: University Press).

Omi, M. and H. Winant (1995) *Racial Formation in the United States*, 2nd edn. (London/New York: Routledge).

Pakulski, J. and M. Waters (1996) *The Death of Class* (Thousand Oaks, CA: Sage).

Palmer, G. (2010) 'Governing Bodies', in Kraidy and Sender (eds), *The Politics of Reality Television*, pp. 65–77.

Pfister, J. (1997) 'On Conceptualising the Cultural History of Emotional and Psychological Life in America', in J. Pfister and N. Schnog (eds), *Inventing the Psychological: Towards a Cultural History of Emotional Life in America* (New Haven, CT/London: Yale University Press).

Priest, P. J. (1995) *Public Intimacies: Talk-Show Participants and Tell-All TV*. The Hampton Press Communication Series (Cresskill, NJ: Hampton Press).

Raphael, C. (1997) 'Political Economy of Reali-TV', *Jump Cut*, 41: 102–9.

Rieff, P. (1966) *The Triumph of the Therapeutic: Uses of Faith after Freud* (New York: Harper and Row).

Rose, N. (1990) *Governing the Soul: The Shaping of the Private Self* (London/New York: Free Association Books).

——— (1998) *Inventing Ourselves: Psychology, Power, and Personhood* (London/New York: Cambridge University Press).

Savage, M., J. Barlow, P. Dickens and T. Fielding (1992) *Property, Bureaucracy and Culture: Middle-Class Formation in Contemporary Britain* (London: Routledge).

Shattuc, J. (1997) *The Talking Cure: TV Talk Shows and Women* (London/New York: Routledge).

Skeggs, B. (2004) *Class, Self, Culture* (London: Routledge).

Skeggs, B. and H. Wood (2008) 'The Labour of Transformation and Circuits of Value "around" Reality Television', *Continuum: Journal of Media and Cultural Studies*, 22(4): 559–72.

——— (2009) 'The Moral Economy of Person Production: The Class Relations of Self-Performance on "Reality" Television', *The Sociological Review*, 57(4): 626–44.

Smith, M. J. and A. F. Wood (2003) *Survivor Lessons: Essays on Communication and Reality Television* (Jefferson, NC: McFarland).

Torgovnik, M. (1991) *Gone Primitive* (Chicago: Chicago University Press).

Turner, G. (2006) 'Celebrity, the Tabloid and the Democratic Public Sphere', in P. D. Marshall (ed.), *The Celebrity Culture Reader* (New York/London: Routledge), pp. 487–500.

Wray, M. (2006) *Not Quite White: White Trash and the Boundaries of Whiteness* (Durham, NC: Duke University Press).

Wray, M. and A. Newitz (eds) (1997) *White Trash: Race and Class in America* (London/New York: Routledge).

15/Imogen Tyler

Pramface Girls: The Class Politics of 'Maternal TV'

Pramface. Noun: A teenage mother, usually from a council housing estate. Coined by the online gossip site, popbitch, and originally a woman with the facial looks of a poor single mother. Derog. (Peevish's online slang dictionary 2011)

The seven-second pre-credit sequence of Episode 3, Series 2 of the British reality television show *Underage and Pregnant* (BBC 3, 2010) opens with ambient music and a close-up shot of a baby sucking a plastic dummy (soother) in a pushchair. The camera zooms out and tilts upwards to reveal two teenage girls who are sharing a cigarette as they manoeuvre the pram along an alleyway. The girls are framed against a row of brown stone-faced terraced houses and a grey wet sky. The music fades and a young female voice with a broad Yorkshire accent and flat vowels speaks over the opening visual sequence, 'When my dad left, that is when I started being a bad girl [laughs]'. The camera cuts mid-sentence to a close-up of the younger of the two girls, who sits on a bedroom floor in her school uniform, her knees drawn up to her chest and her face framed by a baby's cot and a bed full of soft toys. This brief sequence communicates what Beverley Skeggs and Helen Wood (2009) have termed 'a moral subject semiotics': a conjunction of signs, bodies and landscape which compose a familiar assemblage of classed and gendered values. The visual semiotics of this sequence are easy for a British television audience to decode: bleached hair, sports clothing, baby in pushchair, dummy,

'Becca and Michelle' pre-credit
sequence of Episode 3, Series 2,
Underage and Pregnant (BBC 3, 2010)

Cathy Come Home (Ken Loach, 1966)

cigarettes, broken home, regional accents, terraced houses, underage sex. This televisual grammar of working-class motherhood cites the visual iconography of the social-realist television drama of 1960s Britain, typified by Ken Loach's *Cathy Come Home* (BBC, 1966). Loach's powerful drama fashioned a bleak (but beautifully shot) decaying post-industrial landscape, in which pinch-faced homeless mother Cathy (Carole White) pushed a pram through pot-holed terraced streets and past factory gates.

Anita Biressi and Heather Nunn have described social-realist television drama as 'overtly politicized ... media engagement that rooted documentary practice in (albeit flawed) desires to change social policy, uncover invisible lives and challenge an inequitable social system' (Biressi and Nunn 2005: 10). Reality TV draws on many of the techniques of social realism, such as the use of hand-held cameras, the employment of non-actors and an improvised, unscripted 'home-made' aesthetic. Both genres (problematically) portray 'the British working class from the point of view of the social outsider or "cultural tourist"' (Creeber 2009: 435). However, reality television has none of the political aspirations of social-realist drama; made by independent production companies, it is driven by profit (Creeber 2009). The unwed or homeless mother of social realism was quintessentially a 'good mother' who was represented as a victim of historical social circumstances and outmoded social mores. The depiction of her poverty and stigmatisation was designed to raise political consciousness. In reality TV, she has metamorphosed into the 'pramface girl', a figure who dramatises what Skeggs and Wood have described as 'class inequality displayed as subjectivity' (Skeggs and Wood 2009: 639). In neo-liberal Britain, poverty is not perceived or represented as a social problem but as an individual failing, and in the case of teen motherhood as a pathological subjectivity.

The term 'pramface' surfaced in popular culture in 2003 as a slur to describe young celebrity mothers from working-class backgrounds with 'a face better suited to pushing a pram round a housing estate'.[1] It is now employed as a term of abuse for young working-class mothers who are perceived as a drain on the welfare state. The pramface girl is figured as a work-shy and feckless teen mother, a character who has purposefully squandered opportunities for social mobility in meritocratic Britain and has 'chosen' a life of poverty, state dependence and redundancy for herself and her children.[2] This chapter tracks the televisual life of 'the pramface girl', for while this figure circulates within a wide range of popular media, her *raison d'être* is reality TV, and in particular the reality sub-genre I term 'maternal TV'. Focusing on the most successful teen mother reality show in the UK, *Underage and Pregnant*, this chapter examines the meaning of this distinctly neo-liberal figuration of working-class motherhood and explores how reality TV transforms having a baby into a 'class act'.

Researching the Social Life of Reality TV

This chapter draws on extra-textual sources, including interviews with seven participants in the pro-gramme and audience commentary from blogs and social networking sites. Through this mix of close textual analysis and social research methods, I have attempted to capture *the social life of reality TV*. As Wood and Skeggs insist, reality television is 'a frame of reference through which we and our forms of identity (as audience *and* potential performers) are increasingly and normatively mediated' (Wood and Skeggs 2010: 94). In other words, reality TV is not (simply) representational in respect of pre-vailing social relations and systems of value, but is fundamentally *constitutive* of contemporary social life. As Wood and Skeggs suggest of their audience research, 'mediated worlds and lived worlds are simultaneously experienced in significant and dynamic moments of connection' (ibid.: 104). The blur-ring of mediated and lived experience is evident when one tries to delineate reality TV, a ubiquitous form sustained by such a huge range of public and commercial industries that it simply cannot be understood in terms of television content alone, or even in the interaction between televisual texts and audiences: rather, 'reality' is better understood as the axiomatic system of media culture. For real-ity media are not only thoroughly embedded in everyday social practices, but are productive of 'tele-visual sociality'. One of the most significant developments in the phenomenal ascendance of reality TV is its extension into online formats through the development of Web 2.0 digital technologies. Social networking sites, in particular, play a pivotal role in the production, circulation and reception of reality TV.

The empirical research for this chapter took place when the second series of *Underage and Pregnant* was being aired in the UK (July–September 2010), which meant that I was able to track in 'real time' the online audience responses posted on message boards, blogs and social networking sites. Although a rich analysis of this audience data is beyond the scope of this chapter, while researching the 'online life' of *Underage and Pregnant*, it became apparent how the exaggerated char-acters on reality TV operate for audiences as vehicles for communicating values and beliefs. For example, the ways in which reality show participants' and viewers' 'likes' or 'dislikes' operate as signs of taste which are instrumentalised in everyday conversational practices of distinction-making (Tyler and Bennett 2010). While many responses to the participants in *Underage and Pregnant* reit-erate the kinds of (often negative) judgments incited by the text, discussion threads offer a fascinat-ing insight into how the televisual characterisations become animated in struggles over identity and value. This online research revealed how differently positioned viewers negotiate dominant specta-torial positions through articulations of identification and dis-identification with the caricatured rep-resentations and 'performances' of the young mothers on screen. This finding echoes those of Skeggs and Wood's reality TV audience research project (2004–8)[3] in which reality participants represent complex figures of identification and dis-identification, the meaning and value of which is highly dependent on the classed, gendered, parental and racialised positioning of the audience (Skeggs, Wood and Thumim 2008). Wood and Skeggs conclude that 'reality television creates a structure of immanence for viewers through which there is rarely a singular stable "reading" of a programme, but rather a set of immediate affective moments through which our audiences experience and locate themselves in the unfolding drama' (Wood and Skeggs 2010: 104). My online research further reveals how reality television extends beyond immediate contexts of screening and viewing, as characters and storylines are reanimated in sometimes unanticipated ways.

As well as exploring audience responses to *Underage and Pregnant*, I was able to use social networking sites to contact and interview seven of the teen mothers who had participated in the programme. These interviews ranged from short exchanges to longer conversations which took place over a period of weeks. Significantly, these online research methods parallel those used by television production companies to recruit participants. 'Youth orientated' reality TV is completely enmeshed with social networking media, from the very early stages of production, through recruitment, marketing and reception. For teenagers with high levels of internet access, social networking is a technology deeply embedded in their everyday lives and accessed via personalised media technology. Young people use social networking sites, such as MySpace, Bebo and Facebook, predominantly as a means of interacting with their peers. The nature of these communications is such that they are inevitably informal. This medium lends itself to new forms of intimacy and immediacy, one of the many features that social networking sites share with reality TV.

Many teenagers engage in practices of 'friending' with relatively little thought as to the consequences of exposing their private lives, thoughts and feelings in what is a privately owned for-profit information domain. One participant described to me the way in which she felt she was 'ensnared' by a researcher working for *Underage and Pregnant* after being 'friended' by her online. Another stated: 'I think they exploited my interest in the media and this is how *they hooked me* in the first place, because it actually all began when I started speaking to a researcher on Bebo' (my emphasis). Both social networking sites and reality TV are examples of *active surveillance media* in which participants 'volunteer' to participate. As Michael Bullock writes:

> The emergence of social networking sites such as Facebook, MySpace and Twitter […] among a myriad of others, hails the beginning of a new era of 'opt in' surveillance where users are encouraged to share their personal activities, information, and thoughts with their peers and even people they have no connection to. (Bullock 2009: 28)

This raises a series of ethical questions about the use of social networking as a research method and the relationship between academic research and television production research methods. However, this online research also revealed some of the ways in which social networking is also enabling of political communities, and creates spaces within which young mothers are able to acquire capital and recognition outside dominant systems of representation and social control. The combination of online ethnography and participant interviews enabled me to track how reality TV participants employ social networking to respond to their negative framing within programming: three participants in *Underage and Pregnant* went to some lengths to intervene in online chatroom debates with audiences about their negative representation, while all of the participants discussed aspects of their participation in the show with each other, and with friends and audiences in social network sites. This highlights how social networking operates as a 'back-channel' for participants to 'recode' themselves.[4] Through their online dialogues and posts, and in their interviews with me, the young women rationalise and begin to 'theorise' their positioning within the programme, critiquing television production codes and editorial decision-making, and introducing alternative perspectives on specific sequences, shots, narrative, events and takes.

Maternal TV

'Maternal TV' is a proliferating reality subgenre and includes 'correctional' parenting shows such as *Supernanny* (Channel 4 2004–),[5] and hospital-based childbirth reality shows such as *One Born Every Minute* (Channel 4, 2010). There has been a growing focus within this genre on 'teen' parenting. In the UK, this includes programmes such as: *Baby Borrowers* (BBC 3, 2007), *Kimberley: Young Mum 10 Years On* (Channel 4, 2009), *Help! I'm a Teen Mum* (ITV, 2007), *Kizzy: Mum at 14* (BBC 3, 2007), *The Trouble with Girls: Three Girls and Three Babies* (BBC 3, 2009), *Teen High Mum* (BBC 3, 2009), *18 Pregnant Schoolgirls* (BBC 3, 2009), *Pregnancy: My Big Decision* (BBC 3, 2009), *Young Mum's Mansion* (BBC 3, 2009) and *Pramface Babies* (ITV, 2009). While this chapter focuses on British Maternal TV, these reality programmes are also in the ascendance in the USA where the most prominent examples are MTV's *16 and Pregnant* (2008 and 2010) and spin-off, *Teen Moms* (2009–10). *Teen Moms* was MTV's most successful show in 2009 and in the top three US cable shows for the year, attracting an average of 3.3 million viewers, franchised worldwide and dubbed 'the teen mom phenomenon' (Goldberg 2010).

Underage and Pregnant

Underage and Pregnant is commissioned and broadcast by BBC 3, the public broadcaster's 'youth channel', which targets a television audience of sixteen- to thirty-four-year-olds and is described in a BBC press release as a programme that 'goes beyond the statistics and tabloid headlines to reveal the real story of life as a pregnant schoolgirl and teenage mum'.[6] This chapter focuses on Series 2 of *Underage and Pregnant* screened in the summer and autumn of 2010. This second series has proved a huge ratings success, regularly pulling in audiences of a million. As I finished this chapter, the production company (Mentorn Television) had begun to recruit participants for a third series. The term 'underage' in the title is a reference to the fact that the girls were all under the British legal age for consensual sexual relations between a man and a woman when they became pregnant. The choice of the word 'underage', rather than young or teenage in the title, has a lurid quality that from the outset undermines the claim of the programme-makers that they want to get 'behind the sensational headlines'.[7] *Underage and Pregnant* does not focus on the medical aspects of pregnancy and birth, but is concerned with documenting the teenagers' changing body-image, their friendships, sexual and family relationships, and issues around money and education. In some episodes, the drama centres on families coming to terms with teen pregnancy and preparing for the birth, while others focus on the ways in which the young mothers are coping, or failing to cope, with a newborn infant. Each episode is 30 minutes long, an individual storyline compressed into approximately 15 minutes of footage. The participants I interviewed said that filming for an individual episode took place over a period of approximately four months, with film crews spending in total between five and seven days with each participant. The participants are unpaid, receiving only a gift token worth approximately £250 for their participation.

The vast majority of the participants in *Underage and Pregnant* are from backgrounds which are coded as poor, working-class or lower-middle-class, although episodes often feature two teenage mothers who have contrasting storylines in terms of their perceived 'respectability'. As one participant noted, 'In most episodes, one family is always portrayed as uneducated and "working class" whereas the other is supposed to be a bit posher. I think they exaggerate that divide.' Regional accents and architecture are mobilised to reinforce class-based perceptual frames. This foregrounding of class differences is central to the spectatorial pleasure offered by the text and serves to reinforce the understanding that the audience can occupy a secure position from which to make evaluative assessments of the teenage mothers depicted (See Tyler and Bennett 2010; Skeggs 2005). This interpretation was reinforced in interviews with participants, one of whom described how she felt that the representation of her family was distorted to make them appear poor. As she notes: 'They didn't represent my family in an accurate or positive way, always making my family out to be poor. For example, they didn't screen the footage of us all going [abroad on holiday] even though they were filming at the airport with us.'

Edited sequences are threaded together with a voiceover by actress and television celebrity Natalie Cassidy, familiar to British viewers from her role as Sonia Jackson, a working-class character involved in an underage pregnancy storyline in the long-running soap opera *EastEnders*. The use of Cassidy as narrator reinforces the youthful, sympathetic 'big sisterly' mode of address of the programme. However, while Cassidy's softly spoken 'Estuary English' voiceover is sympathetic and neutral in tone, her narration is laid over what Skeggs and Wood term 'judgment shots': visual shots and sequences that incite negative moral judgment (Skeggs, Wood and Thumim 2008). As the series progresses, the familiarity of this ploy means that Cassidy's voiceover acquires a more condescending and ironic tone.

Shame on Her

The encoding of what Skeggs (2005) terms 'person value' through visual sequences of townscapes is a central trope within *Underage and Pregnant*. 'Michela' (Episode 4, Series 2) begins with overhead views of Glasgow, which cut to overhead and extreme long shots of a housing estate before settling on a long shot of the frontage of one house. This bird's-eye narrative perspective is familiar to viewers of British soap operas, such as *EastEnders* which uses satellite footage in the title sequence to zoom into the working-class East End of London, seemingly from outer space, and from *Coronation Street*, where the title montage whisks the viewer over the roofs of Victorian terraced houses in northern England (Lovell 1996). Andrew Higson describes these sequences as 'that long shot of our town from that hill' which form a critical part of 'social realist narrative positioning from outside and above the indus- trial landscape' (Higson 1996: 152). These long shots involve 'an external point of view, the voyeurism of one class looking at another … to read the shot in this way is to identify with a position outside and above' (ibid.: 152).

The voiceover to the opening sequence of this episode of *Underage and Pregnant* informs us that 'Michela lives on an estate near Glasgow with her parents, sister Suzanne and eight-week-old Tamara-Leigh.' The implication is that this is a council estate (referred to in Scotland as schemes): publicly built and subsidised housing, similar to 'projects' in the US. In Britain, council estates were built by regional governments (local councils) primarily between the 1950s and the 80s to supply affordable housing to working-class people whose properties were demolished as part of large-scale inner-city 'slum clearances', or who lived in overcrowded urban areas. The historical association between council estates and slums, and concerted attempts on the part of the middle classes to dif- ferentiate between private estates and council estates, led to the deep stigmatisation of council prop- erties.[8] The focus of pre-credit and opening sequences on housing estates, and other 'working-class landscapes', metaphorically establishes a 'high ground' from which the viewer can pass judgment. These geographical sequences operate as 'psychological landscapes' which connote the personal qualities of the protagonist herself.

Michela's story was one of the more intrusive and disturbing episodes of *Underage and Pregnant*, and includes repeated sequences which shame Michela by dramatising her inadequate mothering. The episode is the only one to feature footage shot at night, while Michela and her baby were sleep- ing. This low-resolution, night-vision footage resembles a sequence from a nature programme and while difficult to see clearly, it is presented through the narrative as visual evidence of Michela's incompe- tence at giving her baby night feeds and proof that she is an 'unfit mother' who is failing to care for her infant. By way of contrast, Michela's mother and sister (who is also a teen mother) are portrayed sym- pathetically in the programme as caring and concerned. In one sequence, a voiceover explains that Michela has been visited by social workers. In a shot/reverse-shot sequence, her older sister (a 'good' mother) asks Michela what the social workers said, and Michela replies, 'Don't know. Wasn't listening to them.' Her cheeks are flushed and she refuses to look at the camera or her sister. Michela's sister then proceeds to admonish her about her maternal failure. The negative judgment incited by this sequence is heightened by the use of subtitles, absent from the rest of the programme, which drama- tise Michela's Glaswegian accent and draw attention to her 'incomprehensible' behaviour.

As Skeggs and Wood write, 'the working-class appear to display and dramatise themselves as inad- equate, in need of self-investment. They are shown to have not just deficit culture, but also deficit sub- jectivity' (Skeggs and Wood 2009: 636). Through the intervention of the expertise of social services, Michela's deficiencies are 'transformed', and at the end of the programme she is depicted as a model cit- izen in a scene in which she talks at a local youth centre to teens, warning them about the difficulties of

'Don't know. Wasn't listening to
them.' Episode 4, Series 2, *Underage
and Pregnant*

motherhood. Each episode of *Underage and Pregnant* follows a similar narrative arc: an initial crisis (pregnancy or new motherhood) leads to conflict in family and other intimate relationships, a crisis which reaches some kind of resolution when the teenage participants become adequate mothers. However, I would argue that these contrived narratives exist largely as a means of legitimising the entertainment garnered from highly selective and often intentionally 'shaming' footage of these young women's lives.

Class Laughter

Laughter is central to processes of class-making, and 'laughter shots' feature regularly in *Underage and Pregnant* (Tyler 2008). For instance, Episode 7 from Series 2 includes a street sequence in which pregnant teenager Chenice and her friend describe how she discovered she was pregnant. This sequence ends with a street-level medium shot of a fast-food restaurant and the words of the narrative voiceover, 'Chenice finally took a pregnancy test in the KFC toilet.' If Michela represents the council estate, then Chenice is encoded in the urban landscape of London, as 'cheap' and 'disposable' like the fast-food restaurant in which she discovered she was pregnant.

Reality TV audiences share and reiterate comic moments online, posting quotes and even sharing funny screen shots on message boards. For example, the comic line 'Chenice finally took a pregnancy test in the KFC toilet' was immediately circulated on Twitter as the programme was screened, surfaced later on Facebook and was mocked and discussed in several audience forums. Winfried Menninghaus (2003) argues that laughing at something is 'an act of expulsion' that closely resembles the rejecting movement of disgust. Disgust and laughter are, he notes, complementary ways of admitting an alterity (Menninghaus 2003: 11). This is explicit in online conversational threads, in which the vocabulary moves seamlessly between comedy and disgust, as seen in one blogger's comment on the Chenice episode, 'omg they are soooo disgusting. lol' [Oh, my God. They are so disgusting. Laugh out Loud]. Laughter has an important function for the reality television audience: it moves us both literally and figuratively, we are averted, moved away from the thing (the object or figure) we laugh at. Laughter is boundary-forming, creating a distance between 'them' and 'us', asserting moral judgments and a superior class position (Tyler 2008).

Chenice finally took
a pregnancy test in the KFC toilet

'Chenice finally took a pregnancy test in the KFC toilet.' Episode 7, Series 2, *Underage and Pregnant*

Laughter also plays a role in Tasha's story in Episode 7, Series 2, which begins with a spectacular series of aerial shots of the famous north of England seaside town Blackpool, a landscape immediately recognisable to British viewers from its promenade and tower. In the case of Tasha's story, this class voyeurism is reinforced by the fact that Blackpool has a long history as a Victorian working-class seaside resort but since the 1960s has been associated with post-industrial decline, unemployment, poverty and other social problems. The pre-credits sequence thus frames Tasha in a social and economic landscape associated with faded glory, poverty and seaside vulgarity. The sequence ends with a close-up shot of a pair of fake leopard-skin boots, before panning up to a young woman pushing a pram, creating a direct visual association between Tasha and Blackpool. The relationship between person and place is further encoded in the opening sequence, which features street-level views of the housing estate on which Tasha lives, the camera lingering on shots of a street, before focusing on a medium close-up of a specific bungalow. The voiceover to this sequence informs us that 'Renting a house across the street from her mum and dad, Tasha survives on benefits.'

Skeggs, Wood and Thumim (2008) develop the term 'judgment shots' to describe the key moments in reality programmes when the audience is incited to respond with judgment to what they are seeing and hearing on screen. In their 'text-in-action' sessions, the audience 'gasped, laughed, tutted, sighed, "ooh"ed and/or "aah"ed' at these moments. These affective responses then often

> translated into judgement through mediating statements such as 'oh my God', which were then converted into moral judgements, such as 'How can they let their children behave like that?', or 'How can they get into that state?', or 'How can they let themselves go?' (Skeggs, Wood and Thumim 2008: 5)

'Tasha is struggling to cope.'
Episode 7, Series 2, *Underage and Pregnant*

Tasha's story features several typical 'judgment shots', the most obvious being the images of piles of clutter and unwashed clothes in her house. These judgment shots operate as audience direction, supporting what Samantha Lyle has termed the 'controlling and pervasive nature of the middle-class gaze', which 'encourages a preferred reading by the audience in terms of classed identities, thus (re)producing symbolic violence through viewer affects' (Lyle 2008: 322). Tasha described how the production crew had filmed her house without her permission:

> They filmed my house when I wasn't in. They didn't ask me if they could film the mess; if they asked I would have sorted it out (obviously it's not like that now) but it was only odd days it was a big mess but it came across that I lived in a pig sty, that bit I was not happy about! As that is the only thing I have been judged on, 'If you are going on TV you don't leave your house in a mess you tidy it up'.

Tasha is deeply concerned about appearing as a respectable young mother and was angry about being represented as slovenly, clearly aware of the kinds of judgment these shots would encourage. She was particularly concerned about inviting the negative judgments of those she described as older mothers. Tasha identifies how the programme has been shot and edited to encourage mockery of her bodily habitus, domestic skills and her environment. As a result, she spent a considerable time on online message boards attempting to wrest back control over her representation. She prepared for the screening of the episode by placing messages on social network sites and message boards advertising the date of the screening and highlighting her anxiety that audiences might 'judge her'. She also responded in 'real time' to comments made on Facebook about her depiction on the programme, sought and received reassurance from Facebook 'friends' and intervened in a range of bulletin and message boards in which audiences had made negative comments about her. She argued with one poster who criticised her portrayal and she created online photo albums composed of shots of her tidy house, emphasising in captions the transformation of rooms which had previously appeared in negative judgment shots in the programme. Through these strategies, Tasha was able, at least partially, to redirect readings of her performance, and to dissipate her anxiety that she might be perceived as unrespectable or a bad mother. Tasha engaged in this as part of the process of participation and clearly enjoyed what she described as 'being famous', campaigning for a 'catch-up' series of *Underage and Pregnant*.

It is important to note, however, that the majority of the young women I interviewed expressed more ambivalence about participation in the programme, enjoying aspects of their exposure on television but also expressing regret at the more negative dimensions of their portrayal, and frustration at their lack of control over the editorial process. While many of them employed online back-channels, few did so with the gusto of Tasha. Other participants felt unable to challenge their negative portrayal at all and believed they had been exploited by the programme-makers. The following comments by one participant summarised some of the young women's feelings of being duped and exploited:

> At first I thought it would be a good idea to be on the programme but when they are actually in your face, telling you what to do and try getting you to saying things you don't want to, it is really difficult. You just don't realise what you've actually said and you also say things to keep them from stop going on. It is only when they show you what is going on TV you realise what you have said and how it will be judged, but by then they will not take anything off because you've signed a document.

Fertility Envy

This chapter emerges out of a larger research project on 'Maternal Publics', which explores the extraordinary proliferation of representations of maternity within popular culture (see Tyler 2010, 2009; Baraitser and Tyler 2010). The fascination with celebrity pregnancy and motherhood, the emergence of 'momoir' literary genres and a focus on the documentation of foetal life, pregnancy and childbirth have all emerged alongside an intensive interest in maternity within reality TV. Much of this maternal publicity is concerned with the *scaling* of maternal bodies: that is, with practices of coding particular kinds of maternity as desirable or abject (Young 1990). Historically, this scaling of maternal bodies is not a new phenomenon, and young unwed working-class mothers have always been a target of social stigma. Nevertheless, the mockery of 'pramface' has a contemporary specificity, and must be read in relation to what Helen Wilson and Annette Huntington have described as new neoliberal norms of femininity, in which the ideal life trajectory of middle-class girls and women conforms to the current governmental objectives of economic growth through higher education and increased female workforce participation (Wilson and Huntington 2005: 59). In *Underage and Pregnant*, the moral worth of participants is often correlated with their educational status: those mothers seen to be continuing in education are able to acquire forms of value and capital, while those seen as 'abandoning' education for motherhood are more harshly judged. However, the pramface is also castigated because she embodies anxiety about the time and place of motherhood in a society obsessed with paid work. Indeed, the 'inappropriate fertility' of teenagers embodied in the figure of the pramface is a symptom of a wider 'fertility anxiety' which haunts middle-class neoliberal femininity. Pramface is not only productive in the wrong way, but worse, she has that which is denied those who (in the words of one of my students) 'do what you are supposed to do, you know, work hard at school, go to university, have a proper career'. The increased visibility of the pregnant body, and an increasingly sexualised consumer culture of pregnant beauty, 'flaunts fertility in your face' and generates widespread 'fertility anxiety' not only among older women, but also among teenagers and young women. Indeed, I want to suggest that the figure of the pramface girl is in fact a site of deep class envy.

Despite attempts to frame *Underage and Pregnant* as sex education, with the production of a complementary teacher's pack for schools, there is little sense that the programme plays any kind of 'contraceptive' function for its audience. On the contrary, what is striking from reading audience comments is how many women identify positively with the young mothers on screen. Particularly noticeable is how many audience members express their own 'fertility envy' of the participants: many blogs and posts attest to the ways in which this and similar programmes make girls and women feel broody. As one teenager viewer states, 'I love this stuff except it makes me want a baby weellll bad' (The Student Room 2010). Furthermore, as Wood and Skeggs (2010) suggest, motherhood becomes a central marker of value and identification which their viewers often mobilised against the stigmatising framing of reality participants. Maternal values and desires allow for a recoding of the young women through positive identifications with their mothering. Therefore, while *Underage and Pregnant* reiterates received mythologies about teen motherhood and the imagined deficiencies of working-class culture, I want to end this chapter with some very preliminary reflections on what this programme also *inadvertently* reveals about how maternity is experienced by some girls as a means of creating value in the context of impossible neo-liberal ideals.

Suzanne Cater and Lester Coleman's (2006) study for the Joseph Rowntree Foundation on 'planned' teenage pregnancy detailed how for many young people parenthood is viewed as 'an opportunity, within their own control, to change their life and to gain independence and a new iden-tity' (Cater and Coleman 2006: 31). This was particularly the case for young people from relatively deprived backgrounds and from areas of Britain where there were limited employment and educa-tional opportunities. In this context, having a baby is experienced by some young people as a rational response to their situation – a means of creating value for themselves and enriching their lives in a social context in which they are positioned as worthless.

> Nobody ever said anything to me at school – like – do you wanna do such and such a job …
> everyone knows you probably couldn't do them types of things round here so maybe that's why they
> don't put it in your head in the first place! [laughs] You'd only be pissed off that you couldn't do it,
> wouldn't ya. I see being a mum as a job though … if I didn't, if I wasn't a mum, I don't think I'd even
> have a job, so it was probably a good decision for me – personally. (Female, aged eighteen, in Cater
> and Colman 2006: 31)

This quotation recalls Chenice in *Underage and Pregnant*. While the audience might have laughed as Chenice describes how she discovered that she was pregnant in a KFC toilet, her account in the same episode of how being pregnant has infused her life with value is deeply affecting. *Underage and Pregnant* does enable some positive readings of teen motherhood as identities of value by revealing the capacity of young women to mother their children, often with limited resources and in the face of incredible social stigma, in ways that are both moving and inspiring. As Skeggs and Wood write,

> people excel at that which they are supposed to fail; they show integrity when they are positioned as trivial; they show good will when put into ridiculous situations which are designed to humiliate. Participants do challenge their coding and loading through their self-performances. (Skeggs and Wood 2009: 640)

Conclusion: Prymface and Proud

This chapter has taken me on a fascinating journey: I have watched many hours of reality TV and have journeyed into an online world where 'proud 'n' pramface' girls poke fun at the 'fertility envy' of 'dried-up' middle-aged women. Despite negative coding in reality TV, the pramface girl moves through media culture in unanticipated ways, and becomes reanimated in deeper struggles over the strictures of 'neo-liberal girlhood'.

'Prymface' was the username of one mother who 'friended' me on Facebook. Prymface, she explained, stands for 'Promoting Respect for Young Mothers'. Through blogging, tweeting and networking with young mothers, Prymface and her network are challenging 'stereotypical views of teenage parents that encourage judgment and discrimination based on age'. Savvy women like Prymface not only actively challenge negative stereotypes, but are taking on politicians, pulling apart policy documents, writing diaries, poems and novels, making films and crucially representing themselves in their own terms.

Notes

1. For the etymology of this term and its implicit reworking of the figure of 'Cathy' from Loach's *Cathy Come Home*, see Dee O'Connell (2003).
2. This chapter develops earlier work on classed maternal figures: see Tyler 2008, 2009, 2010.
3. See ESRC report <http://www.esrc.ac.uk/my-esrc/grants/RES-148-25-0040/read/reports> accessed 2 February 2011.
4. I am grateful to Beverley Skeggs and Helen Wood for this account of my research.
5. For an excellent analysis of *Supernanny* and the new televisual parenting paradigm, see Tracey Jensen (2010).
6. BBC press release [online], 2009. Available at: <http://www.bbc.co.uk/pressoffice/pressreleases/stories/2009/04_april/23/growing.shtml> accessed January 2011.
7. BBC 3's use of sensationalist programme titles has been frequently criticised in public debates. In 2007, another teen mother reality show, *Pramface Mansion*, underwent a last-minute title change to *Young Mum's Mansion* after negative public reactions to the use of the slur 'pramface'.
8. This is evident in the ubiquity of the pejorative slang term 'chav', which is said to be an acronym for, variously, 'Council Housed and Violent', 'Council Housed and Vile' or 'Council House Associated Vermin'. 'Council' is similarly used as a derogatory slang word in its own right to describe somebody who is perceived to be poor or vulgar.

Bibliography

Baraitser, L. and I. Tyler (2010) 'Talking of Mothers', *Soundings: A Journal of Politics and Culture*, 44, Spring: 117–27.

Biressi, A. and H. Nunn (2005) *Reality TV: Realism and Revelation* (London: Wallflower Press).

Bullock, M. L. (2009) 'The Evolution of Surveillance Technology beyond the Panopticon', unpublished thesis. Available at: <http://danm.ucsc.edu/~mbullock/doc/LukeBullock_Thesis.pdf> accessed 13 July 2011.

Cater, S. and L. Coleman (2006) *'Planned' Teenage Pregnancy: Perspectives of Young Parents from Disadvantaged Backgrounds*, Joseph Rowntree Foundation (Bristol: Policy Press).

Creeber, G. (2009) '"The truth is out there! not!": *Shameless* and the Moral Structures of Contemporary Social Realism', *New Review of Film and Television Studies*, 7(4): 421–39.

Goldberg, S. (2010) 'The Teen Mom Phenomena' [online], 10 September. Available at: <http://edition.cnn.com/2010/SHOWBIZ/TV/09/10/teen.mom.mtv/index.html?eref=edition_entertainment> accessed 11 September 2010.

Higson, A. (1996) 'Space, Place, Spectacle: Landscape and Townscape in the "Kitchen Sink" Film', in A. Higson (ed.), *Dissolving Views: Key Writings on British Cinema* (London/New York: Cassell), pp. 133–56.

Jensen, T. (2010) '"What kind of mum are you at the moment?" *Supernanny* and the Psychologising of Classed Embodiment', *Subjectivity*, 3: 170–92.

Lovell, T. (1996) 'Landscapes and Stories in 1960s British Realism', in A. Higson (ed.), *Dissolving Views: Key Writings on British Cinema* (London/New York: Cassell), pp. 157–77.

Lyle, S. (2008) '(Mis)recognition and the Middle-Class/Bourgeois Gaze: A Case Study of *Wife Swap*', *Critical Discourse Studies*, 5(4): 319–30.

Menninghaus, W. (2003) *Disgust: Theory and History of a Strong Sensation*, translated by H. Eiland and J. Golb (New York: SUNY Press).

O'Connell, D. (2003) 'Pity the poor pramface', *Observer* [online], 10 August. Available at: <http://www.guardian.co.uk/politics/2003/aug/10/socialexclusion.advertising> accessed 12 September 2010.

Peevish's online slang dictionary (2011). Available at: <http://www.peevish.co.uk/slang/search.htm> accessed 21 September 2010.

Skeggs, B. (2005) 'The Making of Class through Visualising Moral Subject Formation', *Sociology*, 39(5): 65–82.

Skeggs, B. and H. Wood (2009) 'The Moral Economy of Person Production: The Class Relations of Self-Performance on "Reality" Television', *The Sociological Review*, 57(4): 626–44.

Skeggs, B. , H. Wood and N. Thumim (2008) '"Oh goodness, I am watching reality TV": How Methods Make Class in Multi-Method Audience Research', *European Journal of Cultural Studies*, 11(1): 5–24.

The Student Room (2010) Anon. Blog [online]. Available at: <www.thestudentroom.co.uk> accessed 2 September 2010.

Tyler, I. (2008) '"Chav mum, chav scum": Class Disgust in Contemporary Britain', *Feminist Media Studies*, 8(1): 17–34.

—— (2009) 'Why the Maternal Now?', *Studies in the Maternal* [online], 1(1). Available at: <http://www.mamsie.bbk.ac.uk/back_issues/issue_one/Imogen%20Tyler_1000%20words_new.pdf]> accessed 31 September 2010.

————— (2010) 'Pregnant Beauty: Maternal Femininities under Neo-Liberalism', in R. Gill and C. Scharff (eds), *New Femininities: Postfeminism, Neoliberalism and Identity* (Basingstoke: Palgrave Macmillan), pp. 21–36.

Tyler, I. and B. Bennett (2010) 'Celebrity Chav: Fame, Femininity and Social Class', *European Journal of Cultural Studies*, August, 13(3): 375–93.

Wilson, H. and A. Huntington (2005) 'Deviant (M)others: The Construction of Teenage Motherhood in Contemporary Discourse', *Journal of Social Policy*, 35(1): 9–76.

Wood, H. and B. Skeggs (2010) 'Reacting to Reality TV: The Affective Economy of an "Extended Social/Public Realm"', in M. Kraidy and K. Sender (eds), *Real Worlds: The Global Politics of Reality TV* (New York: Routledge), pp. 93–107.

Young, I. M. (1990) *Justice and the Politics of Difference* (Princeton, NJ: Princeton University Press).

16/Valerie Walkerdine

Shame on You! Intergenerational Trauma and Working-Class Femininity on Reality Television

Introduction

This chapter explores the ways in which current attempts to shame and improve working-class women on British reality television work with regard to affective relations. Drawing on cultural theoretical work on Victorian working-class women as shameful, dirty and to be improved, the chapter explores how this is lived and embodied. Referring to research on intergenerational trauma, particularly the work of Françoise Davoine and Jean-Max Gaudillière (2004) on how unspoken responses to historical danger can be passed down generations, and Bracha Ettinger's (2006) work on the particular role of women in the transmission of affect, I consider how shame and self-improvement are transmitted so that generations of working-class women come to embody a shame ripe for transformation. This makes many transformation-style reality programmes compelling viewing.

The presentation of working-class women on reality television has been the subject of considerable academic debate (see McRobbie 2004; Skeggs 2005; Skeggs and Wood 2008; Tyler 2008; Wood and Skeggs 2004). While many studies have concentrated on the regulation of class and femininity, my aim is to add another dimension to Skeggs' (1997) considerable work on shame and working-class femininity. My argument is that shame and respectability have long antecedents in relation to working-class women, in which the feminine body is understood as always already shameful. My particular interest is in how we might understand the intergenerational transmission of shame in relation to the working-class female body which is always presented as ready and ripe for transformation. This means that the desire to rid oneself of shame and the acknowledgment of shaming as a recognised and even acceptable form of treatment of working-class women are central, providing an address to all women which presents potentially compulsive viewing.

Ringrose and Walkerdine (2008) identified a wide range of reality television programmes which focused on shaming and improving working-class women based on the concept of the makeover (and see Palmer in this volume). Moseley (2000) has pointed to the makeover takeover of British television, while Wood and Skeggs (2004) argue that participants are urged to escape their identified lack through the cultural self-knowledge of television's expert mediators. Ringrose and Walkerdine point to a central dynamic within makeover shows of the transformation of an abject subject (Kristeva 1982). Skeggs and Wood (2008) also argue that while some shows seem to offer a redemptive narrative of transformation, most actually forestall the possibility by putting forward a familiar story of lack of taste, of pathological culture and bad choice, which are barriers to the possibility of becoming a subject who can correctly choose the course of their own life. Expert knowledges offer up a melancholic, endlessly prolonged, possibility for transforming the abject working-class woman. Thus, Ringrose and Walkerdine cite programmes which include *Supernanny* (Channel 4, 2004), *Little Angels* (BBC 3, 2004–6), *House of Tiny Tearaways* (BBC 3, 2005–), *Honey We're Killing the Kids* (BBC 3, 2005), *Jamie's School Dinners* (Channel 4, 2005), as well as a number of dieting programmes such as *Diet Doctors Inside and Out* (Five, 2006), *You Are What You Eat* (Channel 4, 2004–7), and finally appearance makeover shows such as *10 Years Younger* (Channel 4, 2003–) and *What Not to Wear* (BBC 1, 2001–). Ringrose and Walkerdine also point to programmes in which working-class women attempt to improve themselves through getting a better job and have to undergo an Eliza Dolittle-type transformation of appearance and demeanour to get work (*Get Your Dream Job*, BBC 3, 2006). Similarly, the transformation of manners and appearance are also demanded in *Ladette to Lady* (ITV 1, 2005–) where unruly young working-class women are put through a finishing school.

As Ringrose and Walkerdine argue, these programmes reflect shifts in modes of governance in which citizens are made to be responsible for their own regulation, usually presented as an effect of neo-liberalism. In neo- or advanced liberalism (Rose 1990; Walkerdine and Bansel 2009), liberal modernity is intensified, as citizens are supposed to adopt a reflexive selfhood through which they must constantly adapt and invent themselves in response to the labour market. While class is still an issue, it often becomes glossed over as individual responsibility as the pathologised subject fails to discipline and manage themselves in the correct way. This results in pathological child-rearing, a dirty kitchen, fat children, eating unhealthy food, and lack of aspiration and motivation to change and succeed. While self-realisation is what is expected of the life project and one in which success is judged by the psychological capacities to succeed, the ability to handle uncertainty and the precariousness of never knowing where work will come from is to be experienced as a personal failing. In this account, psychology has a special role to play by offering an individual explanation, a restorative practice and expert knowledge to help ensure successful change and adaptation. Neo-liberal subjects are enjoined to shape themselves through practices of consumption into people who can succeed and, moreover, be the object of their own dreams. This, of course, fits well with how we might understand the address of reality television to female spectators in the present. Other writers on reality television have developed an understanding of the genre as *the* vehicle of current neo-liberal political trends (See Palmer 2003; Ouellette and Hay 2008).

In this chapter, however, I want to think about the way in which, contrary to much work on the 'nowness' of neo-liberalism, it is clear that the shaming and denigration of working-class women can be shown to have begun with the inception of class as a mode of stratification and regulation. My particular concern is to think about how we might understand contemporary televisual modes of shaming as having an affective history which means that working-class women across generations have been, and still are, suffused with shame and the need for transformation. Thus, it is my argument that current reality television practices are popular because they work on an already embodied and transmitted shame passed down generations in families and in wider social, cultural and bodily practices. In order to understand this, I will refer to work on history and intergenerational transmission of trauma.

Victorian Working-Class Women's Sexuality

Foucault reminds us in the first volume of the *History of Sexuality* (1998) that the Victorians did not repress, but rather medicalised, sexuality. However, this work does not address the complex way in which class was produced as a mode of regulation in this period which pathologised working-class women's sexuality, understanding them as dirty, amoral and potentially as amateur or professional prostitutes, and who were also often the object of middle- and upper-class men's transgressive desires. Pamela Fox argues that in Victorian novels, the sexual interest and prurience of upper-class men in the 'dirty' servant conflates actual physical dirt with desired masculine 'dirty fantasies':

> Dirt and sexuality become conflated, negating working-class females' femininity. She thus has no recourse but to yearn for a mode of subjectivity which represents a splitting of herself, which allows her to divide her sexual identity along physical and metaphysical lines. (Fox 1994: 102)

The working-class woman is, by implication, already dirt; all she can do is strive to be as pure as possible – a mode of moral regulation through which she must regulate herself or at least avoid the designation of dirty which has been projected onto her. This creates a set of practices in which the working-class woman must constantly guard against the markers of dirt appearing on her body. She must know how to be sexy enough but not too much, to look good but not cheap, and so on. Judith Walkowitz, in *City of Dreadful Delight* (1992), argues that the woman in public was a crucial accompaniment to the male flâneur in Victorian London, adding that working-class women were seen as both endangered and as a source of danger, typified by the figure of the prostitute. Littlewood and Mahood state:

> Let anyone walk certain streets of London, Glasgow or Edinburgh, of a night, and without troubling his head with statistics, his eyes and ears will tell him at once what a multitudinous amazonian army the devil keeps in constant field service, for advancing his own ends. The very stones seem alive with lust, and the very atmosphere is tainted. (Littlewood and Mahood 1991: 160)

Yet Roberts (1995) tells us that childhood was short-lived for Victorian working-class women, according to oral testimonies. Girls learned a habit of obedience, seldom criticised their parents and submitted their wishes to family needs. Family members had to help each other to survive harsh and difficult conditions in which there was no pleasure in work and even a glimpse of sexual knowledge was a dangerous source of shame. Yet, of course, the very difficult conditions in which women lived did mean that they sometimes needed to engage in temporary prostitution. Constant danger and threat of poverty was set against a fierce attempt to stay both respectable and sexually ignorant. This is established against the allure of Otherness for upper-class men and the pathologisation and harassment of women who did work as prostitutes. No wonder then, as Walkowitz (1992) tells us, that working-class women were seen as both the threat and the source of danger.

While it is not possible in this chapter to trace the lines of descent of these kinds of designations from the nineteenth century to the present, and acknowledging that forms of regulation of sexuality have changed considerably, it is fair to argue that even today working-class women's sexuality is equally pathologised. For example, in terms of the overt public display of drunken sexuality, the danger of being a 'ladette', the need to walk a tightrope between dressing up and dressing down and of being too crass, flashy and overtly sexual (Ringrose and Walkerdine 2008; Walkerdine 2011; McRobbie 2009). Skeggs' (1997) classic work on respectability shows us how working-class women are afraid to enter an upmarket department store for fear of not appearing respectable enough. Layton (2006) demonstrates how American middle-class shoppers clearly differentiate between stores by class, whereby working-class shops are experienced by middle-class shoppers who grew up working class as 'painfully familiar' and by upper-class shoppers as simply alien: 'for both groups, entering the store might reactivate all they have split off to attain what they have, and both groups' emotional response suggest a fear of contagion with the lower classes' (Layton 2006: 41). For those born into the upper class, the affect is revulsion, while for those who grew up in a working-class environment, it is shame and humiliation. Layton argues that we can think of this in terms of a dynamic normative unconscious in which we have to suppress or split off those feelings, desires and attributes that are understood as not part of a proper way of being human. Following Bourdieu (1984), she argues that doxa is transmitted in conflictual relational experiences and held in place by emotions such as shame, anxiety and love.

It is my contention that working-class women have, since the inception of class as a category of regulation, lived their bodies as simultaneously oversexed, dirty and showy, with the trope of respectability, and later upward mobility, as a way of trying at least to look like a lady. While 'respectable' working-class women may strive to behave correctly, those who are already pathologised may act out the role that has been assigned and projected onto them. Nowhere is this more apparent than in Bernard Shaw's *Pygmalion* (or the film *My Fair Lady*, 1964), in which Eliza Dolittle is transformed from a woman in a public space (a flower seller) to a figure resembling royalty, while being taught to speak using received pronunciation. Professor Higgins' experiment with Eliza, of course, does not actually allow her to move entirely out of her class: having sworn at the races, she is subsequently saved by marrying Higgins, himself not an upper-class man. In other words, while moral danger and regulation are always on the cards, transformation carries with it the peril of simply 'passing' for middle or upper class, and the working-class woman constantly runs the risk of being found out. Thus, the working-class woman must still walk a tightrope which demands that she regulate herself, prove herself worthy of a family or a job, wear sexy but not cheap clothes, and sound like a lady not a 'ladette'. However, she can never actually escape her place at the intersection of these projections with her fantasies of somehow 'making it'.

As Layton (2006) says, the projections have to be internalised or introjected. The psychoanalyst Christopher Bollas (2003) argues that feelings and experiences from parents can be transmitted to children wordlessly in the form of projective identifications. Children can feel that something is an issue without understanding why, because it has been transmitted wordlessly by the previous generation. Thus, it seems plausible to argue that the experience of working-class women in relation to shame about their bodies and sexualities could be transmitted wordlessly down to future generations of women and men. Of course, this does not exclude overt regulation, nor practices of sexual and moral regulation, or of cultural and media transmission. However, intergenerational transmission allows us to think about how such affects become central to the ways in which working-class women experience themselves, as well as how they are experienced by middle-class Others.

What a potent mix then for television to exploit! If all women, regardless of their class, experience the shame – be they embodiments of it or those trying to avoid it, or indeed those who are terrified of being tainted by it – this creates a great deal of potential pleasure in viewing reality television. We may feel excited by the possibilities of transformation; we may feel that if we do not transform ourselves we will be discovered or cast out; or we may opt for a display which brazenly rejects this transformation. We might enjoy watching a working-class woman getting her comeuppance, or relish the fact that a middle-class home is after all dirty, or the children wild; and so, we are pleased to watch humiliation, as moral regulators ourselves (Walkerdine and Lucey 1989).

My aim here, then, is to further develop this line of argument by referring to a body of psychoanalytic work which considers the intergenerational transmission of historical trauma. While this work has been largely applied to war and genocide, I suggest that it is possible to apply it to the transmission of shame across generations of working-class women (and indeed middle-class women, though from a different position) which has been harnessed by reality television.

Affect, Shame and Makeover Television

A considerable amount of work on reality television has been generated by the 'turn to affect' (Clough and Halley 2007). In particular, several studies investigate the ways in which reality television works on emotion, affect and intimacy. One of the important emphases of this work is the suggestion that while television might be a site for self-regulation, it works not simply discursively, but by pulling the viewer in through emotional attachments. The long tradition of psychoanalytic study of the media also worked with notions of identification with programmes. However, feminist approaches which assumed that media texts produced subjects through their incorporation into the filmic or televisual fantasy scenario were countered by other feminist approaches to fantasy which argued for its active use by women (Geraghty 1991). In fact, these positions were not nearly as polarised as was often assumed. Nevertheless, there was an agreed assumption that 'meaning' was emitted from the media text. In the turn to affect, we can understand shame, for example, as being transmitted rather differently. For example, Misha Kavka (2008) surveys a number of approaches to the study of affect and argues that television watching produces shame (the eyes dropping and head bowing) because, unlike reading, it is considered a trashy escape. 'The promise of affective charge', she argues, 'is why we watch television in the first place.' She adds that:

> The shame associated with television thus arises from its peculiar positioning between affect and reality: too
> ironically aligned with reality to offer a 'proper' escape to the realm of subjectivity, interiority and
> imagination, television is nonetheless too affectively engaging to be informative of the real world. The shame
> of caring about what we see on TV emerges from this cusp. (Kavka 2008: 46)

In this view, shame is interrelational because it happens in anticipation of the response of others. While those participants on reality television may engage in 'unabashed exhibitionism', says Kavka, and one might imagine that they are shamed, it is the viewers who are the more deeply exposed because of their own shame in watching. The affective reality of the exposure is relayed back to them. This approach is interesting, but it assumes that shame is created simply by watching a low-status medium. This means that the issues of the historicity of shaming are eluded. Rather, I want to argue that reality television works affectively by mobilising that history of shaming already embodied by working-class women who are desired by middle- and upper-class men as transgressive and regulated by middle-class women since the inception of class. Affect does not simply work because it is projected at the viewer, but also because the female viewer already embodies the shame: it is transmitted down generations in which constantly shifting practices of censorship and regulation serve to shame and make abject the working-class female body, a body which must always be ready to be shamed and thus transformed by a process of gentrification or respectabilisation.

Ladette to Lady

In order to discuss this in more depth, I will refer to the British television series *Ladette to Lady*, which seems to spectacularly visualise and make entertainment and humour out of the processes I have been describing. *Ladette to Lady* is a British reality television series modelled on the *Pygmalion* narrative which was screened on ITV 1 over five successive series (2005–10). In each case, young working-class women who are known to engage in heavy drinking and exhibitionist sexuality are brought to a country house where they are drilled in the manner of a finishing school in order to make them into women who, like Eliza Dolittle, might pass as ladies in a county-set social occasion. (The last two series used young Australian women.)

The format of the series is to take 'rough' young women and train them in deportment, elocution, dress, manners and etiquette, as well as domestic skills such as flower arrangement, cookery and entertaining. They are exposed to various tests and each week one young woman leaves the programme. Their own clothes are exchanged for a rather frumpish uniform, with hair pulled into headbands and Queen Elizabeth II-type headscarves on outings to the country. The course is run not by a Professor Dolittle but by three upper-class women. Humiliation and shaming are a central part of the way that the programme works. As the director of the school says to one young woman, 'You're a little piece of scum.' Or, as she puts it to one of the upper-class guests at a post hunt social, 'You try to teach these girls manners – awful!'

The young women can often be spirited, recognising their exploitation as women, sexist double standards, the boorish behaviour of some men (who indeed seem to typify the desires presented by Walkowitz) and the need to be tough in a tough world, and they display exuberance if given a chance to experience exhilaration. But the task of teaching them to behave like ladies is as humiliating, cruel and remorseless as it ever was in *Pygmalion*. Moreover, one suspects that while these young women are indeed transformed by the end of the show, they are more likely to be employed as the service workers for the wealthy than marry an upper-class man.

In the latest version of the series featuring Australian working-class women, the upper-class men made lewd jokes and deliberately led the young women in games that required exhibitionism and drinking. As the women themselves said, how was being a lady getting away from that kind of behaviour? In addition, the young women were encouraged to be demure and docile, to show psychological vulnerability, despite references to the very hard lives and stories presented by the young women. Kavka's explanation that as viewers we are shamed by watching such young women, both by experiencing their shame and by being caught in the shameful act of watching it, fails to engage with the inherent shame carried by classed female bodies which resonates both with those who are and are not working class. Angela McRobbie (2009) reads working-class 'ladettes' being loud and 'getting their tits out' after drunken nights as giving in to patriarchy by having to attract men while at the same time having to behave like the lads. But such young women have long been read as over the top, oversexed and vulgar, outside the norms of respectable femininity. We might, in fact, read the difficulties associated with this positioning of white working-class women as a play on, and intensification of, the very oversexualisation of which they are routinely accused, and therefore against which they have had to constantly to defend themselves since the nineteenth century. This is not to say that such young women are not caught by the complexities of male desire or that they are in any sense free; after all, they are trapped at the bottom end of the job market. But I wonder if the acts express a longing to be 'larger than life', to be 'seen' in a space other than one that, as McRobbie (2009) shows us, is so often a very familiar cramped space of humiliating normalisation (Walkerdine 2011).

As viewers, we are caught inside the very issues facing such women – how to be seen and how to avoid shame and humiliation. It is precisely because experiences like these are embodied that the female body can experience these affects in relation to viewing this type of programme. In Deleuze's sense, such meanings are already immanent within the programmes and embodied shame is not simply a bowed head or a blushing face, but the result of a body condemned over generations for being dirty, a dirt conflated with sexuality. As Fox (1994) notes, this negates the sexuality of working-class women, so that all they can long for is a splitting, a respectability, a certain purity, a position long put forward by reformers. In *Ladette to Lady*, precisely similar reformist tactics are at work. Young women who have tried to engage with the fact that they are considered dirt by exhibiting and revelling in their dirtiness in order to keep shame at bay are enjoined by upper-class women to behave with decorum in the face of men's dirty fantasies. Thus, shame is not simply an aspect of watching television but is embodied in the historical practices which have positioned working-class women and their bodies as dirt.

What does it feel like to embody dirt? How might such women affectively experience their designation as dirt? My argument is that this way of experiencing and regulating the dirty body is not new but re-emerges when we long to be accepted, not to be shamed and rejected, or to feel, along with the 'ladettes', the desire to break free. If this phenomenon has existed since the inception of class-ification, it is also passed down generations from one body to another. To understand this, we must turn to those who have worked on intergenerational transmission. We need to see just how bodies not only keep experiencing shame, but how this shamefulness is passed around between women and men, and down generations, for whom practices and ways of embodying respectability come to be central.

Intergenerational Transmission

Françoise Davoine and Jean-Max Gaudillière (2004) are psychoanalysts working with historical trauma and psychosis. They were trained in a Lacanian tradition but have developed Lacan by historicising the central concepts of the Real, the Imaginary and the Symbolic. For them, the central concept in moving beyond structuralism and into history is the issue of trust. They argue that Lacan's ideas were formed at the moment of structuralism, which led him to stress transhistorical universals of language and kinship and to ignore history. Their own revision utilises his tripartite framework of Real, Imaginary and Symbolic, but renders them rather differently. They stress the primacy of oral language as the medium through which ordinary people communicate, which includes gestures, songs, sayings, etc. and how these are passed down generations. In particular, they understand the oral tradition as pagan and hence in opposition to the power of the Church to define language. Therefore, oral transmission interferes with written transmission and they note the creative power of oral stories. For them, the Real is that which cannot be symbolised and is therefore transmitted and expressed through the body, through affect. Like the annihilation anxieties discussed by other psychoanalytic traditions (Walkerdine 2010), it is that which cannot be represented because it has never *been* represented which is significant. It has instead been experienced through the body and certainly has meaning. This Real, then, is the historical experience which cannot be spoken but is nevertheless transmitted intergenerationally through bodily affective connections. It breaks the social link which binds one generation to another and unites communities. In addition, they argue that Lacan took for granted that the Symbolic Order was functioning and that trust equally was functioning. But in many difficult circumstances, trust crumbles and so we cannot take it for granted – we have to assume a break in the social link which has to be mended. For Davoine and Gaudillière, the social link is fundamentally about trust and is contained in discourse, because trust involves talking together: it is a relationship with an Other. Anxiety is produced by the absence of trust. If we historicise trust and anxiety in this way, we could see that what surfaces as anxiety about looks, bodies, sexuality, parenting, etc. relates to a historical absence of trust which existed within class stratification itself. This is visible in the ways in which working-class women have had to hold all the anxieties, revulsion, fear, disgust and desire about them that are circulated in the public sphere. Anxiety is related to the state of mind that corresponds to uncertainty, generating a traumatic memory.

The place of anxiety is where the social link has broken, where trust no longer exists and so has been excised or cut out from history. As I have already stated, children are researchers of the unusual, who recognise when something is not quite right, especially when adults try to hide it.

They sense things affectively but do not understand what they mean, except that mistrust and there-fore anxiety is communicated by this unknown thing which is not quite right. Lilian Rubin (1991) demonstrates this process in her study of working-class families in the USA.

The transmission of working-class shame in this approach can be understood as the creation of an affective bodily response, an anxiety created by the production of classed relations in which working-class women can neither trust nor be trusted. This anxiety is lived not as a repression but as a terrifying bodily experience in which the boundaries of the body are hard to contain because of very primitive anxieties. I think we might assume, given the work of Roberts (1995), that the obe-dience demanded of working-class girls within their families – the strict morality, the ignorance about sex, the submission to authority – was designed to keep them pure and safe and to survive in very terrifying circumstances. Of course, this is not to say that the moral regulation by fathers of their daughters was not draconian or bullying, but more that such families had to live in a context in which trust could only be maintained within the family and working-class community. Tight controls and regulation can form what Esther Bick (1968) calls a second skin, a form of protection against the pos-sibility of dissolving and annihilation (Walkerdine and Jimenez 2011). Tight regulation binds women, allowing them to feel safe if they stick to the rules, but it does nothing to give them back the trust which class divisions have taken away.

Davoine and Gaudillière argue that intergenerational transmission of historical trauma works by the impossibility of conveying to the next generation the experience which cannot be named or thought because it is too painful. The catastrophe happened before the 'subject of speech' existed (i.e. in the historical experience of the previous generation), but it is transmitted in numerous ways even though there is no gaze, no voice or no word. To illustrate their position, they recount the story of Gilda. During World War II, her father was the only survivor of his army unit which was massa-cred during the battle of El Alamein in 1942. By a quirk of fate he was absent that day, assigned to duties elsewhere. He had to tell the bereaved families how their sons died. Gilda tells the analysts that she 'often wondered if I was not one of them. My father considered me his little soldier. We were poor; he wanted me to be first in school, and I was' (Davoine and Gaudillière 2004: 31).

What Gilda experienced as the need to fight on, never to give up, to be top of her class, was somehow connected to her father's projection onto his daughter of the desire to protect all those soldiers whose lives had been so brutally cut short. Only his soldiering daughter could keep alive the memory which haunted him and which could never be allowed to die but had to be passed on to the next generation, even though Gilda at that time knew nothing of her father's history. What she experienced, therefore, was a demand to soldier on and to succeed that she did not understand. He does not communicate to her the horrors of what he felt, but rather makes demands on Gilda which in effect keep the soldiers alive (his little soldier) and translate into an attempt to avoid any possible failure by coming top of the class. Gilda knows bodily that all is not right, that something else is being communicated which she cannot name, and she becomes psychotic. Davoine and Gaudillière see this as Gilda carrying the historical secret for him. As we know only too well, such historical secrets are indeed passed on in many families, not only about war, but for our purposes here, in par-ticular, illegitimacy, prostitution, poverty and many kinds of class shame. It is through such wordlessly expressed historical traumas, I would suggest, that working-class women across generations continue to experience feelings about their appearance, bodies, sexualities, etc. which may defy their attempts to rationalise them.

The Matrixial

To develop this line of thinking further, I would like to refer to the Israeli analyst Bracha Ettinger (2006), who is particularly concerned with the role of the maternal in the intergenerational transmission of trauma and how the feminine body acts as a site through which classed historical experience moves between bodies. Developing the concept of the matrixial, Ettinger reminds us that 'matrix' comes from the Latin for womb, and so the matrixial space is a womb-like space, a feminine space in which something is gestated. She extends this concept of gestation into what she calls 'the matrixial borderspace': 'joint corporeal resistance, shared affective experiences, exchanges of phantasy that relate to non-Oedipal sexual difference and interconnectivity' (Ettinger 2006: 69).

Ettinger's view that woman is a subject and not simply a container is crucially important for how we think 'woman'. In so many approaches, 'woman' is understood as the universal container which makes separation possible. This is common to all object relations' approaches but is also common to most Western philosophy (Walkerdine 2006). Ettinger is at pains to show how the matrixial is an active position in which affective connections are made, rather than simply a place of containment. This adds an important dimension to our discussion. I have stressed the centrality of attempts to cope with and defend against annihilation anxiety in the transmission of shame across generations. Like Ettinger's concept of the matrixial, I have stressed these as active affective connections. This helps us to move away from a position in which femininity itself is seen as the universal way of containing anxiety and promoting separation and individuation. So, the matrixial is an active system of connections across subjects, modelled on the notion of the active feminine prenatal encounter in which connections are made not through words but fluids, feelings and physiological responses.

Just as the womb provided a permeable membrane linking the mother to the foetus, the matrixial borderspace is a space of affective connection between people, and particularly between women. In developing her work in relation to the transmission of trauma across generations, Ettinger tries to understand how memories and feelings are passed down generations who have experienced trauma (in her case the Shoa), resulting in an embodied connection for people who are several generations removed from the trauma but nevertheless still feel its effects. For Ettinger, the matrixial works as an inter- and intra-subjective transhistoric space of connection. Is this a way of explaining how many shared connections are made? She identifies a process of multidirectional change where things get transformed via the borderlinks and become thresholds through which elements known and unknown pass. These are associated with particular affects – awe, alertness, astonishment, compassion – and induce instances of the co-emergence of meaning. Multiple and plural matrixial subjectivity is also singular and partial. The matrixial awareness of the links with intimate strangers is the feminine dimension, but it is not simply the province of women because we have all experienced it; it exists as archaic traces. Ettinger's work therefore suggests that experiences can be shared affectively and that they can pass down generations (encrypted unsymbolised events belonging to someone else) through a process which could be described as an affective history.

Returning to Reality Television

What I have attempted to provide in this chapter is a way of understanding what might make reality television programmes which focus on class shame compelling viewing for women. In doing this, I have moved away from a simple reading of the television text (though this is, of course, central) to an attempt to understand how the embodied experience of viewing might work through shame. Furthermore, I have argued that this shame might have been intergenerationally transmitted as silent and encrypted embodied messages which transmit not only ways of doing things, but unspoken and spoken anxieties about women's bodies and sexuality. These are experienced as a desperate need to behave, and look at and regulate the body, in a certain way; to attempt to evade the wordless anxiety that accompanies transgression, an anxiety ultimately about annihilation, passed silently from mother and father to daughter and son over a long period of historical time. While shame and anxiety are transmitted bodily, their emergence is social and historical and relates to the regulation of working-class female sexuality in the Victorian period.

In this chapter, I have proposed an understanding of the intergenerationally transmitted affective experience of shame as generated historically, and experienced and embodied personally, which ultimately resists any attempt to wish it away by simply defining it as ideological.

Bibliography

Bick, E. (1968) 'The Experience of the Skin in Early Object-Relations', *International Journal of Psycho-Analysis*, 49: 484–6.

Bollas, C. (2003) *Being a Character* (London: Brunner-Routledge).

Bourdieu, P. (1984) *Distinction: A Social Critique of the Judgement of Taste*, translated by R. Nice (Cambridge, MA: Harvard University Press).

Clough, P. and J. Halley (eds) (2007) *The Affective Turn: Theorizing the Social* (Durham, NC: Duke University Press).

Davoine, F. and J. M. Gaudillière (2004) *History beyond Trauma* (New York: Other Press).

Ettinger, B. (2006) *The Matrixial Borderspace* (Minneapolis: University of Minnesota Press).

Foucault, M. (1998) *The History of Sexuality Vol. 1: The Will to Knowledge* (London: Penguin).

Fox, P. (1994) *Class Fictions: Shame and Resistance in the British Working-Class Novel, 1890–1945* (Durham, NC: Duke University Press).

Geraghty, C. (1991) *Women and Soap Opera* (Oxford: Blackwell).

Kavka, M. (2008) *Reality Television, Affect and Intimacy: Reality Matters* (Basingstoke, Hants.: Palgrave Macmillan).

Kristeva, J. (1982) *Powers of Horror: An Essay in Abjection* (New York: Columbia University Press).

Layton, L. (2006) 'That Place Gives Me the Heebie-Jeebies', in L. Layton, Nancy Caro Hollander and Susan Gutwill (eds), *Psychoanalysis, Class and Politics: Encounters in the Clinical Setting* (Hove, E. Sussex: Routledge), pp. 51–65.

Littlewood, B. and L. Mahood (1991) 'Prostitutes, Magdalenes and Wayward Girls: Dangerous Sexualities of Working Class Women in Victorian Scotland', *Gender and History*, 3(2): 160–75.

McRobbie, A. (2004) 'Notes on *What Not to Wear* and Post-Feminist Symbolic Violence', *Sociological Review*, 52(2): 97–109.

———— (2009) *The Aftermath of Feminism: Gender, Culture and Social Change* (London: Sage).

Moseley, R. (2000) 'Makover Takeover on British Television', *Screen*, 41(3): 299–314.

Ouellette, L. and J. Hay (2008) *Better Living through Reality TV* (Oxford: Blackwell).

Palmer, G. (2003) *Discipline and Liberty: Television and Governance* (Manchester: Manchester University Press).

Ringrose, J. and V. Walkerdine (2008) 'Regulating the Abject: The TV Make-over as Site of Neo-Liberal Reinvention toward Bourgeois Femininity', *Feminist Media Studies*, 8(3): 227–46.

Roberts, E. (1995) *Women's Work, 1840–1940* (Cambridge: Cambridge University Press).

Rose, N. (1990) *Governing the Soul: The Shaping of the Private Self* (London: Routledge).

Rubin, L. (1991) *Worlds of Pain* (New York: Basic Books).

Skeggs, B. (1997) *Formations of Class and Gender: Becoming Respectable* (London: Routledge).

———— (2005) 'The Making of Class and Gender through Visualizing Moral Subject Formation', *Sociology*, 39(5): 965–82.

Skeggs, B. and H. Wood (2008) 'The Labour of Transformation and Circuits of Value "around" Reality Television', *Continuum: Journal of Media and Cultural Studies*, 22(4): 559–72.

Tyler, I. (2008) '"Chav Mum, Chav Scum": Class Disgust in Contemporary Britain', *Feminist Media Studies*, 8(1): 17–34.

Walkerdine, V. (2006) *Minding the Gap: Thinking Subjectivity beyond a Psychic/Discursive Division*, public lecture, ESRC Identities and Social Action Programme and Centre for Psycho-Social Studies, University of the West of England, Bristol.

———— (2010) 'Communal Beingness and Affect: An Exploration of Trauma in an Ex-Industrial Community', *Body & Society*, March, 16(1): 91–116.

———— (2011) 'Review of A. McRobbie: *The Aftermath of Feminism: Gender, Culture and Social Change*', *Sociology*, 45: 700–6.

Walkerdine, V. and P. Bansel (2009) 'Neo-Liberalism, Work and Subjectivity: Towards a More Complex Account', in M. Wetherell and C. Mohanty (eds), *Identities Handbook* (London: Sage), pp. 492–508.

Walkerdine, V. and L. Jimenez (2011) *Gender, Work and Community after De-industrialisation: A Psychosocial Approach to Affect* (Basingstoke, Hants.: Palgrave Macmillan).

Walkerdine, V. and H. Lucey (1989) *Democracy in the Kitchen* (London: Virago).

Walkowitz, J. (1992) *City of Dreadful Delight: Narratives of Sexual Danger in Late-Victorian London* (Chicago: University of Chicago Press).

Wood, H. and B. Skeggs (2004) 'Notes on Ethical Scenarios of Self on British "Reality" TV', *Feminist Media Studies*, 4(1): 205–8.

17/Lisa Blackman

'This is a matter of pride': *The Choir: Unsung Town* and Community Transformation

Introduction

This chapter will take the British reality television three-part series *The Choir: Unsung Town* as its starting point to think through the role of affect for understanding engagement with televisual products. The pioneering practices of the choirmaster-turned-transformational coach, Gareth Malone, made the area of South Oxey in Hertfordshire his target. Known for its high unemployment and relative deprivation, it sits adjacent to areas in the county associated with wealth and privilege. The distinction between working-class South Oxey and its middle-class neighbours is established at the beginning of the series, where South Oxey becomes redolent of the lack of opportunity, hope and pride that characterise the youth of that area. Malone's challenge is to get the young and old singing, and this practice is presented by the participants, Malone and the series as an important element in processes of community regeneration and transformation. I will argue in this chapter that the practice of singing, and particularly the practices of community choir singing, introduces elements to our understandings of transformation that extend beyond the usual psychotherapeutic logic that has become characteristic of the reality television format. This extension requires an engagement with concepts and theories that have been obscured by the focus on the textual and discursive elements of reality television, which tend to overlook the complex relationships engendered between bodies and affect.

This focus on the more affective basis of the logic of transformation, as it is enacted in this particular series, will foreground work that has been more marginal in our understandings of the psychosocial significance of reality television. This includes work on muscular bonding, the community ego, affective contagion, the somatically felt body and attention to more rhythmic forms of communication (see Blackman 2008a). All of these concepts and ideas point towards aspects of reality television that occur within a register of feeling, affect and emotion and which connect reality television to working-class rituals such as collective singing in the pub and at working men's clubs. These rituals arguably enhance and expand participants' sense of well-being and connection and are felt in and through the body, connecting this series to other popular formats such as *X Factor* (2004–) and *Strictly Come Dancing* (2004–) that similarly focus on practices such as singing and dancing in order to effect change and transformation.

The focus on the body and its potential for mediation will bring work on reality television to bear on other technologies of the social which work primarily through a suggestive ontology and take us back to theories prominent during the nineteenth century (Tarde 1969; James and Sidis quoted in Blackman 2010). These theories of 'affective transfer' became increasingly marginalised with the rise of the psychological sciences and the authorisation of a foundational ontology which understood the human subject primarily as a rational, unified, autonomous and self-contained subject. The chapter's re-engagement with this work will discuss ways in which the concept of mediation can be extended to capture the remaking of working-class pride that becomes lived as the 'buzz' and achievement of the show, which is difficult to describe, but profoundly witnessed by the participants and viewers alike.

Televisual Affect

There is a growing body of literature within television studies which is beginning to consider the role of televisual affect within our consumption of media forms and practices (Skeggs, Thumim and Wood 2008; Wood and Skeggs 2004; Kavka 2008; Gorton 2009). This work recognises the importance of the registers of emotion, feeling and affect within televisual engagement and problematises the binary that has framed audience reception studies between those audiences considered passive and those seen as active. Historically, this binary has been class-based, with the supposed mindless (working-class) masses considered overly suggestible to media influence, and the ideal middle-class media consumer represented as able to resist and engage critically with what is presented to them on the screen or over the airwaves (see Blackman and Walkerdine 2001). Kristyn Gorton's (2009) re-evaluation of this historically sedimented binary argues that the audience(s) must be considered both active *and* passive, and that a focus on emotion discloses the criticality of audiences while at the same time acknowledging their emotional involvement. Taking this further, Skeggs, Thumim and Wood (2008) argue that the very methodological practices used in audience research presume certain forms of cultural capital and competence that might not be so easily available to working-class participants. The recovery of emotion as an important yet neglected, or even denigrated, aspect of media consumption also works to revalue media forms and practices which have been associated with working-class tastes and habits, such as reality TV, and importantly invite a consideration of how we frame our research objects and subjects through our conceptual and methodological choices.

Rather than being considered shallow, superficial entertainment, reality TV has been positioned by many media academics as an example of neo-liberal forms of social governance. As a technology of citizenship, reality TV is seen to circulate idealised norms of citizenship through which participants are judged, positioned and invited to act upon themselves and others in order to effect change and transformation (Hay 2000; Ouellette 2009; Couldry 2009; see the chapters by Couldry and Palmer in this volume). These processes involve marking out what Ouellette (ibid.: 239) terms 'risky deviants' and 'self-made victims', which, as many authors have argued, require making class-based distinctions couched in a combination of morality discourses and therapeutic language and concepts (McRobbie 2005; Biressi and Nunn 2005; Jensen 2010). Differences to middle-class consumer, citizen and lifestyle

norms are understood to be enacted through forms of symbolic violence, which involve the denigration of working-class tastes and habitus and their replacement with those consistent with the
'choice-making neo-liberal' (Couldry 2009; Ouellette 2009: 233). Reality television formats operate
much like electronic versions of the self-help instruction manual, offering a rationalistic discourse of
self-transformation and reinvention consistent with those found across other media cultures which
operate through a psychotherapeutic logic (see Blackman 2004; Blackman and Walkerdine 2001;
Rose 1999). However, what has been given less attention in this work is the circulation, cultivation
and focus on affectivity within reality TV and how we might understand this (also see Skeggs, Thumim
and Wood 2008). In an interesting shift linking affect and suggestion, Gorton (2009) refigures suggestion as not simply evidence of working-class susceptibility or vulnerability to media influence, but
rather as a technology of the social that works through encouraging intensity, intimacy, connection
and belonging. This chapter is specifically interested in this aspect of reality TV.

Kavka (2008) similarly repositions reality TV as a form of mediated intimacy, which, although technologically mediated, is achieved through the denial or ignoring of the process of mediation itself.
This is interesting, because it ties work on reality television to work on remediation (Bolter and
Grusin 2000), and also repositions television as a medium of tele-presence: that is, a medium that
brings things close (Sconce 2000; Andriopolous 2005). This 'liveness effect' (Kavka 2008: 17) is attributed to television's capacity to collapse space and time, and to produce the sense of an imagined
community of belonging; the sense that one is there in a shared yet mediated space. These are the
very attributes, of course, that are heightened within reality television. Rather than primarily being
involved in the production of meaning, reality television is seen to produce *resonances*. The question
then becomes how to understand the significance and production of televisual resonance(s)?
Kavka turns to contemporary work on affect to address this, offering what she terms a theory of
affectivity or mattering, drawing from psychoanalysis, the seminal work of Brian Massumi (2002), as
well as the work of Silvan Tomkins (Sedgwick and Frank 1995) on 'affect contagion'.

Although affect is often posited as a kind of formless or amorphous process felt through intensities and captured through emotion (Massumi 2002; Blackman and Venn 2010), Kavka combines this
processual account of affect with a more psychoanalytic approach that explores how affects can be
channelled or materialised such that television becomes a social conduit for the circulation, transmission and embodiment of affective intensities. The television screen is viewed as a technology of
mediation that is generative of affect, providing an interface for affect to take form. Kavka suggests
that affect has 'object-potential, as opposed to (being) object-less or independent of the social world'
(Kavka 2008: 30). In other words, affect requires mediation in order to be felt. Thus, affective intensities or resonances can be produced without their necessarily being an ideological/discursive chan-
nelling or structuring of meaning capturing such intensities. It represents what Kavka terms a 'different
way of knowing' that is felt but perhaps difficult to articulate.

Kavka's focus on positioning reality TV within a public sphere governed less by rationalistic discourse and more by 'affective transmissions' shifts the focus away from normalising discourses and
more towards the situational. As Kavka (2008: 92) argues, 'we identify, and identify with, the situation
through its affective resonance: this is what it feels like to be someone sitting around a kitchen table

negotiating a fellow inmate's upset/anger/sense of exclusion'. It is the performance or enactment of the various dilemmas, contradictions and difficulties of negotiating our relational subjectivities that generate the feelings that are transmitted across the screen and which we as viewers experience as resonances. It is what we might call the ecology, setting or milieu that is generative of affect.

Although Kavka is not explicit about the ontology of relationality that is crucial to her analysis, one might argue, following many philosophers and theorists who have developed relational ontologies of subjectivity, that it is not simply that we are governed in relation to the fiction of autonomous selfhood, but rather that we live, differentially, a specific epistemology of neo-liberal personhood (also see Blackman 2004). This epistemology is characterised by the strange paradox that rather than being or becoming a self-contained, self-regulating subject, we continually negotiate being 'one yet many' (see Blackman 2008b). Although we may have come to inhabit bodies as if we are self-enclosed, separate, autonomous units – what Teresa Brennan (2004) has termed affective self-containment and Cohen (2009) calls 'biopolitical individualization' – this does not capture the thoroughly singular-plural beings that we are (Nancy 2000). This work directs us towards co-extensivity: the milieus or settings within which subjectivities are co-enacted, co-constituted and co-produced. Vikki Bell (2007) develops some of these relational ways of thinking about subjectivity in order to theorise culture and performance. I want to turn to this work briefly, as it sets out some of the issues that I am interested in exploring in relation to reality TV, and specifically the relation between class and affectivity within *The Choir*.

Culture and Performance

Bell (2007) critiques Foucauldian genealogical work, with its focus on historical discontinuities, arguing that it obscures the forms of felt, carnal connections which are transmitted across generations. She suggests that studies of the performative have tended to focus on the circulation, regulation and reproduction of norms, rather than on the embodied relations and dispositions which are transmitted across generations but which might be governed more by silence or strategic amnesia (also see Cho 2008; Walkerdine 2010 and Walkerdine in this volume). As many scholars of class have shown, one of the most salient embodied dispositions which have marked working-class subjects is shame (Skeggs 1997, 2004; Walkerdine 1990). The complex ways in which shame is produced, transmitted and circulated across generations opens up the question of what Bell terms 'performative routedness' (Bell 2007: 32). Turning to critical race studies and Gilroy's (1993) illuminating work on diaspora, she re-establishes the importance in this context of exploring how this background of felt dispositions is commemorated and routed. In this sense, forms of subjectivity are produced and enacted through an engagement with those embodied relations which might be felt, but which are difficult to articulate or are articulated or passed between people through silence or condensed words like 'crap'. As Charlesworth argues: 'The silences and ellipses in people's speech are their implicit, unknowing recognition of the background; those moments when the unsaid, unspoken, passes between people, manifesting in knowing silences and appropriate gestures' (Charlesworth 2000: 113).

Bell describes these as 'those relations that are neither simply of identification nor of alterity, that is, those of genealogical connection' (Bell 2007: 33). In other words, these forms or practices appeal in some sense to people's felt embodied dispositions which disclose their 'generational, carnal connection' (ibid.: 37). Bell only gives one brief example of how such a frame would enable the analysis of forms of cultural performance or communication which respond, often in non-linguistic ways, to the generational ties and connections formed around trauma or shame. It is within this context that I want to reposition certain reality television genres as enacting the conditions within which such performative routedness might take place. This extends Kavka's (2008) focus on the 'situational' to consider the important place of intergenerational carnal connection within genres of reality TV which focus on self and community transformation.

Bell draws upon Hamera's (2005) discussion of the 'performance of amnesia', which focuses on how embodied forms of performance (in this case Cambodian dance) allow bodies to 'speak what they can't' (Pollack 2005: 76). This is about the communication and transmission of intergenerational forms of trauma that appear to be 'unrepresentable' (if we remain at the level of signification), and that are usually contained through a logic of silence. The family that Hamera attempts to interview have been displaced through forced migration to LA following the genocides carried out by the Khmer Rouge in the 1960s in Cambodia. What characterised the Sems family was their unwillingness or inability to articulate the trauma surrounding these events, which Hamera links to their survival and sanity.

What is interesting about the significance of the practice of dance in the Sems' family life was that the Khmer movements performed by the parents allowed them to embody the traumas and communicate with those who did not survive, and therefore to afford the possibility of intergenerational communication and transmission. The Sems described how the voices they heard while dancing communicated the traditional Khmer dance movements to them. In this context, the dance was a relational practice that afforded a 'with-ness'; and that allowed connections of lineage and continuity to be forged and embodied. Thus, the dance was not the expression of an individual psyche-in-trauma, but rather a form of affective symbiosis which allowed a reaching-toward the unrepresentable and unknowable. This reaching-toward was not characterised by a singular body reaching out to another singular body through a discrete sensory motor-system. Rather, the dancing bodies were always in excess of themselves and importantly communicated with 'others' through the embodied experience of voice-hearing (see Blackman 2001). I think this work is instructive for considering some of the processes of transformation that appeared to be experienced by the participants in *The Choir*, and potentially witnessed by viewers. I will explore this in the next section in the context of what has come to be known as the 'makeover'.

Makeover TV

Meredith Jones has defined 'makeover culture' as a logic circulating across a variety of media, cultural and technological forms and practices that valorise and reward 'processes of working on the self' (Jones 2008: 11). Ultimately, it is the capacity of the self to undergo transformation, albeit with the help of others (human and non-human), and the experience of such transformation as somehow revealing a true or authentic self that is a key characteristic of such genres. Thus, the logic of makeover culture, according to Jones (ibid.) and others such as Cressida Heyes (2007), is precisely the contradiction between the body-as-labour; the idea that bodies are processes that are characterised by change, mutation and permeability; and how such processual views are limited by the assumption that what these processes reveal is a self that was already there waiting to be disclosed or revealed. This account of makeover cultures, which reality television has been aligned to, has been extended in other makeover genres to consider community or group transformation. The ethic of self-improvement that governs such shows is more relational; relations that do not rely on competition or competitiveness. Rather than focusing upon 'individual body-projects', the shows create groups who are taken to be connected in some way. What becomes important to such shows is creating the conditions within which individuals will come to see themselves as group members, as existing in relation to some greater whole or entity. See, for example, NBC's *School Pride* (2010), where groups of local volunteers repair and mend their inner-city schools in a bid to help the community.[1] Through the creation of a group entity, certain forms of transformation are afforded and in some cases this might be aligned to community regeneration or transformation.

The Choir: Unsung Town aired on British television in 2009 on BBC 2 and followed a 'makeover logic'. It combined elements of the usual makeover format (see Jones 2008) with a focus on what we might term the more *affective* basis of practices of community regeneration and transformation. The goal of the show was to get members of a working-class community in South Oxey to sing together as a choir, where the atomisation of the members of the community and their failure to take pride in their surroundings was presented as a key hurdle to community regeneration. Choir singing was offered as a practice and technique that would allow the development of self-determination, courage, fortitude and citizenship which would enable new community relations to be forged. Primarily, this involved the remaking of working-class shame into pride. Thus, regeneration for the area was presented in the show as one that was chiefly bound up with how the community members felt about themselves and their surroundings, particularly as a community who felt Othered in relation to the adjacent very middle-class areas of Hertfordshire characterised by privilege, wealth and opportunity.

The processes of remaking community presented in the show were not focused upon improving relative wealth or material privileges, but rather creating a sense of belonging, togetherness, loyalty and bonding, which primarily occurred through the registers of affect, emotion and feeling. South Oxey is a good example of a 'new estate': that is, an area characterised by new housing estates built by the council following World War II (Clapson 1999). It also features on the website Chavtown, billed as one of the worst places in Britain to live, where the social figure of the Chav is used on the site to denigrate the area and enact reactions of disgust towards the working classes (see Tyler 2008). Set within this context, *The Choir* provides the conditions for what might appear, if we remain at the level of representation, further acts of symbolic violence, performed within the setting of the show by the very middle-class, white, young choirmaster, Malone.

Indeed, the dynamics that characterise the relationship between Malone, as the middle-class out-sider, and the working-class participants on the show provide some of the dramatic tensions that are played out during the series. The choir rehearsals are beset by many of the participants' refusal to accept Malone's challenge to 'get the town singing'. The most marked example of this was non-attendance of the rehearsals, which prompted Malone to visit some of the participants in their homes in order to persuade them of the value of joining in. The movement between South Oxey as an area of relative deprivation, the rehearsal room, which was located in a local school, and the homes of some of the participants is reminiscent of the observational documentary techniques used in 'fly-on-the-wall' accounts of working-class lives (see Hill 2005). What is interesting about Malone, as the choirmaster-turned-transformational coach, within this context are the terms used to describe him by the participants. His ability to induce commitment from the young and old to the practice of choir singing was generated through his charisma, rather than his class privilege.

The concept of charisma to describe personality is interesting, because it conjures up a kind of incorporeal aura which allows affect and feeling to transmit between subjects but not in any direct or obvious way (see Susman 1979). Indeed, we might relate the concept of charisma to Mike Featherstone's (2010) concept of the 'body-without-image' which he develops to understand the relationship between body and affect. 'Body-without-an-image' refers to the more non-visual, felt sense we have of both our own and others' bodies, and primarily concerns the movement of affect between bodies that is felt but difficult to articulate. The analysis of Malone as somebody who is able to induce affective commitment is beyond the scope of this chapter, but it does point towards a repositioning of Malone as not simply a middle-class cultural intermediary, but rather as a figure who appeals on the very non-representational levels that arguably the show enacts.[2] Indeed, his success in getting the town to sing together culminated with the choir, made up of 256 people, singing at the Royal Albert Hall in London, and organising and singing at a choral festival staged for 6,000 mem-bers of the local community.

Community Transformation

In this section, I focus on the final episode of the show, which documented some of the community reactions to taking part in the programme. Within the conventions of reality TV formats, this is con-stituted as the 'reveal' of the show, which often within makeover television follows a before/after logic (Moseley 2000) that focuses on the participants' experience of taking part in the practices and processes of transformation. In the case of *The Choir*, this took place after the festival performance, when participants, both young and old, were asked how it had felt to take part in the transformation. Following the staging of the choral event, members of the choir and of the local community who had come to the concert were interviewed to gauge their reactions. These reactions were interspersed with footage of Gareth Malone being hugged and embraced by choir members, and close-ups of the emotional expressions of participants as they voiced what being part of the choir had meant to them. In the case of some participants, their backstories had become part of the wider narrative: this included a young man with a history of long-term unemployment, and an older man, recently bereaved. What marked their responses was a sense of renewed hope, connection, expansion and above all pride, and that their changed feelings corresponded to the remaking of South Oxey and primarily the remaking of the estate that they felt had been made possible by the experience.

Particularly salient was the sense of achievement participants felt about taking part in the show, and the inchoate terms they used to describe their experiences and feeling of being part of a community-in-the-making. The experience was repeatedly described as expansive but the felt dimensions of this expansiveness were difficult to capture and articulate. As with the title of the show, the participants described the singing as expressing elements of connection and belonging that deeply resonated with them, although they couldn't necessarily capture what it was about 'singing the town' which had produced such feelings. The 'buzz' of the experience expressed by many discloses the atmosphere that the communal singing experience had produced. This included statements such as: 'You don't know what you've done for me'; 'feeling part of the family'; 'the best experience of my life' and 'it filled a massive void in my life'. One elderly resident said that it was something she would never have dreamed about in South Oxey. She movingly relayed to the camera how 'all you ever heard was the bad about South Oxey. Now they can say the good about South Oxey, can't they?' In the words of another resident, the programme put 'us on the map at last'.

The remaking of the psychic geography of the area is in sharp contrast to its association with the working-class disgust directed at the area through the website Chavtown. The remaking of place was particularly about the enactment of tight bonds between members of the community, most of whom did not know each other, and had little to do with one another prior to the programme. As one choir member said, 'I feel really part of it, part of the community; the community has totally come together. I feel – it's just amazing. I've never experienced this here before.' So, we can clearly see that rather than some imagined community coming together, the affective basis of the practice of community choir singing created the possibility of the mobilisation, connection and distribution of relations of entanglement among people and place that produced particular situated responses to felt senses of shame. This was primarily expressed through the feelings of happiness and pride that were echoed by the wider population of South Oxey who came to the staging of the choral event. As one young woman expressed, 'Just seeing people together here, it's just really nice. It makes you feel quite proud to come from South Oxey actually, which not many people would say.'

What I want to do in the rest of this chapter is first to introduce some elements that might help us understand the felt dimensions of this experience of community transformation. I will then draw out the methodological implications of this for researching reality television. As well as offering what might be recognised as a typical 'makeover' format, I will argue that The Choir also affords the possibility for the enactment of forms of performative routedness. The remaking or transformation of shame into pride, which is characteristic of the transformational logic performed on the show, is primarily enabled through embodied practices such as singing. Singing has a long history within the British working-class trade union movement, where music has been used as an organising tool for developing a sense of belonging and community among members (Hill 2004). As we have seen, the show chiefly foregrounds the affective basis of community development enabling new relations of entanglement to be forged among people, places, entities and objects. It primarily allows the remaking of communal connections in new housing areas and estates which obscure the felt, carnal relations that might have bound working-class communities together in the past.

The importance of 'holding together' for communities with long histories of deprivation, neglect and poverty cannot be underestimated and has been identified as an important component of regeneration practices in areas formally defined by industrial modes of working. Walkerdine (2010) focuses upon the practices which allow an ex-industrial community in South Wales to retain a sense of togetherness in the face of the decimation of the industrial modes of working that historically brought the community together as a particular kind of collective entity. She describes this as the practice and development of a 'community ego'. What becomes important is the psychic geography of a place and how this can be forged and enacted through embodied practices and relations. The argument I am making, of course, might be critiqued by positing the show as a nostalgic search for an authentic sense of community that simply does not exist any more (see Biressi and Nunn 2005), or in the terms laid out by the neo-liberal thesis that reality television is problematically rein- forcing the repeal of state support. However, I am more interested in thinking about the role reality televison might play in engaging with memories which are shared, plural, co-constituted and which might be felt rather than easily articulated. The importance of memory as *felt* and as 'non-inscribed' directs our attention to where these memories might be found, and how the past might be brought into the present, demonstrating, perhaps, the capacity of the reality television format to animate place in ways that take us beyond the usual psychotherapeutic logic.

This particular approach to the problem of memory within mediated environments such as real- ity television is aligned to work on memory-as-ghosting or haunting (Abraham and Torok 1994; Cho 2008). These are memories that are trans-generational and which are transmitted by mediums and practices other than the speaking subject: this might include film, television, photographs, fiction and less inscribed, more embodied practices of remembering. Connerton (1989) suggests that non- inscribed practices of memory transmission have a rhythmic quality to them. Unlike inscribed mem- ories, which become organised and discursively produced and legitimated through particular codes and nosographic categories, non-inscribed memories are performed and ritualised through specific rhythms of everyday life.

Similarly useful for this kind of conceptual framing, the idea of suggestion that had been mobilised in early sociology and social psychology was one that understood communication through a con- cept of the affective or what we might term a feeling body. In early mass psychology, for example, a very particular kind of *feeling* body was viewed as an integral part of the way in which imitative processes were seen to reproduce themselves between actors within a field of complex social processes. Appeals to reason and rationality, didactic command and instruction, and staged forms of persuasion would miss the mark, and even make followers more resistant to change and transfor- mation. What were needed were appeals to the heart, to feeling, to passion, to the imagination: to a realm of affect which was co-present with the psychic and emotional rather than the intellect and reasoning (Moscovici 1985).

We might extend this in the context of researching class and reality television by considering contemporary work in body studies, which is developing a number of key concepts in order to approach the affective body, and studies on mediated memory that originate within analyses of technologically mediated environments (see Blackman and Harbord 2010). One of the overwhelming statements made in relation to *The Choir* was that 'they loved singing, they absolutely loved singing'. This directs our attention away from textual analyses of televisual affect and more towards reality television as technologically mediated environments, for both participants and viewers alike, which disclose the body's potential for mediation (see Skeggs, Thumim and Wood 2008). As with the work of Skeggs, Thumim and Wood (ibid.), this might involve exploring the relationship between technologically mediated events, such as the close-up shot, and non-verbal gestures created within the televisual encounter.

Work in body studies has identified the importance of approaching bodies as 'somatically felt', drawing attention to the importance of techniques and practices which work to expand and augment the body's potential for connection and extension. This includes work on marching and muscular bonding (McNeill 1995), synaesthesia (Freund 2009), movement (Sheets-Johnstone 1999) and the 'tactile-kinesthetic' body which is under-researched within media studies more generally (also see Blackman 2008a; Tambornino 2002). The challenge is to develop methods which can engage with the processes that underpin mediation, which importantly include the experiences of participants, as well as those viewers who gain pleasure from their own viewing.

Conclusion

There has been a renewed interest in the ideas of 'government by suggestion' that we find in mass psychology and that have also been revitalised through the contemporary interest in the work of the French sociologist and philosopher Gabriel Tarde (see Gibbs 2008; Blackman 2007). As Gibbs argues, if crowds were once considered sites of affect contagion, then how might we think about technologies of mediation, such as television, within the present? One of the arguments made by Tarde (1969) was that with the rise of communication technologies such as radio and the printing press, for example, people no longer needed physical proximity in order for affect contagion to take place. In that sense, work on televisual affect takes us back to these arguments and, as we have seen, to reconsider the role of television as a technology of suggestion. One of the problems, I would argue, with some of the engagements on televisual affect within studies of reality television is the reliance on the work of Silvan Tomkins (Sedgwick and Frank 1995). In her fascinating genealogy of shame and guilt, Ruth Leys explores the influence of Tomkins in the many reconsiderations of shame that have taken place within queer, feminist and cultural theory. As Leys argues, Tomkins' work represents an anti-intentionalist approach to affect, where affects are produced as 'automatic, reflex-like corporeal' responses (Leys 2007: 125). Affect contagion is reduced to 'the biological' despite the many critiques of this work that she painstakingly outlines. The approach to 'contagion' or affective transfer that I have started to develop in this chapter retains an important focus on the intergenerational transmission of shame (as also developed by Walkerdine in this collection), which importantly cannot be reduced to the biological, although it is embodied in complex ways.

It is not simply that reality television allows the discharge of affects, but rather that the performative dimensions of reality television potentially allow an engagement with embodied relations and dispositions that are difficult to articulate but that are felt nonetheless. These relations, however, need some kind of performative routedness to take form; they are socially and historically located and generated, and this is perhaps one of the most interesting aspects of reality television that deserves further attention. This will entail more of an engagement with embodiment and corporeality, and particularly in how we might rethink memory, habit, affect and suggestion as thoroughly relational, intergenerational and mediated processes of self- and social (trans)formation that cannot be reduced to a neo-liberal psychotherapeutic logic.

Notes

1. <http://www.nytimes.com/2010/10/17/arts/television/17school.html> accessed 11 February 2011.

2. Malone's unlikely star quality is commented upon by Tim Dowling in a *Guardian* feature on *The Choir: The Unsung Town*: 'The real star, of course, is Malone, who remains one of the most strangely beguiling presences television has ever uncovered: impish but laconic, funny and yet still resolute, reserved but shameless, camp but dignified – and clearly a bloody good choirmaster. The choir loves him, kids love him, old women love him, young women love him, Matty loves him, and I am going to be him for Halloween.' (*Guardian*, Wednesday, 2 September 2009).

Bibliography

Abraham, M. and M. Torok (1994) *The Shell and the Kernel: Renewals of Psychoanalysis* (Chicago: University of Chicago Press).

Andriopolous, S. (2005) 'Psychic Television', *Critical Inquiry*, 31(3): 618–38.

Bell, V. (2007) *Culture and Performance: The Challenge of Ethics, Politics and Feminist Theory* (Oxford/New York: Berg).

Biressi, A. and H. Nunn (2005) *Reality TV: Realism and Revelation* (London/New York: Wallflower Press).

Blackman, L. (2001) *Hearing Voices: Embodiment and Experience* (London/New York: Free Association Books).

——— (2004) 'Self-Help, Media Cultures and the Production of Female Psychopathology', *European Journal of Cultural Studies*, 7(2): 219–36.

——— (2007) 'Reinventing Psychological Matters: The Importance of the Suggestive Realm of Tarde's Ontology', *Economy and Society*, 36(4): 574–96.

——— (2008a) *The Body: The Key Concepts* (Oxford/New York: Berg).

——— (2008b) 'Affect, Relationality and the Problem of Personality', *Theory, Culture and Society*, 25(1): 27–51.

——— (2010) 'Embodying Affect: Voice-Hearing, Telepathy, Suggestion and Modelling the Non-Conscious', *Body & Society*, Special Issue on Affect, 16(1): 163–92.

Blackman, L. and J. Harbord (2010) 'Technologies of Mediation and the Affective: A Case Study of the Mediated Environment of Mediacityuk', in D. Hauptmann and W. Niedich (eds), *Cognitive Architecture: From Bio-Politics to Noo-Politics. Architecture and Mind in the Age of Information and Communication* (Amsterdam: 010), pp. 302–23.

Blackman, L. and C. Venn (2010) 'Affect', *Body & Society*, Special Issue on Affect, 16(1): 1–6.

Blackman, L. and V. Walkerdine (2001) *Mass Hysteria: Critical Psychology and Media Studies* (Basingstoke, Hants./New York: Palgrave).

Bolter, J. D. and R. Grusin (2000) *Remediation: Understanding New Media* (Cambridge, MA: MIT Press).

Brennan, T. (2004) *The Transmission of Affect* (Ithaca, NY/London: Cornell University Press).

Charlesworth, S. (2000) *A Phenomenology of Working-Class Experience* (Cambridge: Cambridge University Press).

Cho, G. (2008) *Haunting the Korean Diaspora: Shame, Secrecy and the Forgotten War* (Minneapolis: University of Minnesota Press).

Clapson, M. (1999) 'Working-Class Women's Experiences of Moving to New Housing Estates in England since 1919', *20th Century British History*, 10(3): 345–65.

Cohen, E. (2009) *A Body Worth Defending: Immunity, Biopolitics and the Apotheosis of the Modern Body* (Durham, NC: Duke University Press).

Connerton, P. (1989) *How Societies Remember* (Cambridge, New York/Port Chester/Sydney: Cambridge University Press).

Couldry, N. (2009) 'Teaching Us to Fake It: The Ritualized Norms of TV's "Reality" Games', in S. Murray and L. Ouellette (eds), *Reality TV: Remaking Television Culture* (New York/London: New York University Press), pp. 82–99.

Featherstone, M. (2010) 'Body, Image and Affect in Consumer Culture', *Body & Society*, Special Issue on Affect, 16(1): 193–221.

Freund, P. (2009) 'Social Synaesthesia: Expressive Bodies, Embodied Charisma', *Body & Society*, 15(4): 21–31.

Gibbs, A. (2008) 'Panic!: Affect, Suggestion and Mimesis in the Social Field', *Cultural Studies Review*, 14(4): 130–46.

Gilroy, P. (1993) *The Black Atlantic: Modernity and Double Consciousness* (Cambridge, MA: Harvard University Press).

Gorton, K. (2009) *Media Audiences: Television, Meaning and Emotion* (Edinburgh: Edinburgh University Press).

Hamera, J. (2005) 'The Answerability of Memory: "Saving" Khmer Classical Dance', in A. Abbas and J. Nguyet (eds), *Internationalizing Cultural Studies: An Anthology* (Oxford: Blackwell Publishing), pp. 95–105.

Hay, J. (2000) 'Unaided Virtues: The Neo-Liberalization of the Domestic Sphere', *TV and New Media*, 1(1): 53–73.

Heyes, C. (2007) *Self-Transformations: Foucault, Ethics and Normalised Bodies* (London/New York: Routledge).

Hill, A. (2005) *Reality TV: Audiences and Popular Factual TV* (London/New York: Routledge).

Hill, J. (2004) 'The IWW and the Making of a Revolutionary Working-Class Counterculture', review, *MLN*, 119(5): 1120–4.

Jensen, T. (2010) 'What Kind of Mum Are You at the Moment? *Supernanny* and the Psychologising of Classed Embodiment', *Subjectivity*, 3(2): 170–92.

Jones, M. (2008) *Skintight: An Anatomy of Cosmetic Surgery* (Oxford/New York: Berg).

Kavka, M. (2008) *Reality TV, Affect and Intimacy: Reality Matters* (Basingstoke, Hants./New York: Palgrave Macmillan).

Leys, R. (2007) *From Guilt to Shame: Auschwitz and After* (Princeton, NJ: Princeton University Press).

McNeil, W. H. (1995) *Keeping Together in Time: Dance and Drill in Human History* (Cambridge, MA: Harvard University Press).

McRobbie, A. (2005) *The Uses of Cultural Studies* (London: Sage).

Massumi, B. (2002) *Parables for the Virtual: Movement, Affect, Sensation* (Durham, NC: Duke University Press).

Moscovici, S. (1985) *The Age of the Crowd: A Historical Treatise on Mass Psychology* (Cambridge/New York: Cambridge University Press).

Moseley, R. (2000) 'Makeover Takeover on British Television', *Screen*, 41(3): 299–314.

Nancy, J. L. (2000) *Being Singular-Plural* (Stanford, CA: Stanford University Press).

Ouellette, L. (2009) 'Take Responsibility for Yourself: *Judge Judy* and the Neo-Liberal Citizen', in S. Murray and L. Ouellette (eds), *Reality TV: Remaking Television Culture* (New York/London: NYU Press), pp. 223–42.

Pollack, D. (2005) 'Introduction', in A. Abbas and J. Nguyet (eds), *Internationalizing Cultural Studies: An Anthology* (Oxford: Blackwell Publishing), pp. 71–8.

Rose, N. (1999) *Powers of Freedom: Reframing Political Thought* (Cambridge: Cambridge University Press).

Sconce, J. (2000) *Haunted Media: Electronic Presence from Telegraphy to Television* (Durham, NC/New York: Duke University Press).

Sedgwick, E. and A. Frank (eds) (1995) *Shame and Its Sisters: A Silvan Tomkins Reader* (Durham, NC/London: Duke University Press).

Sheets-Johnstone, M. (1999) *The Primacy of Movement* (Amsterdam/Philadelphia: John Benjamin's Publishing Co.).

Skeggs, B. (1997) *Formations of Class and Gender: Becoming Respectable* (London/New York: Sage).

———— (2004) *Class, Self, Culture* (London: Routledge).

Skeggs, B., N. Thumim and H. Wood (2008) '"Oh goodness, I am watching reality TV": How Methods Make Class in Audience Research', *European Journal of Cultural Studies*, 11(1): 5–24.

Susman, W. (1979) '"Personality" and the Making of Twentieth-Century Culture', in J. Higham and P. Conkin (eds), *New Directions in American Intellectual History* (Baltimore, MD: Johns Hopkins University Press).

Tambornino, J. (2002) *The Corporeal Turn: Passion, Necessity, Politics* (New York/Oxford: Rowman and Littlefield).

Tarde, G. (1969) *On Communication and Social Influence* (Chicago/London: Chicago University Press).

Tyler, I. (2008) '"Chav mum, chav scum": Class Disgust in Contemporary Britain', *Feminist Media Studies*, 8(1): 17–34.

Walkerdine, V. (1990) *Schoolgirl Fictions* (London: Verso).

———— (2010) 'Communal Beingness and Affect: An Exploration of Trauma in an Ex-Industrial Community', *Body & Society*, Special Issue on Affect, 16(1): 91–116.

Wood, H. and B. Skeggs (2004) 'Notes on Ethical Scenarios of Self on British "Reality" TV', *Feminist Media Studies*, 4(2): 205–8.

Index

Page numbers in **bold** type indicate more detailed analysis; those in *italics* denote illustrations; *n* = endnote